Elements of
VEDIC
ASTROLOGY

Volumes 1 & 2 Combined

Dr. K S Charak
M.S. (SURGERY)
F.R.C.S. (U.K.)

UMA
Publications

Elements of
Vedic Astrology

Volumes 1 & 2 Combined

© Dr. K.S. Charak

First Edition	:	June 1995
Second Edition	:	September 1996
Third Edition	:	September 1998
Fourth Edition	:	July 2006
Fifth Combined Edition	:	July 2021

ISBN 9789381769102

Published by:

UMA Publications
23 Doctors Apartments, Vasundhara Enclave, Delhi-110 096, India
E-mail: kscharak@gmail.com

Printed by:

CreateSpace, An Amazon.com Company

Dedicated

to the memory of my brother

Bishan S. Charak

whom I lost to the USA

Preface to the Fifth Edition

The *Elements of Vedic Astrology* has remained the most acclaimed, appreciated and relished work on the principles of the Parashari system of astrology. During the past over twenty-five years, the book has gone through four editions and several reprints while its popularity amongst the students and teachers of Vedic astrology has remained undiminished. The main reason for the supremacy that this work enjoys is the comprehensive coverage of this vast subject in a highly organized, scientific and compact manner, in a language that is easy to understand and appealing to the reader of this subject.

This work has been earlier presented in two volumes. We are pleased to present to the world of astrology the fifth edition of this highly admired work in a more compact, slightly larger in dimensions, single volume which the reader should find easier to handle. The text has been completely revised and additional notes added at several places to elucidate the points which we felt needed additional clarification. It is hoped that this work continues to captivate the reader of this exalted subject as ever before.

I must put on record my acknowledgement of the help renderd by our friend Rajeev Jhanji in bringing out this work in its present format and in offering, from time to time, valuable inputs to improve the content of the text.

July 18, 2021   DR. K.S. CHARAK
23 Doctors Apartments   MS (Surgery); FRCS (UK)
Vasundhara Enclave
Delhi - 110096 (India)

Preface to the First Edition

Teaching astrology to highly educated and elite classes of students in the Bharatiya Vidya Bhavan, New Delhi, has imposed great demands on the teaching faculty here to maintain and upgrade their quality of teaching. A direct consequence of this has been the production of several high standard books by the faculty members. Stress has been placed on illustrating the various astrological principles and techniques by suitable examples. The scientific basis of astrology has been proved repeatedly by illustrating the principles which give replicable results.

Study of Vedic astrology demands an elementary knowledge of astronomy and some basic techniques concerned with the preparation of horoscopic charts. Understanding the static promise in a horoscope, and the dynamic aspect of timing the fruition of such promise, are areas which demand deeper study. Vedic astrology has at its disposal innumerable techniques which can be employed for virtually infallible results. Not all techniques are to be used by every practitioner of Vedic astrology on all horoscopes. But a knowledge of most of these is desirable. Eventually, each astrologer develops his standard technique which suits him the best.

Elements of Vedic Astrology is directed towards providing the basic principles of Vedic astrology. It highlights the scientific basis of astrology. The initial few chapters are directed towards clarifying the fundamental principles of astrology. The basic concepts of astronomy as are relevant to a study of astrology are described clearly. An example of the highly evolved ancient Indian method of teaching has been taken from a celebrated scripture; it highlights the simple yet lucid style of imparting scientific-spiritual instruction to a disciple. Some important areas of astrology concerned with the characteristics of rashis, houses and planets, the nature of planets, and the significations of houses and planets, have all been described in great details. Two chapters have been devoted to the techniques of casting a horoscopic chart. It may be pertinent to point out here that an understanding of the manual method of casting of a horoscope has vast advantages and must be mastered fully. Reliance may later be placed on computerised calculations if so desired.

Subtle areas of astrology, like the planetary states (Avasthas) and the sub-planets, have been discussed briefly and areas for further research indicated. The use of vargas, or subtle divisions, has been explained. The Vimshottari dasha system has been dealt with in details while the Yogini dasha has been described briefly in order to provide an additional confirmatory tool. A vast amount of information gathered from standard classical texts of astrology in respect of the placement of planets in different houses or rashis, and the various planetary influences on them, has been provided.

The stature of a horoscope is reflected in the presence or absence of the all-important planetary yogas in a horoscope. These must be recognised at the outset, and their quality judged, in order to assess the potential inherent in a chart. Three full chapters have been devoted to this aspect along with illustrative examples.

Determination of longevity is a tricky area in astrology. Some standard methods of calculating the span of life along with their pitfalls have been described.

Specialised predictive areas of Vedic astrology have been touched briefly in order to acquaint the reader of such additional predictive tools. These include medical astrology, horary astrology, transits, annual charts and Ashtakavarga. One chapter has been devoted to the Muhurta or electional aspect of astrology. Greater understanding of these areas necessitates further study, an aspect which has been hinted at appropriately.

The book deals solely with the Parashari system which is the most prevalent system of Vedic astrology. No attempt has been made to transgress into the other parallel system known as the Jaimini system which is less in vogue, is less well understood, and needs a lot of research before being universally applicable.

The work is primarily meant for those who want to learn astrology from the very beginning, and pursue it seriously in a scientific manner. It will serve as a stepping stone for those who want to eventually go into specialised branches of astrology. It is also aimed to help those who intend to indulge in astrological research in hitherto unexplored areas like the vargas, the sub-planets, or the planetary states, etc.

My efforts will be more than rewarded if this work fulfils its intended aims.

May 25, 1995   Dr. K.S. Charak
72 Gagan Vihar
Delhi - 110051 (India)

Contents

...I...
Vedic Astrology: An Introduction

ॐ सह नाववतु। सह नौ भुनक्तु। सह वीर्यं करवावहै।
तेजस्वि नावधीतमस्तु। मा विद्विषावहै॥
ॐ शान्तिः शान्तिः शान्तिः॥

Aum! May He protect us both (the teacher and the disciple) together. May He sustain us both together. May we attain vigour together. May the learning of us both be resplendent. May we harbour no mutual ill will.

Aum! Peace! Peace! Peace!   Kathopanishad

Astrology is as old as the Vedas themselves. The Vedas, which are the sacred Hindu scriptures, embody eternal knowledge. Strict moral and spiritual practices along with a deep study are the prerequisites to understand the essence of the Vedas. To the uninitiated, the Vedas might appear as nothing more than ritualistic oblations to air, water and thunder, etc. Deep truths, however, begin to unfold to the true seeker as his search goes on.

In times of yore, sincere seekers of truth and knowledge in India used to spend years and years at the feet of their 'gurus', learning the meanings hidden in the Vedas.

In order to decipher what lies concealed in the Vedas, a study of certain subjects is considered a prerequisite. These subjects are called the 'Vedangas' or the body organs of the Vedas. There are six such Vedangas. They are:

(i)   *Shiksha*, which deals with an understanding of the Vedic 'Varnas', 'Swaras' and 'Matras', and thus with the technique of correct pronunciation.

(ii) *Chhanda*, dealing with the appropriate lyrical utterance of the Vedic 'Suktas'.

(iii) *Vyakarana*, expounding the grammatical aspects of the language.

(iv) *Nirukta*, which explains the difficult words, 'padas' and 'mantras'.

(v)   *Kalpa*, dealing with the understanding of Sutras and the use of Mantras, hence concerned with the ritualistic aspect of the Vedas.

(vi) *Jyotisha* or astrology.

Of the body called the Vedas, astrology represents the 'eyes', with its capacity to 'see' the past, the present and the future. Astrology is considered as the most important of the Vedangas.

What is Astrology?

Astrology is a scientific study and application of the language of the heavenly bodies. These heavenly bodies, determined on the basis of astronomy and mathematics, are mapped in the form of a horoscope. Their specific locations in the horoscope indicate specific happenings in the case of individuals, of multitudes and of geographical regions. Whether the Sun, the Moon, the planets and the stars themselves influence the terrestrial phenomena, or they only indicate such phenomena by their various dispositions, is immaterial. What is important to us is that variations in their disposition determine variations in the events on the earth; the correlations are only too strong to be brushed aside by the critics of astrology.

Who should practise astrology?

In the ancient times, a strict code of conduct was demanded of those who practised astrology. A guru would teach astrology only to a deserving disciple who would adhere to such a code of conduct. The guru-shishya (i.e., the teacher-disciple) tradition is already long over in India. With changing times, it has become difficult to find an appropriate 'guru' and a deserving 'shishya' to pursue this sacred study within the rules laid by the sages of yore. It is, however, quite in order to be aware of this ancient code of conduct. Varahamihira, the celebrated authority on astrology, prescribes the following qualifications for an astrologer:

(a) *Physical features*: According to the said author, the physical features reflect the inner nature of a man. The astrologer must be good to look at, with all his body parts complete and healthy. He should be of sound health, with sound hands, feet, nails, chin, teeth, ears, forehead and head, and having a loud and impressive voice.

(b) *Moral soundness*: He should be truthful, gentle, bereft of cravings and aversions, clean of heart, not inclined to be critical of the qualities of others, and devoid of base and worldly distractions.

(c) *Behaviour in an assembly*: He should be clever, able to express himself, bold in an assembly, not intimidated by his fellow astrologers, dignified, and aware of the constraints of social and historical circumstances.

(d) *Proficiency in the subject of astrology*: He should be well-read, and proficient in the three branches of astrology known as the Ganita, the Samhita and the Hora. He must have studied the five Siddhantas (or mathematical treatises). His mathematical proficiency must include a knowledge of the various divisions of time, from the gross ones like the *Yuga* to the finer ones. He must also possess knowledge of the various divisions, including the finest ones, of the zodiac.

(e) *Proficiency in various branches of astrology:* The astrologer is required to possess a knowledge of different aspects of astrology which deal with propitiation of planets, rendering the planets beneficial or hostile, conducting religious ceremonies, and rituals which help neutralise the natural calamities.

(f) *Defence of astrology:* The astrologer must be able to answer queries, and also pose relevant questions where appropriate. When necessary, he should be able to dazzle others by his knowledge, only to increase the dignity of astrology.

(g) *More about the qualities of an astrologer:* The astrologer must possess knowledge of solar, civil, nakshatric and lunar time measures; of intercalary months; of the sixty Samvatsaras, the yugas, years, months, days and Horas; of varying opinions on varying aspects of mathematical astronomy; of various dispositions of planets, including their exaltations, debilitations, fast and slow motions, their conjunctions as well as planetary warfares; of latitudes and longitudes of places on the surface of the earth; of the movements of the nakshatras; of the rising and setting of signs, Charakhandas for different latitudes, etc. He should be highly confident and a clear expounder of the Shastras.

The sage Parashara advocates a similar code of conduct for astrologers, stressing particularly on the necessity for technical, intellectual and moral excellence; the capacity to weigh the pros and cons of a situation, along with an ability to synthesize a coherent prediction based on a sound knowledge of the principles, sometimes apparently contradictory, of astrology.

Sub-divisions of Astrology

There are three main sub-divisions of astrology.

1. *Samhita*: This deals with collectivity or multitudes. It encompasses such varied areas as weather forecasts, agricultural produce, natural disasters, floods, famines, wars, earthquakes, cyclones, market trends, changes in government, national and international events, and virtually anything that influences the masses. The annual world predictions which are generally based either on the Hindu New Year commencing on the Chaitra Shukla Pratipada, or on the Solar Ingress into Mesha, fall under the Samhita astrology.

2. *Siddhanta or Tantra or Ganita*: This deals with the mathematical aspects of astrology. There are several treatises on Siddhanta astrology but five, among them, are considered as particularly important. They are:

   (a) Surya Siddhanta
   (b) Paulisha Siddhanta
   (c) Romaka (or Lomasha) Siddhanta
   (d) Vasishtha Siddhanta
   (e) Paitamaha Siddhanta

A proficiency in these is considered as a prerequisite for a good astrologer, according to the celebrated Varahamihira.

3. *Hora*: It deals with:

   (a) Individual horoscopes, or Jataka, or natal charts.

   (b) Muhurta or electional astrology, which concerns itself with the election of favourable planetary dispositions to achieve specific accomplishments in day-to-day life.

Astrology and Science

Study of astrology has been branded by the neo-scientists as a belief in superstition. Greater criticism has been heaped on astrology by those who have never bothered to study the subject. Many critics have questioned the basis of astrology, ignoring the fact that an understanding of a basis has to succeed and not precede an observation. The basis of gravitational pull was determined after the existence of the force of gravitation was recognised. Anyone who studies astrology with an open mind cannot but appreciate the fact that astrology is a highly developed science.

By definition, science means a knowledge ascertained by observation and experiment, critically tested, systematised and brought under general principles. Astrology strictly fulfils all these criteria. Two aspects of astrology deserve a special mention:

(a) *The cause-and-effect phenomenon*: Critics of astrology boast that physical sciences depend upon a cause and effect relationship, which astrologgy apparently lacks. They, however, fail to appreciate that astrology is a cosmic science and not bound by the limitations of a laboratory. In physical sciences, there may be a gross cause or a subtle cause, producing a physically visible or gross effect. Gravitation, which is a subtle cause, produces a gross effect of attracting a physical body towards the earth. In the case of astrology, the cause is always subtle while the effect is appreciable and predictable according to rules which have been developed and refined over the centuries. The subtle cause in case of astrology is the cosmic force represented by the disposition of the various heavenly bodies or 'planets'. Physical scientists can only trace the cause from the apparent effect.

It may be noted, however, that astrology deals with a multitude of phenomena on the earth. This being so, there are numerous parameters and a methodology more elaborate than any known physical science can boast of. Making correct predictions, therefore, is difficult and demands hard labour on the part of an astrologer. Unfortunately, the failure of an astrologer has been often misinterpreted as a failure of the science.

(b) *The phenomenon of replication*: Astrology is also criticised on the ground that its principles do not yield results which can be invariably replicated or reproduced. Physical sciences can, on the other hand, boast of a reproducibility of their various principles. *It may be pointed out here that every correct astrological prediction, in fact, underscores the principle of replication in astrology.* Since astrology is a complex science, its every known principle has to be applied carefully, considering the numerous parameters and weighing the various pros and cons. In the ancient Indian scriptures, for example, numerous astrological dicta lie hidden. Unfolded and carefully applied today, they prove their eternal applicability and give dazzling results which the open minded scientists of today can only marvel at. It is no coincidence that a planetary combination present at the time of the Mahabharata war, and described by Karna to lord Krishna, also obtained, in a modified form, in 1914 when the World War I started; in 1942 when World War II was in progress, and again in 1971 at the time of the Indo-Pak conflict. During all these occasions, India got involved in the mess quite intimately. In 1965 too, when India and Pakistan clashed, a similar but modified planetary disposition arose. Before heaping any criticism on astrology, it will be interesting to watch when such a combination is likely to obtain in future, and in what form.

Astrology and Karma

Karma is the sum total of one's physical, mental and spiritual functions. The world goes on because there is a role of free will assigned to human beings. Where does then astrology fit in, deal as it does with predestination? Is there a conflict between belief in astrology and in free will? How can scriptures lay emphasis on both if they are mutually conflicting?

Astrology is based on the relationship of cause and effect. If there is an effect, there must be a cause preceding it. Thus, if an event good or bad happens today, there must be a cause for it, whether or not that cause is appreciable. Certain functions or Karmas produce an immediate result. Still others obtain fruition after a longer time period. Still others may take several years or decades (or even longer) to materialise. If one believes in the law of cause and effect, then the ambience of one's birth and the subsequent opportunities or their lack cannot be a matter of mere chance. This takes us to a belief in birth and rebirth. Karmas done in one birth must manifest sometime in a later birth.

The past karmas produce limitations for us because they yield certain results which influence our future karmas. We do have a free will, but within the limitations precribed by the results of our past actions. Karmas in fact manufacture destiny.

An astrologer can point out which of the results from the past karmas can be overcome, and which cannot be overcome and, therefore, have to be suffered. A karma done is like a missile fired; it may or may not be neutralised by a counter-missile, depending upon the relative strength of the two.

Astrology and Genetic Link

A fascinating aspect of astrological study is the link that exists between members of the same family. This is an area of research also. Just as certain blood groups cannot exist amongst the children of particular parents, so also certain planetary combinations cannot obtain in certain families. Study of horoscopes belonging to a family indicate similarities which can be easily appreciated. This aspect of astrology has a vast possible usage.

Interlinked Destinies

Different individuals who are linked to each other in one way or the other show distinct similarities in their horoscopic charts. An event which is visible in the horoscope of a child can also be seen in the horoscopes of his parents as well as siblings. People who come in closer contact in mutual relationships or business partnerships show striking similarities in their charts at appropriate periods. Just as particles of similar densities sink to a similar extent on centrifugation, so also people who have similar pursuits tend to get grouped together.

Composite Approach for Astrological Predictions

In the ancient times, astrology was studied and practised in a highly scientific manner. Just as in medical sciences of today where multiple investigative tools are employed to diagnose a disease, in astrology too several different methods used to be employed. As the ancient tradition disappeared, astrology shrank into a family tradition, getting confined to a few families only. Its approach became more and more rigid. Until recently, many astrologers have been using only limited methods to make only a limited range of predictions.

Lately, however, highly educated people have started studying astrology giving it a modern and scientific look. This sacred subject is now taught in institutions like any other modern science. No longer is astrological study subject to limitations of method and approach. A highly effective composite approach for astrological predictions has been thus revived. Any given event is confirmed in a horoscopic chart by using a host of available techniques, like the use of both the Parashari and the Jaimini systems, the application of various dashas and the use of several divisional charts and of Ashtakavarga. Besides, the same event is often studied in the charts of those closely related to or associated with the native. This increases the success of predictions and proves the superiority of astrology as a scientific discipline.

In the pages that follow, an earnest attempt will be made to explain some of the elements of this sacred science.

7

...II...
Elementary Concepts
of Astronomy - I

सहस्रयुगपर्यन्तमहर्यद्ब्रह्मणो विदुः ।
रात्रिं युगसहस्रान्तां तेऽहोरात्रविदो जनाः ॥

Those who know of the day of Brahma as of a duration of a thousand ages and the night (too) of a thousand ages, they (verily) know the (essence of) day and night.   Gita VIII/17

Vedic astrology is based on a very sound understanding of astronomy. In ancient India, astronomy was a highly developed subject. A knowledge of astronomy was considered essential for an astrologer. To the ancient Vedic astrologer, such phenomena as the rotation and the revolution of the earth, the formation of seasons, the occurrence of eclipses, the concepts of solar and lunar months, the equinoxes, and the subtle concepts of disposition of planets and stars in the sky, were all well known. Without the availability of the present day sophisticated instruments and telescopes, he was able to decipher fine variations in the disposition of heavenly bodies. The fact that he could take into consideration such fine divisions of time as is possible only through the electronic / atomic clocks of today is marvellous.

Earth as the centre

The Vedic astrologer was aware that nothing in the universe was stationary. It was, therefore, irrelevant to attempt to pick up a fixed point in the sky, and consider the movements of earth and other heavenly bodies in relation to such a point. In any case, it was more convenient to imagine himself as the central point with the rest of the universe in constant motion around himself. He, therefore, considered the position and movement of all heavenly bodies in relation to the earth itself which was his residence. It is no wonder then that Indian astronomy and astrology consider the earth as the centre, and all other heavenly bodies moving around it in one manner or the other. The Indian astronomy is thus *geocentric, and not heliocentric* which latter considers the Sun as the centre. The Indian astronomer does appreciate the Sun to be the centre of the solar system, but he also appreciates that the Sun, the solar system, as well as the stars are all moving. For him, the point of relative fixity at the centre of heavenly bodies in the galaxy was the pole star, called as the *Dhruva*. With such profound appreciation of astronomy, it is preposterous on the part of anyone to attribute ignorance of the earthly movements to the ancient Indian astronomer.

The Zodiac

Imagine a belt or a path in the sky, some 18 degrees of arc in width, running around the earth in an east-west direction. Groups of stars, to all appearance fixed, are studded along this imaginary belt. Twenty seven (or twenty eight!) such groups of stars are recognised in Vedic astrology. Because of lack of apparent motion, these are called as *Nakshatras*. This imaginary belt, with nakshatras studded on it, is called the *zodiac*.

The zodiac forms the reference point for fixing up the position of any planet or star in the sky. Since it encircles the earth, it is comprised of 360 degrees. The twenty-seven nakshatras being evenly placed on it each have a span of 13˙20' arc. The various nakshatras are numbered from one to twenty-seven.

In contrast to the fixed nakshatras, there are the moving heavenly bodies called the Grahas. These move along the zodiac from the west to the east. They derive their name from the fact that, while moving against the background of the nakshatras, they appear to get hold of one nakshatra after the other (graha = to catch hold of). Vedic astrology recognises nine grahas. They are the Sun, the Moon, Mars, Mercury, Jupiter, Venus, Saturn, Rahu and Ketu. Of these, the Sun is a star, the Moon is a satellite of the earth, Rahu and Ketu are mere mathematical points on the zodiac, while the remaining ones

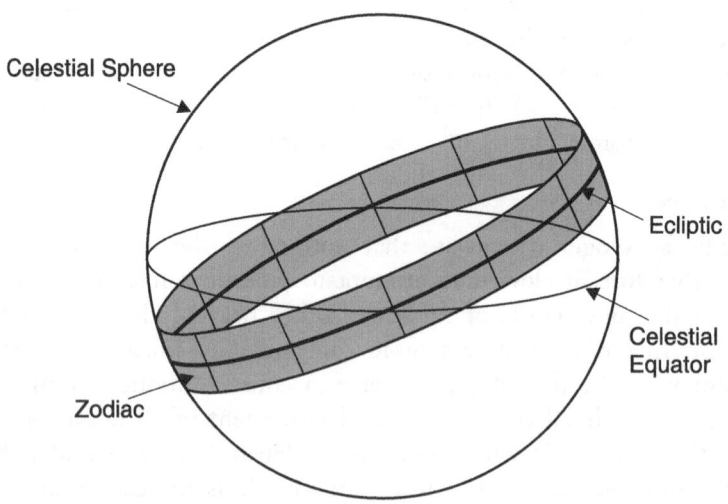

The zodiac is a band 18° wide and placed obliquely to the equator. It is divided into twelve equal parts called Rashis or twenty-seven equal parts called Nakshatras. The ecliptic passes through the centre of this band.

are planets. For the sake of descriptive convenience, we shall refer to all of these as 'planets'. These planets (appear to) revolve around the earth while staying within the limits of the zodiac.

The apparent path of the Sun along the zodiac is known as the ecliptic. The ecliptic passes through the centre of the zodiac. It is inclined at an angle of 23°28' to the plane of the equator.

We have deliberately refrained from considering the extra-Saturnine planets, called Uranus, Neptune and Pluto. These do not form a part of Vedic astrology.

Signs or Rashis

When the zodiac is divided into twelve equal parts, each such part has an extension of 30 degrees of the arc. Such a division is called a *Sign or Rashi*. A sign consists of two and a quarter nakshatras. A particular group of stars in the zodiac is considered as the starting point of the zodiac. From this point, the twenty-seven nakshatras or the twelve signs begin. A planet located anywhere along the zodiac may be considered as located in a particular sign, depending upon which twelfth division of the zodiac it is in; it may be considered as being located in a particular nakshatra too, depending upon which twenty seventh division of the zodiac it is in.

The planets from the Sun to Saturn have been allotted the ownership of these signs. While the Sun and the Moon own one sign each, the remaining planets own two signs each. Rahu and Ketu are generally not allotted ownership of these signs. The names of the twelve signs, their planetary lords, and their extent in the zodiac, etc., are given in Table II-1.

Table II-1

	Sign	English equivalent	Symbol	Lord	Extent in degrees
1.	Mesha	Aries	♉	Mars	0- 30
2.	Vrisha	Taurus	♈	Venus	30- 60
3.	Mithuna	Gemini	♊	Mercury	60- 90
4.	Karka	Cancer	♋	Moon	90-120
5.	Simha	Leo	♌	Sun	120-150
6.	Kanya	Virgo	♍	Mercury	150-180
7.	Tula	Libra	♎	Venus	180-210
8.	Vrishchika	Scorpio	♏	Mars	210-240
9.	Dhanu	Saggitarius	♐	Jupiter	240-270
10.	Makara	Capricorn	♑	Saturn	270-300
11.	Kumbha	Aquarius	♒	Saturn	300-330
12.	Meena	Pisces	♓	Jupiter	330-360

Nakshatras

The twenty-seven nakshatras also extend along the zodiac from 0° to 360°. They too are owned by planets. In the case of nakshatras, the planets Rahu and Ketu are also allotted the ownership. Each nakshatra is further divided into four parts called the *padas or charanas*. There are thus 108 nakshatra padas or quarters in the twenty-seven nakshatras. Each nakshatra quarter measures 3°20'. The relation of nakshatras with rashis, and their extent and owners, are shown in Table II-2.

Table II-2
Rashis, Nakshatras and Nakshatra Lords

Rashis	Nakshatras	Extent s d m	Pada	Lord
1. Mesha	1. Ashwini	0^{s}13°20'	4	Ketu
	2. Bharani	0^{s}26°40'	4	Venus
	3. Krittika	1^{s}0°0'	1	Sun
2. Vrisha	3. Krittika	1^{s}10°0'	3	Sun
	4. Rohini	1^{s}23°20'	4	Moon
	5. Mrigasira	2^{s}0°0'	2	Mars
3 Mithuna	5. Mrigasira	2^{s}6°40'	2	Mars
	6. Ardra	2^{s}20°0'	4	Rahu
	7. Punarvasu	3^{s}0°0'	3	Jupiter
4. Karka	7. Punarvasu	3^{s}3°20'	1	Jupiter
	8. Pushya	3^{s}16°40'	4	Saturn
	9. Ashlesha	4^{s}0°0'	4	Mercury
5. Simha	10. Magha	4^{s}13°20'	4	Ketu
	11. P Phalguni	4^{s}26°40'	4	Venus
	12. U Phalguni	5^{s}0°0'	1	Sun
6. Kanya	12. U Phalguni	5^{s}10°0'	3	Sun
	13. Hasta	5^{s}23°20'	4	Moon
	14. Chitra	6^{s}0°0'	2	Mars
7. Tula	14. Chitra	6^{s}6°40'	2	Mars
	15. Swati	6^{s}20°0'	4	Rahu
	16. Vishakha	7^{s}0°0'	3	Jupiter
8 Vrishchika	16. Vishakha	7^{s}3°20'	1	Jupiter
	17. Anuradha	7^{s}16°40'	4	Saturn
	18. Jyeshtha	8^{s}0°0'	4	Mercury
9 Dhanu	19. Moola	8^{s}13°20'	4	Ketu
	20. P Asadha	8^{s}26°40'	4	Venus
	21. U Asadha	9^{s}0°0'	1	Sun

Rashis	Nakshatras	Extent s d m	Pada	Lord
10 Makara	21. U Asadha	9ˢ10°0'	3	Sun
	22. Shravana	9ˢ23°20'	4	Moon
	23. Dhanistha	10ˢ0°0'	2	Mars
11. Kumbha	23. Dhanistha	10ˢ6°40'	2	Mars
	24. Sata Bhishaj	10ˢ20°0'	4	Rahu
	25. P Bhadrapada	11ˢ0°0'	3	Jupiter
12. Meena	25. P Bhadrapad	11ˢ3°20'	1	Jupiter
	26. U Bhadrapad	11ˢ16°40'	4	Saturn
	27. Revati	12ˢ0°0'	4	Mercury

A segment of the zodiac extending from 276°40'0" to 280°53'20" (equivalent to 6°40'0" to 10°53'20" in the Makara rashi), involving the last quarter of the twenty first (i.e. Uttarashadha) nakshatra and the beginning of the twenty-second (Shravana), is sometimes considered as a separate nakshatra by the name *Abhijit*. This addition changes the number of nakshatras to twenty-eight. In such a situation, Abhijit is considered as the twent-second nakshatra, and the subsequent six nakshatras (from Shravana onwards) assume changed numbers (from 23 to 28, instead of 22 to 27).

The geocentric astronomical framework

In order to understand the very basic astronomical concepts, as pertinent to an understanding of Vedic astrology, it is important to understand certain facts about the earth, the movements of the earth, and the apparent movement of the planets around the earth. Explanation of a few definitions is also in order.

Earth as a sphere: The earth is spherical. It rotates from *west to east* around its axis. The *axis of the earth* is an imaginary line which, passing through its centre, connects its two poles, the *north pole and the south pole*. Another imaginary line running across the largest circumference of the earth, equidistant from its poles and running in an east-west direction, is called the *equator*. The terrestial equator is considered as the zero degree of latitude. Parallels drawn to the equator, either north or south of it, indicate the north or south latitudes, from zero degree at the equator to 90 degrees at either pole.

Imaginary lines can also be drawn on the surface of the earth connecting the north pole to the south pole. Encompassing the circumference of the earth, these correspond to the 360 degrees of *longitude*. They are also known as the *terrestrial meridians*. Ancient Vedic astrologers considered the terrestrial meridian passing through Ujjain as the zero degree longitude. At present, the meridian passing through Greenwitch in England is regarded as corresponding to zero degree of longitude.

The longitudes are marked from zero degree to 180 degrees east or west, depending upon whether a place falls to the east or to the west of Greenwitch.

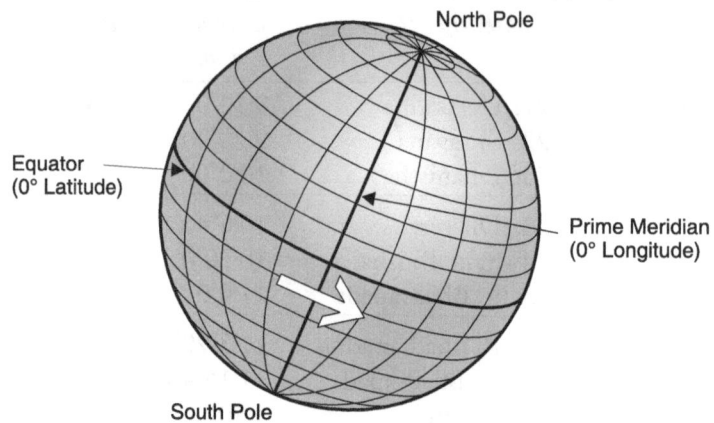

The equator divides the earth into northern and southern hemispheres. Latitudes and longitudes help locate a place on the surface of the earth. Arrow shows the direction of earth's rotation from west to east.

The latitude and the longitude of a place are the co-ordinates which help to locate the place accurately on the surface of the earth. The 360 degrees of terrestrial longitude represent a time span of 24 hours. One hour thus corresponds to 15 degrees, and one degree of terrestrial longitude represents 4 minutes of time.

The great and the small circles: A *great circle* is any circle the plane of which passes through the centre of a sphere. Equator is a great circle on the earth, equidistant from the north and south poles.

Any circle the plane of which does not pass through the centre of a sphere is called a *small circle*. As the equator corresponds to zero degree latitude, all parallels to it are small circles, which represent the north or south latitudes.

Imaginary extensions into space: The space around the earth extends to an infinite extent. To us, the extension of space upto the zodiac is of primary importance.

Celestial Sphere is an imaginary projection of the earth in all directions upto infinity. An extension of the plane of terrestial equator into space is called the *celestial equator*. Any great circle that joins the celestial north and south poles is called a *meridian*. The meridian of a place corresponds to the terrestrial longitude. The meridian passing through Greenwitch corresponds to zero degree of longitude, and is termed as the *principal meridian* or the *standard meridian*. The angular distance between the principal meridian and the meridian of a given place (i.e., the angle subtended by the principal meridian and the meridian of a given place, at the centre of the earth) is called the longitude of a place.

The Sun crosses the meridian of a place at mid-day. The intersection of the ecliptic (i.e., the sun's apparent path around the earth) with the meridian of a place is termed as the *midheaven* which in other words corresponds to the *Bhava-Madhya (midpoint) of the tenth house* of a horoscope. The meridian of a place thus passes, around the earth, through north pole, midheaven (10th house or zenith), south pole, nadir (4th house) and back to the north pole.

Declination and right ascension: Just as parallels of latitude and meridians of longitude help to locate a place on the surface of the terrestrial sphere, so do their extensions in the form of parallels of *declination* and meridians of *right ascension* help to locate heavenly bodies on the celestial sphere.

Declination of a planet is the angle subtended by it and the celestial equator at the earth. The declination of a planet, thus, corresponds exactly with the terrestrial latitude. A planet at the terrestrial equator is said to possess zero degree declination.

Right ascension of a planet is its angular distance, measured eastwards along the celestial equator, from the vernal equinox to the point where a perpendicular drawn through the said planet falls on the celestial equator.

Equator and Ecliptic; formation of seasons: The earth rotates on its own axis in twenty-four hours. Along with this rotation, it also revolves around the Sun in one year or 365.2422 days (365 days 5 hours 48 minutes 46 seconds). This span of time is called a tropical year. The path of the earth around the Sun appears to us, from the earth, as the Sun's path around the earth, and is called the ecliptic.

The equator runs around the middle of earth in an east-west direction and divides the earth into a *northern hemisphere* and a *southern hemisphere*. The ecliptic, or the Sun's path, in the apparent east-west direction, does not lie along the equator but is obliquely placed to it. Half of the Sun's path thus lies to the north of the equator and a half of it to the south of the equator.

Aryabhatta wrote over fifteen centuries ago:

> "One half of the ecliptic, running from the beginning of the sign Aries to the end of the sign Virgo, lies obliquely inclined (to the equator) northwards. The remaining half (of the ecliptic) running from the beginning of the sign Libra to the end of the sign Pisces, lies (equally inclined to the equator) southwards."

The Sun thus happens to cross the equator twice a year, giving rise to what are termed as the two equinoxes. The *vernal equinox* happens around the 21st March, when the Sun is on its northerly course. The *autumnal equinox* occurs around 23rd September when the Sun is on its southerly course. On these two occasions, the day and night all over the globe are of equal duration. The Sun is vertically above the equator at this time. The declination of the Sun at these occasions is zero as it corresponds to the terrestrial equator which represents zero degree latitude.

After vernal equinox, the Sun progressively attains north declination until it reaches a maximum of 23°28'. This occurs around 21st June and is known as the *summer solstice*. The Sun is vertically above the tropic of Cancer at this time. The northern hemisphere experiences the longest day and the shortest night on this occasion. The reverse holds true for the southern hemisphere.

After the autumnal equinox, the Sun pursues a southward course and attains a maximum south declination of 23°28' at the time of *winter solstice*.

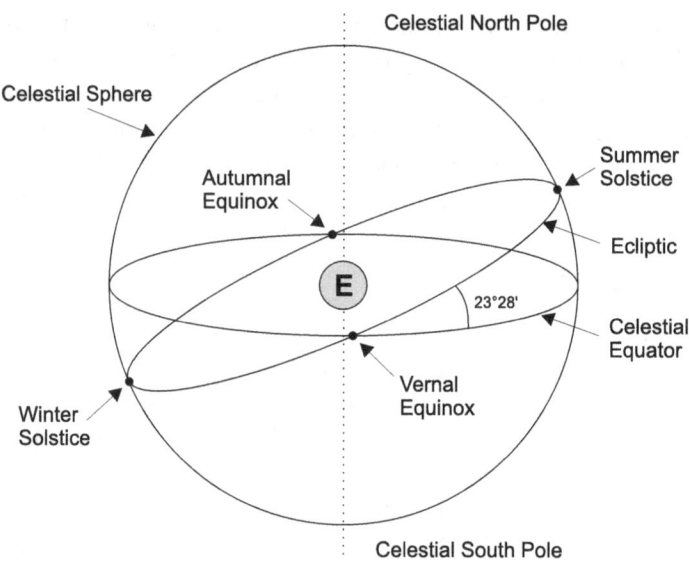

The ecliptic is inclined to the equator at an angle of 23°28'. It crosses the equator at two points, the vernal equinox and the autumnal equinox. The north and south poles of the earth correspond to the celestial north and south poles.

This happens around 22nd December. The Sun is vertically above the tropic of Capricorn, at this time. The northern hemisphere experiences the shortest day and the longest night on this occasion. The reverse holds true for the southern hemisphere.

The obliquity of the ecliptic to the equator thus results in the *formation of seasons*. When it is winter in the northern hemisphere, it is summer in the southern hemisphere. When it is summer in the northern hemisphere, it is winter in the southern hemisphere.

The horizon: It is the great circle which represents the meeting line of the earth and the sky. It varies according to the position of the observer on the surface of the earth. For example, for an observer at the north pole of the earth, the horizon corresponds with the equator while the southern hemisphere remains out of view. For one standing at the equator, the great circle passing through the poles represents the horizon; the two poles lie on the horizon in this case. For any intermediate positions, the horizon too varies accordingly. More and more of the southern hemisphere moves out of the horizon as the observer moves northward, and more and more northern hemisphere moves out of the horizon as the observer moves southward.

The point of the celestial sphere which is directly overhead for the observer is called as the *zenith*. This is at right angles to the observer's horizon. Its opposite point is known as the *nadir*. The great circle that passes in a north-south direction through the zenith and the nadir, through the celestial north and south poles (i.e., the north and south poles of the equator) and through the north and south points of the horizon is called the *meridian* which has been already referred to.

The rising and setting of signs

As already mentioned, the ecliptic passes through the centre of the zodiacal belt which extends some 8° to 9° on its either (north as well as south) side. The planets remain within the limits of the zodiac. The earth rotates around its axis once in twenty-four hours *from west to east.* As a consequence, all heavenly bodies appear to revolve around the earth from east to west once in twenty-four hours. The zodiac, with the nakshatras and rashis fixed upon it, also appears to revolve around the earth once in twenty-four hours. Thus all the signs and nakshatras on the zodiac appear to successively rise in the eastern horizon and set at the western horizon once in twenty-four hours. Six of the twelve signs appear at the eastern horizon during the day-time and the remaining six during night-time. The following points are of importance:

1. The sign that rises at the eastern horizon, at a given moment of time, is of primary importance and called the *ascendant or the lagna.* It is the sign where the ecliptic cuts the eastern horizon. In a horoscope this represents the first house.

2. The sign seventh from the ascendant is the descendant or the setting sign. That is, when a particular sign is rising in the eastern horizon, its opposite sign is setting in the western horizon. It is the sign where the ecliptic cuts the western horizon. In a horoscope this represents the seventh house.

3. The points where the meridian cuts the ecliptic are the zenith (above the earth) and the nadir (below the earth, exactly opposite to the zenith) The zenith (mid-heaven) represents the tenth house in a horoscope, while the nadir represents the fourth house.

4. Each sign takes time to rise at the horizon from zero degrees to 30 degrees. All signs are not of equal duration so that some signs take longer to completely rise above the horizon compared to the others.

5. Signs can be divided into three groups, depending upon their rising periods (rashi maanas).

Group A	Mesha	Kanya	Tula	Meena
Group B	Vrisha	Simha	Vrishchika	Kumbha
Group C	Mithuna	Karka	Dhanu	Makara

A sign belonging to one group takes the same time to rise as another belonging to the same group *at the equator.* The six signs from Karka to Dhanu lengthen and the remaining six shorten as one proceeds from the equator to the north pole. On the other hand, the signs from Makara to Mithuna lengthen, while the remaining ones shorten, as one proceeds from the equator to the south pole.

6. *For any given latitude, the rising period for different signs is fixed.*

7. As one moves away from the equator, certain signs lengthen while the

others shorten as far as their rising period is concerned. That is, certain signs remain longer on the horizon than the others.

8. Six signs elapse between sunrise and sunset, while the remaining six signs do so between sunset and sunrise.

9. This means that in winter, when the days are shorter, the six zodiacal signs that rise successively during the day have a shorter time duration, while the remaining six have a longer time duration. This gives rise to signs of short ascension and those of long ascension.

10. Signs of long ascension in the northern hemisphere are: Karka, Simha, Kanya, Tula, Vrishchika and Dhanu.

   These are signs of short ascension for the southern latitudes

11. Signs of short ascension in the northern hemisphere are: Makara, Kumbha, Meena, Mesha, Vrisha and Mithuna.

   These are the signs of long ascension for the southern latitudes.

12. As one nears the poles, certain zodiacal signs fail to rise.

The concept of sidereal time

The earth rotates around its axis in 24 hours, in what may be termed a mean solar day. In other words, the mean solar day is a function of earth's rotation in relation to the Sun. Considered with reference to any fixed star in the zodiac, the earth completes its one rotation in approximately 23 hours and 56 minutes (23 hours, 56 minutes, 4.09 seconds, to be precise). One rotation of the earth in relation to a fixed star is called a *sidereal day*. Said in another manner, a sidereal day is the time interval between two successive transits of a fixed star over the meridian of a place. A sidereal day is 3 minutes and 56 seconds (or roughly 4 minutes) shorter than the mean solar day.

   A sidereal day consists of 24 sidereal hours. Time reckoned according to this method is called the *sidereal time*. Since the sidereal time considers the angular rotation of the earth in relation to the fixed stars of the zodiac, *the earth will attain the same position with reference to the zodiac every day at the same sidereal time. In other words, for any location, for the same sidereal time, the disposition of the signs of the zodiac (including the rising sign, the setting sign, the tenth house, the 4th house, etc.) will be the same.* This is the reason why it is essential to obtain the correct sidereal time for the purposes of erecting an astrological chart for any given moment of mean solar time as provided by the watch.

   Why is the mean solar day longer than the sidereal day?

   By the time the earth rotates once, with reference to a fixed star, i.e., in one sidereal day, the Sun has moved by approximately 1° further along the zodiac. In order for the earth to achieve the same position with reference to the Sun, it has to rotate an extra 1° thereby consuming approximately 4 additional minutes each day.

Precession of Equinoxes

The earth revolves around the Sun once in 365 days 5 hours 48 minutes and 46 seconds. Considered from the earth, the Sun appears to complete one round of the ecliptic during this period. This is called a *tropical year*. In the span of a tropical year, the earth regains its original angular position with the Sun. It is also called the year of seasons since on this Earth-Sun cycle depends the occurrence, and timing, of seasons. If we consider the revolution of the Sun around the earth from one vernal equinox (around 21st March, when the day and night all over the globe are equal) to the next vernal equinox, it takes one tropical year to do so.

However, if at the end of a tropical year from one vernal equinox to the next, we consider the position of the earth *with reference to a fixed star of the zodiac*, the earth appears to lie some 50.26 seconds of celestial longitude to the west of its original position. In order for the earth to attain the same position with respect to a fixed star after one revolution, it takes a time span of 365 days 6 hours 9 minutes and some 9.5 seconds. This duration of time is called a *sidereal year*. The sidereal year is just over 20 minutes longer than the tropical year; this time difference is equivalent to 50.26 seconds of celestial longitude.

Each year, the Vernal equinox will fall short by 50.26 seconds along the zodiac reckoned along the fixed stars. This continuous receding of the Vernal equinox along the zodiac is called as the *precession of equinoxes*.

Cause of the precession: The earth rotates around its axis like a spinning top. In doing so, its north pole (and, therefore, the celestial pole), describes a circle of some 47 degrees around the pole of the ecliptic. This, in other words, means that the plane of the equator intersects the plane of the ecliptic at a constantly shifting point. This point, the first point of Aries or the vernal equinox, goes on receding westward at a rate of approximately 50.26 seconds of arc each year. This is called the precession of the equinoxes. *The result of this precession is a slow increase in the right ascensions of almost all fixed stars in the zodiac.* This precession

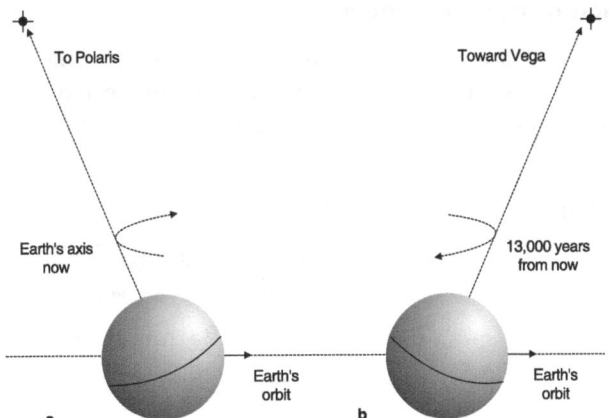

The wobble of earth's axis in a clockwise direction causes the precession of equi-noxes. The axis now points towards Polaris (a); in approximately 13,000 years, it will have moved to a point within a few degrees from Vega (b).

takes some 25,800 (or approximately 26,000) years to complete one circle. As will be seen, an appreciation of this precession is of paramount importance in the understanding of the basic concepts of Vedic astrology.

Fixed and Movable zodiacs: The *fixed or the sidereal zodiac* considers the nakshatras as its basis. Its first degree begins as the first degree of Mesha (Aries) from a particular point in the Revati group of stars. There is another zodiac, however, which is reckoned from the Vernal equinoctial point; here the first point of Aries begins from the Vernal equinox. This is called the *movable or the tropical zodiac*. As has been seen, the movable zodiac continues to recede westward along the stars which characterise the fixed zodiac.

Ayanamsha; the Sayana and the Niryana systems. It has been seen that because of the precession of equinoxes at a rate of 50.26 seconds per year, the distance between the Vernal equinox (the 1st point of the movable zodiac) and the 1st point of Mesha (Aries) on the fixed zodiac has been progressively increasing. This distance at any given epoch is called as the *Ayanamsha*. The ayanamsha thus indicates the difference between the fixed zodiac and the movable zodiac. The system that considers the fixed zodiac is called the *Niryana (without ayana!) system*, while the one that considers the movable zodiac is called the *Sayana (with ayana!) system*. The Niryana values of planetary longitudes can be obtained by subtracting the ayanamsha for a given time from the Sayana longitudes.

The Niryana and the Sayana zodiacs coincided in the year 285 AD when the ayanamsha was zero. At the rate of precession of equinoxes stated above, the ayanamsha on the 1st of January, 1995 is 23°47'26". The equinoctial precession completes one round in aproximately 26,000 years, as mentioned earlier, so that the fixed and movable zodiacs coincide regularly after this time span. The ayanamsha reckoned on the basis of considering the year 285 AD as the year when the Sayana and the Niryana zodiacs coincided is called the *Chitrapaksha ayanamsha*.

Ancient method of time reckoning

The Vedic seers had an elaborate method of reckoning time. They combined genius with religion so that it appealed to the intellectual and the devoted alike. There were several methods of reckoning time. One standard method was as follows:

1 Asu (or Prana)	=	4 (sidereal) seconds
6 Asus	=	1 sidereal Pala (or Vighati or Vinadi or 24 seconds)
60 Palas	=	1 Ghati (24 minutes)
60 Ghatis	=	1 day (24 hours)
30 days	=	1 month
12 months	=	1 year
43,20,000 years	=	1 Yuga

72 Yugas	=	1 Manu
14 Manus	=	1 Kalpa (or 1008 Yugas)
2 Kalpas	=	A day and night of Brahma
30 day-nights of Brahma	=	1 month of Brahma
12 months of Brahma	=	1 year of Brahma
100 years of Brahma	=	Life of Brahm (or 1 Mahakalpa)

In addition to the above, the following methods of reckoning of time were used for astrological purposes:

1. Sidereal day = Time interval between one star-rise to the next.
2. Civil day = Time interval between one sunrise to the next.
3. Lunar month = One new moon to the next.
4. Solar month = Interval between entry of Sun from one sign to the other.
5. Solar year = Period of one solar revolution.
6. Jupiterian (Barhaspatya) year = Period of Jupiter's motion through a sign.

Circular divisions

Measures of angles have been similarly described by Vedic astronomers.

60 Pratatparas	=	1 Tatpara
60 Tatparas	=	1 Vilipta (or Vikala or second)
60 Vilipta	=	1 Lipta (or Kala or minute)
60 Lipta	=	1 Lava (or bhaga or amsha or degree)
30 Lavas	=	1 Rashi (Sign)
12 Rashis	=	1 celestial circle or a revolution

Planets and the zodiac

The planets revolve around the Sun at different velocities in elliptical orbits. They also appear to revolve around the earth in elliptical orbits. Says Parashara:

"Although the grahas proceed towards the east, they appear as if they are moving in the westward direction, under the influence of the 'force of flow'."

The following three factors are of importance:

I. *The rotation of the earth from west to east direction.* Even as this causes the day as well as the night, it also makes the planets appear to be moving from east to west across the earth.

II. *Daily revolution of the zodiac from east to west*: The rotation of the earth makes the whole zodiac also appear as if it is making one daily revolution around the earth. In one day-night duration, all the signs of the zodiac (and all the nakshatras) successively rise in the east and set in the west.

III. *The movement of the planets from west to east*: Although the daily rotation of the earth makes the Sun and other planets appear to be moving from east to west, in effect they move from west to east along the zodiac. Thus a planet in Mesha will actually proceed to Vrisha, and then to Mithuna, and so on.

Order of the planets: Aryabhata describes the order of planets thus:

"Beneath the asterisms lie (the planets) Saturn, Jupiter, Mars, the Sun, Venus, Mercury and the Moon (one below the other); beneath them all lies the earth....."

Planets as lords of days and Horas: Aryabhata continues:

"The (above mentioned) seven planets beginning with Saturn, which are arranged in the order of increasing velocity, are the lords of the successive Horas. The planets occurring fourth in order of increasing velocity are the lords of the successive days, which are reckoned from sunrise."

There are 24 Horas in a day, each Hora being (approximately!) equivalent to an hour. The first Hora on a day, starting from sunrise, belongs to the lord of the day itself. Subsequent Horas follow in the order as given above, i.e., Saturn, Jupiter, Mars, Sun, Venus, Mercury, Moon, Saturn, etc., until the end of day at next sunrise.

From Saturn, the fourth in order is the Sun; therefore, the Sun is the lord of the day following the day of Saturn. That is, Sunday follows Saturday. From the Sun, the fourth in order is the Moon. Therefore, Sunday is followed by the day of the Moon, i.e., Monday.

Inner and Outer planets: The planets Mercury and Venus have their orbits between the Sun and the earth. They are called *inner or inferior planets*. These planets cannot go far away from the Sun. Mercury can only move a maximum of 27 degrees from the Sun and Venus a maximum of 47 degrees from the Sun.

The planets Mars, Jupiter and Saturn, whose orbits lie outside the orbit of the earth, are called *outer or superior planets*.

Retrogression and direct motion: Planets move along the zodiac from west to east, around the Sun. However, when seen from the earth, sometimes their motion appears to be occurring in a reverse direction against the background of the stars. This apparent motion in the reverse direction is called as retrogression of planets and has special significance in predictive astrology. Rahu and Ketu, which are not true planets, however, always move in retrograde direction (see Chapter III).

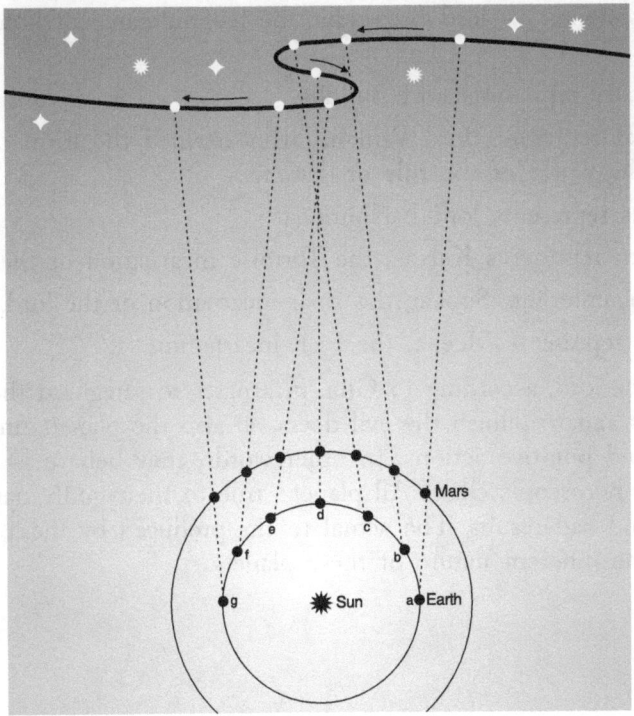

Phenomenon of apparent retrogression in an outer planet as viewed from the earth.

Combustion of planets: Planets when too close to the Sun become invisible and are labelled as *combust*. A combust planet loses its strength and tends to behave adversely according to predictive astrology. Aryabhata has the following to say about combustion:

> 'When the Moon has no latitude (i.e., when it is at zero degree of latitude) it is visible when situated at a distance of 12 degrees from the Sun. Venus is visible when 9 degrees distant from the Sun. The other planets taken in the order of decreasing sizes (viz., Jupiter, Mercury, Saturn and Mars) are visible when they are 9 degrees increased by twos (i.e., when they are 11, 13, 15 and 17 degrees) distant from the Sun.'

The degrees as mentioned above are generally taken as the limits within which the respective planets are said to be combust.

Planets as gods

Planets represent concentrations of energy. They influence the terrestrial phenomena by their disposition in the heavens. The sage Parashara, the father of Vedic astrology as understood and practised today, considers the planets as the representatives of gods. According to him:

(i)   The Sun represents lord Rama.

(ii)   The Moon represents lord Krishna.

(iii)   Mars stands for lord Narsimha, the half human-half lion form of the lord.

(iv)   Mercury represents lord Buddha.

(v)   Jupiter represents lord Vamana, who attained the form of a dwarf to rid the world of the rule of demons.

(vi)   Venus represents lord Parshurama.

(vii)   Saturn represents Kurma, the Tortoise incarnation of the lord.

(viii)   Rahu represents Sookar, the Boar incarnation of the lord.

(ix)   Ketu represents Meena, the Fish incarnation.

Even as the lord, according to Gita, incarnates to safeguard the interests of the righteous and to punish the evil-doers, so also the planets undertake their benevolent and punitive actions. In other words, they behave as benefics and malefics in a horoscopic chart. All planets, true to their godly nature, produce both good and bad results. The actual results produced by them manifest according to the inherent nature of these planets.

...III...
Elementary Concepts
of Astronomy - II

अव्यक्ताद्व्यक्तयः सर्वाः प्रभवन्त्यहरागमे ।
रात्र्यागमे प्रलीयन्ते तत्रैवाव्यक्तसंज्ञके ॥

*At the coming of (Brahma's) day, all manifestation springs forth from the
unmanifested (Brahma); at the coming of (Brahma's) night it all merges in
the same unmanifested.*

Gita VIII/18

The Panchanga

Knowledge of astrology finds its daily use in indian homes. All the Vedic
rituals and even day to day pursuits make use of a knowledge of astrology.
While predictive astrology was mainly restricted for the kings in ancient times,
practical astrology in the form of what we call today as electional astrology
was of concern to the lay man as well. The Indian almanac which details
information about the various festivals, rituals and planetary combinations for
the purpose of election of a suitable moment, and has been in use since times
immemorial, is called a *Panchanga*.

A Panchanga consists of five parts:

1. *Tithi* or the lunar date;
2. *Vaara* or the day of the week;
3. *Nakshatra* or the lunar asterism;
4. *Yoga*; and
5. *Karana*.

While *Vaara* or the day of the week is a function of the Sun alone, the
other four parts of the Panchanga depend upon the disposition of the Moon
alone or the Moon-Sun duo. The Moon thus has a special significance in
Vedic astrology, besides the Sun. In India, traditionally the birthdays are also
observed and celebrated based on the tithi and nakshatra operating at the
time of birth of the native.

Lunar months

The Moon goes around the earth once in a lunar month. Like other planets, it moves from west to east along the zodiac although the rotation of the earth makes it appear to be moving in the reverse direction. One revolution of the Moon around the earth produces what is called a *lunar month*. There are the following types of lunar months:

1. *The Sidereal month*: This is a period of time during which the Moon makes one round of the zodiac, as observed from the earth. Its duration is equivalent to 27.3217 mean solar days (or 27 days 7 hours 43 minutes approximately). During this period the Moon, when observed against a fixed star, moves round the zodiac once and returns to the same star.

2. *The Synodic month*: This is a period of time which elapses between one New Moon and the next. Its duration is 29.5306 mean solar days (or 29 days 12 hours 44 minutes approximately). The synodic month is also called a *lunation*. A New Moon indicates a conjunction of the Sun and the Moon. The synodic month is larger than a sidereal month because it indicates the relation of the Moon with the Sun. During one revolution of the Moon, the Sun too moves along the zodiac by slightly less than one sign. To catch up with the Sun (in order to complete a synodic month) the Moon, therefore, has to take some extra time.

3. *The Nodical month*: The intersection of the ecliptic by the Moon's path results in the formation of the ascending and the descending nodes of the Moon, respectively known as Rahu and Ketu. They move in the reverse or retrograde direction along the zodiac. A nodical month is the time that the Moon takes to complete one round from Rahu to Rahu. Since Rahu moves in a retrograde direction, it meets the Moon slightly earlier along the zodiac. The duration of the nodical month is approximately 27.2122 mean solar days.

4. *The Anomalistic month*: This is the duration of time that the Moon takes to complete one revolution around the earth, in its orbit from perigee to perigee. Its duration is approximately 27.5546 mean solar days.

Note:

The Moon loops around the earth in an elliptical orbit, just as the earth does around the Sun. The orbit itself is in constant flux due to perturbations caused by the Sun and the planets. *Perigee* is the point at which a body (the Moon in this case!) in orbit around the earth is at the least distance from the earth. Its reverse is called as *Apogee*, which signifies that a body in orbit around the earth is at its farthest from the earth.

An anomalistic lunar month is the lunar equivalent to the solar *anomalistic year* which indicates the passage of the Sun around the earth from perigee to perigee (or, in fact, the passage of the earth around the Sun from perihelion to perihelion!).

Perihelion and *Aphelion* are the equivalents of perigee and apogee, with the Sun (Helios=Sun) as the centre and the planets orbiting around it.

Cycles of the Moon

A lunar year, generally considered for astrological purposes, is a synodic year consisting of twelve synodic months amounting to a duration of approximately 354 days. It contains 360 tithis or lunar dates (30 tithis in a synodic month). This year falls short of a solar year, of about 365.25 days, by about eleven days.

If a totally lunar calender were followed, the various seasons would fail to coincide with the lunar months, since a lunar year would end eleven days earlier than a solar year. This would mean a difference of over a month every three solar years. In order to compensate for this, and to make the solar and lunar calenders function side by side, a luni-solar concept has been developed so that an extra lunar month is considered approximately every three years, or earlier. This extra lunar month which is periodically taken into consideration in order to bring harmony between the solar and the lunar calenders is called an *intercalary month*. The use of various 'Yugas' consisting of three year cycles, five year cycles, eight year cycles, eleven year cycles, nineteen year cycles and thirty year cycles, etc., signified brilliant attempts by Indian pre-Vedic astronomers to harmonise the solar and lunar years. The nineteen year cycle appears to be the most accurate 'observed' Yuga or cycle. It consists of seven intercalary months over a period of nineteen solar years. This in other words means that in a period of 228 solar months, there are 235 lunar (synodic months (New Moons or Full Moons).

The Metonic Cycle: Consistent with the above observations is the discovery by Meton (433 BC) that there occur 235 lunations in a period of nineteen solar years. It will be seen that total number of days in nineteen years (19 x 365.2422) comes to 6939.60 days. Total number of days in 235 lunar synodic months (235 x 29.5306) comes to 6939.69 days. The two figures are remarkably close. This means that a period of nineteen years or 228 solar months (19 x 12.228) is equal to 235 lunar months or 19 lunar years plus seven lunar months. We have already observed above that there occur seven intercalary months in nineteen years.

The nineteen years luni-solar cycle is so accurate that the tithis or lunar dates recur or fall on similar days after exactly nineteen years. Even such astronomical phenomenon as the eclipses recur after nineteen year intervals with fair precision.

Adhika-Maasa or the Intercalary month: The Sun changes its sign or rashi every month. The day it enters a sign is called as its ingress into that sign. A lunar month in which there is no solar ingress into a sign is considered an intercalary month. An intercalary month occurs once in 32 (solar) months and 16 days. This means that roughly once in three years there is an intercalary month; during this year, there are thirteen lunar months.

Kshaya Maasa or Omitted month: This happens when there are two solar ingresses (i.e., the Sun enters two signs) during one lunar month. This happens very infrequently. When there is an omitted month, there occur two intercalary months during one year.

Paksha: A paksha consists of fifteen lunar dates. Two pakshas make a lunar month. A *Krishna-paksha* extends from Poornima (or Full Moon) to Amavasya (or New Moon). A *Shukla-paksha* extends from New Moon to Full Moon.

Moon's Nodes

The Moon's apparent path intersects the ecliptic obliquely at two points called the *nodes*. This is similar to the Sun's path or ecliptic intersecting the equator at an oblique angle. The point where the Moon crosses the ecliptic from south to north is called the *ascending node* or *Rahu*. Where it crosses the ecliptic from north to south is called the *descending node* or *Ketu*. These two points are six signs or 180 degrees apart. Just as the equinoctial point shifts westwards on the ecliptic, so also the Moon's orbit intersects the ecliptic at a constantly shifting point. Thus, Rahu and Ketu go on receding or shifting westward along the ecliptic. Their movement is, therefore, constantly retrograde. They complete one round of the zodiac in approximately eighteen years and ten days.

Rahu and Ketu, though only astronomical points, have a special status in Vedic astrology. They are treated as grahas or planets, like any other planet.

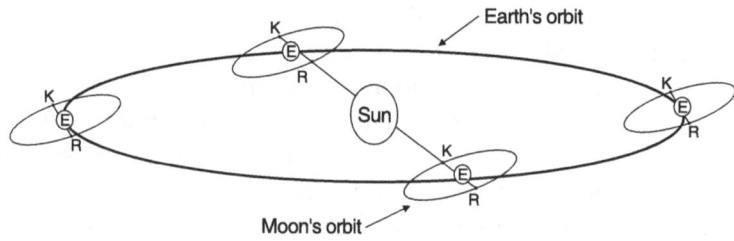

The orbit of the earth around the Sun and that of the Moon around the earth. Rahu and Ketu are formed where the Moon's orbit intersects the apparent path of the Sun around the earth.

The Eclipses

There are two kinds of eclipses:

1. Solar eclipses, and

2. Lunar eclipses.

A *solar eclipse* occurs when the shadow of the Moon falls on the earth. This means that at the time of a solar eclipse, the Moon happens to lie between the Sun and the earth. This occurs on a New Moon day, when the Sun and the Moon are conjunct and happen to lie on the same side of the earth. Since the orbit of the Moon is tilted at an angle of approximately 5 degrees to the ecliptic, the Sun-Moon-earth trio do not always fall on one straight line on every New Moon day. That is why the eclipse does not occur every time there is a New Moon.

A *lunar eclipse* occurs when the Moon lies opposite to the Sun with the earth intervening between the two. The shadow of the earth falls on the Moon. This happens on a Full Moon day when the Sun-earth-Moon trio fall in one straight line. Again, because of the obliquity of thec Moon's path to the ecliptic, this situation does not arise at every Full Moon.

It has been pointed out that the Moon's path crosses the Sun's path at the ascending and the descending nodes (i.e., Rahu and Ketu). The Moon must, therefore, be fairly close to Rahu and Ketu, and the Sun too must be close enough, to ensure that the earth, the Sun and the Moon fall on a straight line. "Swallowed by Rahu" is an expression applied to the eclipsed luminary.

A solar eclipse is likely to occur if a New Moon occurs within 18½ degrees of the node (Rahu or Ketu) and certainly if the distance is less than 15 degrees. A lunar eclipse occurs on a Full Moon day (i.e., the Sun and the Moon are opposite to each other). It is likely to occur when the distance between the Moon and the node is less than 12 degrees, and certainly if it is less than about 9½ degrees. A

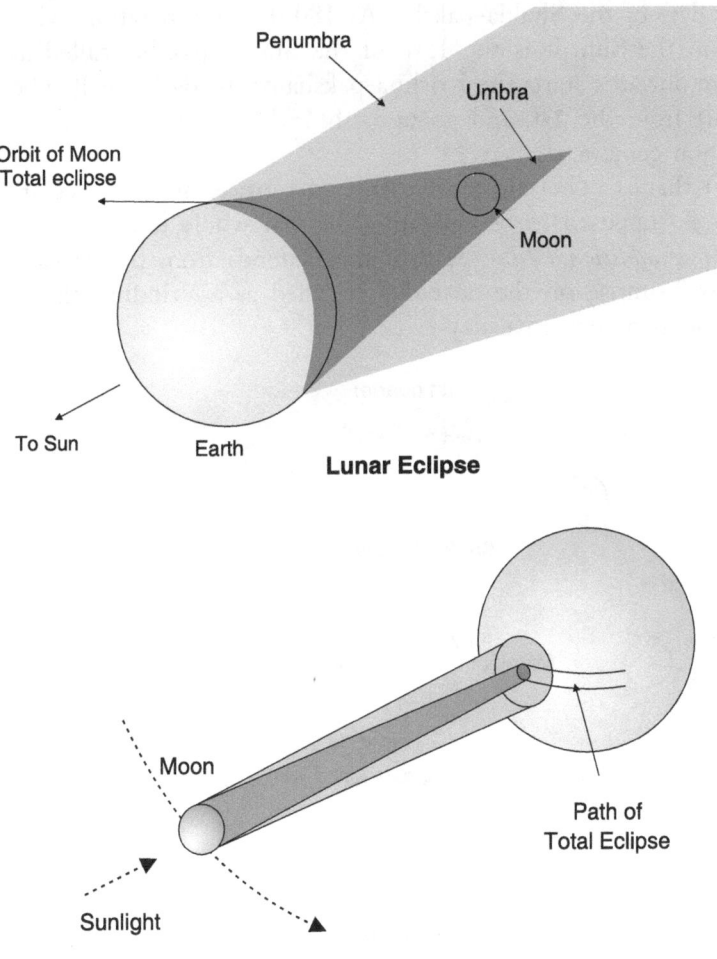

Lunar Eclipse

Solar Eclipse

maximum of sevn eclipses (four or five solar eclipses; three or two lunar eclipses) are possible in any given year.

Tithis or Lunar Dates

There are thirty lunar dates or tithis, of 12 degrees each (30 x 12 = 360 degrees). A tithi is indicative of the Moon's separation from the Sun. It is obtained by subtracting the longitude of the Sun from the longitude of the Moon, and dividing the above value by twelve. The quotient plus one gives the number of the tithi operating on any particular day. Thus,

(Moon - Sun) divided by 12

Tithi = Q + 1

The tithis are counted from the 1st of the bright half or Shukla-paksha. The Sun's conjunction with the Moon coincides with the 30th tithi or *Amavasya*. When the Moon overtakes the Sun, but lies within its 12 degrees, it is the 1st lunar date of the Shukla-paksha. At 180 degree separation, with the Moon opposed to the Sun, it is the 15th of the Shukla-paksha, called as *Poornima*. From here onwards starts the Krishna-paksha or the darker half. The tithis here again start from the 1st, and go upto th 15th or Amavasya, when the Moon and the Sun conjoin.

A tithi that is operating at the time of sunrise, on a particular day, is the tithi that is supposed to be operating on that whole day.

Vriddhi or additional tithi: A tithi that extends from before sunrise on one day to after sunrise on the next day is called as a Vriddhi tithi. Such a tithi operates on two successive days.

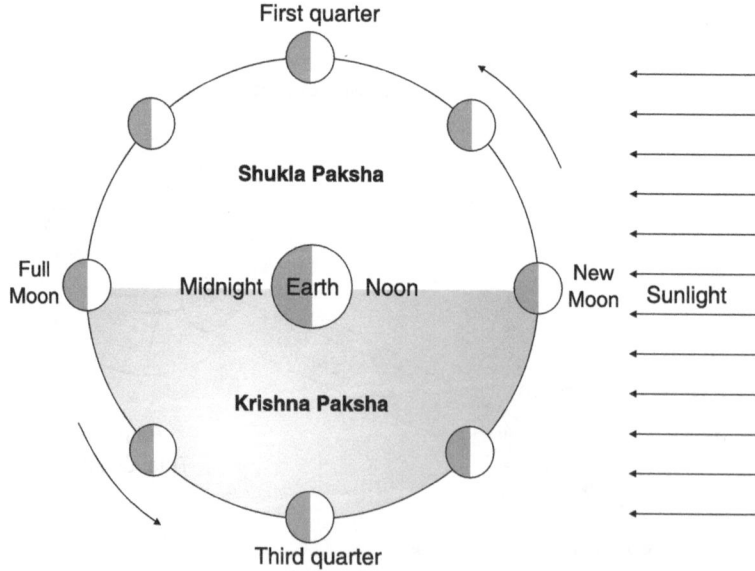

Phases of the Moon

Kshaya or omitted tithi: A tithi that begins after a sunrise and ends before the next sunrise is called a Kshaya tithi. This tithi is supposed to miss its operation during that lunar cycle.

Tithi is extremely important in performing day to day rituals and ceremonies, and in electional astrology.

Yogas

There are twenty seven Yogas. Each one measures 13°20' of arc (360° ÷ 27 = 13°20'). A Yoga indicates a sum of the longitudes of the Moon and the Sun in multiples of 13°20'. Although this measure of a Yoga is the same as that of a Nakshatra (which has been already dealt with), there is no link between the two. Add the Niryana longitudes of the Sun and the Moon and divide by 13°20'. The quotient plus one gives the number of the Yoga from the first one (Vishkumbha) onwards. The twenty-seven Yogas are listed below.

1.	Vishkumbha	15.	Vajra
2.	Preeti	16.	Siddhi
3.	Ayushman	17.	Vyatipata
4.	Saubhagya	18.	Variyana
5.	Shobhana	19.	Parigha
6.	Atiganda	20.	Shiva
7.	Sukarma	21.	Siddha
8.	Dhriti	22.	Sadhya
9.	Shoola	23.	Shubha
10.	Ganda	24.	Shukla
11.	Vriddhi	25.	Brahma
12.	Dhruva	26.	Indra
13.	Vyaghata	27.	Vaidhriti
14.	Harshana		

Yogas, like tithis, find extensive use in electional astrology and day to day rituals.

Karana

A *Karana* is half a tithi, or 360 minutes (6 degrees) of arc. In thirty tithis comprising a lunar month, there are sixty half-tithis or Karanas.

There are four Karanas that occur only once in a lunar month. They are the fixed Karanas and called as:

1. *Shakuni*: assigned to the latter half of the 14th day of Krishna-paksha.

2. *Chatushpada*: assigned to the first half of the Amavasya (15th day of Krishna-paksha).

3. *Naga*: assigned to the latter half of the Amavasya.

4. *Kimstughna*: assigned to the first half of the first day of the Shukla-paksha.

The remaining seven Karanas recur eight times during rest of the lunar month. Their names are:

1. Bava
2. Balava
3. Kanlava
4. Taitila
5. Gara
6. Vanija
7. Vishti

These Karanas recur in regular order starting from the second half of the first day of Shukla-paksha until the first half of the 14th day of the Krishna-paksha.

Karanas too find their use in rituals as well as electional astrology.

Some Astronomical Facts about Planets

The following is a very brief description of the planets (the Sun, the Moon, the planets and Rahu-Ketu) which are of relevance in Vedic astrology.

SUN

This is the most important of the nine grahas (or "planets"). In fact, the Sun is our nearest star in space with planets revolving around it. It is the source of all the natural light and heat of the earth. It provides the centripetal force to balance the centrifugal force generated by the planets going around it. Its diameter is 1.392 million kilometres, which is almost 109 times the diameter of the earth. The mass of the Sun is some 323,000 times the mass of the earth. It has extremely high surface and core temperatures, and goes on producing immense amounts of energy. At one time the Sun was considered the centre of the universe (this does not appear to be the view ever held by the Vedic scholars!). Now we know that it lies near the edge of a spiral arm of the Milky Way galaxy, lying some 30,000 light years away from the galactic centre, and sharing the general rotation of the galaxy.

MOON

It is a satellite of the earth. In Vedic astrology it is of paramount importance. It is the fastest moving of the 'grahas' and has the usual west to east movement along the zodiac. It has a relatively small size, its diameter being only about 3476 kilometres. Its average distance from the earth is about 384,400 kilometres (or roughly 239,000 miles). It always presents the same face toward the earth. This is possible by the fact that it takes the same time to rotate once on its axis as it does to revolve once around the earth in its orbit (i.e., 27.32 days). Since the rotation around the axis is a uniform motion, while the motion in orbit is not, we are sometimes able to see an extra strip of the Moon's surface on one side or the other. Some 59% of the total surface of the Moon may thus be visible to us on the earth at one time or the other. This phenomenon is called *Liberation*.

The luminosity of the Moon is caused by light from the Sun. It is the varying relative positions of the Sun and the Moon that produce the phases of the Moon. These lunar phases, earlier discussed as tithis, are extremely important in Vedic astrology.

MARS

Mars is the first of the outer planets and the fourth in order of distance from the Sun (the others being Mercury, Venus and the earth). Its orbit is highly elliptical (compared to the near circular orbit of the earth), so that at its closest position to the earth it may only be about 56 million kilometres from the earth, while at its farthest it may reach 100 million kilometres. The brilliance of Mars in the sky thus depends upon its location in the orbit. Mars is only twice as large as our Moon, its diameter being 6786 kilometres. It is at a mean distance of 227.8 million kilometres from the Sun.

The synodic period of Mars is 780 days, which is the interval between Martian oppositions to the Sun, with the earth lying in between. Mars rotates on its own axis in 1.026 days and has an orbital period (i.e., period of sidereal revolution) of 687 days (1.881 years). Mars has two small satellites called Phobos and Deimos.

MERCURY

Mercury is the planet nearest to the Sun. Its proximity to the Sun makes it extremely hot. It has a very eccentric orbit so that its minimum distance from the Sun (perihelion) is much less than its maximum distance (aphelion). *It may be noted that a planet has its maximum orbital speed at perihelion and minimum at aphelion.* Its mean distasnce from the Sun is approximately 58 million kilometres. Mercury has a diameter of about 4870 kilometres, and its orbit has a maximum inclination of about 7 degrees on either side of the ecliptic. Mercury rotates once around its axis in 58.65 days which is quite precisely two-thirds of its orbital period of about 88 earth days.

JUPITER

Jupiter is the largest planet of the solar system, its mass exceeding that of all the other planets combined. Its rapid spin (once in about 9 hours and 50 minutes) has caused it to bulge at its equator (diameter approx. 143,000 kilometres) and to flatten at the poles (diameter approx. 133,000 kilometres). It is 318 times as massive as the earth but less than a thousandth part of the Sun. Its mean distance from the Sun is 778 million kilometres. It has an orbital period of 11.86 earth years.

Being far away from the Sun, Jupiter is a cold planet with its gaseous cloud having a temperature of some 140°C below freezing point. There are several satellites (perhaps upto sixteen!) which circle around Jupiter.

VENUS

Venus is the second nearest planet to the Sun. Its dense cloudy atmosphere reflects light extremely efficiently and accounts for the brilliance of this planet in the sky. The maximum inclination of its orbit is about 3°24' on either side of the ecliptic. It is located at a mean distance of 108 million kilometres, and has a diameter of about 12,000 kilometres.

The rotation period of Venus is 242.6 days. An important fact about the rotation of Venus is that it is *retrograde*, that is opposite to the general direction of rotations in the solar system. The orbital period of Venus is about 224.7 days.

SATURN

It is the last of the naked eye planets. Its mean distance from the Sun is 1426 million kilometres. Its rotation period is approximately 10 hours 14 minutes, and its orbital period is 29.46 years. Saturn has a diameter of over 120 thousand kilometres at the equator. Being further away from the Sun, Saturn is a cold planet. It is larger than the rest of the planets (except Jupiter) and is about 95 times as massive as the earth. Its characteristic feature is the presence of rings around it. At least twenty satellites are known to revolve around the planet.

The *extra-saturnine planets* (Uranus, Neptune and Pluto) need the help of a telescope for their identification. They do not form a part of predictive Vedic astrology and are, therefore, not treated of here.

...IV...
Vedic Method of Instruction:
An Illustration

सहस्ररश्मिः शतधा वर्तमानः प्राणः प्रजानामुदयत्येष सूर्यः ।

It is the Sun that rises – the Sun that possesses a thousand rays, exists in a hundred forms and is the life of all creatures.

Prashna Upanishad I/8

Ancient Indian teaching methods involved a personal instruction by the teacher to his disciple. The teacher, called as 'Guru', would generally live in seclusion, away from city life, and have a select group of disciples, called 'Shishyas'. It would only be the good fortune of a 'shishya' if he managed to secure a good 'guru'. Similarly, a great 'guru' would strive to find a deserving disciple. The teacher-disciple relation used to be a highly affectionate relationship, with the teacher commanding the same, nay more, reverence from his disciples as the latter owed to their parents.

The ancient historical records of India find their place in the *Puranas*. In these Puranas, generally there is a story being told by an elevated sage to one or more seekers of knowledge. In one of the earliest of the Puranas, called the *Shri Vishnu Purana*, there is a dialogue between the celebrated sage Parashara and his worthy disciple Maitreya. The disciple wants to know from his teacher the method of the Creation, the cycles of creation and annihilation, and the cause behind these cycles. Sage Parashara happened to be the father of sage Vyasa, the compiler of the Mahabharata as well as the Vedas and several Puranas. The Mahabharata coincided with the beginning of the Kali era which is equivalent to 3102 BC. In other words, this dialogue between Parashara and Maitreya is well over five thousand years old.

During their discussion, sage Parashara briefly mentions about the Sun god, the nakshatras and the zodiacal signs. This happens in *Canto 2, Chapter 8 of the Shri Vishnu Purana*. Those shlokas (reverent stanzas) as are relevant to our subject are being presented here, along with author's comments, in order to show the profundity of knowledge possessed by the Vedic scholars, as also their simple and lucid method of instruction.

It may be clarified here that, except where specifically indicated, all discussion considers the tropical or Sayana zodiac and not the sidereal or Nirayana zodiac, for reasons not too difficult to appreciate.

Shloka 11

अहोरात्रव्यवस्थानकारणं भगवान्रविः।
देवायानः परः पन्था योगिनां क्लेशसङ्क्षये॥११॥

The Sun god is the cause of occurrence of the day and the night. He, for the liberated yogi, is the channel to higher regions.

Comments: The rotation of the earth, or the apparent movement of the Sun across the heavens around the earth, leads to the formation of the day and the night.

The second part of the shloka corroborates the view of the Gita that elevated liberated souls take to the path of the Sun to reach the higher regions. Illustrating subtle truths through a flavour of religious philosophy is a typical Indian method of teaching.

Shloka 12

दिवसस्य रविर्मध्ये सर्वकालं व्यवस्थितः।
सर्वद्वीपेषु मैत्रेय निशार्धस्य च सम्मुखः॥१२॥

O' Maitreya! The Sun god remains in all regions in mid-heaven at mid-day; in the opposing ones, at midnight.

Comments: Mid-heaven for any place is the meridian which is crossed by the Sun at mid-day. For those places which are located exactly opposite, the same position is achieved at midnight. When the Sun is at mid-heaven, a zenith for a given place, it is at nadir for a place located exactly opposite, and vice versa. In a horoscopic chart, the mid-heaven indicates the 10th house, and the nadir the 4th house.

Shlokas 13, 14

उदयास्तमने चैव सर्वकालं तु सम्मुखे।
विदिशासु त्वशेषासु तथा ब्रह्मन् दिशासु च॥१३॥
यैर्यत्र दृश्यते भास्वान्स तेषामुदयः स्मृतः।
तिरोभावं च यत्रैति तत्रैवास्तमनं रवेः॥१४॥

In a similar manner, sunrise and sunset are opposite to each other. O' Brahmin! Residents of all directions and angles, where (at the end of the night) they see the Sun they call it sunrise, and where (at the end of the day) they see the Sun disappear they call it the sunset.

Comments: Just as zenith and nadir are opposite positions, so are the sunrise and the sunset. The sunrise and the sunset are different for different places; these are terms which are used by different people for convenience to describe what looks like the appearance and the disappearance of the Sun. In a horoscope, the rising (of a sign) coincides with the first house, and the setting with the seventh house.

Shloka 15

नैवास्तमनमर्कस्य नोदयः सर्वदा सतः ।
उदयास्तमनाख्यं हि दर्शनादर्शनं रवेः ॥ १५ ॥

Ever consistent in its position, the Sun god in effect neither rises nor sets. Only His being seen or being lost to vision are labelled as His rise and His setting.

Comments: The sage clarifies the relatively fixed position of the Sun compared to the Earth. The Sun remains where it is, and what appears as rising or setting is not primarily a function of the Sun. It is the rotation of the earth which makes the Sun appear and disappear at regular intervals.

Shloka 18

उदयास्तमनाभ्यां च स्मृते पूर्वापरे दिशौ ।
यावत्पुरस्तात्तपति तावत्पृष्ठे च पार्श्वयोः ॥ १८ ॥

The very rising and setting of the Sun has caused the east and the west directions. In effect, the way He illumines the east, even so He does the west, as well as the south and the north.

Comments: The east and west directions are dependant upon the directions of the apparent rise and the setting of the Sun. On its own part, the Sun has nothing to do with these as he illumines all the areas equally. The north, south, east and west directions are a consequence of earth's rotation.

Shloka 26

एवं पुष्करमध्येन यदा याति दिवाकरः ।
त्रिशद्भागन्तु मेदिन्यास्तदा मौहूर्तिकी गतिः ॥ २६ ॥

Thus, when, after reaching the middle of the Pushkaradweepa, the Sun traverses the thirtieth part of (Its apparent course around) the earth, Its movement is considered to be of one Muhurta.

Comments: A Muhurta is a unit of time. It is equal to one-thirtieth part of the duration of a day-night, which is sixty Ghatis or twenty four hours. A Muhurta is equal to two Ghatis or 48 minutes.

Shloka 27

कुलालचक्रपर्यन्तो भ्रमन्नेष दिवाकरः ।
करोत्यहस्तथा रात्रि विमुंचन्मेदिनीं द्विज ॥ २७ ॥

O' Dwija! Like one revolving at the circumference of a potter's wheel, this Sun traverses all the thirty parts of the Earth (i.e., 30 parts of the zodiac) in one day-night.

Comments: As has been commented above, a Muhurta is a unit of time and not an arc of the zodiac. Since the movements of the Sun, as well as other planets, is not uniform or linear, the Sun neednot traverse an arc equal to one-thirteeth part of the zodiac in one Muhurta. But during one day-night, the Sun does go round the earth once. There are thus thirty Muhurtas in a span of one day-night.

Shloka 28

अयनस्योत्तरस्यादौ मकरं याति भास्करः ।
ततः कुम्भं च मीनं च राशे राश्यन्तरं द्विज ॥ २८ ॥

O' Dwija! At the beginning of the Uttarayana, the Sun, first of all, goes to the Makara rashi (the sign Capricorn). Thereafter, He goes to Kumbha (Aquarius) and Meena (Pisces), traversing one rashi after the other.

Comments: Uttarayana is the northerly course of the Sun. It begins from the moment the Sun enters the sign Capricorn around 22nd December, i.e., when it has attained the maximum south declination of 23° 28'. The northern hemisphere has the shortest day and the longest night at this time. The Sun next passes through Kumbha and Meena.

Shloka 29

त्रिष्वेतेष्वथ भुक्तेषु ततो वैषुवतीं गतिम् ।
प्रयाति सविता कुर्वन्नहोरात्रं ततः समम् ॥ २९ ॥

Having savoured of these three rashis, the Sun, equalising the day and night takes recourse to a balanced pace (at the beginning of the sign Mesha).

Comments: That is, the Sun causes a balance at the time of its entering the sign Mesha or Aries. This happens around 21st March when the day and night are equal, and the Sun has attained zero declination. In general discussions, the planets are considered as masculine. Their passage through rashis, generally held to be feminine, is considered as an act of savouring or relishing these rashis.

Shlokas 30-31

ततो रात्रिः क्षयं याति वर्द्धतेऽनुदिनं दिनम् ॥ ३० ॥
ततश्च मिथुनस्यान्ते परां काष्ठामुपागतः ।
राशि कर्कटकं प्राप्य कुरुते दक्षिणायनम् ॥ ३१ ॥

Thereafter, the night progressively shortens and the day lengthens. Quitting the Mithuna (Gemini) rashi (after traversing Mesha and Vrisha - Aries and Taurus), having attained the culmination of Uttarayana, he reaches the Karka (Cancer) rashi and begins the Dakshinayana.

Comments: Zero degree Mesha is the position of vernal equinox. Thereafter, the Sun continues its northerly course through Vrisha and Mithuna, until it attains a maximum north declination of 23˚28' at the beginning of Karka when the northern hemisphere has the longest day and the shortest night. This happens around 21st June. Thereafter, the Sun commences the Dakshinayana or its southerly course.

Shlokas 32-33

कुलालचक्रपर्यन्तो यथा शीघ्रं प्रवर्तते।
दक्षिणप्रक्रमे सूर्यस्तथा शीघ्रं प्रवर्तते॥ ३२॥
अतिवेगितया कालं वायुवेगबलाच्चरन्।
तस्मात्प्रकृष्टां भूमिं तु कालेनाल्पेन गच्छति॥ ३३॥

Just as one sitting at the circumference of a potter's wheel moves very fast, so the Sun crosses the Dakshinayana at a faster pace. Thus He traverses His eminent path at a rapid pace, in a short span of time, as if driven by the force of a fast wind.

Comments: The Sun's path is the twelve signs of the zodiac. The sage here points to the last day of the Dakshinayana, or winter solstice, when the Sun traverses the day at a faster pace. This holds true for the northern hemisphere where, at the end of Dakshinayana or the beginning of Uttarayana, the day is short and the night long. This is further explained in the subsequent Shlokas.

Shloka 34

सूर्यो द्वादशभिः शैघ्र्यान्मुहूर्तैर्दक्षिणायने।
त्रयोदशार्धमृक्षाणामह्ना तु चरति द्विज।
मुहूर्तैस्तावदृक्षाणि नक्तमष्टादशैश्चरन्॥ ३४॥

O' Dwija! While in Dakshinayana, due to His fast pace during the day, the Sun traverses the thiteen-and-a-half nakshatras in twelve Muhurtas. But during the night, due to Its slower pace, It traverses as many nakshatras in eighteen Muhurtas.

Comments: The following facts emerge from this Shloka:

1. It is the last day of the Dakshinayana that is meant here.

2. The Sun has to traverse half the zodiac (thirteen-and-a-half nakshatras, equivalent to six rashis or signs) during day time and the remaining half during night-time.

3. Since at the end of the Dakshinayana, the day is the shortest and the

night the longest, the six signs of the zodiac that emerge at the horizon during day-time, one after the other, do so at a faster pace.

4. Since the end of the Dakshinayana or the beginning of the Uttarayana coincides with the Sun's entry into Makara, the six signs starting from Makara (which rises with the sunrise at the time of shifting from Dakshinayana to Uttarayana) have a shorter duration while the remaining six (from Karka onwards) have a longer duration.

   The signs Karka (Cancer) to Dhanu (Sagittarius) are thus the *signs of long ascension*, while those from Makara (Capricorn) to Mithuna (Gemini) are the *signs of short ascension*. At the time of winter solstice, the signs of long ascension rise during the night and those of short ascension rise during the day.

5. The preceding two shlokas apply to the northern hemisphere. The reverse holds true for the southern hemisphere. Thus, in the southern hemisphere, the signs Karka to Dhanu are the signs of short ascension while those from Makara to Mithuna are those of long ascension.

   The longest day in the northern hemisphere coincides with the shortest day in the southern hemisphere. Or, the longest night in the northern hemisphere coincides with the shortest night in the southern hemisphere.

6. The sage apparently had his hermitage in some part of north India where the duration of the day could reach upto 12 Muhurtas (nine hours and thirty-six minutes) and that of the night upto 18 Muhurtas (fourteen hours and twenty four minutes) at the end of Dakshinayana.

Shloka 35

कुलालचक्रमध्यस्थो यथा मन्दं प्रसर्पति।
तथोदगयने सूर्यः सर्पते मन्दविक्रमः ॥ ३५ ॥

The Sun moves at a lower pace during the Uttarayana, like one settled at the middle portion of the potter's wheel.

Comments: As is apparent in the subsequent shlokas, it is the end of the Uttarayana or the summer solistice which is meant here.

Shlokas 36-38

तस्माद्दीर्घेण कालेन भूमिमल्पां तु गच्छति।
अष्टादशमुहूर्तं यदुत्तरायणपश्चिमम् ॥ ३६ ॥
अहर्भवति तच्चापि चरते मन्दविक्रमः ॥ ३७ ॥
त्रयोदशार्द्धमहा तु ऋक्षाणां चरते रविः।
मुहूर्तैस्तावदृक्षाणि रात्रौ द्वादशभिश्चरन् ॥ ३८ ॥

Therefore, at this time, He traverses a smaller circumference of the earth in a very long time, so that the last day of Uttarayana is of a duration of eighteen Muhurtas. On this day too, the Sun, moving at a very slow pace, traverses the thirteen-and-a-half nakshatras, constituting half the

zodiac, in one day's time. At night, however, He crosses the same number
of nakshatras in twelve Muhurtas.

Comments: The last day of Uttarayana is the reverse of the last day of
Dakshinayana. The signs of long ascension (from Karka to Dhanu) rise during the day while those of short ascension (from Makara to Mithuna) rise
during the night.

Shloka 39-40

अतो मन्दतरं नाभ्यां चक्रं भ्रमति वै यथा।
मृत्पिण्ड इव मध्यस्थो ध्रुवो भ्रमति वै तथा॥३९॥
कुलालचक्रनाभिस्तु यथा तत्रैव वर्तते।
ध्रुवस्तथा हि मैत्रेय तत्रैव परिवर्तते॥४०॥

Just as the nave of a wheel rotates at a very slow pace along with the slow
rotation of the central portion of the wheel (compared to its mid-portion
and the circumference), so also the Dhruva (the pole star) located in the
centre of the Jyotisha-Chakra rotates at a very slow pace. Maitreya! Just
as the central axis of the potter's wheel rotates around itself, the Dhruva
too rotates on itself in a similar manner.

Comments: The pole star (called as Dhruva in the Puranas because of its
fixed position) is very close to the true position of the north celestial pole. It
is only about 1˚ away from the true north pole. The pole star is considered
as the nave of a huge celestial wheel. Innumerable invisible spokes are supposed to issue forth from it to attach individually to the innumerable stars and
planets which all revolve around it, along with the rotation of the pole star
around its axis. Thus the various heavenly bodies retain their relative angular
relationship with each other as well as the pole star.

Shloka 41

उभयोः काष्ठयोर्मध्ये भ्रमतो मण्डलानि तु।
दिवा नक्तं च सूर्यस्य मन्दा शीघ्रा च वै गतिः॥४१॥

Revolving in a circular fashion between the northern and southern
limits, the pace of the Sun, during the day and night, varies between
slow and fast.

Comments: This is self-explanatory in view of the comments made earlier.

Shloka 42

मन्दाहि यस्मिन्नयने शीघ्रा नक्तं तदा गतिः।
शीघ्रा निशि यदा चास्य तदा मन्दा दिवा गतिः॥४२॥

In whichever Ayana, the Sun's pace is slower during the day, Its pace at
night is faster. And whenever Its pace at night is faster, Its pace during
the day is slower.

Comments: Same thing said in two ways. The reverse of the above observation too holds true.

Shloka 43-45

एकप्रमाणमेवैष मार्गं याति दिवाकरः।
अहोरात्रेण यो भुङ्क्ते समस्ता राशयो द्विज॥४३॥
षडेव राशीन् यो भुङ्क्ते रात्रावन्यांश्च षड्दिवा॥४४॥
राशिप्रमाणजनिता दीर्घह्रस्वात्मता दिने।
तथा निशायां राशीनां प्रमाणैर्लघुदीर्घता॥४५॥

O' Dwija! The Sun always traverses the same distance. In a day-night span, He savours of all the (twelve) rashis. The Sun enjoys its course through six rashis during the day and six rashis during the night. Variations in the duration of the day depend upon the extent of the rashis. Variations in the duration of the night too depend upon the extent of the rashis.

Comments: Earlier it was stated that the Sun travelled through thirteen-and-a-half nakshatras during the day and a similar number of them at night. That means six rashis during the day and six during the night. This has been explained earlier.

It must be emphasised that it is not the Sun that traverses these rashis during the day-night span. It is the twelve rashis that successively rise at the eastern horizon during the twenty four hours. The Sun only appears to move around the earth. However, in a horoscope, the Sun passes through six houses of the chart as the six signs rise during the day; similarly it passes through six houses of the horoscopic chart as the other six signs rise during the night. The location of the Sun in a horoscope thus indicates the time of the day the horoscope is cast for.

When the signs of long ascension rise during the day, the day is longer and the night shorter. When those of short ascension do so, the day is shorter and the night longer.

Shlokas 46-47

दिनादेर्दीर्घह्रस्वत्वं तद्भोगेनैव जायते।
उत्तरे प्रक्रमे शीघ्रा निशि मन्दा गतिर्दिवा॥४६॥
दक्षिणे त्वयने चैव विपरीता विवस्वतः॥४७॥

Upon His course through the rashis depend the prolixity and brevity of the day and night. While in (at the end of!) Uttarayana the Sun's pace is faster during the night and slower during the day, during the (concluding part of) Dakshinayana the reverse is true.

Comments: The reverse holds true for the southern latitudes. Repetition of the same concept emphasises the significance inherent in it.

Shloka 68

कर्कटावस्थिते भानौ दक्षिणायनमुच्यते।
उत्तरायणमप्युक्तं मकरस्थे दिवाकरे॥६८॥

Sun's entry into Karka is called Dakshinayana and His entry into Ma-
kara indicates Uttarayana.

Comments: Self-explanatory.

Shloka 69

त्रिशन्मुहूर्तं कथितमहोरात्रं तु यन्मया।
तानि पंचदश ब्रह्मन् पक्ष इत्यभिधीयते॥६९॥

Brahmin! The day-night consisting of thirty Muhurtas that I have already
described, such fifteen day-nights constitute a 'Paksha'.

Comments: Half the lunar cycle, from New Moon to Full Moon or from
Full Moon to New Moon, is also called a Paksha. It is *Krishna Paksha* between Full Moon and New Moon, and *Shukla Paksha* between New Moon
and Full Moon.

Shloka 70

मासः पक्षद्वयेनोक्तो द्वौ मासौ चार्कजावृतुः।
ऋतुत्रयं चाप्ययनं द्वेऽयने वर्षसंज्ञिते॥७०॥

Of two Pakshas is a month. Two solar months make a Ritu and three
Ritus make an Ayana; and two Ayanas give rise to a Varsha (year).

Comments: A Ritu means a season. There are six Ritus of two months
each. They are as under:

Name of Ritu or season	Approx period		Equivalent months of Saka Era (National calendar)	Planetary Lord of the Ritu
	From	To		
1. Vasanta	Mar 21	May 20	Chaitra-Vaishakha	Venus
2. Grishma	May 21	Jul 20	Jyeshtha-Ashadha	Mars/Sun
3. Varsha	Jul 21	Sep 21	Shravana-Bhadrapad	Moon
4. Sharad	Sep 22	Nov 20	Ashwin-Kartika	Mercury
5. Hemanta	Nov 21	Jan 20	Margashirsha-Pausha	Jupiter
6. Shishira	Jan 21	Mar 20	Magha-Phalguna	Saturn

An Ayana comprises the six month period of the Sun's northerly (Uttarayana)
or southerly (Dakshinayana) course. Two Ayanas or 'six-months' make a year.
The Sun in Uttarayana (roughly) corresponds with the three Ritus: Shishira,
Vasanta and Grishhma. Its Dakshinayana phase (similarly) corresponds with
the remaining three Ritus: Varsha, Sharada and Hemanta.

Shloka 71

> संवत्सरादयः पंच चतुर्मासविकल्पिताः।
> निश्चयः सर्वकालस्य युगमित्यभिधीयते॥७१॥

Five types of Varshas (years), variously worked out on the basis of the four types of months, are called a 'Yuga'. This Yuga is the basis of all time determination (like intercalary months, etc.).

Comments: This concept of five year cycles or Yugas is different from a 'Yuga' already described. Here, a year consists of 366 days. The Yuga or lustrum thus has 1830 days. During this period there are 61 *Savana* (civil) months of 30 days each. A solar month consists of 30 1/2 civil days. Also, there are (approximately) 62 lunar (synodic) months during this period accounting for about two intercalary months.

The four types of months are:

1. *Saura*: Based on solar revolution of one year. The sojourn of the Sun through one zodiacal sign constitutes one such month.

2. *Savana*: Consisting of 30 Savana (or civil) days. One Savana day is the duration of time from one sunrise to the next.

3. *Lunar*: A period of one New Moon to the next.

4. *Naakshatra or Sidereal*: Based on the sidereal day which is equivalent to one star-rise to the next.

Shloka 72

> संवत्सरस्तु प्रथमो द्वितीयः परिवत्सरः।
> इद्वत्सरस्तृतीयस्तु चतुर्थश्चानुवत्सरः।
> वत्सरः पंचमश्चात्र कालोऽयं युगसंज्ञितः॥७२॥

The first of these (Varshas or years) is called 'Samvatsara', the second 'Parivatsara', the third Idvatsara, the fourth Anuvatsara, and the fifth Vatsara. This (whole) period (of five years) is known as a 'Yuga'.

Comments: According to the Narada Samhita, five years make a Yuga. The presiding deities of the five years that comprise a Yuga are respectively Agni (Fire), Surya (the Sun), Chandra (the Moon), Brahma and Shiva. Then there are twelve Yugas (making a cycle of sixty years).

The sixty-year cycles are called as the Jupiterian cycles or Jupiter's years. Different methods of their calculation are followed in North and South India. In North India, the Jupiterian years are determined by the entry of Jupiter, by mean motion, into different zodiacal signs beginning from the sign Kumbha (Aquarius). In South India, the Jupiterian year starts from April 13 or 14 (the day of Sun's entry into the sign Mesha of the Niryana zodiac). In either case the order of the sixty years is the same, considering Prabhava as the first year.

The following is a list of the Jupiterian years, and the equivalent years of the Christian era, according to the South Indian usage. The years of Christian era considered here are from 1951 to 2010.

1.	Prabhava	- 1987		31.	Hemalamba	- 1957
2.	Vibhava	- 1988		32.	Vilamba	- 1958
3.	Shukla	- 1989		33.	Vikari	- 1959
4.	Pramoda	- 1990		34.	Sharvari	- 1960
5.	Prajapati	- 1991		35.	Plava	- 1961
6.	Angiras	- 1992		36.	Shubhakrita	- 1962
7.	Shrimukha	- 1993		37.	Shobhakrita	- 1963
8.	Bhava	- 1994		38.	Krodhi	- 1964
9.	Yuvan	- 1995		39.	Vishvavasu	- 1965
10.	Dhata	- 1996		40.	Parabhava	- 1966
11.	Ishana	- 1997		41.	Plavanga	- 1967
12.	Bahudhanya	- 1998		42.	Kilaka	- 1968
13.	Pramathi	- 1999		43.	Saumya	- 1969
14.	Vikrama	- 2000		44.	Sadharna	- 1970
15.	Vrisha	- 2001		45.	Virodhakrit	- 1971
16.	Chitrabhanu	- 2002		46.	Paridhavi	- 1972
17.	Subhanu	- 2003		47.	Pramadi	- 1973
18.	Tarana	- 2004		48.	Ananda	- 1974
19.	Parthiva	- 2005		49.	Rakshasa	- 1975
20.	Avyaya	- 2006		50.	Nala	- 1976
21.	Sarvajit	- 2007		51.	Pingala	- 1977
22.	Sarvadhari	- 2008		52.	Kalyanakrit	- 1978
23.	Virodhi	- 2009		53.	Siddhartha	- 1979
24.	Vikrita	- 2010		54.	Raudra	- 1980
25.	Khara	- 1951		55.	Durmati	- 1981
26.	Nandana	- 1952		56.	Dundubhi	- 1982
27.	Vijaya	- 1953		57.	Rudhirodgari	- 1983
28.	Jaya	- 1954		58.	Raktakshi	- 1984
29.	Manmatha	- 1955		59.	Krodhana	- 1985
30.	Durmukha	- 1956		60.	Kshayakrit	- 1986

Shloka 76-79

प्रथमे कृत्तिकाभागे यदा भास्वांस्तदा शशी।
विशाखानां चतुर्थेंऽशे मुने तिष्ठत्यसंशयम्॥ ७६॥
विशाखानां यदा सूर्यश्चरत्यंशं तृतीयकम्।
तदा चन्द्रं विजानीयात्कृत्तिकाशिरसि स्थितम्॥ ७७॥
तदैव विषुवाख्योऽयं कालः पुण्योऽभिधीयते।
तदा दानानि देयानि देवेभ्यः प्रयतात्मभिः॥ ७८॥
ब्राह्मणेभ्यः पितृभ्यश्च मुखमेतत्तु दानजम्।
दत्तदानस्तु विषुवे कृतकृत्योऽभिजायते॥ ७९॥

Muni! When the Sun is in the first part of the Krittika nakshatra (equivalent to the concluding part of Mesha) and the Moon decidedly in the fourth quarter of Vishakha (the beginning of Vrishchika), or when the Sun is in the third quarter of the Vishakha nakshatra (equivalent to the concluding part of Tula) and the Moon is in the beginning of the Krittika (end of Mesha), there occurs the most sacred of moments called the 'Vishuva' (or equinox). This time is appropriate for making offerings, etc., in respect of the Devas, the Brahmins and the Pitras (Manes). It is as if at this time the Devas would receive offerings with their mouths open. One who bestows charities at the time of 'Vishuva' himself achieves satiation.

Comments: Here is a clue to the time when the text of the *Shri Vishnu Purana* must have been put in written form. Prior to that, such texts were passed on from generation to generation through individual memory.

In the above Shlokas, the Niryana or sidereal position of the Sun at the time of two equinoxes is mentioned. In case of vernal equinox, the Sun has been mentioned as being in the first part of Krittika nakshatra equivalent to sign Mesha (Aries) 26°40' to 30°0'. Adding the Ayanamsha of 23°27'26" at the end of 1994, we get the Sayana or tropical position of the Sun at 50°27'26" to 53°47'26". We are aware that vernal equinox occurs at tropical zero degree of Aries. Thus, this 1st point of Aries has receded from anywhere between 50°27'26" to 53°47'26" since the *Shri Vishnu Purana* must have been compiled in its present form. Considering a mean value of 50.26" as the annual recession or precession of the equinoxes (approx 71.63 years a degree) the above range of precession works out to be equivalent to approximately 3614 years to 3852 years (about 1858 to 1620 years BC). Since Parashara was anterior to the Mahabharata war, which occurred more than five thousand years earlier, at the time of the beginning of Kaliyuga, obviously this Purana was passed on from one generation to the next through oral transmission. When it was actually put in written form, the Vernal equinox must have been occurring at the sidereal position of the Sun as mentioned above.

The autumn equinox has been mentioned as occuring at the time when the Sun was in Tula (Libra) 26°40' to 30°0'. This again works out to the same value.

That the Kali era, signifying the commencement of the Kaliyuga, started over five thousand years ago has been asserted by Aryabhata who was born in 476 AD and whose fifteen hundredth anniversary was celebrated in 1976. Says he:

"When three quarter yugas (viz., Krita, Treta and Dwapara) had passed and also 3600 years (in the fourth, viz., the Kaliyuga), then 23 years had passed after my birth."

Adding 23 years to his year of birth, we get the year 499 AD. If we substract 499 years of Christian era from the total Kali years at that time, we get (3600 minus 499) the value of 3101 years. The beginning of the Kali era has been known to coincide with the year 3102 BC.

...V...
Of Signs, Houses and Planets

नैव स्त्री न पुमानेष न चैवायं नपुंसकः ।
यद्यच्छरीरमादत्ते तेन तेन स रक्ष्यते ॥

Neither is this surely a woman, nor is this a man, nor even is this a eunuch. It is protected by the very bodies which it acquires.

Shvetashvatara Upanishad V/10

We have already seen that there are twelve signs of the zodiac. One of the signs happens to be the sign rising at the eastern horizon at the time of birth. This rising sign is called the *lagna or the ascendant*. The lagna happens to be the first house of the horoscope. By this is meant that the houses and signs do not coincide. The first house has the label of the sign rising at the time of birth, the second bears the label of the sign that will rise next, and so on.

The nine grahas (from the Sun to Ketu) or 'planets' are the occupants of these houses. The houses represent certain characteristics. The signs falling in these houses also represent certain characteristics, and the two intermingle to indicate something newer. Then the planets which occupy them inflict further modifications.

In order to be able to make any fruitful predictions, it is essential to understand the meanings of the signs, houses and planets. These are briefly indicated in the pages that follow.

A Horoscopic Chart

Before going further, it is important to appreciate how a horoscopic chart looks like.

A. *North Indian Chart* is the one in which the order of the houses is fixed. It consists of four central rhomboidal houses (which are numbered 1, 4, 7 and 10, starting from the upper central rhomboid) and eight triangular houses. The sign rising at the time of birth is marked in the first house

46

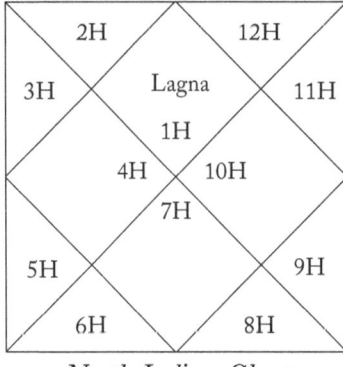

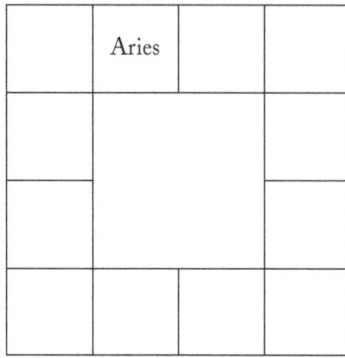

North Indian Chart *South Indian Chart*

or the upper central rhomboid, and the remaining signs marked in regular order in an anti-clockwise direction.

B. *The South Indian Chart* has the signs in a fixed order in the chart. The lagna is marked in the appropriate sign. The remaining houses are counted in a clock-wise manner.

C. *An Eastern Indian Chart*, often used in Bengal and Orissa, also has the signs in a fixed order in the chart. The ascendant is marked in the appropriate sign. The re-maining houses are counted in an anti-clockwise direction.

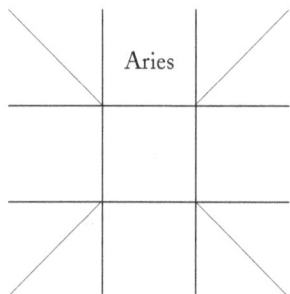

Whatever the type of horo-scopic chart preferred, the planets are placed in the houses bearing the signs in which the planets are located astro-nomically.

East Indian Chart

The process of working out the lagna and the position of planets has been dealt with in Chapters VIII and IX.

The Signs (or Rashis)

The signs of the zodiac have special features which are being described here.

1. *Appearance and Habitat*: The twelve signs of the zodiac each have a specific appearance and a habitat. This may be best described by reproducing a dialogue between sage Pulastya and sage Narada, as mentioned in the *Vamana Purana*.

   Pulastaya addresses Narada, saying, "Sage Narada! Now I narrate to you how these various signs look like, as also the areas they reside in or haunt.

   "The sign Mesha resembles a ram. It circulates among the goats, the sheep and regions holding wealth and precious stones. It wanders on grassy lands, and around lakes surrounded by vegetation.

"The sign Vrisha resembles a bull. Cowhouses and farmlands are its place of residence.

"A man and a woman bearing a trumpet and a harp represent the sign Mithuna whose places of residence are the couch and the lounge. It circulates amongst the singers, the dancers and the sculptors. This dual sign haunts the sports lovers and the pleasure houses.

"Karkata has the appearance of a crab and lives in water. Its places of residence include water-filled garden beds, river banks and un-inhabited lands.

"Simha (resembling a lion) resides in the mountains, forests, caves, inaccessible places, deep ditches and the living places of hunters.

"Kanya (consists of a woman) standing in a boat and holding corn and a lamp in her hand, inhabits women's pleasure rooms.

"Narada! Tula is represented by a man holding a balance in his hand, and its residences include lanes, bazaars, towns, routes and buildings.

"Vrishchika resembles the scorpion in appearance. It moves in crevices and pits. Its areas of residence include poisons, animal excreta, stones and insects.

"Of Dhanu, the legs are like those of a horse. It is radiant and holds a bow and arrow. Well versed in horse riding, in handling of arms and in doing daring and brave deeds, it resides in elephants, chariots, etc.

"O Brahmin! The mouth of Makara is like that of a deer, shoulders like those of a bull and eyes like those of an elephant. It moves in the rivers and resides in the ocean.

"Kumbha resembles a man wearing wet clothes and holding on his shoulders an empty pitcher. It moves in gambling houses and resides in drinking dens.

"The sign Meena consists of two fishes lying side by side, the head of one being beside the tail of the other. It circulates in the places of pilgrimmage and in the oceans. It haunts pious places, temples of gods and houses of Brahmins."

2. *Parts of the body*: The various signs from Mesha onwards represent (1) head, (2) face, (3) shoulders, (4) chest, (5) heart and stomach, (6) abdomen, (7) lower abdomen and groin, (8) external genitalia, (9) thighs, (10) knees, (11) calves, and (12) feet.

3. *Stature: Of short stature* are signs Mesha, Vrisha, Kumbha and Meena (i.e., 1,2, 11 and 12). *Of tall stature* are the signs Simha, Kanya, Tula and Vrishchika (i.e., 5, 6, 7 and 8).

Of even stature are the signs Mithuna, Karka, Dhanu and Makara, (i.e., 3, 4, 9 and 10).

Note: Stature here has nothing to do with signs of long ascension and those of short ascension.

4. *Diurnal strength: Strong during night* are the signs Mesha, Vrisha, Mithuna, Karka, Dhanu and Makara. Except Mithuna, they rise by the hind side (*Prishtodaya*). *Strong during day* are Simha, Kanya, Tula, Vrischhika, Kumbha and Meena. Except Meena, they rise by the head (*Sheershodaya*).

Mithuna too rises by the head.

Meena rises both by the head and the tail (*Ubhayodaya*).

5. *Malefic/Male*: Odd signs, viz., 1, 3, 5, 7, 9 and 11.

6. *Benefic/Female*: Even signs, viz., 2, 4, 6, 8, 10 and 12.

7. *Movable or otherwise*:

Signs 1, 4, 7 and 10 are *movable*; they indicate change and mobility.

Signs 2, 5, 8 and 11 are *fixed*; they indicate stability and fixity.

Signs 3, 6, 9 and 12 are *mixed*; they indicate a balance between the fixed and movable signs.

8. *Directions*:

East	:	signs 1, 5 and 9.
South	:	signs 2, 6 and 10.
West	:	signs 3, 7 and 11.
North	:	signs 4, 8 and 12.

9. *Inherent nature*:

Fiery	:	signs 1, 5 and 9.
Earthly	:	signs 2, 6 and 10.
Airy	:	signs 3, 7 and 11.
Watery	:	signs 4, 8 and 12.

10. *Biological characters*:

Quadrupeds	:	signs 1, 2, 5, posterior half of 9, and anterior half of 10.
Bipeds	:	signs 3, 6, 7, 11, and anterior half of 9.
Insect (*Keeta*)	:	signs 4 and 8.
Those inhabiting water	:	signs 12, and rosterior half of (*Jalachara*) 10.

11. *Constituent character*:

    Mineral (*Dhatu*)   :   signs 1, 4, 7 and 10.

    Vegetable (*Moola*)   :   signs 2, 5, 8 and 11.

    Animal (*Jeeva*)   :   signs 3, 6, 9 and 12.

12. *Caste*:

    Kshatriya   :   signs 1, 5 and 9.

    Vaishya   :   signs 2, 6 and 10.

    Shudra   :   signs 3, 7 and 11.

    Brahmin   :   signs 4, 8 and 12.

13. *Lords*:

Of the twelve signs, starting from Mesha, the lords are respectively Mars, Venus, Mercury, the Moon, the Sun, Mercury, Venus, Mars, Jupiter, Saturn, Saturn and Jupiter.

The Houses

The twelve houses of a horoscope deal with all conceivable aspects of life. The most important of all houses is the lagna or the first house. The remaining houses are basically related to the first house only. The planets in the horoscopic chart are subservient to the lagna, and their original nature undergoes modifications depending upon the lagna.

1. The *Kendras* (or Quadrants): Houses 1, 4, 7 and 10. These are highly significant houses.

2. The *Panapharas* (or Successant Houses): Houses 2, 5, 8 and 11.

3. The *Apoklimas* (or Cadent Houses): Houses 3, 6, 9 and 12.

4. The *Trikonas* (or Trines): Houses 1, 5 and 9. These are highly auspicious and, along with the Kendras, determine the health, wealth, status, dignity, rise and virtue of a native. The lagna, being both a kendra and a trikona, is the most significant of all houses.

5. The *Upachayas*: Houses 3, 6, 10 and 11. These houses indicate struggle, competition and material achievement.

6. The *Trika Houses*: Houses 6, 8 and 12. These are considered bad houses (Duhsthanas). They indicate debt, disease, loss and misery.

7. The *Ayu-sthanas* (or houses of longevity): Houses 8 and 3 (8th from the 8th). They indicate the length of life and, therefore, also the death.

8. The *Maraka-sthanas* (or killer houses): Houses 2 and 7.

9. *The two halves of a horoscope*:

   (a) Houses 1 to 7 indicate the *invisible half* and houses 7 to 1 indicate the *visible half* of the horoscope.

   (b) Houses 10 to 4 indicate the *eastern half* and houses 4 to 10 indicate the *western half* of the horoscope.

The significations of the twelve houses have been listed elsewhere.

The Planets

Nine main planets are employed in Vedic astrology. Their English equivalents and symbols are given in Table V-1.

Table V-1

Vedic Name	English equivalent	Symbol
Ravi (Surya)	Sun	☉
Chandra	Moon	☽
Mangala	Mars	♂
Budha	Mercury	☿
Guru (Brihaspati)	Jupiter	♃
Shukra	Venus	♀
Shani	Saturn	♄
Rahu	Rahu (Dragon's head)	☊
Ketu	Ketu (Dragon's tail)	☋

1. *Physical Attributes*

   The Sun has a square build, scanty but curly hair, lovely appearance, good intelligence, impressive voice, medium stature, red eyes, dark red complexion, strong bones, bilious nature, firm temperament and saffron robes.

   The Moon has a slim but roundish body, beautiful appearance, lovely eyes, sweet tongue, phlegm and wind in his composition, white complexion, short curly hair, amiable nature, Sattvika inclination, discriminating wisdom, restless nature, excessive sexual urge, white robes.

   Mars is characterised by fierce red eyes, short stature, tough and youthful body, fickle but generous disposition, short but shining and curly hair, valorous nature, Tamasika inclination, eagerness to hurt, easy excitability, bilious disposition and fair complexion.

   Mercury has a slim and beautiful body, large reddish eyes, dark green complexion, healthy skin, medium height, clear and witty speech, expression with multiple meanings, Rajasika inclination, plenty of energy, bile, wind and phlegm in his composition, and green robes.

   Jupiter has a big belly and a fat body, pale eyes, virtuous disposition, phlegmatic temperament, knowledge of scriptures and sciences, bright yellow complexion, Sattvika inclination, sharp intelligence, keenness in religious pursuits, forgiving nature and yellow-coloured dress.

Venus is dark brown and handsome, of symmetrical limbs and dark curly hair, writer of poetry, and has an amorous disposition. He has long arms, broad chest, excessive seminal fluid, windy and phlegmatic temperament, Rajasika inclination, grace, vigour, wisdom and intelligence, and multi-coloured robes.

Saturn has a tall, lean and weak body, dark complexion, stiff hair and limbs, large teeth, lazy disposition, windy temperament, cruel nature, Tamasika inclination, lame, dark and shabby robes.

Rahu and Ketu have a bluish complexion resembling smoke, wild in bearing, intelligent, and of windy disposition.

2. *Planetary Lordship*

The Sun owns	Simha
The Moon owns	Karka
Mars owns	Mesha and Vrishchika
Mercury owns	Mithuna and Kanya
Jupiter owns	Dhanu and Meena
Venus owns	Vrisha and Tula
Saturn owns	Makara and Kumbha

3. *Castes*

Brahmins	:	Jupiter, Venus
Kshatriyas	:	Sun, Mars
Vaishyas	:	Moon, Mercury
Shudra	:	Saturn

4. *Essential nature*:

Sattvika (good and noble) :	Sun, Moon, Jupiter
Rajasika (active and just) :	Mercury, Venus
Tamasika (dark and base) :	Mars, Saturn

5. *Rulership in respect of the Kaala-Purusha (or the time personified)*:

Sun	:	Soul
Moon	:	Mind
Mars	:	Essence
Mercury	:	Speech
Jupiter	:	Wisdom and comforts
Venus	:	Seminal fluid
Saturn	:	Miseries

6. *Social status*

King	:	Sun, Moon
Commander-in-chief	:	Mars
Heir-apparent	:	Mercury
Ministers	:	Jupiter, Venus
Servant	:	Saturn
Army	:	Rahu and Ketu

7. *Gender*

Masculine	:	Sun, Mars, Jupiter
Feminine	:	Moon, Venus
Eunuchs	:	Mercury, Saturn

8. *Rulership over body constituents*

Sun	:	Bones
Moon	:	Blood
Mars	:	Marrow
Mercury	:	Skin
Jupiter	:	Fat
Venus	:	Seminal fluid
Saturn	:	Nerves

9. *Places represented*

Sun	:	Temple
Moon	:	Watery place
Mars	:	Place of fire
Mercury	:	Playground
Jupiter	:	Treasure house
Venus	:	Bedroom
Saturn	:	Dirty places, sites of refuse disposal

10. *Directions*

Sun	:	East
Moon	:	North West
Mars	:	South
Mercury	:	North
Jupiter	:	North East
Venus	:	South East
Saturn	:	West
Rahu	:	South west

11. *Directional strength*

Mercury, Jupiter	:	East (Lagna or the 1st house)
Sun, Mars	:	South (10th house)
Moon, Venus	:	North (4th house)
Saturn	:	West (7th house)

12. *Benefics and Malefics*

Natural benefics : Moon, Mercury, Jupiter, Venus

Natural malefics : Sun, Mars, Saturn, Rahu, Ketu

The waning Moon and afflicted Mercury too behave as malefics.

13. *Exaltation, Debilitation and Moola Trikona*

Planets are strong and favourable when placed in their exaltation signs or in Moola Trikona signs. Six signs or 180 degrees away from its exaltation point lies the debilitation point of a planet.

Table V-2
Exaltation, Debilitation and Moola Trikona of Planets.

Planet	Exaltation	Debilitation	Mooltrikona
The Sun	Aries 10°	Libra 10°	Leo 0°-20°
The Moon	Taurus 3°	Scorpio 3°	Taurus 4°-20°
Mars	Capricorn 28°	Cancer 28°	Aries 0°-12°
Mercury	Virgo 15°	Pisces 15°	Virgo 16°-20°
Jupiter	Cancer 5°	Capricorn 5°	Sagittarius 0°-10°
Venus	Pisces 27°	Virgo 27°	Libra 0°-15°
Saturn	Libra 20°	Aries 20°	Aquarius 0°-20°

14. *Natural Mutual Relationship of Planets.*

Planets according to their nature, are disposed as friends or enemies or neutrals towards other planets. A planet in its friend's house is more comfortable and can express itelf more freely than the one in an enemy's house. The great Varahamihira sponsors the view of Satyacharya in determining the natural mutual relationship of planets. According to this view, a planet's friends are the lord of its exaltation sign as also the planets owning houses 2, 12, 5, 9, 4 and 8 from its Moola Trikona sign. Table V-3 shows the natural mutual relationship of planets according to the above view.

TABLE V-3
Natural mutual relationship

Planet	Friends	Enemies	Neutrals
The Sun	Mon, Mar, Jup	Ven, Sat	Mer
The Moon	Sun, Mer	–	Mars, Jup, Ven, Sat
Mars	Sun, Mon, Jup	Mer	Ven, Sat
Mercury	Sun, Ven	Mon	Mars, Jup, Sat
Jupiter	Sun, Mon, Mar	Mer, Ven	Sat
Venus	Mer, Sat	Sun, Mon	Mars, Jup
Saturn	Mer, Ven	Sun, Mon, Mar	Jup

15. *Temporal relationship*

Besides their natural disposition as friends, enemies or equals (neutrals) towards each other, planets become friends or enemies of each other depending upon their location in a horoscopic chart.

Temporal friends: Planets located in houses 2, 12, 3, 11, 4 and 10 from any planet become its temporal friends.

Temporal enemies: Planets located in houses 1 (i.e., conjunction), 7 (opposition), 5, 9, 6 and 8 from any planet become its temporal enemies.

16. *Five grades of relationship*

On the basis of their natural and temporal disposition towards each other, planets may have any of the five grades of relationships given below:

	Natural	*Temporal*	*Resultant relationship*
1.	Friend	Friend	Bosom friend
2.	Friend	Enemy	Neutral
3.	Neutral	Friend	Friend
4.	Neutral	Enemy	Enemy
5.	Enemy	friend	Neutral
6.	Enemy	Enemy	Bitter enemy

17. *Aspects, Combustion and Retrogression*

Planets exert their influence on the houses and planets that they aspect. All planets fully aspect the seventh house, or planets located therein, from their own position. In addition, the outer planets (Mars, Jupiter and Saturn) have been granted special aspects. Thus Mars also fully aspects houses 4 and 8, Jupiter houses 5 and 9, and Saturn houses 3 and 10. The remaining planets cast a quarter glance on houses 3 and 10, half an aspect on houses 5 and 9, and three-quarter aspect on houses 4 and 8.

Planets when close to the Sun tend to lose their strength and vitality, and are considered to be *combust*. A combust planet loses its capacity to do good and produces adverse results. Planets also become *retrograde* when, during their motion, they appear to be moving in a reverse direction. The Sun and the Moon do not become retrograde while Rahu and Ketu (almost) always move in a retrograde direction. A retrograde planet produces unexpected results and is generally adverse for health.

...VI...
Nature of Planets

सदृशं चेष्टते स्वस्याः प्रकृतेर्ज्ञानवानपि।
प्रकृतिं यान्ति भूतानि निग्रहः किं करिष्यति॥

The man of knowledge too acts in accordance with his own nature. All beings follow their nature. What can obstinacy accomplish? Gita III/33

Analysis of a horoscopic chart requires a thorough understanding of the nature of planets. It is on the basis of a proper knowledge of the nature of planets that good and bad results can be predicted with any accuracy. Before venturing into predictive aspect of astrology, it is imperative on the part of a practitioner of astrology to spend some time mastering the principles that govern the benevolence and malevolence of planets.

Planets may be benefic or malefic by nature. Or they become benefic or malefic depending upon the nature of the rising sign in a horoscope. Benefic and malefic planets produce their results when their appropriate dashas operate. Dashas thus help us in the timing of events.

The nature of various planets is determined on the basis of standard astrological principles mentioned by the classical writers. These principles have been discussed in details in the *Essentials of Medical Astrology* by the author. The following account is primarily a reproduction of the same principles.

Malefics and Benefics by nature

Planets may be malefic or benefic depending upon their inherent nature. Thus, Jupiter, Venus, waxing Moon and well-associated Mercury are natural benefics. Similarly, the Sun, Mars, Saturn, Rahu and Ketu, waning Moon and afflicted Mercury are natural malefics. The Moon and Mercury are naturally weak. The Moon though a mild and benevolent planet, behaves as a malefic when too close to the Sun. Mercury gets influenced too easily; it thus behaves as a benefic under benefic influence and as a malefic under malefic influence. Rahu and Ketu too can behave as benefics especially when placed in the signs of Jupiter and Mercury.

Benefics and Malefics for different Lagnas

Parashara's Principles

Planets behave as benefics and malefics depending on the houses they own. The ownership would naturally vary from one lagna to the other. In other words, for a given lagna, certain planets will behave as benefics while others will behave as malefics or neutrals. This will be independant of their inherent nature as already described. Planets thus are subservient to the lagna. On the basis of the principles discussed hereunder, a natural benefic may assume the role of a malefic while a natural malefic may assume a benefic role. The standard principles in this regard, as laid down by the sage Parashara in his celebrated Brihat Parashara Hora Shastra are being given below.

Principles - Part I

(a) Natural benefics as lords of quadrants (houses 1,4,7 and 10) shed their beneficence.

(b) Natural malefics as lords of quadrants shed their malefic nature.

   Note :

   (i) Natural benefics are the Moon, Mercury, Jupiter and Venus; natural malefics are the Sun, Mars, Saturn, Rahu and Ketu.

   (ii) Lordship of quadrants has a neutralising influence on the nature of planets. The natural benefics thus lose the capacity to give benefic results, while the natural malefics lose their capacity to do harm.

   (iii) Only the ownership of quadrants does not convert benefics into malefics, and vice versa.

(c) Lords of trines (houses 1,5 and 9) give benefic results no matter whether by their inherent nature they are benefics or malefics.

   Note : Lord of the lagna is both the lord of a quadrant and a trine. It is thus supposed to give benefic results irrespective of it's inherent nature.

(d) Lords of the third, the sixth and the eleventh houses are always malefic.

(e) Lords of the second, the twelfth and the eighth houses behave as neutrals. They give results according to their location as well as association.

   Note : Lords of the 2nd, 12th and 8th houses are impressionable neutrals.

Principles - Part II

The twelve houses in a horoscope have been divided into four groups above: (a) the quadrants; (b) the trines; (c) the 3, 6, 11 group; and (d) the 2, 12, 8 group. In each group the relative strength of the various house lords is described thus:

(a) Of the lords of the quadrants, the 4th lord is more powerful than the lagna lord; the 7th lord is more powerful than the 4th lord; and the 10th lord is more powerful than the 7th lord.

(b) Of the trine lords, the 5th lord is more powerful than the lagna lord, while the 9th lord is more powerful than the 5th lord.

(c) Of the 3, 6, 11 group, the sixth lord is more powerful than the 3rd lord while the 11th lord is more so than the 6th lord.

(d) Of the 2, 12, 8 group, the 12th lord is more powerful than the 2nd, while the 8th lord is more so than the 12th.

Principles - Part III

The lord of the 8th house, though considered a neutral above, has a special propensity to do evil. The eighth house represents obstructions, obstacles, failures, intrigues, ailments, death and the like. The following points must be remembered while considering the 8th house.

(a) Eighth house is the 12th from 9th (indicating loss of Bhagya); hence its lord is ever malefic.

Note :

(i) Twelfth house from lagna indicates loss. Twelfth house from any house indicates loss of that house. Since the ninth house stands for Bhagya (luck), virtues, pious deeds, religious inclinations, father, etc., the twelfth from it (i.e., the 8th) indicates the loss of all these. Loss of fortune or luck is considered the biggest loss.

(ii) When the 8th lord is also the lagna lord, the benefic nature of the lagna lordship prevails, and the 8th lord tends to behave as a benefic unless it is particularly afflicted or ill-placed.

(b) The eighth lord is still more malefic when it also lords over the 3rd or the 11th house.

Note :

(i) For Pisces ascendant, Venus is the lord of the third and the 8th houses and is bad.

(ii) For Virgo ascendant, Mars is the lord of the third and the eighth houses and, therefore, adverse.

(iii) For Taurus ascendant, Jupiter is the lord of the 8th and the 11th houses, and is adverse.

(iv) For Scorpio ascendant, Mercury as the lord of the 8th and the 11th houses is bad.

(c) The eighth lord becomes a benefic when it also owns a trine.

Note:

(i) Jupiter and Mercury for Leo and Aquarius ascendants respectively own the 5th and 8th houses, and behave as benefics.

(ii) For Gemini ascendant, Saturn as the lord of the 8th house as well as the 9th house (a trine) does not become an outright benefic, and, according to the Bhavartha Ratnakara, gives mixed results only.

(d) The evil effects of the eighth house lordship do not apply to the Sun or the Moon.

Note : The Moon is the 8th lord for Sagittarius ascendant, and the Sun for Capricorn ascendant. According to the sage Parashara, the Sun and the Moon remain un-afflicted by the eighth house lordship. This, however, may not hold true in actual practice, at least in medical astrology.

Principles - Part IV

(a) When a planet owns both a quadrant and a trine, it becomes particularly useful and is called a Raja-yoga-karaka (doer of great benefit). It gives additional benefit if it is also located in a quadrant or a trine.

Note :

(i) Mars for Cancer and Leo ascendants, Venus for Capricorn and Aquarius ascendants, and Saturn for Taurus and Libra ascendants, become Yoga-karakas because of the ownership of a trine and a quadrant.

(ii) Some people doubt the efficacy of Saturn as a benefic for Taurus ascendant despite its ownership of the 9th and the 10th houses (a trine and a quadrant respectively). This is because the 9th lord is considered a Badhaka (an obstructing agent) for a fixed lagna like Taurus. This, however, is not the view of Parashara which, in our opinion, is more authentic.

(b) Only the ownership of a quadrant does not convert a malefic into a benefic. The malefic must also own a trine to completely shed its malevolence.

Note : Saturn, as the lord of the 10th and the 11th houses for Aries ascendant, as lord of the 3rd and the 4th houses for Scorpio ascendant, and as the lord of the 6th and the 7th houses for Leo ascendant, remains a malefic despite owning a quadrant in each case.

(c) The blemish of kendra lordship (ownership of quadrants), as applicable to benefics, increases progressively from the Moon, to Mercury, to Jupiter, to Venus.

60

(d) Full Moon, Mercury, Jupiter and Venus, in this order, are progressively more powerful as benefics.

(e) Waning Moon, the Sun, Saturn and Mars, in this order, are progressively more powerful as malefics.

Principles - Part V (Raja Yogas)

When the lord of a quadrant is in some way related to the lord of a trine, a Raja Yoga (or a highly benefic combination) is formed. Benefic combinations in a horoscope neutralise affliction and are good for remaining free from disease. Relationship between any two house lords can be in one of the following ways:

(a) By location in the same house (conjunction).

(b) By mutual aspect.

(c) By an exchange of houses (Parivartana Yoga).

(d) When one of them is placed in the other's house and this latter aspects the former.

   Note : When the lords of quadrants and trines are related in one of the ways indicated above, they still do not produce a Raja yoga if they also own the Papasthanas (adverse houses), i.e., houses 3, 6 and 11.

Principles - Part VI (Rahu and Ketu)

(a) Rahu and Ketu give results according to the house where they are located, and according to the planet (i.e., the lord of a house) whom they join.

(b) Rahu and Ketu become Yogakarakas (productive of Raja Yoga) in the following situations:

   (i) When they are placed in a quadrant, and join a trine lord; or

   (ii) When they are placed in a trine, and join a quadrant lord.

(c) Rahu also behaves as Saturn and Ketu also as Mars.

Trika Houses and their Lords

Houses 6, 8 and 12 are known as Trika houses. While these houses and their lords, as well as the planets that associate with these houses and their lords, are productive of adverse results, they are particularly adverse in relation to health. The sixth house and the sixth lord, among other things, indicate disease and accidents. The eighth house and the eighth lord indicate chronic disease, incurable disease, or death. The twelfth house and its lord indicate suffering and also hospitalisation. The dasha periods of the planets associated with these houses and their lords must be carefully watched for determining illness.

The Marakas (Death Inflictors)

The Marakas are planets which are supposed to cause death. It has already been stated that the eighth house governs longevity. The eighth from the 8th (i.e., the third house) is the alternate house of longevity. We are also aware that the twelfth house from any house signifies the loss of that house. Twelfth from the eighth house is the 7th house; twelfth from the third house is the 2nd. The 2nd and the 7th houses thus indicate loss of longevity, in other words death. These houses are called the Maraka houses. Planets which (i) own these houses, (ii) occupy these houses, or (iii) associate with the lords of these houses assume the role of Marakas or death inflictors. The dashas and antardashas of these planets are significant in causing death. It may be remembered, however, that death does not occur every time the dashas and antardashas of these planets operate; under normal circumstances, these dashas disturb health.

It is appropriate to study a chart carefully and work out the span of life according to the standard principles of astrology. Death during childhood must be excluded by judging the horoscope for Balarishta. Thereafter, the length of life must be classified as being Alpayu (short life; upto 32 years), Madhyayu (medium life; 64 years) or Poornayu (long life; 100 years). It is the coinciding of a maraka dasha with the culmination of the span of life that causes death. At other times, the dashas of marakas should be watched for health.

It is not necessary that the time of death will always coincide with the dashas and antardashas of planets concerned with the second and seventh houses or their lords. Other planets too can assume this role when the dashas of the marakas stated above are not operating. In this connection, the following factors are of importance:

(a) Lord of the twelfth house;

(b) Planets associated with the lord of the twelfth house;

(c) Antardashas of the 6th, 8th or 12th lords operating in the dasha of a maraka planet;

(d) Lords of the 2nd and 12th houses from the Moon if they happen to be malefics;

(e) Saturn assumes the most potent maraka status when associated with planets having maraka potential.

(f) Death sometimes occurs in the dasha or antardasha of the most malefic planet in the horoscope.

Note :

(a) Saturn and Rahu can behave as unqualified killers if their dasha and antardasha are operating at a time coinciding with the expected span of life.

(b) A maraka planet does not kill in its dasha, in the antardasha of a benefic planet related to it. It can, however, kill in the antardasha of an unrelated malefic planet.

(c) Lords of the 2nd and the 12th houses become potent marakas in their mutual dasha-antardashas.

(d) Similarly, lords of the 6th and the 8th houses can cause death in their mutual dasha-antardashas.

(e) Dasha of the 8th lord occupying the ascendant is also important.

(f) If two or more sons of a native run the Rahu dasha simultaneously, it forebodes death for the native. This is a marvellous example of the principle of inter-related destinies.

Relationship of Planets to Various Lagnas

It is appropriate now to tabulate the relationship of planets to the various lagnas on the basis of the aforesaid principles.

	Lagna	Benefics	Malefics	Marakas	Yogakaraka
1.	Mesha	Sun, Jup	Mer, Ven, Sat	Ven	-

(i) Mere conjunction of Jupiter and Saturn (9th and 10th lords) does not produce a Raja Yoga.

(ii) Jupiter becomes malevolent if ill-associated.

(iii) Mars tends to behave as a benefic on account of the lagna lordship.

	Lagna	Benefics	Malefics	Marakas	Yogakaraka
2.	Vrisha	Sun, Sat	Mon, Jup, Ven	Mars (Mon,Jup,Ven)	Sat

(i) Mercury is partly beneficial.

(ii) Even Venus is not too good for Taurus ascendant.

	Lagna	Benefics	Malefics	Marakas	Yogakaraka
3.	Mithuna	Ven	Sun, Mars, Jup	Mon	-

(i) Combination of Saturn (9th lord) and Jupiter (7th & 10th lord) does not produce a Rajayoga.

(ii) Jupiter as a benefic is the lord of two quadrants (excluding the lagna). It is particularly liable to the blemish of kendra lordship. Such blemish is applicable to Mercury & Jupiter only.

(iii) Mercury is neutral. Saturn may give mixed results.

	Lagna	Benefics	Malefics	Marakas	Yogakaraka
4.	Karka	Mon, Mars, Jup	Mer, Ven	Sat	Mars

(i) Sun acts as a benefic or malefic depending upon its association.

	Lagna	Benefics	Malefics	Marakas	Yogakaraka
5.	Simha	Sun, Mars, Jup	Mer, Ven, Sat	Sat	Mars

(i) Combination of Jupiter (5th lord) and Venus (10th lord) does not produce a Rajayoga.

(ii) The Moon (12th lord) gives results depending upon its association.

Lagna	Benefics	Malefics	Marakas	Yogakaraka
6. Kanya	Mer, Ven	Mon, Mars, Jup	Ven	-

(i) Association of Venus (9th lord) and Mercury (10th lord and Lagna lord) produces a Rajayoga.

(ii) The Sun (12th lord) gives results based on its association.

(iii) Mercury as lagna lord and lord of the 10th house (the most powerful quadrant) becomes a benefic while Jupiter (4th and 7th lord) suffers from the blemish of lordship of two kendras.

Lagna	Benefics	Malefics	Marakas	Yogakaraka
7. Tula	Mer, Sat	Sun, Mar, Jup	Mar	Sat

(i) Venus is neutral.

(ii) Combination of the Moon (10th lord) with Mercury (9th lord) produces a Rajayoga.

Lagna	Benefics	Malefics	Marakas	Yogakaraka
8. Vrishchika	Mon, Jup	Mer, Ven, Sat	Ven	-

(i) Mars is neutral (cf. Venus for Taurus lagna).

(ii) The Sun-Moon (10th lord and 9th lord respectively) association produces a Rajayoga.

Lagna	Benefics	Malefics	Marakas	Yogakaraka
9. Dhanu	Sun, Mar	Ven	Ven, Sat	-

(i) Jupiter is neutral as is the Moon.

(ii) Sun-Mercury (9th and 10th lords) association produces a Rajayoga.

Lagna	Benefics	Malefics	Marakas	Yogakaraka
10. Makara	Mer, Ven	Mon, Mar, Jup	Mar (and other malefics)	Ven

(i) The Sun is a neutral.

(ii) Saturn (2nd lord) itself is not a maraka as it is the lord of the lagna also.

Lagna	Benefics	Malefics	Marakas	Yogakaraka
11. Kumbha	Ven, Sat,	Mon, Mar, Jup	Sun, Mar, Jup	Ven

(i) Mercury is mediocre, perhaps more beneficial than harmful.

Lagna	Benefics	Malefics	Marakas	Yogakaraka
12. Meena	Mon, Mar, Jup	Sun, Mer, Ven, Sat	Mer, Sat	-

(i) Mars is not a maraka despite being the second lord. (cf. Venus for Virgo ascendant)

(ii) Association of Mars (9th lord) and Jupiter (10th lord as well as lagna lord) produces a Rajayoga.

(iii) Compare this with the role of Venus and Mercury in the case of Virgo ascendant.

Miscellaneous Adverse Factors

While the above information must suffice to decide about the nature of a planet, there are other factors too which need attention. This is particularly true of the adverse factors since a knowledge about them is of importance in obtaining the warning signals and taking appropriate remedial measures. Some such sensitive adverse factors are mentioned below. It is stressed, however, that the aim of making a mention of these is not to frighten a consultor but to help him to the utmost extent by advising appropriate corrective steps.

1. *The twenty-second Drekkana* : The twenty-second Drekkana is the Drekkana that falls exactly seven houses away from the lagna. It thus falls in the 8th house on the same degrees as those of the lagna. Place the degrees of the lagna in the sign occupying the 8th house of the birth chart and determine its Drekkana. The lord of that sign and the planets falling in that sign in the Drekkana chart are evil and capable of causing death and disease. When a Drekkana chart is cast, the 8th house of this chart indicates the 22nd Drekkana. The lord of this house as well as the planets falling in that house prove malefic.

2. *The sixty-fourth Navamsha*. Whereas the 22nd Drekkana is calculated from the lagna, the 64th Navamsha is calculated from the Moon. It falls exactly seven houses away from the Moon. Place the degrees of the Moon in the sign 8th from it, and determine the Navamsha of that sign. The lord of that Navamsha is the lord of the 64th Navamsha, and, along with planets falling therein in the Navamsha chart, behaves as a malefic. In the usual Navamsha chart, the sign falling in the 4th house from the Moon happens to be the 64th Navamsha; its lord as also its associates, and the planets falling in that house in the Navamsha chart behave as evil planets.

3. *Sarpa Drekkana*. The second and third Drekkanas of the sign Karka, the first and the second of the sign Vrishchika, and the last Drekkana of the sign Meena are termed the Sarpa (serpent) Drekkanas. Planets falling in these Drekkanas tend to produce ill health during their periods and sub-periods if other factors also indicate thus.

...VII...
Significations of Houses and Planets

यद्यदाचरति श्रेष्ठस्तत्तदेवेतरो जनः ।
स यत्प्रमाणंकुरुते लोकस्तदनुवर्तते ॥

Whatever a great man does, the same is done by others too. Whatever standard he sets, the same the world follows.   *Gita III/21*

The twelve houses of the zodiac represent all the aspects of existence at the terrestrial as well as the individual level. Likewise, the nine planets also indicate the varied areas of existence. In order to analyse a horoscopic chart, it is essential to understand what the different houses of the horoscope, and the nine planets located therein, signify. An understanding of the interaction between planets and houses, integrated with the dasha systems and other specific techniques, provides a basis for accurate predictions.

An attempt is being made here to provide adequate information about all that the planets and the houses signify. However, this information is not exclusive, particularly in view of the fact that several new meanings must emerge when the standard principles are applied in the modern context. It only underlines the fact that astrology is ever a live and expanding subject.

Significations of the Twelve Houses

The houses from the lagna to the seventh represent the right half of the body of the native (and the left half of the body of his spouse). Those from the seventh to the lagna represent his left half, and the right half of his spouse.

First House : Body, fame, character, strength, courage, knowledge or lack of it, residence, place of birth, dignity, honour, ancestry, livelihood, the beginning, the present, wisdom, wealth, comforts and discomforts, self-respect, peace of mind, happiness and un-happiness, detachment, virtues and vices, health of parents.

In medical astrology : Body in general, limbs, complexion, marks or moles on the body, sound and unsound health, skin texture, longevity, sleep, head, brain, texture of hair, stamina.

Second House: Wealth, speech, physical enjoyments, trading in ornaments, pearls and diamonds, buying or selling in general, accumulation of wealth, earning through self-effort, acquisitions from father, truthfulness and falsehood, inclinations, food, taste, clothes, eloquence, humility, steadiness of mind, learning, education, letters, anger, deceitfulness, family members, friends, enemies, servants, close followers, self-control, death.

In medical astrology : Face, teeth, tongue, oral cavity, nose, nails, speech, eyes (right eye).

Third House: Courage and valour, physical fitness, hobbies, talent, education, good qualities, siblings, longevity of parents, tolerance, capability, quality and nature of food, selfishness, sports, fights, refuge, trading, dreams, sorrows, stability of mind, neighbourhood, near relations, friends, army, inheritance, orna-ments, cleverness, short journeys.

In medical astrology : Ears (right ear), neck, throat, shoulders, bones, upper limbs, mental instability, physical growth, longevity.

Fourth House: Near and dear ones, caste and ancestry, mother, relatives on mother's side, lands and houses, agriculture, farming, gardens, orchards, installations, buildings, parliament, favours from the ruler, medicine, education, knowledge of land and geography, hidden treasures, comforts and discomforts, courage, faith, victory and defeat, perfumes, clothes, milk, digging, agricultural produce, vehicles, possession of cattle, horses and elephants.

In medical astrology : Chest, lungs, heart, breast, potent medicine.

Fifth House: Progeny, father, mental ability, learning, knowledge, scholarship, character, conception, prosperity, acqui-sitions through wife, fascination (for women), sharp wisdom, discrimination and analytical skill, capability, devotion to gods, means of earning, official seal, good or bad memory, speculation, humiliation, authorship, Shruti (Vedas), Smriti, knowledge of mantras, karmas of past lives.

In medical astrology : Heart, upper abdomen, liver, gall bladder, mind, mental illness, problems related to pregnancy.

Sixth House: Enemies, opposition, mental agitation, injuries, accident, disease, wounds sustained in war, loans, debts, losses, disappointments, obstacles, poisons, slanders, humiliation, cruelty, indulgence in prohibited acts, theft, quarrels, imprisonment, maternal uncles, maternal aunt, step-mother, pets, cattle, quadrupeds, flavours of food, servants, subordinates, nuisances in general.

In medical astrology : Intestines, umbilical region, phlegmatic illness, tuberculosis, eye disease, poisoning, accidents, operations.

Seventh House: Spouse, sex partner, marriage, adultery, lust or passion, nature and character of spouse, sexual union, secret love affairs, journey, deviation from one's path, partnership in business, overt enemies, quarrels, theft, loss of memory, recovery of lost wealth, progress, attainment of status, grandfather, brother's son, death.

In medical astrology : Lower urinary tract, anal canal, semen, seminal vesicles, urethra, prostrate, sexual act.

Eighth House: Marital status of a woman, longevity, death, obstacle, disgrace, defeat, discontinuity, suddenness, unexpectedness, misery, loss of memory, sin, killing a living being, capital punishment, nature of death, place of death, wickedness, father's indebtedness, deviation from expected norms, frightful place, difficult route, crevices, finding faults, humiliation, wife's wealth, sudden unexpected gain, hidden talents, spiritual pursuits and attainments, inheritance, son of the elder sister.

In medical astrology : External genitalia, incurable or chronic disease, loss of a limb, longevity, cause of death, severe mental anguish.

Ninth House: Virtuous deeds, pilgrimages, worship, religious inclination, devotional and religious learning, karmas of the present birth, splendour, association with the virtuous, auspiciousness, the preceptor or guru, father, austerity, penance, charity, kindness, wisdom, knowledge, devotion towards the preceptor, spiritual initiation, mental quietude, fame and fortune, progeny, temples, Vedic rituals, long journeys, travel by the sea.

In medical astrology : Hips, thighs, nourishment.

Tenth House: Profession, function, source of livelihood, governmental service, honour from the king, business, status, wealth, political power, fame, progress, nature of work, professional inclination, the treating physician, hidden treasure, prescribed course, teaching capability, self-control, dominance, sacrificing nature, proficiency, father's wealth and well-being, foreign travel, financial status, place of residence, performance of sacred and religious deeds.

In medical astrology : Knee joint, knee cap.

Eleventh House: Gains of all nature, income, acquisition, fulfilment of desires, nature of earning, arrival, rewards, recognition, favours from the ruler, special status, proficiency, learning, ancestral property, fondness for precious stones, lost wealth, pursuit of pious and religious deeds, profits and returns, elder brother, paternal uncle, longevity of mother, material enjoyments.

In medical astrology : Legs, left ear, left upper limb, recovery from disease.

Twelfth House: Expenditure, loss of wealth, spending money for prescribed or prohibited pursuits, pleasures of the bed, bedroom, mental anguish, loss of sleep, physical disease, wickedness, penury, loss or disease of a limb, loss of authority, imprisonment, confinement in an enemy's house, loss of spouse, exit from the world, emancipation, renunciation, distant travel, foreign land, emigration, loss in travel, paternal property, spiritual learning, secret learning, fear from overt and covert enemies.

In medical astrology : Sleep disorders, mental imbalance, hospitalisation, feet, left eye, death.

Significations of the Planets

Planets too, like houses, have their significations. They are as follows:

The Sun: Physical strength, dominance, influence, courage, valour, bitter taste, land, enlightenment, soul, father, father's comforts, king, royal favours, kingly pursuits, high status, undisguised conduct, mental purity, kingdom, travelling, summer (Grishma), heat, fire, stones, trees with thorns, grass, forests, mountains, eastern direction, half a year, river banks, body, face, anger, indignation, hostility, good nature, administration, leader, physician, competence, gold, copper, pearls, ruby, ornaments, timber, quadruped, short stature, thick yarn, victory, devotion to lord Shiva, Kshatriyas (the 2nd in order in the four-castes system), red cloth, saffron, lotus, cow with its calf, the world of mortals.

In medical astrology : Soundness of health, old age, stomach, bile, heart, right eye, bones, fever, inflammation, diseases of the head, headache, baldness, biliary disease, injuries from falls, epilepsy, injuries sustained from quadrupeds.

The Moon: Mother, comforts to and from mother, beauty, facial lustre, gracefulness, fame, happiness, vehicles, mind, mental capabilities, intelligence, sense of humour, woman's inclination, mental agility, nature of an individual, contentment, laziness, sleep, liquids,water, milk, curd, honey, saline, eating, delicious fruits, fish and aquatic animals, snakes and other reptiles, flowers, perfumes, blossoms, fine clothes, white colour, crystals, silver, bronze, pearls, royal insignia, well, tank, lake, expanses of water, pilgrimage, pleasures, splendour, shyness, modesty, mildness, kindness, love, lover, affection, royal favour, wheat, white rice, sugarcane, salt, Brahmins, north-west direction, rainy season (Varsha), a muhurta (a time period equivalent to 48 minutes), middle age, world of the Manes.

In medical astrology : Mental llness, epilepsy, ulcers, acidity, phlegmatic disorders, pleurisy, tuberculosis, blood disorders, breast, left eye, malarial fever, fevers associated with chills and rigors, sleep disorders, menstrual problems, disease of shoulders, fear from watery animals.

Mars: Courage, valour, aggressiveness, anger, physical strength, pride, arrogance, combat, administrative capability, capacity to award punishment, skill in the use of weapons, risky ventures, archery, leadership, dominance, fame, victory, army, fort, cruelty, adultery, strength of the enemy, king, a fool, arguments, injury, surgery, criticism of others, sword, an axe or hatchet, knife, leadership of a village or a town, royal, famous, commander of an army, independance, controlling wild animals, non-vegetarian food, fickle nature, heat, summer (Grishma), southern direction, burns, fire, steadfastness, service of the ruler, home, a house, land, soil, burnt place, earthenware, goldsmith, gold, copper, good food, craving, persistence, obstinacy, speech, siblings (especially younger ones), snake, red colour, blood, gore, red clothes, red flowers, poison, bitter taste, pungent taste, sight, day, tree.

In medical astrology : Bile, marrow, haemoglobin (red pigment in the blood), muscles, menstrual cycle in women, accidents, injuries, burns, surgical operations, biliary disease, blood disorders, cuts and wounds, dysuria, head injuries, physical fitness and vitality.

Mercury: Education, knowledge, learning, sholarship, grammar, mathematics, astrology, astronomy, writing, script, philosophical knowledge, oratory, speech, good conversation, power of expression, witty language, intelligence, humility, fear, discrimination, editorship, printer, a minister, conversation studded with multiple meanings, a trader, commerce, treasury, pilgrimage, temples, bad dreams, sculptor, religious rites, devotion, mental quietude, fickleness, friends, black magic, self control, birds, horses, knowledge of scriptures and Vedanta, renunciation, skill in mantras, yantras as well as tantric pursuits, dancing, substances of mixed hues, eunuch, Shudras (the last in order in four-caste system), seasons, autumn (Sharad), skin moisture, northern direction, green colour, a prince, a youth, a child, maternal uncle, maternal grandfather, younger coborns, physician, towers of temples, dust, balanced outlook, skill in precious stones, crosswise looks.

In medical astrology : Skin, diseases of the skin, navel, sexual organs, neck, throat, nose, lungs, mental aberrations, nervous breakdown, speech disorders, vertigo, impotence.

Jupiter: Successors, sons and daughters, grandchildren, disciples, wealth, treasure, classical learning, philosophical learning, judicial learning, Sanskrit language, higher education, astrology, astronomy, grammar, Shastras, logic, religious study, Dharma or righteous conduct, status, grandfather, elders, teachers, Brahmins (the 1st in order in four-caste system), old age, place of pilgrimage, sharp intellect, wisdom, proficiency, eloquence, fame and renown, capacity to understand, self-respect, arrogance, indignation, writer of books, long poems, mantras or incantations, lecturing and delighting an audience, helpful nature, a man of law, a judge, devotion, beneficence, penance, self control, royal throne, physical health, valour, progress, understanding the minds of others, knowledge of scriptures, decorations, yellow cloth, yellow topaz, yellow colour, precious stones, gold, honey, turmeric, salt, cows, buffaloes, elephants, chariot, mansion, elder brother, friends, north-east direction, early half of winter (Hemanta), spending on sacred deeds, charities, trader, fat in the body.

In medical astrology : Diseases of liver and gall bladder, obesity, diabetes, pancreas and spleen, disease of digestive organs, knee, anaemias, ear trouble, laziness, chronic disease.

Venus: Wife, woman, marriage, conjugal bliss, sexual adventures, romantic conversation, amorous sports, love sports in water, overindulgence in sex, sexual perversions, romance, adultery, possessing many women, beauty, youth, fame, flowers, love of fragrances, tenderness, dealing in perfumes, clothes and articles of beauty, pride in ancient culture, servants, fortune, kingdom, royal favours, radiance, ornaments, talents, wealth, knowledge of the scriptures, diamonds, pearls, cotton, physical comforts, fame, fine arts, music, dance, singing, poetry, drama, vehicles, elephants, horses, cattle, playing on flute or violin, voluptuous gait, well-proportioned limbs, spring season (Vasanta), south-east direction, middle age, agriculture, family members, bedroom, white flowers, ghee, curd, gold, silver, land, good fortune, good food, the Vaishyas (3rd in order in the four-caste system).

In medical astrology : Venereal disease, eye disease, diseases of the urinary system, intestinal disease, diabetes, typhoid, appendicitis, exhaustion.

Saturn: Longevity, sufferings, misery, ill-health, obstruction, sorrow, distress, death, humiliation, servility, stupidity, covetousness, allegation, punishment, incarceration, outcaste, a maid servant, separation, slavery, falsehood, illiteracy, exhaustion, exertion, indignation, ugliness, dirty dress, shabby looks, eunuch, illegitimate, sins, cruelty, skill in law and judiciary, renunciation, detachment, philosophical attitude, directed downwards, Shudras, western direction, second half of winter (Shishira), means of livelihood, old age, infamy, firmness, indebtedness, penury, income, association with the wicked, benefit from inferiors, hunter, a wanderer, horses, elephants, goats, buffaloes, asses, dogs, oil, wood, black metal, iron, lead, black grains, precious stones, ashes, agriculture or farming, sexual indulgence, happiness from a woman, long lasting, the servant class, multitudes, labourers.

In medical astrology : Chronic disease, incurable disease, legs, feet, tendons, skin, ugly hair, lameness, mutilated limbs, amputation, depression, insanity, idiocy, exhaustion and fatigue.

Rahu: Sudden happening, disinclination, faulty logic, harsh speech, irreligious, adultery with a wicked woman, falsehood, sin, wickedness, royal status, royal insignia, benefits from outcastes, foreign travel or residence, long travel, pilgrimage, a muhurta (48 minutes), air, space, breathing, old age, hesitation, poison, snakes, reptiles, south-west direction, wandering in difficult terrain, going to the mountains, maternal grandfather, gambling, blue cloth, dark flower, emerald, dense forest, sudden disaster, technical eduction.

In medical astrology : Bones, chronic disease, incurable disease, insanity, hiccup, phobias, leprosy, weeping wounds, poisoning, snake bites, malignant tumors.

Ketu: Knowledge of the self, renunciation, knowledge of the mantras and tantras, secret learning, detachment, bath in holy rivers, pilgrimage, penance, hunger, vow of silence, Vedantic philosophy, disease, physician, a flag, association with hunters, fortune, suffering, luxuries, paternal grandfather, vultures, dogs, deer, cocks, pain, injury, surgical treatment, horned animals, thorn, stone, trouble from enemies.

In medical astrology : Chronic disease, tuberculosis, viral diseases, eruptive fevers, epidemics, worm infestations, non-healing wounds, mental instability, diseases causing diagnostic confusion.

Planets as Significators for Houses

Each of the twelve houses has one or more significators or Karakas for it. A significator is an additional indicator of the functions of a house. A house may have more than one significator. The various significators for different houses are as follows:

Lagna	=	Sun
Second House	=	Jupiter
Third House	=	Mars
Fourth House	=	Moon, Mercury
Fifth House	=	Jupiter
Sixth House	=	Mars, Saturn
Seventh House	=	Venus
Eighth House	=	Saturn
Ninth House	=	Sun, Jupiter
Tenth House	=	Sun, Mercury, Jupiter, Saturn
Eleventh House	=	Jupiter
Twelfth House	=	Saturn

Predictive use of significators

A significator for a house must be considered when events pertaining to a house are being judged. For example, when one wants to know about mother (4th house), the Moon (significator for 4th house as well as mother) must also be examined. Or while judging in respect of brother (3rd house), Mars (significator for 3rd house as well as brother) must also be judged. Besides, the following scheme must be adhered to:

1. Whatever is considered from the 9th (father), the 10th and the 11th houses from the lagna, must also be examined from the 9th, 10th and 11th *from the Sun.*

2. Whatever is considered from the 1st, the 2nd, the 4th, the 9th and the 10th houses from the lagna, must also be considered from similar houses *from the Moon.*

3. Whatever is considered from the 3rd from lagna, must also be considered from the 3rd house *from Mars.*

4. Whatever is considered from the 6th house (disease, enemy, maternal uncle) from the lagna must also be judged from the 6th *from Mercury.*

5. For progeny, consider the 5th house from lagna and the 5th *from Jupiter.*

6. For spouse, consider the 7th from lagna and the 7th *from Venus.*

7. Indications of the 8th (death, longevity) and the 12th from the lagna must be considered from such houses *from Saturn* also.

8. Whatever be the indications of the house, these must also be judged from the lord of that house.

...VIII...
Casting a Horoscope:
Midpoints of Houses

केनेषितां वाचमिमां वदन्ति चक्षुः श्रोत्रं क उ देवो युनक्ति।

By whom is this speech willed that people utter? Who is the effulgent being who directs the eyes and the ears.   Kena Upanishad I/1

A horoscope is a graphic representation of the signs of the zodiac and the planets located in those signs. For any given moment, the sign that rises at the eastern horizon is considered the beginning point or the first house of the horoscopic chart. The subsequent signs represent the subsequent houses of the horoscope.

The first house or the rising sign is labelled as *the lagna* or the *ascendant*. This is the most important, since all subsequent astrological exercises are based on this particular point. It will be remembered that the earth rotates once in 24 hours on its axis, from west to east, thereby causing one apparent revolution of the zodiac around it. *All the twelve signs of the zodiac thus rise at the eastern horizon, reach the mid-heaven, set at the western horizon and again proceed to their starting point once in twenty four hours.* The lagna is that specific degree on the zodiac which rises at one particular moment of time. It is *a still picture of the zodiac along with its planets, with the lagna corresponding with the rising degree of the zodiac*, that constitutes a horoscope.

The lagna in the horoscope, according to Vedic astrology, represents the mid-point of the first house, also called as the Bhava-Madhya of the lagna or lagna-spashta. A part of the house thus precedes this point and a part succeeds it. This is not so in western astrology where the cusp of a house is the starting point of that house.

Importance of Time

Since the zodiac is constantly moving around the earth, its angular position, and that of the rashis and nakshatras attached on it, is constantly changing.

It is this regular change from moment to moment which differentiates one horoscope from the other and, therefore, one person from the other. This underlines the significance of noting down the correct time of an epoch, e.g., the birth time in case of the native's birth chart, for casting a correct horoscope.

Recording of time

The ancient Indian method of recording the birth time considered the beginning of day from the moment of sunrise. This has been in vogue in India until recently. The more widely used method, however, is the modern method which recognises the passage of the Sun across the meridian or mid-heaven to correspond with *local noon*, and across the nadir or lower meridian to correspond with *local midnight*. The time reckoning is done from midnight to midnight.

Standard time, local time, zonal time

The time of an epoch is recorded by a watch or a clock. The clock generally follows what is called the *standard time* of a place, which is nothing but the local time of a particular place, within the country, which has been considered a reference point for all time reckoning for tht country. The standard time has a relation with the *Greenwich Mean Time* (GMT) which is but the local mean time (LMT) for zero degree longitude. Places east of Greenwich are ahead of GMT and those west of Greenwich are behind GMT in their time reckoning.

It may be appreciated that time reckoning is a function of the rotation of the earth. One rotation in 24 hours is equivalent to 360° of longitude. Thus each fifteen degrees of longitude correspond to one hour of time, or each degree to four minutes of time. In India, the standard time is reckoned from a place 82.5 degrees east of Greenwich which, at a rate of four minutes per degree of longitude, corresponds to five hours and thirty minutes of time. Being east of Greenwich, Indian Standard Time (IST) is five and a half hours ahead of the GMT.

Some very large countries use different time zones or zones separated generally by 15° of longitude. Each zone has its own *zonal time* which is like a standard time for that particular zone. Thus there may be several standard times in one country, as happens in the USA or Russia. A sound understanding of these time zones is essential in order to obviate mistakes in casting astrological charts.

Another pitfall is the use of *summer time* (or daylight saving time) in certain countries, where all clocks are advanced (generally) by one hour during the summer months. One must be aware of the actual dates of the year when changes from normal to the summer time, and vice versa, are effected. If such details are omitted, gross mistakes may occur in the casting and subsequent analysis of a horoscope.

Data required for casting a horoscopic chart

In order to cast a horoscopic chart, the following three things are required:

1. Date of birth (or of an epoch).

2. Time of birth: Standard time or local time; information about any zonal time or summer time.

3. Place of birth: the latitude and the longitude of the place of birth.

The purpose of the above data is to obtain the correct moment of time so that an accurate horoscopic chart can be constructed for a given location.

Equipment needed for casting a chart

This is as follows:

1. *Ephemeris* for the appropriate year (*of birth*): An ephemeris is an astronomical almanac detailing the daily position of the Sun, the Moon, the planets and the stars, etc. In the west, *Raphael's Ephemerides*, are generally held as the standard ephemerides. These give the Sayana or the tropical position of the planets, etc. In India, *Lahiri's Indian Ephemeris*, based on the Chitrapaksha Ayanamsha, is the best and gives the Niryana or the sidereal positions of the planets, etc., which are better suited for Vedic astrology. Lahiri's Ephemerides are available for each year, as well as in the form of condensed ephemeris.

2. *Tables of Ascendants* : These are ready-made tables which give data about calculating the degree of the ascendant for varying latitudes. In India, Lahiri's tables based on the Niryana system are the most popular and are highly recommended. However, any tables based on the Sayana system are equally good. As the difference between the Sayana and the Niryana systems is that of the Ayanamsha only, it is quite in order to work out the ascendant on the Sayana basis and subtract the Ayanamsha from it to obtain the Niryana values.

   The above mentioned tables also help one to calculate the tenth house or the meridian. From this, the remaining house cusps can be calculated.

3. *Gazetteer* for finding latitude and longitude of the place of birth. This information, pertaining to major cities of India and abroad, is tabulated at the end of the 'Tables of Ascendants' referred to above.

Steps in Calculating the Ascendant

The important steps involved in calculating the ascendant at a particular place, for a given moment, are given below.

1. *Local mean time of the place of birth:* From the time of birth available as a standard time (e.g., Indian Standard Time) or a zonal time, determine the

local mean time (LMT) of birth or the local time of birth for the place in question by applying the appropriate correction.

If the place in question falls to the east of the meridian of reference for a country, add four minutes for each degree of difference of longitude between the place and the reference point. If it falls to the west, substract at the rate of four minutes per degree of difference of longitude.

The ascendant or the rising sign is based on the local time and not on the standard or zonal time for a country or a zone.

2. *Sidereal time*: From the LMT, determine the sidereal time. This is important because the tables of ascendants are based on the sidereal time. As has been already pointed out, *for the same sidereal time for a given latitude, the time of rising as well as the span of the various signs of the zodiac is the same.*

The value of sidereal time available from ephemeris or from the 'Tables of Ascendants' is for 12 noon, local mean time, of each day. Around autumn equinox, these values coincide while around vernal equinox they are about twelve hours apart. It will be recalled that a sidereal day is about 4 minutes shorter than a civil day of 24 hours. This difference of 4 minutes for every 24 hours of the clock time amounts, approximately, to 10 seconds for every one hour of the clock (i.e., 4 minutes divided by 24 hours).

To obtain the sidereal time of birth, one has first to note the sidereal time at 12 noon local mean time. The next step is to consider whether the local mean time of birth falls in the forenoon (between midnight and 12 noon) or in the afternoon (between 12 noon and midnight). In case of a forenoon birth, subtract as many hours and minutes from the value of the sidereal time available from the ephemeris, as the birth time is before 12 noon; in case of an afternoon birth, add as many hours and minutes to the available sidereal time as the birth is after 12 noon. In addition, subtract or add, as above, a time period at a rate of (approx.) 10 seconds for each hour subtracted or added above. This gives the correct sidereal time of birth.

3. *Working out the Ascendant*: On the basis of the sidereal time of birth, and the latitude of the place, the exact degree of the lagna or the ascendant is worked out.

Generally the tables of ascendants are based on the Sayana system, so that an appropriate ayanamsha has to be subtracted to obtain the Niryana values. Lahiri's tables, however, have a Niryana basis. These tables have been constructed on the basis of the year 1938 AD. For periods before or after that year, appropriate corrections in respect of equinoctial precession have to be applied.

The Tenth House

The 'Tables of Ascendants' also gives a table for calculating the tenth house of a horoscope. Since we use the sidereal time, for reason mentioned earlier, for a given sidereal time the midpoint of the tenth house (as any other house midpoint!) is the same for all places falling on the same latitude. Also, the tenth house represents the upper meridian or zenith. Therefore, its midpoint will be the same for all places falling on the same longitude for a given moment of time. It is thus understandable that when we use the sidereal time, the midpoint of the tenth house for a given sidereal time of birth is the same at all places (all latitudes and longitudes) on earth.

Bhava-Madhya of the remaining houses

Described here is the standard method of determining the midpoints of various houses in Vedic astrology.

Six signs added to the lagna-spashta (the sign and degrees of ascendant) gives the midpoint of the 7th house or the descendant.

Six signs added to the midpoint of the tenth house gives the midpoint of the 4th house or nadir, a lower meridian.

One-third the difference between the ascendant and the tenth house, when added to the midpoint of the 10th house gives the midpoint of the 11th house; two-thirds this difference added to the 10th house gives the midpoint of the 12th house.

One-third the difference between the lagna and the 4th house, when added to the lagna, gives the midpoint of the 2nd house; two-thirds this difference added to the lagna gives the midpoint of the 3rd house.

Bhava-Madhyas of the 5th, 6th, 8th and 9th houses are obtained by adding six signs respectively to the midpoints of the 11th, 12th, 2nd and 3rd houses.

Bhava-Sandhis or junctional points of the houses

Midway between the midpoint of the 12th house and the lagna is the junctional point of the lagna and the 12th house.

Midway between the lagna and the 2nd house is the junctional point of the lagna and the 2nd house.

Between the above mentioned two junctional points is the extent of the lagna.

The junctional points of the remaining houses, and their extents can be similarly worked out.

Calculating the Ascendant and the 10th house – an example

Let us now take a practical example, and cast the lagna and the 10th house for a native born on January 4, 1995 (Wednesday) at 2:52 PM (IST) at latitude 28°N39' and longitude 077°E13'.

Step 1

From the Indian Standard Time of birth (2:52 PM), obtain the local mean time by subtracting 4 minutes per degree of longitude that the place in question falls to the west of the standard meridian for India (viz., 82°E30').

		h	m	s
IST	=	2	52	00
Correction for place :		–	21	08
(82°30' – 77°13' = 5°17'; 5°17' x 4 = 21m 8s)				
LMT	=	2h	30m	52s

Note : This value may be rounded off to *2h 31m* for convenience.

Step 2

Obtain the sidereal time for January 4, 1995 at 2h 31m LMT. This is done from the ephemeris or from the 'Tables of Ascendants'.

		h	m	s
Sidereal time for 12 noon on January 4, 1995	=	18	53	35
Correction for the above longitude	=		+	03
Corrected sidereal time for 12 noon	=	18h	53m	38s

Since the time of birth falls 2 hours and 31 minutes after 12 noon, we have to add this period as well as a time value of about 10 seconds per hour of this time or about 25 seconds (for 2hours and 31 minutes).

Thus, sidereal time for		h	m	s
2h:31m PM (LMT) on January 4, 1995	=	18	53	38
	+	2	31	00
	+			25
	or	21h	25m	03s

Note : This may be rounded off to 21h 25m for convenience.

As already indicated, for births occurring before 12 noon, a corresponding amount of time has to be subtracted from the sidereal time for 12 noon. Let us prsume that, instead of occurring 2 hours and 31 minutes after 12 noon, the birth occurred the same number of hours and minutes before noon (i,e., at 9:29 am) on January 4, 1995. The corresponding period will have to be subtracted from the corrected sidereal time for 12 noon. We will then have :

Sidereal time for 9:29 AM (LMT)		h	m	s
on January 4, 1995	=	18	53	38
	–	2	31	00
	–			25
	or	16h	22m	13s

Step 3

From the 'Tables of Ascendants', find out the ascendant for the latitude of the place, for the sidereal time obtained above.

In case the Sayana tables are available, the midpoint of the ascendant obtained will be its Sayana value. The value of ayanamsha for the year of birth is to be subtracted from this to obtain the Niryana lagna, as is required in Vedic astrology.

If Lahiri's tables with Niryana basis are available, the lagna degree available will be for the year 1938 AD to which appropriate ayanamsha correction for the year 1995 AD (the year of birth of the native) will need to be applied.

The calculation hereunder is based on Lahiri's Tables with a Niryana basis. In the relevant tables for latitude 28°N39':

(i) Ascendant for Sidereal time 21h 28m	=	1ˢ	13°	12'
(ii) Ascendant for Sidereal time 21h 24m	=	1ˢ	12°	09'
(iii) Change in ascendant for 4 minute change in sidereal time	=		1°	03'
(iv) Change in ascendant for 1 minute change in sidereal time (1°03' divided by 4)	=		0° 15' 45"
(v) Ascendant for Sidereal time 21h 25m	=	1ˢ	12° 24' 45"
(vi) Ayanamsha correction for the year 1995	=		− 48'
(vii) Therefore, the correct ascendant	=	1ˢ	11° 36' 45"

or Vrisha 11° 36' 45".

Step 4

The tenth house is similarly obtained from the tables which are appropriate for all places on earth. Referring to the said tables we find :

(i) Tenth house for Sid. time 21h 28m	=	9ˢ	26° 35' 00"
(ii) Tenth house for Sid. time 21h 24m	=	9ˢ	25° 34' 00"
(iii) Change in 10th house for 4m change in Sidereal time	=		1° 1'
(iv) Change for 1m change in Sid. time	=		15' 15"
(v) Tenth house for Sid. time 21h 25m	=	9ˢ	25° 49' 15"
(vi) Ayanamsha corr. for 1995 AD			− 48'
(vii) Thus, the tenth house	=	9ˢ	25° 1' 15"

or Makara 25° 1' 15".

Calculating the remaining houses and their juctional points

Having determined the lagna and the tenth house, it is easy to determine the remaining houses. Here the lagna is 1ˢ11°36'45" and the 10th house is 9ˢ25°1'15".

(i) *Seventh house* : Adding 6 signs (180 degrees) to the lagna we get the midpoint of the 7th house. In the present example it will be: 7ˢ11°36'45"

(ii) *Fourth house* : Adding 6 signs (180 degrees) to the midpoint of the 10th house, we get the midpoint of the 4th house. Thus the 4th house Bhava-Madhya here is: 3ˢ25°1'15".

(iii) *Houses eleven and twelve* : The difference between the lagna and the tenth house (i.e., lagna-spashta minus the 10th house; 3ˢ16°35'30" in our example) is divided by three, and the result obtained (1ˢ5°31'50") added to the 10th house to get the 11th house; and to the 11th house to get the 12th house. In our example.,

11th house	=	11ˢ	0°	33'	5"
12th house	=	0ˢ	6°	4'	55"

(iv) *Houses two and three* : One-third the difference between the lagna and the fourth house (i.e., Bhava-Madhya of the 4th house minus the lagna, or 2ˢ13°24' 30", divided by 3 giving us a value of 0ˢ24°28'10") is added to the lagna to obtain the 2nd house, and again to the 2nd house to obtain the 3rd house. In our example,

2nd house	=	2ˢ	6°	4'	55"
3rd house	=	3ˢ	0°	33'	5"

(v) *Remaining houses* : Houses 5, 6, 8 and 9, are obtained by adding six signs to the houses 11, 12, 2 and 3 respectively. The Bhava-Madhyas of the various houses in the example under consideration may be tabulated as follows (Table VIII-1).

Table VIII-1

House	Bhava–Madhya	House	Bhava–Madhya
	s d m s		s d m s
1st house	1 11 36 45	7th house	7 11 36 45
2nd house	2 6 4 55	8th house	8 6 4 55
3rd house	3 0 33 5	9th house	9 0 33 5
4th house	3 25 1 15	10th house	9 25 1 15
5th house	5 0 33 5	11th house	11 0 33 5
6th house	6 6 4 55	12th house	0 6 4 55

The Bhava-Sandhis or junctional points of the various houses are obtained easily by determining the mid-point between the adjacent houses. For example,

(i) The mid-point between the 12th house (0ˢ6°4'55") and the Lagna (1ˢ11°36'45") is 0ˢ23°50'50", being half the distance between the midpoints of the two houses.

(ii) Similarly, the mid-point between lagna (1ˢ11°36'45") and the 2nd house (2ˢ6°4'55") is 1ˢ23°50'50" being half the distance between the midpoints of the two houses.

(iii) The first house thus extends from 0ˢ23°50'50" to 1ˢ23°50'50".

(iv) The junctional points between all the other houses, and thus the extent of each house, can be determined in a similar manner.

Table VIII-2 shows the beginning, the midpoint (Bhava-Madhya) as well as the end of the various houses for the chart under consideration.

Table VIII-2

House	Beginning				Bhava–Madhya				End			
	s	d	m	s	s	d	m	s	s	d	m	s
1st House	0	23	50	50	1	11	36	45	1	23	50	50
2nd House	1	23	50	50	2	6	4	55	2	18	19	0
3rd House	2	18	19	0	3	0	33	5	3	12	47	10
4th House	3	12	47	10	3	25	1	15	4	12	47	10
5th House	4	12	47	10	5	0	33	5	5	18	19	0
6th House	5	18	19	0	6	6	4	55	6	23	50	50
7th House	6	23	50	50	7	11	36	45	7	23	50	50
8th House	7	23	50	50	8	6	4	55	8	18	19	0
9th House	8	18	19	0	9	0	33	5	9	12	47	10
10th House	9	12	47	10	9	25	1	45	10	12	47	10
11th House	10	12	47	10	11	0	33	5	11	18	19	0
12th House	11	18	19	0	0	6	4	55	0	23	50	50

Note : The midpoint (Bhava-madhya), as mentioned above, does not fall at the exact mid-point of the arc or the extent of a house. Each house thus has two parts: the Poorva Bhaga or the first part, and the Uttara Bhaga or the subsequent part.

Ascendant for a foreign birth

Lahiri's 'Tables of Ascendants' can also be used for births outside India. The method employed for the purpose is the same. One has to arrive at the correct sidereal time of birth of the native. This needs an understanding of the standard time for the country of birth, as also the appropriate time zone if the country has more than one standard time. This may be illustrated with an example.

Let us consider a birth occurring in New York (USA), Lat. 40°N43', Long. 074°W00' on May 22, 1949 at 11:43 PM (Eastern Daylight Saving Time, EDT).

Since the daylight saving time (the summer time) is one hour ahead of the normal time, the actual normal time of birth is 10:43 PM.

LMT   =   10:43 PM + 4 minutes
    =   10:47 PM.

Note : New York falls in a zone, five hours behind the GMT. While five hours are equivalent to 75° of longitude (one hour is equivalent to 15 degrees, or one degree is equivalent to 4 minutes), New York is only 74° West of GMT. Thus it lies 1° east of the reference point (75°W) of its zonal time. Thus 4 minutes are added to the zonal time to obtain the local mean time.

Referring to the *Tables of Ascendants*, we have

			h	m	s
(i)	Sidereal time for 12 hour noon, local mean time, on May 22	=	3	57	43
(ii)	Correction for the year 1949	+			31
(iii)	Sid. time on May 22, 1949 at 12 noon LMT =		3h	58m	14s

(iv) We need the sidereal time for 10h 47m (PM) local time. Since this time is after 12 noon by 10h 47m, it is to be added to the above value of Sid. time, after adding the correction at a rate of approx. 10s per hour of time.

		h	m	s
Local Time	=	10	47	00
correction for 10h 47m	+		1	47
Corrected local time	=	10	48	47

(v)	Therefore the sidereal time	=	3h	58m	14s
		+	10	48	47
			14h	47m	01s

(vi) This is the Indian sidereal time (for 82°E30'). For New York, a correction needs to be applied at a rate of 0.66 seconds per degree of longitude. This amounts to +1m 43s.

So the corrected sidereal time will be: 14h 48m 44s

(vii) For this sidereal time, the ascendant is worked out as already described, using the tables relevant to the latitude of New York. The Tenth house and the remaining houses are also worked out as already described.

Ascendant for Southern Latitudes

Lahiri's Tables have been constructed for northern latitudes. For southern latitudes, tables specifically prepared for the same may be used. However, Lahiri's tables too can be used, with slight modification, for the southern latitudes. The method for this is as follows:

1. Determine the sidereal time of birth as explained above.

2. Add to it 12 hours. Subtract 24 should the result exceed 24 hours.

3. Determine the ascendant as for a northern latitude, using the time value obtained above.

4. To the ascendant obtained thus, add six signs. Subtract 12 if the result exceeds 12 signs.

This will be the ascendant for the corresponding south latitude.

Note : In the southern latitudes, the duration of signs is different from that in northern hemisphere. Signs of long ascension in the northern hemisphere become those of short ascension in the southern hemisphere.

Thus Mesha measures in northern hemisphere, what Tula mea-sures in the southern hemisphere. This holds true for other signs too. By adding 12 hours to the sidereal time of birth and calculating the ascendant on the basis of tables for northern latitudes, we are actually calculating the sign opposite to the real ascendant in the southern latitude. To this ascendant thus obtained, we add six signs to get the real ascendant.

Ancient Indian Method of Calculating the Bhava-Madhya of the Lagna

It is not our aim to go into the details of this method. Only the principles are being enumerated as follows:

1. *Concept of the day* : The day, for purposes of astrology extends from sunrise to sunrise, and consists of 60 Ghatis. There is thus the importance of the time of sunrise which must be calculated accurately. It is the visibility of the upper limb of the disc of the Sun that coincides with the sunrise.

2. *Ishta-kaala* : The time of birth is reckoned in Ghatis and Vighatis,etc., from the time of sunrise, and not from midnight onwards as we are accustomed to do these days. This is called the Ishta-kaala.

3. *Oblique ascension or Rashi Maana* : This is the duration of time which a sign takes to completely rise above the horizon. *This refers to the signs of the tropical or Sayana zodiac.* The Rashi-Maana is expressed in the time unit called Asu (referred to in an earlier chapter) which is equal to 4 seconds. Six Asus or 24 seconds make a Pala or Vighati. The Rashi-Maana of the various signs of the zodiac (Sayana) at zero degree latitude (equator) are as follows:

| Signs (Sayana) | | | | Rashi–Maana in | |
				Asus	Vighatis
Mesha	Kanya	Tula	Meena	1670	278
Vrisha	Simha	Vrishchika	Kumbha	1795	299
Mithuna	Karka	Dhanu	Makara	1935	322

4. *Rashi-Maana for other latitudes* : This needs an understanding of the ascensional differences or *Charkhandas* for different latitudes. When Charakhandas for a given latitude are subtracted from signs Makara to Mithuna, or added to signs Karka to Dhanu one gets the Rashi-Maana for the various Sayana rashis for that latitude. For southern latitudes, the addition and substraction are reversed. An elaborate discussion on the method of determining the Charkhandas for various latitudes is beyond the scope of this work.

5. *The Sayana Sun at sunrise* : From a Panchanga, the position of the Sayana Sun at sunrise is found out. Generally the position of the Sun at sunrise is given on Niryana basis in the Panchangas. This can be converted to Sayana value by adding the Ayanamsha for the particular year or month of birth. This provides the sign that the Sun is in *at sunrise*. The duration of this sign being known, it is possible to work out how much of this sign has yet to rise above the horizon and how much time it will take to do so. After that time period, the next sign will rise and take the time that we know. In this way, the rising sign for the appropriate Ishta Kaala is worked out. This is the Sayana lagna.

6. *Niryana lagna* : Subtract the ayanamsha from the Sayana lagna. This gives the Niryana lagna.

84

...IX...
Casting a Horoscope:
Longitudes of Planets

आदित्यानामहं विष्णुज्र्योतिषां रविरंशुमान्।
मरीचिर्मरुतामस्मि नक्षत्राणामहं शशी॥

Of the Adityas I am Vishnu; of the lights (I am) the radiant Sun; of the winds I am Marichi; of the nakshatras I am (their lord) the Moon.

Gita X/21

After determining the lagna, or the ascendant, the next step is the calculation of the longitudes of planets, also called as Graha-sphutas. These longitudes indicate the astronomical location of planets in the zodiac. Since a horoscope is a graphic representation of planetary disposition at a given moment, it is imperative that a correct calculation for planetary positions be carried out.

The position of planets is given in various almanacs or Panchangas. In India, there are several hundred different Panchangas published from different places. Many of these used to give planetary longitudes at the time of local sunrise, generally on four occasions during a lunar month, viz., the 8th lunar date of the dark half, the New Moon day, the 8th lunar date of the bright half, and the Full Moon day. Lately, most of these have switched on to the Indian Standard Time, giving planetary positions generally at 5:30 AM which is equivalent to 12 midnight GMT.

In India, the ephemeris most popular with the English knowing reader is the Lahiri's Indian Ephemeris which is published annually. It gives planetary positions according to the Niryana or Sidereal system, for 5:30 AM (IST). It makes use of the Chitrapaksha ayanamsha. Ephemerides based on the Sayana or the tropical system can also be used. They give the Sayana positions of planets which need to be converted to the Niryana values by subtracting the ayanamsha value for the appropriate year of birth.

Use of Standard Time

We have used local mean time for the calculation of the cusp of the ascendant, as well as other cusps. That was because the rising of signs at any place is dependant upon the local time of that place. Thus, for any given time of a clock, different signs will rise at different places on the earth.

The longitude of a planet is the angular distance that the planet makes with the centre of the earth. This relationship is the same for all places on the surface of the earth. In other words, at any given moment, the planetary positions for all places on the earth are the same. Lahiri's ephemeris gives planetary positions (Niryana) for 5:30 AM (IST). Therefore, for calculation of planetary positions for any given moment, the IST must be used. In other words, for the calculation of planetary longitudes, the same time measure must be employed as has been employed by the ephemeris in use.

Longitudes of Planets: Steps in calculation

Let us calculate the longitudes of planets for the native born on January 4, 1995 at 2:52 PM (IST) at Delhi (same data as used in the example for calculating the cusps for the lagna and the houses, Chapter VIII)

We know that Lahiri's ephemeris gives planetary positions for 5:30 AM (IST) on a daily basis. Our epoch (2:52 PM on January 4, 1995) falls between 5:30 AM of January 4, 1995 and 5:30 AM of January 5, 1995. Let us consider the longitude of the Sun.

Consider the time of birth as the time elapsed since 5:30 AM (for which planetary positions are available). This will be:

2:52 PM − 5:30 AM	=	9h 22m.			

Position of the Sun (see ephemeris)		s	°	'	"
at 5:30 AM on January 5, 1995	=	8	20	22	40
at 5:30 AM on January 4, 1995	=	8	19	21	30
Motion of Sun in 24 hours	=		1°	1'	10"

Motion of the Sun in the time elapsed from 5:30 AM to the time of birth (i.e., 9h 22m)	=			23'	52"
Adding this to the longitude of the Sun at 5:30 AM on January 4, 1995 we get	=	8ˢ	19°	45'	22"

This is the longitude of the Sun for the above mentioned time of birth. Longitudes of the remaining planets can be similarly calculated.

Longitude of Retrograde Planets

A retrograde planet moves in the reverse direction and, instead of increasing, its longitude decreases as the time elapses. Rahu and Ketu often move in retrograde direction only. Other planets, except the Sun and the Moon, are subject to retrogression from time to time.

For the birth data given above, Mars is also retrograde. Let us calculate the position of Mars.

Longitude of Mars :

		s	°	'	"
on January 5, 1995	=	4	8	51	00
on January 4, 1995	=	4	8	52	00
Movement in 24 hours	=		–	1'	00"
Movement for the elapsed time (i.e., 9 hours 22 minutes)	=		–		23"

Adding this to the longitude of Mars on January 4, 1995, we get 4ˢ8°51'37" as the longitude of Mars for the said time of birth.

Thus, in case of retrograde planets, the movement proportionate to the elapsed time gets subtracted from the given longitude.

The longitudes of all the planets, based on the above birth data, may be tabulated below:

		s	°	'	"
1.	Sun	8	19	45	22
2.	Moon	9	29	02	36
3.	Mars (R)	4	08	51	37
4.	Mercury	9	02	07	51
5.	Jupiter	7	11	36	41
6.	Venus	7	03	13	15
7.	Saturn	10	14	29	20
8.	Rahu	6	18	57	29
9.	Ketu	0	18	57	29

Note : Rahu and Ketu are 180 degrees or six signs apart. Ketu's position is obtained by adding 6 signs to the longitude of Rahu.

Considering Vrisha as the lagna arrived at in the preceding chapter, for the same birth data, the basic horoscopic chart (or the Rashi chart) may be depicted as below.

Lahiri's ephemeris which gives planetary positions for 5:30 am (IST) can also be used in case of foreign births. In such cases, the time of birth (expressed as the standard time or the zonal time) must be converted to its equivalent Indian Standard Time for determining the planetary positions.

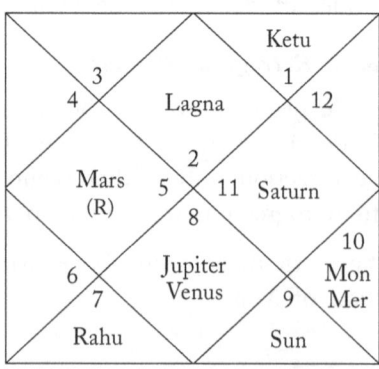

...X...
Vargas or Subtle Divisions

पश्यामि देवांस्तव देव देहे सर्वांस्तथा भूतविशेषसङ्घान्।
ब्रह्माणमीशं कमलासनस्थमृषींश्च सर्वानुरगांश्च दिव्यान्।।

*In Your body, O Lord, I see all the gods and the varied multitudes of
beings as well, and Brahma (the Creator) seated on the lotus throne, and
all the sages as also races of the serpents divine.*   Gita XI/15

It is easy to appreciate that any given sign remains on the horizon for an
average of two hours, plus or minus a few minutes. This means that all
persons born during that time will have a similar planetary disposition in their
charts. Also, a given sign rises on the horizon at approximately the same time
(with a difference of approx. 4 minutes) on the subsequent day also. It is
possible that the planetary disposition as well as the rising sign may remain
unaffected even if the two births happen a day apart. In cases of twins too,
where the rising signs and the planetary positions are likely to be similar,
segregation of the natives appears difficult.

One of the very brilliant methods of overcoming the diffi-culties mentioned
above is the use of vargas or subtle divisions. Each sign is divided into a
specific number of parts. Thus, the lagna or the rising sign falls in a specific
area of a division. In any given division or varga, the placement of the lagna
and the planets forms that specific varga or divisional chart.

Parashara describes sixteen divisions called as the Shodasha-vargas. These
vargas not only help segregate the apparently similar charts, they also specifically
deal with specific areas of a native's life. Thus, the use of vargas is essential
in order to make accurate and specific predictions.
The sixteen vargas of Parashara are as follows:

1. Rashi or the complete sign of 30°.
2. Hora or one-half of a sign (15°).
3. Drekkana or one-third of a sign (10°).
4. Chaturthamsha or one-fourth of a sign (7°30').
5. Saptamsha or one-seventh of a sign (4°17'8.5").

6. Navamsha or one-ninth of a sign (3°20').
7. Dashamsha or one-tenth of a sign (3°).
8. Dwadashamsha or one-twelfth of a sign (2°30').
9. Shodashamsha or one-sixteenth of a sign (1°52'30").
10. Vimshamsha or one-twentieth of a sign (1°30').
11. Chaturvimshamsha or one-twentyfourth of a sign (1°15').
12. Bhamsha (Sapta-vimshamsha) or one-twentyseventh of a sign (1°6'40").
13. Trimshamsha or one-thirtieth of a sign (1°00').
14. Khavedamsha or one-fortieth of a sign (0°45').
15. Aksha-vedamsha or one-fortyfifth of a sign (0°40').
16. Shashtyamsha or one-sixtieth of a sign (0°30').

These sixteen vargas are briefly described below.

1. *Rashi* : This comprises one full sign of 30 degrees. A rashi chart is the basic horoscope. Here, the lagna depends upon the sign rising at the horizon at the time of birth. The planets are located in the signs which they occupy in the zodiac.

2. *Hora* (Table X-1) : Here, a sign is divided into two parts of 15° each. This is arrived at thus :

   (a) The first 15 degrees in an odd sign belong to the Sun (or the sign Simha) and the second 15 degrees to the Moon (or the sign Karka).

   (b) The first 15 degrees in an even sign belong to the Moon (or Karka) and the second 15° to the Sun (or Simha).

Table X-1
The Hora Chart

Degree↓ Signs→	1	2	3	4	5	6	7	8	9	10	11	12
1st 0°-15°	S	M	S	M	S	M	S	M	S	M	S	M
2nd 15°-30°	M	S	M	S	M	S	M	S	M	S	M	S

3. *Drekkana* (Table X-2) : When a sign is divided into three equal parts of 10° each, such parts are called as Drekkanas. In each sign, the first Drekkana belongs to the same sign; the second Drekkana belongs to the sign fifth from it; and the third Drekkana to the sign ninth from it.

Table X-2
The Drekkana Chart

Signs → Drekkana↓	1	2	3	4	5	6	7	8	9	10	11	12
1st 0°-10°	1	2	3	4	5	6	7	8	9	10	11	12
2nd 10°-20°	5	6	7	8	9	10	11	12	1	2	3	4
3rd 20°-30°	9	10	11	12	1	2	3	4	5	6	7	8

4. *Chaturthamsha* (Table X-3) : This comprises one-fourth of a sign, being equivalent to 7°30'. Here, the first 7°30' of a sign belong to the same sign, the second 7°30' (i.e., 7°30' to 15°0') belongs to the sign falling in the fourth house from it; the third (15°0' to 22°30') to the sign seventh from it and the last (22°30' to 30°0') to the sign falling tenth from it.

Table X-3
The Chaturthamsha Chart

Signs → Chaturthamsha↓	1	2	3	4	5	6	7	8	9	10	11	12
0°-7°30'	1	2	3	4	5	6	7	8	9	10	11	12
7°30'-15°0'	4	5	6	7	8	9	10	11	12	1	2	3
15°0'-22°30'	7	8	9	10	11	12	1	2	3	4	5	6
22°30'-30°00'	10	11	12	1	2	3	4	5	6	7	8	9

5. *Saptamsha* (Table X-4) : A sign of 30 degrees is divided into seven equal parts (of 4°17'8.5" each). In odd signs, the seven parts belong to the seven signs falling in regular order from the odd sign concerned. In even signs, the first part belongs to the sign seventh from it, and the remaining six signs follow in regular order.

Table X-4
The Saptamsha Chart

Signs → Saptamsha↓	1	2	3	4	5	6	7	8	9	10	11	12
1. 04°17'08"	1	8	3	10	5	12	7	2	9	4	11	6
2. 08°34'17"	2	9	4	11	6	1	8	3	10	5	12	7
3. 12°51'25"	3	10	5	12	7	2	9	4	11	6	1	8
4. 17°08'34"	4	11	6	1	8	3	10	5	12	7	2	9
5. 21°25'43"	5	12	7	2	9	4	11	6	1	8	3	10
6. 25°42'51"	6	1	8	3	10	5	12	7	2	9	4	11
7. 30°00'00"	7	2	9	4	11	6	1	8	3	10	5	12

6. *Navamsha* (Table X-5) : This is the most important of the divisional charts. Here, each sign is divided into nine equal parts of 3°20' each. In movable signs, the first Navamsha belongs to the same sign, and the remaining eight Navamshas follow in regular order from it. In the fixed signs, the first Navamsha belongs to the sign falling in the ninth house from it. In case of the mixed signs, the first Navamsha belongs to the sign falling in the fifth house from it. It is said that a planet gives its effect more certainly according to its Navamsha than its Rashi position. When a planet occupies the same sign in the Rashi chart as also the Navamsha chart, it is called *Vargottama*, a highly beneficial situation.

90

Table X-5
The Navamsha Chart

Signs → Navamsha↓	1	2	3	4	5	6	7	8	9	10	11	12
1. 3°20'	1	10	7	4	1	10	7	4	1	10	7	4
2. 6°40'	2	11	8	5	2	11	8	5	2	11	8	5
3. 10°00'	3	12	9	6	3	12	9	6	3	12	9	6
4. 13°20'	4	1	10	7	4	1	10	7	4	1	10	7
5. 16°40'	5	2	11	8	5	2	11	8	5	2	11	8
6. 20°00'	6	3	12	9	6	3	12	9	6	3	12	9
7. 23°20'	7	4	1	10	7	4	1	10	7	4	1	10
8. 26°40'	8	5	2	11	8	5	2	11	8	5	2	11
9. 30°00'	9	6	3	12	9	6	3	12	9	6	3	12

7. *Dashamamsha* (Table X-6) : Each Dashamamsha division consist of 3°. In odd signs, the first three degrees belong to the same sign, the next three degrees to the sign falling next in order, and so on. In even signs, the first three degrees belong to the sign falling in the *ninth house* from itself, the next three degrees to the next (or the tenth) sign, and so on. Dashmamsha too appears to be a highly significant divisional chart, next in importance to the navamsha only.

Table X-6 The
Dashamamsha chart

Signs → Dashamamsha↓	1	2	3	4	5	6	7	8	9	10	11	12
1. 0°- 3°	1	10	3	12	5	2	7	4	9	6	11	8
2. 3°- 6°	2	11	4	1	6	3	8	5	10	7	12	9
3. 6°- 9°	3	12	5	2	7	4	9	6	11	8	1	10
4. 9°-12°	4	1	6	3	8	5	10	7	12	9	2	11
5. 12°-15°	5	2	7	4	9	6	11	8	1	10	3	12
6. 15°-18°	6	3	8	5	10	7	12	9	2	11	4	1
7. 18°-21°	7	4	9	6	11	8	1	10	3	12	5	2
8. 21°-24°	8	5	10	7	12	9	2	11	4	1	6	3
9. 24°-27°	9	6	11	8	1	10	3	12	5	2	7	4
10. 27°-30°	10	7	12	9	2	11	4	1	6	3	8	5

8. *Dwadashamsha* (Table X-7) : This comprises of one-twelfth of a sign, and is equivalent to 2°30'. The first Dwadashamsha of a sign belongs to the same sign, the remaining eleven Dwadashamshas fall in subsequent eleven signs in regular order.

Table X-7
The Dwadashamsha chart

Signs → Dwadashamsha↓	1	2	3	4	5	6	7	8	9	10	11	12
1. 0°00'-2°30'	1	2	3	4	5	6	7	8	9	10	11	12
2. 2°30'-5°00'	2	3	4	5	6	7	8	9	10	11	12	1
3. 5°00'- 7°30'	3	4	5	6	7	8	9	10	11	12	1	2
4. 7°30'-10°00'	4	5	6	7	8	9	10	11	12	1	2	3
5. 10°00'-12°30'	5	6	7	8	9	10	11	12	1	2	3	4
6. 12°30'-15°00'	6	7	8	9	10	11	12	1	2	3	4	5
7. 15°00'-17°30'	7	8	9	10	11	12	1	2	3	4	5	6
8. 17°30'-20°00'	8	9	10	11	12	1	2	3	4	5	6	7
9. 20°00'-22°30'	9	10	11	12	1	2	3	4	5	6	7	8
10. 22°30'-25°00'	10	11	12	1	2	3	4	5	6	7	8	9
11. 25°00'-27°30'	11	12	1	2	3	4	5	6	7	8	9	10
12. 27°30'-30°00'	12	1	2	3	4	5	6	7	8	9	10	11

9. *Shodashamsha* (Table X-8) : Here, a sign is divided into sixteen divisions comprising of 1°52'30" each. In movable signs, the first Shodashamsha starts from Mesha; the next one is Vrisha, and so on, until the twelfth which is Meena. From the thirteenth Shodashamsha, the order starts from Mesha again and proceeds in the same manner until the sixteenth Shodashamsha falls in Karka.

In case of fixed signs, the first Shodashamsha is Simha, and the last Vrishchika. In mixed signs, the first Shodashamsha is Dhanu and the last Meena.

Table X-8
The Shodashamsha chart

Signs → Shodashamsha↓	1	2	3	4	5	6	7	8	9	10	11	12
1. 0 - 1°52'30"	1	5	9	1	5	9	1	5	9	1	5	9
2. - 3°45'00"	2	6	10	2	6	10	2	6	10	2	6	10
3. - 5°37'30"	3	7	11	3	7	11	3	7	11	3	7	11
4. - 7°30'00"	4	8	12	4	8	12	4	8	12	4	8	12
5. - 9°22'30"	5	9	1	5	9	1	5	9	1	5	9	1
6. - 11°15'00"	6	10	2	6	10	2	6	10	2	6	10	2
7. - 13°07'30"	7	11	3	7	11	3	7	11	3	7	11	3
8. - 15°00'00"	8	12	4	8	12	4	8	12	4	8	12	4

Signs → Shodashamsha↓		1	2	3	4	5	6	7	8	9	10	11	12
9.	- 16°52'30"	9	1	5	9	1	5	9	1	5	9	1	5
10.	- 18°45'00"	10	2	6	10	2	6	10	2	6	10	2	6
11.	- 20°37'30"	11	3	7	11	3	7	11	3	7	11	3	7
12.	- 22°30'00"	12	4	8	12	4	8	12	4	8	12	4	8
13.	- 24°22'30"	1	5	9	1	5	9	1	5	9	1	5	9
14.	- 26°15'00"	2	6	10	2	6	10	2	6	10	2	6	10
15.	- 28°07'30"	3	7	11	3	7	11	3	7	11	3	7	11
16.	- 30°00'00"	4	8	12	4	8	12	4	8	12	4	8	12

10. *Vimshamsha* (Table X-9) : This is the twentieth division of a sign measuring 1°30' of arc. In movable signs, it starts from Mesha, in fixed signs from Dhanu and in mixed signs from Simha. Subsequent Vimshamshas belong to the signs falling in order subsequently.

Table X-9
The Vimshamsha chart

Signs → Vimshamsha↓		1	2	3	4	5	6	7	8	9	10	11	12
1.	0°00'- 1°30'	1	9	5	1	9	5	1	9	5	1	9	5
2.	1°30'- 3°00'	2	10	6	2	10	6	2	10	6	2	10	6
3.	3°00'- 4°30'	3	11	7	3	11	7	3	11	7	3	11	7
4.	4°30'- 6°00'	4	12	8	4	12	8	4	12	8	4	12	8
5.	6°00'- 7°30'	5	1	9	5	1	9	5	1	9	5	1	9
6.	7°30'- 9°00'	6	2	10	6	2	10	6	2	10	6	2	10
7.	9°00'-10°30'	7	3	11	7	3	11	7	3	11	7	3	11
8.	10°30'-12°00'	8	4	12	8	4	12	8	4	12	8	4	12
9.	12°00'-13°30'	9	5	1	9	5	1	9	5	1	9	5	1
10.	13°30'-15°00'	10	6	2	10	6	2	10	6	2	10	6	2
11.	15°00'-16°30'	11	7	3	11	7	3	11	7	3	11	7	3
12.	16°30'-18°00'	12	8	4	12	8	4	12	8	4	12	8	4
13.	18°00'-19°30'	1	9	5	1	9	5	1	9	5	1	9	5
14.	19°30'-21°00'	2	10	6	2	10	6	2	10	6	2	10	6
15.	21°00'-22°30'	3	11	7	3	11	7	3	11	7	3	11	7
16.	22°30'-24°00'	4	12	8	4	12	8	4	12	8	4	12	8
17.	24°00'-25°30'	5	1	9	5	1	9	5	1	9	5	1	9
18.	25°30'-27°00'	6	2	10	6	2	10	6	2	10	6	2	10
19.	27°00'-28°30'	7	3	11	7	3	11	7	3	11	7	3	11
20.	28°30'-30°00'	8	4	12	8	4	12	8	4	12	8	4	12

11. *Chaturvimshamsha or Siddhamsha* (Table X-10) : Each of these measures 1°15'. There are twenty-four Chaturvimshamshas; they start from Simha in odd signs and from Karka in even signs. Subsequent Chaturvimshamshas follow in regular order.

Table X-10
The Chaturvimshamsha chart

Signs → Chaturvimshamsha↓	1	2	3	4	5	6	7	8	9	10	11	12
1. 0°00'- 1°15'	5	4	5	4	5	4	5	4	5	4	5	4
2. 1°15'- 2°30'	6	5	6	5	6	5	6	5	6	5	6	5
3. 2°30'- 3°45'	7	6	7	6	7	6	7	6	7	6	7	6
4. 3°45'- 5°00'	8	7	8	7	8	7	8	7	8	7	8	7
5. 5°00'- 6°15'	9	8	9	8	9	8	9	8	9	8	9	8
6. 6°15'- 7°30'	10	9	10	9	10	9	10	9	10	9	10	9
7. 7°30'- 8°45'	11	10	11	10	11	10	11	10	11	10	11	10
8. 8°45'-10°00'	12	11	12	11	12	11	12	11	12	11	12	11
9. 10°00'-11°15'	1	12	1	12	1	12	1	12	1	12	1	12
10. 11°15'-12°30'	2	1	2	1	2	1	2	1	2	1	2	1
11. 12°30'-13°45'	3	2	3	2	3	2	3	2	3	2	3	2
12. 13°45'-15°00'	4	3	4	3	4	3	4	3	4	3	4	3
13. 15°00'-16°15'	5	4	5	4	5	4	5	4	5	4	5	4
14. 16°15'-17°30'	6	5	6	5	6	5	6	5	6	5	6	5
15. 17°30'-18°45'	7	6	7	6	7	6	7	6	7	6	7	6
16. 18°45'-20°00'	8	7	8	7	8	7	8	7	8	7	8	7
17. 20°00'-21°15'	9	8	9	8	9	8	9	8	9	8	9	8
18. 21°15'-22°30'	10	9	10	9	10	9	10	9	10	9	10	9
19. 22°30'-23°45'	11	10	11	10	11	10	11	10	11	10	11	10
20. 23°45'-25°00'	12	11	12	11	12	11	12	11	12	11	12	11
21. 25°00'-26°15'	1	12	1	12	1	12	1	12	1	12	1	12
22. 26°15'-27°30'	2	1	2	1	2	1	2	1	2	1	2	1
23. 27°30'-28°45'	3	2	3	2	3	2	3	2	3	2	3	2
24. 28°45'-30°00'	4	3	4	3	4	3	4	3	4	3	4	3

12. *Bhamsha or Sapta-vimshamsha* (Table X-11) : There are 27 Bhamshas (of 1° 6' 40" each) in a sign. In fiery signs (i.e., 1, 5 and 9) they start from Mesha; In earthy signs (i.e., 2, 6 and 10), they start from Karka; In airy signs (i.e., 3, 7 and 11), they start from Tula and in watery signs (i.e., 4, 8 and 12), they start from Makara. The subsequent order is the usual regular order.

Table X-11
The Bhamsha chart

Signs → Bhamsha↓		1	2	3	4	5	6	7	8	9	10	11	12
1.	0 - 1°06'40"	1	4	7	10	1	4	7	10	1	4	7	10
2.	- 2°13'20"	2	5	8	11	2	5	8	11	2	5	8	11
3.	- 3°20'00"	3	6	9	12	3	6	9	12	3	6	9	12
4.	- 4°26'40"	4	7	10	1	4	7	10	1	4	7	10	1
5.	- 5°33'20"	5	8	11	2	5	8	11	2	5	8	11	2
6.	- 6°40'00"	6	9	12	3	6	9	12	3	6	9	12	3
7.	- 7°46'40"	7	10	1	4	7	10	1	4	7	10	1	4
8.	- 8°53'20"	8	11	2	5	8	11	2	5	8	11	2	5
9.	-10°00'00"	9	12	3	6	9	12	3	6	9	12	3	6
10.	-11°06'40"	10	1	4	7	10	1	4	7	10	1	4	7
11.	-12°13'20"	11	2	5	8	11	2	5	8	11	2	5	8
12.	-13°20'00"	12	3	6	9	12	3	6	9	12	3	6	9
13.	-14°26'40"	1	4	7	10	1	4	7	10	1	4	7	10
14.	-15°33'20"	2	5	8	11	2	5	8	11	2	5	8	11
15.	-16°40'00"	3	6	9	12	3	6	9	12	3	6	9	12
16.	-17°46'40"	4	7	10	1	4	7	10	1	4	7	10	1
17.	-18°53'20"	5	8	11	2	5	8	11	2	5	8	11	2
18.	-20°00'00"	6	9	12	3	6	9	12	3	6	9	12	3
19.	-21°06'40"	7	10	1	4	7	10	1	4	7	10	1	4
20.	-22°13'20"	8	11	2	5	8	11	2	5	8	11	2	5
21.	-23°20'00"	9	12	3	6	9	12	3	6	9	12	3	6
22.	-24°26'40"	10	1	4	7	10	1	4	7	10	1	4	7
23.	-25°33'20"	11	2	5	8	11	2	5	8	11	2	5	8
24.	-26°40'00"	12	3	6	9	12	3	6	9	12	3	6	9
25.	-27°46'40"	1	4	7	10	1	4	7	10	1	4	7	10
26.	-28°53'20"	2	5	8	11	2	5	8	11	2	5	8	11
27.	-30°00'00"	3	6	9	12	3	6	9	12	3	6	9	12

13. *Trimshamsha* (Table X-12) : Literally speaking, it is con-sidered as one-thirtieth division of a sign. Actually, however, each sign is divided into five unequal parts, each part belonging to one of the five planets from Mars to Saturn. In odd signs, the first five degrees belong to Mars, the next five degrees to Saturn, the next eight degrees to Jupiter, the subsequent seven degrees to Mercury, and the last five degrees to Venus. This order gets reversed in case of even signs where the planets Venus, Mercury,

Jupiter, Saturn and Mars respectively own five degrees, seven degrees, eight degrees, five degrees and five degrees, in a sign.

Table X-12
The Trimshamsha Chart

	ODD Signs (1, 3, 5, 7, 9, 11)		EVEN Signs (2, 4, 6, 8, 10, 12)	
Trimshamsha↓	Degrees	Lord	Degrees	Lord
1.	0-5	Mars	0-5	Venus
2.	5-10	Saturn	5-12	Mercury
3.	10-18	Jupiter	12-20	Jupiter
4.	18-25	Mercury	20-25	Saturn
5.	25-30	Venus	25-30	Mars

14. *Khavedamsha* (Table X-13): This is the one-fortieth division of a sign, measuring 0°45' of an arc. In odd signs, the first Khavedamsha is Mesha; in even signs it is Tula. The remaining divisions follow in regular order in both cases.

Table X-13
The Khavedamsha chart

Signs → / Khavedamsha ↓	1	2	3	4	5	6	7	8	9	10	11	12
1. 00°00'-00°45'	1	7	1	7	1	7	1	7	1	7	1	7
2. 00°45'-01°30'	2	8	2	8	2	8	2	8	2	8	2	8
3. 01°30'-02°15'	3	9	3	9	3	9	3	9	3	9	3	9
4. 02°15'-03°00'	4	10	4	10	4	10	4	10	4	10	4	10
5. 03°00'-03°45'	5	11	5	11	5	11	5	11	5	11	5	11
6. 03°45'-04°30'	6	12	6	12	6	12	6	12	6	12	6	12
7. 04°30'-05°15'	7	1	7	1	7	1	7	1	7	1	7	1
8. 05°15'-06°00'	8	2	8	2	8	2	8	2	8	2	8	2
9. 06°00'-06°45'	9	3	9	3	9	3	9	3	9	3	9	3
10. 06°45'-07°30'	10	4	10	4	10	4	10	4	10	4	10	4
11. 07°30'-08°15'	11	5	11	5	11	5	11	5	11	5	11	5
12. 08°15'-09°00'	12	6	12	6	12	6	12	6	12	6	12	6
13. 09°00'-09°45'	1	7	1	7	1	7	1	7	1	7	1	7
14. 09°45'-10°30'	2	8	2	8	2	8	2	8	2	8	2	8
15. 10°30'-11°15'	3	9	3	9	3	9	3	9	3	9	3	9
16. 11°15'-12°00'	4	10	4	10	4	10	4	10	4	10	4	10
17. 12°00'-12°45'	5	11	5	11	5	11	5	11	5	11	5	11
18. 12°45'-13°30'	6	12	6	12	6	12	6	12	6	12	6	12
19. 13°30'-14°15'	7	1	7	1	7	1	7	1	7	1	7	1

96

Signs → / Khavedamsha ↓	1	2	3	4	5	6	7	8	9	10	11	12
20. 14°15'-15°00'	8	2	8	2	8	2	8	2	8	2	8	2
21. 15°00'-15°45'	9	3	9	3	9	3	9	3	9	3	9	3
22. 15°45'-16°30'	10	4	10	4	10	4	10	4	10	4	10	4
23. 16°30'-17°15'	11	5	11	5	11	5	11	5	11	5	11	5
24. 17°15'-18°00'	12	6	12	6	12	6	12	6	12	6	12	6
25. 18°00'-18°45'	1	7	1	7	1	7	1	7	1	7	1	7
26. 18°45'-19°30'	2	8	2	8	2	8	2	8	2	8	2	8
27. 19°30'-20°15'	3	9	3	9	3	9	3	9	3	9	3	9
28. 20°15'-21°00'	4	10	4	10	4	10	4	10	4	10	4	10
29. 21°00'-21°45'	5	11	5	11	5	11	5	11	5	11	5	11
30. 21°45'-22°30'	6	12	6	12	6	12	6	12	6	12	6	12
31. 22°30'-23°15'	7	1	7	1	7	1	7	1	7	1	7	1
32. 23°15'-24°00'	8	2	8	2	8	2	8	2	8	2	8	2
33. 24°00'-24°45'	9	3	9	3	9	3	9	3	9	3	9	3
34. 24°45'-25°30'	10	4	10	4	10	4	10	4	10	4	10	4
35. 25°30'-26°15'	11	5	11	5	11	5	11	5	11	5	11	5
36. 26°15'-27°00'	12	6	12	6	12	6	12	6	12	6	12	6
37. 27°00'-27°45'	1	7	1	7	1	7	1	7	1	7	1	7
38. 27°45'-28°30'	2	8	2	8	2	8	2	8	2	8	2	8
39. 28°30'-29°15'	3	9	3	9	3	9	3	9	3	9	3	9
40. 29°15'-30°00'	4	10	4	10	4	10	4	10	4	10	4	10

15. *Aksha-vedamsha* (Table X-14) : Each sign here is divided into forty-five parts, of 0°40' arc. In movable signs the first such division falls in Mesha; in fixed signs in Simha; and in mixed signs in Dhanu. The remaining divisions follow the usual regular order.

Table X-14
The Akshavedamsha chart

Signs → / Akshavedamsha ↓	1	2	3	4	5	6	7	8	9	10	11	12
1. 00°00'-00°40'	1	5	9	1	5	9	1	5	9	1	5	9
2. 00°40'-01°20'	2	6	10	2	6	10	2	6	10	2	6	10
3. 01°20'-02°00'	3	7	11	3	7	11	3	7	11	3	7	11
4. 02°00'-02°40'	4	8	12	4	8	12	4	8	12	4	8	12
5. 02°40'-03°20'	5	9	1	5	9	1	5	9	1	5	9	1
6. 03°20'-04°00'	6	10	2	6	10	2	6	10	2	6	10	2
7. 04°00'-04°40'	7	11	3	7	11	3	7	11	3	7	11	3
8. 04°40'-05°20'	8	12	4	8	12	4	8	12	4	8	12	4

Signs → Akshavedamsha↓	1	2	3	4	5	6	7	8	9	10	11	12
9. 05°20'-06°00'	9	1	5	9	1	5	9	1	5	9	1	5
10. 06°00'-06°40'	10	2	6	10	2	6	10	2	6	10	2	6
11. 06°40'-07°20'	11	3	7	11	3	7	11	3	7	11	3	7
12. 07°20'-08°00'	12	4	8	12	4	8	12	4	8	12	4	8
13. 08°00'-08°40'	1	5	9	1	5	9	1	5	9	1	5	9
14. 08°40'-09°20'	2	6	10	2	6	10	2	6	10	2	6	10
15. 09°20'-10°00'	3	7	11	3	7	11	3	7	11	3	7	11
16. 10°00'-10°40'	4	8	12	4	8	12	4	8	12	4	8	12
17. 10°40'-11°20'	5	9	1	5	9	1	5	9	1	5	9	1
18. 11°20'-12°00'	6	10	2	6	10	2	6	10	2	6	10	2
19. 12°00'-12°40'	7	11	3	7	11	3	7	11	3	7	11	3
20. 12°40'-13°20'	8	12	4	8	12	4	8	12	4	8	12	4
21. 13°20'-14°00'	9	1	5	9	1	5	9	1	5	9	1	5
22. 14°00'-14°40'	10	2	6	10	2	6	10	2	6	10	2	6
23. 14°40'-15°20'	11	3	7	11	3	7	11	3	7	11	3	7
24. 15°20'-16°00'	12	4	8	12	4	8	12	4	8	12	4	8
25. 16°00'-16°40'	1	5	9	1	5	9	1	5	9	1	5	9
26. 16°40'-17°20'	2	6	10	2	6	10	2	6	10	2	6	10
27. 17°20'-18°00'	3	7	11	3	7	11	3	7	11	3	7	11
28. 18°00'-18°40'	4	8	12	4	8	12	4	8	12	4	8	12
29. 18°40'-19°20'	5	9	1	5	9	1	5	9	1	5	9	1
30. 19°20'-20°00'	6	10	2	6	10	2	6	10	2	6	10	2
31. 20°00'-20°40'	7	11	3	7	11	3	7	11	3	7	11	3
32. 20°40'-21°20'	8	12	4	8	12	4	8	12	4	8	12	4
33. 21°20'-22°00'	9	1	5	9	1	5	9	1	5	9	1	5
34. 22°00'-22°40'	10	2	6	10	2	6	10	2	6	10	2	6
35. 22°40'-23°20'	11	3	7	11	3	7	11	3	7	11	3	7
36. 23°20'-24°00'	12	4	8	12	4	8	12	4	8	12	4	8
37. 24°00'-24°40'	1	5	9	1	5	9	1	5	9	1	5	9
38. 24°40'-25°20'	2	6	10	2	6	10	2	6	10	2	6	10
39. 25°20'-26°00'	3	7	11	3	7	11	3	7	11	3	7	11
40. 26°00'-26°40'	4	8	12	4	8	12	4	8	12	4	8	12
41. 26°40'-27°20'	5	9	1	5	9	1	5	9	1	5	9	1
42. 27°20'-28°00'	6	10	2	6	10	2	6	10	2	6	10	2
43. 28°00'-28°40'	7	11	3	7	11	3	7	11	3	7	11	3
44. 28°40'-29°20'	8	12	4	8	12	4	8	12	4	8	12	4
45. 29°20'-30°00'	9	1	5	9	1	5	9	1	5	9	1	5

16. *Shashtyamsha* (Table X-15) : This is the sixtieth division of a sign and measures 0°30' of arc. Being very fine, it needs a very accurate time recording in order to be correct. Sage Parashara lays a lot of stress on the predictive utility of this sub-division. In practice, however, it is rare to be so accurate in one's time recording as to find a correct Shashtyamsha. The first Shashtyamsha in a sign starts from the same sign. The subsequent Shashtyamshas belong to the subsequent signs that follow in regular order.

Table X-15
The Shashtyamsha Chart

Signs → Shashtyamsha↓	1	2	3	4	5	6	7	8	9	10	11	12
1. 00°00'-00°30'	1	2	3	4	5	6	7	8	9	10	11	12
2. 00°30'-01°00'	2	3	4	5	6	7	8	9	10	11	12	1
3. 01°00'-01°30'	3	4	5	6	7	8	9	10	11	12	1	2
4. 01°30'-02°00'	4	5	6	7	8	9	10	11	12	1	2	3
5. 02°00'-02°30'	5	6	7	8	9	10	11	12	1	2	3	4
6. 02°30'-03°00'	6	7	8	9	10	11	12	1	2	3	4	5
7. 03°00'-03°30'	7	8	9	10	11	12	1	2	3	4	5	6
8. 03°30'-04°00'	8	9	10	11	12	1	2	3	4	5	6	7
9. 04°00'-04°30'	9	10	11	12	1	2	3	4	5	6	7	8
10. 04°30'-05°00'	10	11	12	1	2	3	4	5	6	7	8	9
11. 05°00'-05°30'	11	12	1	2	3	4	5	6	7	8	9	10
12. 05°30'-06°00'	12	1	2	3	4	5	6	7	8	9	10	11
13. 06°00'-06°30'	1	2	3	4	5	6	7	8	9	10	11	12
14. 06°30'-07°00'	2	3	4	5	6	7	8	9	10	11	12	1
15. 07°00'-07°30'	3	4	5	6	7	8	9	10	11	12	1	2
16. 07°30'-08°00'	4	5	6	7	8	9	10	11	12	1	2	3
17. 08°00'-08°30'	5	6	7	8	9	10	11	12	1	2	3	4
18. 08°30'-09°00'	6	7	8	9	10	11	12	1	2	3	4	5
19. 09°00'-09°30'	7	8	9	10	11	12	1	2	3	4	5	6
20. 09°30'-10°00'	8	9	10	11	12	1	2	3	4	5	6	7
21. 10°00'-10°30'	9	10	11	12	1	2	3	4	5	6	7	8
22. 10°30'-11°00'	10	11	12	1	2	3	4	5	6	7	8	9
23. 11°00'-11°30'	11	12	1	2	3	4	5	6	7	8	9	10
24. 11°30'-12°00'	12	1	2	3	4	5	6	7	8	9	10	11
25. 12°00'-12°30'	1	2	3	4	5	6	7	8	9	10	11	12
26. 12°30'-13°00'	2	3	4	5	6	7	8	9	10	11	12	1
27. 13°00'-13°30'	3	4	5	6	7	8	9	10	11	12	1	2
28. 13°30'-14°00'	4	5	6	7	8	9	10	11	12	1	2	3

Signs → Shashtyamsha↓		1	2	3	4	5	6	7	8	9	10	11	12
29.	14°00'-14°30'	5	6	7	8	9	10	11	12	1	2	3	4
30.	14°30'-15°00'	6	7	8	9	10	11	12	1	2	3	4	5
31.	15°00'-15°30'	7	8	9	10	11	12	1	2	3	4	5	6
32.	15°30'-16°00'	8	9	10	11	12	1	2	3	4	5	6	7
33.	16°00'-16°30'	9	10	11	12	1	2	3	4	5	6	7	8
34.	16°30'-17°00'	10	11	12	1	2	3	4	5	6	7	8	9
35.	17°00'-17°30'	11	12	1	2	3	4	5	6	7	8	9	10
36.	17°30'-18°00	12	1	2	3	4	5	6	7	8	9	10	11
37.	18°00'-18°30'	1	2	3	4	5	6	7	8	9	10	11	12
38.	18°30'-19°00'	2	3	4	5	6	7	8	9	10	11	12	1
39.	19°00'-19°30'	3	4	5	6	7	8	9	10	11	12	1	2
40.	19°30'-20°00'	4	5	6	7	8	9	10	11	12	1	2	3
41.	20°00'-20°30'	5	6	7	8	9	10	11	12	1	2	3	4
42.	20°30'-21°00'	6	7	8	9	10	11	12	1	2	3	4	5
43.	21°00'-21°30'	7	8	9	10	11	12	1	2	3	4	5	6
44.	21°30'-22°00'	8	9	10	11	12	1	2	3	4	5	6	7
45.	22°00'-22°30'	9	10	11	12	1	2	3	4	5	6	7	8
46.	22°30'-23°00'	10	11	12	1	2	3	4	5	6	7	8	9
47.	23°00'-23°30'	11	12	1	2	3	4	5	6	7	8	9	10
48.	23°30'-24°00'	12	1	2	3	4	5	6	7	8	9	10	11
49.	24°00'-24°30'	1	2	3	4	5	6	7	8	9	10	11	12
50.	24°30'-25°00'	2	3	4	5	6	7	8	9	10	11	12	1
51.	25°00'-25°30'	3	4	5	6	7	8	9	10	11	12	1	2
52.	25°30'-26°00'	4	5	6	7	8	9	10	11	12	1	2	3
53.	26°00'-26°30'	5	6	7	8	9	10	11	12	1	2	3	4
54.	26°30'-27°00'	6	7	8	9	10	11	12	1	2	3	4	5
55.	27°00'-27°30'	7	8	9	10	11	12	1	2	3	4	5	6
56.	27°30'-28°00'	8	9	10	11	12	1	2	3	4	5	6	7
57.	28°00'-28°30'	9	10	11	12	1	2	3	4	5	6	7	8
58.	28°30'-29°00'	10	11	12	1	2	3	4	5	6	7	8	9
59.	29°00'-29°30'	11	12	1	2	3	4	5	6	7	8	9	10
60.	29°30'-30°00	12	1	2	3	4	5	6	7	8	9	10	11

Note : In the Tajika system or the Hindu method of annual horoscopy, some additional and special divisional charts are utilised. Those have not been mentioned here.

Application of the Sixteen Vargas

The sixteen vargas of a horoscope are supposed to deal with specific areas as mentioned below.

1.	Lagna or the Rashi Chart	:	Physical well being of the native.
2.	Hora	:	Wealth and prosperity.
3.	Drekkana	:	Brothers and sisters, and their well being.
4.	Chaturthamsha	:	Luck; also residence.
5.	Saptamsha	:	Children and grand-children.
6.	Navamsha	:	Spouse.
7.	Dashamsha	:	Any specific benefit; profession of the native.
8.	Dwadashamsha	:	Father and mother.
9.	Shodashamsha	:	Pleasures and troubles from vehicles, horses, elephants, etc.
10.	Vimshamsha	:	Spiritual pursuits, penance.
11.	Chaturvimshamsha	:	Education, learning.
12.	Bhamsha	:	Strength and weakness.
13.	Trimshamsha	:	Miseries, troubles.
14.	Khavedamsha	:	Auspicious and inauspicious hap-penings.
15.	Akshavedamsha	:	All things combined.
16.	Shashtyamsha	:	All things combined.

Note :

1. Navamsha is the most commonly used divisional chart which is of extreme practical utility. The promise in the Rashi chart must be confirmed in the Navamsha chart before making any prediction. It is said that the planets give their results according to their disposition in the Navamsha in preference to their indications in the Rashi chart.

2. *Manasagari* has the following areas allotted to seven of the divisional charts.

(a)	Lagna	:	Body and character.
(b)	Hora	:	Wealth.
(c)	Drekkana	:	Results of past karmas.
(d)	Sapthamsha	:	Number of brothers & sisters.
(e)	Navamsha	:	All things combined.
(f)	Dwadashamsha	:	Spouse.
(g)	Trimshamsha	:	Death.

3. Sapthamsha may also be employed to ascertain the character or temperament of the native.

4. Khavedamsha and Akshavedamsha are also used to determine the overall strength of planets.

Sub-groups of the 16 vargas

Those versed in astrology do not always use all the sixteen vargas as mentioned above. Out of these, four groups may be con-sidered. In each group, the relative significance of the different divisional charts varies. It is customary to consider the combined value of the various divisional charts in any of the four groups as equal to 20 units. These four groups, and the relative value of the vargas constituting them, are as follows:

A. *Shadvargas or six divisions* :

	Varga	Relative value
1.	Rashi	6
2.	Hora	2
3.	Drekkana	4
4.	Navamsha	5
5.	Dwadashamsha	2
6.	Trimshamsha	1
	Total	20 units

B. *Saptavargas or seven divisions* :

	Varga	Relative value
1.	Rashi	5
2.	Hora	2
3.	Drekkana	3
4.	Saptamsha	2.5
5.	Navamsha	4.5
6.	Dwadashamsha	2
7.	Trimshamsha	1
	Total	20 units

C. *Dashavargas or ten divisions* :

	Varga	Relative value
1.	Lagna	3
2.	Shashtyamsha	5
3.	Hora	1.5
4.	Drekkana	1.5

5. Saptamsha	1.5	
6. Navamsha	1.5	
7. Dashmamsha	1.5	
8. Dwadashamsha	1.5	
9. Shodashamsha	1.5	
10. Trimshamsha	1.5	
Total	20	units

D. *Shodashvargas or all sixteen divisions :*

Varga	Relative value
1. Rashi	3.5
2. Hora	1
3. Drekkana	1
4. Trimshamsha	1
5. Navamsha	3
6. Shodashamsha	2
7. Shashtyamsha	4
8. Chaturthamsha	0.5
9. Saptamsha	0.5
10. Dashamsha	0.5
11. Dwadashamsha	0.5
12. Vimshamsha	0.5
13. Chaturvimshamsha	0.5
14. Bhamsha	0.5
15. Khavedamsha	0.5
16. Akshavedamsha	0.5
Total	20 units

Note : It is important to realise the relative importance of the Shashtyamsha (one-sixtieth division) among the Dashavargas and the Shodashvargas. However, being a very subtle division, depending on the most accurate time recording, the Shashtyamsha is hardly ever used in practice.

...XI...
The Sub-Planets

धूमेनाव्रियते वह्निर्यथादर्शो मलेन च।
यथोल्बेनावृतो गर्भस्तथा तेनेदमावृतम्॥

*As fire is obscured by smoke, and as a mirror by dust, as an embryo
is enveloped by its coverings, so is this (wisdom) obscured by that
(passion).* Gita III/38

There are certain mathematical points which are of particular significance
in Vedic astrology. These points do not have any physical existence. They,
however, function as minor grahas or subplanets. They are also called as *'Aprakasha
grahas'* or non-luminous planets. Since their calculation and interpretation add
an extra burden on the astrologer, most astrologers do not use them routinely
in their practice. The subplanets, however, offer a very fertile area for research.

The subplanets may be discussed under three distinct heads.

I. The Gulikadi Group

This group consists of five subplanets. To calculate their position, the day (i.e.,
the time duration from sunrise to sunset) is divided into eight equal parts. The
first part belongs to the lord of the day itself (e.g., the Sun for Sunday, the Moon
for Monday, Mars for Tuesday, etc.). Subsequent parts belong to the remaining
six planets. The eighth part is without a lord. The part ruled by Saturn is called
Gulika (or Maandi); that ruled by Jupiter is called *Yamakantaka*, the one ruled
by Mars is called *Mrityu*, the one falling under the Sun is called as *Kaala or
Kaala-Vela*, and the one ruled by Mercury is known as *Ardhaprahara*.

If the birth has taken place at night, its duration (i.e., the duration of time
from sunset to sunrise) is divided into eight parts. The first part belongs to
the planet falling fifth in order from the day lord (e.g., Jupiter for Sunday,
Venus for Monday, Saturn for Tuesday, etc.). The remaining parts are ruled by
the six remaining planets, leaving the eighth part without a lord again. The
various subplanets coincide with the parts belonging to their ruling planets.

Cast an ascendant for the beginning of Saturn's part. This gives the longitude of Gulika. Ascendants cast for the commencing moments of the parts

belonging to other planets give longitudes of the respective subplanets.

Maandi: Some people differentiate between Gulika and Maandi. According to them, when the day and night are of 30 Ghatis (12 hours) each, for a day birth, the Maandi rises at the end of 26 Ghatis on Sunday, at 22 Ghatis on Monday, at 18 Ghatis on Tuesday, at 14 Ghatis on Wednesday, at 10 Ghatis on Thursday, at 6 Ghatis on Friday, and at 2 ghatis on Saturday. In case of night time birth, consider the values given for the day falling fifth from itself, e.g., 10 Ghatis from the onset of night on Sunday, 6 Ghatis on Monday, 2 Ghatis on Tuesday, 26 Ghatis on Wednesday, and so on.

When the duration of the day or of night is different from 30 Ghatis, appropriate alterations must be made. An 'ascendant' calculated for the specific time indicated above gives the position of Maandi.

The formula for the calculation of time of rise of Maandi is:

(a) *Day time birth* :

$$\frac{\text{Duration of day in Ghatis}}{30} \times 26, 22, 18, 14, 10, 6, \text{ or } 2$$

depending upon the day of birth from Sunday onwards.

(b) *Night time birth* :

$$\frac{\text{Duration of night in Ghatis}}{30} \times 10, 6, 2, 26, 22, 18, \text{ or } 14$$

depending upon the day of birth from Sunday onwards.

II. The Dhoomadi Group

Here the following five subplanets are obtained by manipulation of the longitude of the Sun.

(a) *Dhooma* : Longitude of the Sun plus $4^s13°20'$ yields Dhooma, which is a representative of Mars.

(b) *Vyatipata (or Pata)* : 12 signs minus Dhooma yields Vyatipata, a representative of Rahu.

(c) *Parivesha (or Paridhi)* : Add six signs to Vyatipata to obtain Parivesha ruled by the Moon.

(d) *Inderchapa (or Chapa, or Kodanda)* : Represented by Venus, Inderchapa is obtained by subtracting Parivesha from 12 signs.

(e) *Ketu (or Upaketu)* : This is obtained by adding $16°40'$ to Inderchapa. It represents Ketu. Ketu increased by one sign yields the longitude of the Sun.

III. The Prana-Pada

A Pranapada sign is equivalent to 15 Palas (or Vighatis). Each Pala (24 seconds of clock time) is thus equal to two degrees of Pranapada. To get the position of Pranapada, the following steps must be gone through:

1. Obtain the Ishta-Kaala or the time of birth since sunrise, expressed in Ghatis and Palas.

2. Convert the Ishta-Kaala into Palas and multiply by two. This gives the Pranapada degrees (one may convert these into signs and degrees by dividing these by 30).

3. The Pranapada is obtained as follows:

   (i) *The Sun in a movable sign* :

   Pranapada degrees + longitude of the Sun

   (ii) *The Sun in a fixed sign* :

   Pranapada degrees + longitude of the Sun + 240 degrees (9th house from the Sun)

   (iii) *The Sun in a mixed sign* :

   Pranapada degrees + longitude of the Sun + 120 degrees (5th house from the Sun)

The result gives the position of Pranapada in degrees, which can be converted into signs. Multiples of 12 signs must naturally be deleted.

Gulika in Different Houses

Gulika is considered the son of Saturn. It is a highly malefic subplanet. Its results in different houses are being briefly described. Like all malefics, it causes beneficial results in houses 3, 6 and 11.

First House : Sickly, sinning, stupid, ill-tempered, exces-sive sexual urge.

Second House : Disabled, miserable, wretched nature, shameless, poor, and indulgent in immoral acts.

Third House : Good looking, leader of a village, virtuous, respected by the ruler, wealthy, long lived, and without brothers.

Fourth House : Bereft of all comforts, ailing, sinful, and tormented by excess of Vaata and Pitta.

Fifth House : Destitute, immoral, short-lived, jealous, impotent, irresolute, controlled by his wife, speaks ill of others, an atheist; adverse for progeny.

Sixth House : Healthy, destroyer of his foes, good in looks, liked by females, courageous, and kind to others.

Seventh House : Subdued by his wife, a sinner, weak of limb, adulterous, stupid, ungrateful, bereft of friends, lives off his wife's earnings.

Eighth House : Miserable, tormented by hunger, cruel, very ill-tempered, devoid of wealth and virtue.

Ninth House	:	Indulgent in wicked deeds, cruel, lacking common sense, a back biter, may hurt his parents and preceptors.
Tenth House	:	Blessed with sons, varied comforts, inclined towards religious pursuits. According to another reading, the native gives up his prescribed duties and performs shameful acts.
Eleventh House	:	Happy, wealthy, good looking, a leader, of a diminutive body, and widely respected. Adverse for elder brother.
Twelfth House	:	Indulgent in low deeds, wicked, ill-looking, defective of a limb, lazy, associates with fallen women.

Gulika associated with other planets

Sun	:	Hates his father; short life to father.
Moon	:	Adverse for mother.
Mars	:	Devoid of younger brother; separation from brother.
Mercury	:	Insane.
Jupiter	:	Indulges in blasphemous heresy.
Venus	:	Associates with women of easy morals; sexually transmitted disease.
Saturn	:	Chronic illness, short life.
Rahu	:	Suffers, and causes, illness through poisons.
Ketu	:	Suffers, and causes, injury through fire.

The results of other subplanets have been described by sage Parashara and others. They constitute areas of research, which are beyond the scope of this work.

Note : Aspects of planets modify the above mentioned results substantially.

...XII...
Planetary States of Being

या निशा सर्वभूतानां तस्यां जागर्ति संयमी।
यस्यां जाग्रति भूतानि सा निशा पश्यतो मुनेः ॥

*What is night for all beings is the time of waking for the disciplined one;
what is the time of waking for (all) beings is the night for the sage of
vision.*   Gita II/69

Results arising from various planets are said to be dependant upon certain
planetary states or *Avasthas*. A consideration of these planetary avasthas
sheds light on some subtle predictive principles. Not much research seems
to have been done about the avasthas of planets as applicable to predictive
astrology although several classical writers, from Parashara downwards, have
mentioned of them.

Avasthas of planets can be grouped under several heads. They are being
briefly described here according to information derived mainly from Parashara.

I. Baladi-Avasthas or Physical States

Planets belong to one of the five avasthas dependent upon which one-fifth portion of a sign they occupy. These five avasthas are called as:

1. *Balavastha or state of childhood* : 0° to 6° in an odd sign and 24° to 30° in
   an even sign.

2. *Kumaravastha or state of boyhood* : 6° to 12° in an odd sign and 18° to 24°
   in an even sign.

3. *Yuvavastha or state of adulthood* : 12° to 18° in odd as well as even signs.

4. *Vridhavastha or state of old age* : 18° to 24° in odd signs and 6° to 12° in
   even signs.

5. *Mritavastha or state of death* : 24° to 30° in an odd sign and 0° to 6° in
   an even sign.

A planet in its Balavastha fulfils only one-quarter of its promise; one in
Kumaravastha provides for one-half of its promised result; a planet in Yuvavastha

produces full results; one in Vridhavastha produces very little result; and the one in Mritavastha is incapable of any useful function, or may produce only adverse results.

Note :

1. According to the Phaladeepika, a planet in Balavastha indicates progressive benefits, in Kumaravastha comforts, in Yuvavastha royalty and in Vridhavastha death and the like. The one in Mritavastha is dead and functionless.

2. The above results must not be applied literally.

3. No planet can be functionless and each must produce good and bad results according to various factors affecting it. The above mentioned results may not be taken as the final word.

4. It is important to correlate the above indications with the dashas of planets. Two possible applications that could be studied are:

    (a) Planets in Balavastha may produce their results imme-diately as the dasha starts, and those in the subsequent avasthas do so progressively later, during their indicated dasha periods.

    (b) A planet may produce its results at that time of a native's life span as is indicated by the avastha to which the said planet belongs.

II. Jagradadi-Avasthas or States of Consciousness

Depending upon the level of consciousness of a planet, it may fall into one of the three states.

1. *Jagrad Avastha or state of wakefulness* : This happens when a planet is exalted or located in its own house. A planet in Jagradavastha is capable of yielding full results.

2. *Swapnavastha or dreamful state*: This obtains when a planet is located in the house of a friend or a neutral. A planet in such a state produces medium results.

3. *Sushupti-avastha or state of sleep* : When a planet is either debilitated or in the house of an enemy. Such a planet is incapable of any function.

Note : According to the Jataka Parijata, the above three conditions are based on the location of various planets in the Navamsha chart and not in the Rashi chart. This concept appears more appropriate.

III. Deeptadi-Avasthas or Physical-Mental States

Nine planetary conditions have been described under this head.

1. *Deepta or luminous*: A planet in exaltation or its Moolatrikona. Such a planet in its dasha period ensures high status, courage, valour, wealth, vehicles, royal favours and material comforts.

2. *Swastha or stable* : In its own house. Such a planet during its dasha ensures good health, education, fame, lands, wife, favours from the ruler and inclination toward religious pursuits.

3. *Mudita or delighted* : Located in the house of an adhi-mitra or a bosom friend. Its promises include money, clothes, per-fumes, religious pursuits, vehicles, ornaments, etc.

4. *Shanta or quiescent* : In a friend's house. It gives favours from the king, excessive wealth, comforts, lands, study of scriptures, pleasures from meditation.

5. *Deena or deficient* : A planet in the house of a neutral. It ensures change of work place or residence, opposition to one's near and dear ones, humiliation, sickness, etc.

6. *Duhkhi or tormented* : In the house of an enemy. Such a planet during its dasha gives displacement and foreign journey, separation from near ones, fear from thief, fire and the king.

7. *Vikala or grief-stricken* : Associated with a malefic. This gives mental torment, death or separation from friends, troubles at the hands of wife, children and thieves.

8. *Khala or wicked* : In the sign of a malefic. It leads to quarrels, separation from father, loss of lands and wealth, humiliation at the hands of one's own people.

9. *Kruddha (kopa) or angered* : Associated with the Sun (and combust!). This leads to inclination to perform sinful deeds, loss of money, wife and children, and eye disease.

Note : Several writers have mentioned slightly varying names for these avasthas, and also varying conditions that characterise them. Some of them, picked up from classical works, are as follows :

(a) *Shaanta or Quiescent* : In the vargas of benefics.

(b) *Shakta or powerful* : Not combust. This is the reverse of Kruddha.

(c) *Prapeedit or extremely tormented* : Combust, hence equivalent to Kruddha.

(d) *Khala or wicked* : Defeated in planetary warfare. This has also been labelled as *Peedit or tormented*.

(e) *Deena or deficient* : Debilitated.

IV. Lajjitadi-Avasthas or Mental States

There are six of them.

1. *Lajjita or Abashed* : A planet is said to be in Lajjita-avastha when it occupies the fifth house in association with either of the Sun, Mars, Saturn, Rahu or Ketu.

A planet in Lajjita avastha leads to irreligious inclinations, loss of discrimination, illness to child, aimless wandering, quarrel-some nature, etc.

2. *Garvita or Conceited* : In its exaltation or Moolatrikona.

In the dasha of a planet in Garvita-avastha, one gains royal status, new house, learning, wealth, rise in business and varied comforts.

3. *Kshudhita or Hungry* : When it occupies the house of an enemy and is aspected by or associated with an enemy, particularly if it is associated with Saturn.

In its dasha, a planet in Kshudhita-avastha leads to sorrow, mental torment, trouble from enemies, monetary loss, distorted reasoning and loss of all energy.

4. *Trishita or Thirsty* : Placement in a Jalachara or watery sign, aspected by a malefic, unaspected by a benefic.

In its dasha, one suffers illness from association with women, inclination towards wicked deeds, loss of wealth, weakness, and humiliation.

5. *Mudita or Delighted* : In the house of a friend, associated with or aspected by friendly planets as well as Jupiter.

The dasha of a planet in Mudita-avastha ensures beautiful garments, ornaments, large and spacious house to live in, pleasures from women, lands, residence in royal mansions, annihilation of foes, and progress in studies and learning.

6. *Kshobhita or Agitated* : This happens when the planet is associated with the Sun (combust!) and aspected by malefics and enemy planets.

Its dasha causes penury, distorted logic, varied torments, loss of wealth, disease of the foot, and loss of wealth through royal disfavour.

Note : Planets in Kshudhita and Kshobhita avasthas ruin the houses they occupy.

V. Shayanadi-Avasthas or States of (Mental and Physical) Inclination

There are twelve states which indicate the mental and physical tendencies of planets. They are referred to in the following order.

1. Shayana or 'recumbent'.
2. Upavesha or 'sitting'.
3. Netrapani or 'hands on eyes'.
4. Prakashana or 'luminous'.
5. Gamanechchha or 'eager to go'.
6. Gamana or 'departing'.
7. Sabhayam Vasti or 'being in an assembly'.

8. Agama or 'arriving'.

9. Bhojana or 'eating'.

10. Nrityalipsa or 'desire to dance'.

11. Kautuka or 'delight'.

12. Nidra or 'sleep'.

Method of determining the above avasthas

Go through the following steps in respect of the concerned planet :

(a) *Find the product of the following three values* :

   (i) The number of the nakshatra (counted in the regular order from Ashwini) which the concerned planet is in;

   (ii) The number of the planet in its natural order (considering the Sun as 1, the Moon as 2, etc., until Ketu as 9); and

   (iii) The number of the Navamsha in the sign which the planet is in. Some authorities, instead of considering the number of the Navamsha, take into consideration the actual degree of planetary longitude in the sign of its location.

(b) *Add to the above value, the sum of the following three values.*

   (i) The number representing the native's birth nakshatra (i.e., the nakshatra where the Moon of the native is located in the birth chart);

   (ii) The number representing the sign rising in the lagna (Mesha as 1, Vrisha as 2, etc.); and

   (iii) The Ishta-danda or the number of Ghatis (a ghati is equal to 24 minutes) that have elapsed from the time of sunrise upto the time of birth.

(c) *Divide the result obtained above by 12.* Note the remainder, which gives the number representing one of the above mentioned twelve avasthas.

Determining the Cheshta

After determining a planet's avasthas, as mentioned above, it is required to find out the extent to which an avastha is productive of results. To achieve this, the following steps must be gone through:

(a) Multiply the number representing the above mentioned avastha by the same number. (That is, find the square of the remainder obtained as a final result during the process of determining the avastha).

(b) Add to it the constant which represents the first letter of the native's name. Take the help of the accompanying table in this regard.

Numbers	1	2	3	4	5
First	अ a	इ i	उ u	ए ae	ओ o
letter of	क ka	ख kha	ग ga	घ gha	च cha
the	छ chha	ज ja	झ jha	ट ta	ठ tha
native's	ड da	ढ dha	त ta	थ tha	द da
name	ध dha	न na	प pa	फ pha	ब ba
	भ bha	म ma	य ya	र ra	ळ la
	व va	श sha	ष sha	स sa	ह ha

Note : The Sanskrit alphabet does not exactly correspond with the English alphabet. Those who do not know the first letter of their name, according to the Sanskrit alphabet, need to take appropriate help.

(c) Divide the sum of (a) and (b) by 12 and note the remainder.

(d) To the remainder obtained above, add the kshepaka-constant of the planet. The kshepaka-constants for the planets from the Sun to Ketu, in their natural order, are: 5, 2, 2, 3, 5, 3, 3, 4 and 4 respectively.

(e) Divide the value obtained after step (d) by three. Depending upon the remainder being either 1, 2 or 3 (or zero), the relevant Cheshta is called as *Drishti, Cheshta, and Vicheshta.*

In Drishti, the result of an avastha is ordinary. In Cheshta, the result is intense. In Vicheshta, the avastha produces minimal result.

It is not proposed here to go into further details, regarding these avasthas and their Cheshtas. These form a subject for intense research.

Note :

The use of planetary avasthas in astrology needs a very careful consideration. The results attributed to avasthas, particularly to what we call as the Mritavastha of the Baladi group, could have very different meanings when we take into account the concepts of the Jaimini astrology. According to the Jaimini astrology, a planet which is the farthest advanced in a rashi is known as the Atmakaraka, and is supposed to be the most significant of the planets in the chart. It is in some way equivalent to the lagna lord. According to our concepts of the avasthas, such a planet could well be in the Mritavastha. There seems to be some missing link somewhere. Astrologers are known to have made very successful predictions, especially in timing events, solely on the basis of planetary avasthas, without using any dasha.

See for instance the horoscope of Queen Elizabeth of England who was coronated in 1952-53, and continues to be the queen still. See how many planets are above 20 degrees in her horoscope.

Queen Elizabeth — April 21, 1926

Mercury	Sun		Rahu
Venus			Moon
Lagna Mars Jupiter			
Ketu	Sat (R)		

(North Indian chart)

- 12 Mer
- 11 Venus
- Lagna Mars Jupiter / 10
- Ketu 9
- 8 Sat (R)
- Sun 1
- 7 / 4 Moon
- 2
- 6
- 3 Rahu
- 5

Lagna	1°11'	Mars	28°03'	Venus	21°08'
Sun	7°23'	Mercury	11°51'	Saturn (R)	1°37'
Moon	19°22'	Jupiter	29°41'	Rahu	27°17'

Queen Victoria — May 24, 1819

Rahu Mars Saturn	Mercury Venus	Lagna Sun Moon	
Jupiter			
			Ketu

(North Indian chart)

- 3 / 4
- Lagna Sun Moon / 2
- 1 Mercury Venus
- 12 Mar Sat / Rah
- 5 / 11 / 8
- 6 Ketu / 7
- 9
- 10 Jup

Lagna	10°57'	Mars	26°20'	Venus	5°27'
Sun	10°47'	Mercury	17°36'	Saturn	7°24'
Moon	12°16'	Jupiter	25°35'	Rahu	28°23'

Then again see the horoscope of Queen Victoria who became queen in 1837 and died in 1903, ruling as the world's most powerful queen for 66 long years.

This is being pointed out because the avasthas have some secret and hidden meanings which can be elucidated only after thorough research.

...XIII...
Graha Bala or the Strength of Planets

आपूर्यमाणमचलप्रतिष्ठं समुद्रमापः प्रविशन्ति यद्वत्।
तद्वत्कामा यं प्रविशन्ति सर्वे स शान्तिमाप्नोति न कामकामी॥

He, unto whom all desires enter as do waters into the ever filled and ever consistent sea, attains peace and not he who yields unto his desires.

Gita II/70

Planets produce their results depending upon their strength or weakness in a horoscope. Determination of the exact strength of planets demands an elaborate mathematical exercise. It is proposed here only to give an outline of the method involved in determining the strength of planets. For greater details the reader is referred to appropriate works on the subject.

Units of planetary strength

It is customary to express the strength of planets in Rupas and Shashtyamshas (i.e., units and subunits). Sixty Shashtyamshas (subunits) make a Rupa (a unit).

Shadbala or Six-fold Strength

Six different sources of strength combine to give a planet its actual strength. These six sources of strength, also known as shadbala, are:

   I. Sthana Bala or Positional Strength.
  II. Dig-Bala or Directional Strength.
 III. Kaala Bala or Temporal Strength.
 IV. Cheshta Bala or Motional Strength.
  V. Naisargika Bala or Inherent Strength.
 VI. Drig-Bala or Aspectual Strength (i.e., strength derived from aspects of other planets).

I. Sthana Bala

This is the strength of a planet because of its position. This is comprised of :

1. Uchcha Bala.
2. Sapta-vargaja Bala.
3. Oja-yugama Rashi Bala.
4. Oja-yugama Navamsha Bala.
5. Kendradi Bala.
6. Drekkana Bala.

1. *Uchcha Bala* : This is the strength due to exaltation of a planet. A planet gets one Rupa (or sixty Shashtyamshas) of strength when at its exact point of exaltation. It gets '0' units when at its exact point of debilitation. Between its deep exaltation and deep debilitation (i.e., over a span of six signs or 180 degrees), the strength varies from 60 Shashtyamshas to zero Shashtyamsha. Each three degrees of a planet's longitude thus correspond to a strength of one Shashtyamsha.

2. *Sapta-vargaja Bala* : The Sapta-vargas comprise of the Rashi, Hora, Drekkana, Sapthamsha, Navamsha, Dwadashamsha and Trimshamsha.

   (a) *Rashi chart* The allottment of strength varies with the location of the planet as indicated.

(i)	In its Moolatrikona:	45.000 Shashtyamshas
(ii)	In its own house:	30.000 Shashtyamshas
(iii)	In the house of Adhi-Mitra:	22.500 Shashtyamshas
(iv)	In the house of a Mitra:	15.000 Shashtyamshas
(v)	In the house of a Sama:	7.500 Shashtyamshas
(vi)	In the house of a Shatru:	3.750 Shashtyamshas
(vii)	In the house of Adhi-Shatru:	1.875 Shashtyamshas

   (b) *The remaining six vargas* : In the remaining vargas , the Moolatrikona is not considered. Planets in the remaining six categories receive similar strength as mentioned above.

Own house	30.000 Shashtyamshas
Adhi-Mitra (bosom friend)	22.500 Shashtyamshas
Mitra (friend)	15.000 Shashtyamshas
Sama (equal)	7.500 Shashtyamshas
Shatru (enemy)	3.750 Shashtyamshas
Adhi-Shatru (Bitter enemy)	1.875 Shashtyamshas

3. *Oja-yugama Rashi Bala* : The Moon and Venus in even signs, in the Rashi chart, and the Sun, Mars, Mercury, Jupiter and Saturn in odd signs, each get a strength of 15 Shashtyamshas. Elsewhere they get no strength.

4. *Oja-yugama Navamsha Bala* : The Moon and Venus in even signs, and the Sun, Mars, Mercury, Jupiter and Saturn in odd signs in the Navamsha, each get a strength of 15 Shashtyamshas. Elsewhere they get no strength.

5. *Kendradi Bala* : Planets located in the kendras obtain 60 Shashtyamshas, those in Panpharas 30 Shashtyamshas, and those in Apoklimas obtain 15 Shashtyamshas of strength.

6. *Drekkana Bala* : Male planets (the Sun, Mars and Jupiter) in the first Drekkana, eunuchs (Mercury and Saturn) in the middle Drekkana and female planets (the Moon and Venus) in the last Drekkana obtain 15 Shashtyamshas of strength each. If these planets fall outside the prescribed Drekkanas, they get no strength.

II. Dig-Bala

This is the strength that a planet acquires because of the direction of its placement.

1. *The Sun and Mars* are strong in the south (10th house). This means that when either of them is located at the cusp of the 10th house, it receives one Rupa or 60 Shashtyamshas of strength. In the fourth house, 180 degrees away, each of them receives zero Shashtyamsha of strength. In between they receive proportionate strength at a rate of one Shashtyamsha for every three degrees of arc.

2. *The Moon and Venus* are fully strong in the north (cusp of the fourth house) and obtain no strength in the tenth house.

3. *Mercury and Jupiter* obtain full strength in the east (cusp of the lagna) and no strength in the seventh house.

4. *Saturn* obtains full strength in the west (cusp of the seventh house) and no directional strength in the lagna.

III. Kaala Bala

This is dependant upon the moment of birth. It has nine components.

1. *Nata-Unnata Bala* :

   (a) *The Sun, Jupiter and Venus* obtain 60 Shashtyamshas of strength at exact local noon; they get zero strength at exact local midnight. In between, their strength is altered proportionately.

   (b) *The Moon, Mars and Saturn* obtain 60 Shashtyamshas of strength at exact local midnight; they get zero strength at exact local noon. In between, their strength is altered proportionately.

   (c) *Mercury* always gets 60 Shashtyamshas of strength under this head.

2. *Paksha Bala* :

   (a) *Natural benefics* (The Moon, Mercury, Jupiter and Venus) obtain 60 Shashtyamshas of strength when the Sun and the Moon are 180 degrees apart (i.e., full Moon). When the two luminaries are in exact conjunction, they get zero strength. In between their strength is altered proportionately.

(b) *Natural malefics* (The Sun, Mars and Saturn) obtain full strength (60 Shashtyamshas) when the Sun and the Moon are exactly conjunct (new Moon); at full Moon they get zero strength. In between, their strength is altered proportionately.

(c) Multiply the Paksha-Bala of the Moon, as obtained above, by two. This gives the actual Paksha-Bala of the Moon for purposes of reckoning of strength.

3. *Tri-Bhaga Bala* : Tri-bhaga is one-third of anything.

(a) *For a day-time birth:* Determine the length of the day (sunrise to sunset) and divide it by three.

   (i) Birth in the first one-third : Mercury gets full (60 Shashtyamshas) strength.

   (ii) Birth in the middle one-third : The Sun gets full strength.

   (iii) Birth in the last one-third : Saturn gets full strength.

(b) *For a night-time birth*: Determine the length of the night (sunset to sunrise) and divide it into three portions.

   (i) Birth in the first part: The Moon gets full strength.

   (ii) Birth in the middle part: Venus gets full strength

   (iii) Birth in the last part: Mars gets full strength.

(c) Jupiter always gets full strength (60 Shashtyamsha) under this heading, whatever the time of birth.

4. *Abda Bala* : The lord of the first weekday of the year of birth gets 15 Shashtyamshas of strength. Here it is not the year of the Christian era that is meant. The year in question here is :

(a) either the year of 360 days calculated from the beginning of the creation (for which there are special and tedious methods of calculation involved);

(b) or the solar year which commences with the entry of the Sun into the sign Mesha of the Niryana zodiac.

5. *Maasa Bala* : The lord of the first weekday of the month of birth gets 30 Shashtyamshas of strength. Again, the month in question is not the calendar month of the Christian era. It could be :

(a) either the month of 30 days calculated from the beginning of creation;

(b) or the solar month which commences with the monthly solar ingress into Niryana signs of the zodiac.

6. *Vaara Bala* : The lord of the weekday of birth gets 45 Shashtyamshas of strength.

7. *Hora Bala* : Determine the Hora operating at the time of birth. Its lord gets full strength of 60 Shashtyamshas.

8. *Ayana Bala* : Planets obtain strength by possessing north or south declinations.

   (a) All planets have a strength of 30 Shashtyamshas at zero declination.

   (b) The Sun, Mars, Jupiter and Venus obtain full strength (60 Shashtyamshas) at 24° (approx. 23°27') north decli-nation and zero strength at south declination.

   (c) The Moon and Saturn obtain full strength at 24° (approx. 23°27') south declination and zero strength at north declination.

   (d) Mercury increases in strength as it moves away from the zero declination (30 Shashtyamshas of strength) to either north or south declination (full strength).

   (e) The longitudes of planets considered for determination of the Ayana Bala are the Sayana longitudes. A planet has north declination at its Sayana longitude of 0-180 degrees and south declination at its Sayana longitude of 180-360 degrees.

   (f) The Ayana Bala of the Sun must be doubled.

9. *Yuddha Bala* : Planets other than the Sun and the Moon, are said to be in yuddha (or at war) when they are located within one degree of each other. The planet whose longitude is greater is considered subjugated.

   The strength of the conqueror as well as the conquered is determined by adding their Sthana Bala, Dig-Bala and Kaala Bala (upto the Hora Bala above). According to some, the difference between the two is the Yuddha Bala. This must be added to the Bala of the victor and subtracted from that of the loser. According to others, the difference between the two must be divided by the difference between their disc diameters (9.4 Vikala or seconds for Mars; 6.6 for Mercury; 190.4 for Jupiter; 16.6 for Venus and 158.0 for Saturn) to obtain the Yuddha Bala. This is added to the Bala of the victor and subtracted from the Bala of the loser.

IV. Cheshta Bala

Determination of the Cheshta Bala of a planet needs elaborate understanding of astronomical principles involved in the apparent motion of planets from direct to retrograde, and from the slowest to the fastest. In classical texts the Cheshta Bala of planets has been described thus, depending upon their apparent motion.

	Apparent motion	Strength
(i)	Vakra	60 Shashtyamshas
(ii)	Anuvakra (or Ativakra)	30 Shashtyamshas
(iii)	Vikala	15 Shashtyamshas
(iv)	Madhya	30 Shashtyamshas
(v)	Manda	15 Shashtyamshas
(vi)	Mandatara	7.5 Shashtyamshas
(vii)	Sheeghra	45 Shashtyamshas
(viii)	Ati-sheeghra	30 Shashtyamshas

Note :

(a) The Sun has the same Ayana Bala and Cheshta Bala.

(b) The Moon has the same Paksha Bala and Cheshta Bala.

V. Naisargika Bala

Each planet has its inherent strength. Dividing 60 Shashtyamshas by seven, and multiplying the result successively by one, two, three, four, five, six and seven gives the Naisargika Bala respectively of Saturn, Mars, Mercury, Jupiter, Venus, the Moon and the Sun. The Sun, thus, has the maximum Naisargika Bala (60 Shashtyamshas) and Saturn has the minimum (8.57 Shashtyamshas).

VI. Drig-Bala

Each planet receives positive strength when aspected by a bene-fic and negative strength when aspected by a malefic. The sum total of all aspects on a planet is a measure of its Drig-Bala.

Subtracting the longitude of the aspecting planet from the longitude of the aspected planet gives us the angular distance between the two planets. Mars, Jupiter and Saturn have their special aspects. The aspects of various planets at different arcs are tabulated below.

	Aspect of			
Arc	Mars	Jupiter	Saturn	Remaining planets
0°- 30°	No aspect	No aspect	No aspect	No aspect
60°	One quarter	One quarter	Full	One quarter
90°	Full	Three quarter	Three quarter	Three quarter
120°	Half	Full	Half	Half
150°	No aspect	No aspect	No aspect	No aspect
180°	Full	Full	Full	Full
210°	Full	Three quarter	Three quarter	Three quarter
240°	Half	Full	Half	Half
270°	One quarter	One quarter	Full	One quarter
300°-360°	No aspect	No aspect	No aspect	No aspect

In between the degrees mentioned here, proportionate alterations need to be done.

The sum total of aspects of all the planets on a given planet is a measure of its Drig-Bala. This is positive or negative depending upon whether the benefic aspects or the malefic aspects predominate. The total aspectual strength obtained in respect of each planet, when divided by four, yields positive or negative Drig-Bala in Shashtyamshas. This must be added to or subtracted from the total Bala obtained by adding all the various components of Graha Bala in order to obtain the final actual strength of a planet.

The final strength obtained in Shashtyamshas, when divided by 60 yields the strength in Rupas.

Bhava Bala or the Strength of Houses

This has three components :

1. Strength of the lord of the house , as already discussed.

2. Drig-Bala or strength of aspect, which is positive or negative depending upon the sum total of benefic aspects exceeding the malefic ones or vice versa. The method of determining the Drig-Bala is the same as that in case of planets. In case of houses, their cusps are considered in place of the longitudes of aspected planets.

3. Dig-Bala or directional strength.

Dig-Bala

Parashara says the following in this respect:

"To determine the Bhava Bala of Mithuna, Kanya, Tula, Kumbha and first half of Dhanu (i.e., Dwipada rashis), reduce from them the cusp of the seventh house. For Mesha, Vrisha, Simha, second half of Dhanu and first half of Makara (i.e., Chatushpada rashis), reduce from them the cusp of the fourth house. For Karka and Vrishchika (i.e., Keeta rashis), reduce from these the cusp of the lagna. And for Meena and second half of Makara (Jalachara rashis), reduce the cusp of the tenth house from these. Convert the remainder into degrees and divide by three (to get the strength in Shashtyamshas). If the remainder (before converting into degrees) is more than six, reduce it from 12 signs, and then divide by three after converting into degrees (as above). To this add one-fourth of the aspect of different planets (as was done while determining the aspectual strength of planets) in case of benefic aspects and subtract it in case of malefic aspects. Add to it the strength of the lord of the house" (This gives the total Bhava Bala or the strength of the house).

...XIV...
The Dashas or
Operational Periods of Planets

भूतग्रामः स एवायं भूत्वा भूत्वा प्रलीयते।
रात्र्यागमेऽवशः पार्थ प्रभवत्यहरागमे॥

O Partha! This very multitude of existences coming forth again and again merges helplessly at the onset of night (of Brahma), and (again) manifests at the onset of day.

Gita VIII/19

Application of the dasha system is an extremely brilliant feature of Vedic astrology. Whereas the horoscopic chart, with its planetary positions, provides a static picture of a native's life, the dashas add dynamicity to it. The promise indicated in a horoscope attains fruition when an appropriate dasha ope-rates. The dashas, thus, help in timing the events.

There are numerous dasha systems advocated by sage Parashara. The two very widely used dashas are :

1. The Vimshottari dasha, with a cycle of 120 years; and

2. The Yogini dasha, with a cycle of 36 years.

We have mentioned above about the static and dynamic aspects of chart analysis. It may be important to remind the reader at the outset that the dynamic factor in chart analysis is completed when the dashas are integrated with the gochara, or transit of planets. Since one cycle of the Yogini dasha happens to cover a span of only thirty-six years, a native with an average lifespan may experience two or more cycles of the Yogini dasha in his life-time. Thus similar dashas would get repeated in the life of the individual. It becomes all the more important in such a situation to make a liberal use of transits while using the Yogini dasha for any predictions. The subject of transits is dealt with later in this text, in chapter XXIX.

The Parashari dashas are generally nakshatra based. That is to say, they depend upon the birth nakshatra or the nakshatra of the Moon in the birth chart. Of the two dashas mentioned above, the Vimshottari is the more widely used.

THE VIMSHOTTARI DASHA

The twenty-seven nakshatras are divided into three groups of nine nakshatras each. These are owned by the nine planets (see table II-2). Each planet is allotted a specific number of years over which it operates. The order of the dashas is also fixed. This may be seen in table XIV-1.

Table XIV-1
Vimshottari dasha periods

S.No.	Planet	Nakshatras	Dasha period (years)
1.	Sun	3, 12, 21	6
2.	Moon	4, 13, 22	10
3.	Mars	5, 14, 23	7
4.	Rahu	6, 15, 24	18
5.	Jupiter	7, 16, 25	16
6.	Saturn	8, 17, 26	19
7.	Mercury	9, 18, 27	17
8.	Ketu	1, 10, 19	7
9.	Venus	2, 11, 20	20
		Total No. of years	120

Depending upon the Moon's nakshatra in the birth chart, the dasha of a particular planet operates at the time of birth. Subsequent planetary periods follow according to the order mentioned above.

Balance of dasha at birth

After having decided the planet whose dasha operates at the time of birth, it is important to find out how long that dasha would last. This depends upon the exact location of the Moon in a nakshatra.

Each nakshatra has a span of 13°20'. For the Sun's nakshatra, this 13°20' would mean 6 years; for the Moon's nakshatra, it will mean 10 years; and so on. If the Moon is in the beginning of its nakshatra, a larger portion of the years allotted to it are yet to pass. If it is at the end of the nakshatra, only a small fraction of the total allotted period will remain. The balance of a planet's dasha, thus, is proportionate to the extent of the Moon's nakshatra which is yet to elapse.

The reader may refer to Tables XIV-2 and XIV-3 to work out the balance of Vimshottari dasha operating at the time of birth, depending upon the location of the Moon in different signs. More detailed tables are available in the ephemerides which may be referred to if necessary.

Table XIV-2
Balance of Vimshottari dasha depending upon the longitude of the Moon.

Long of Moon ° '	Moon in			
	Mesha Simha Dhanu	Vrisha Kanya Makara	Mithuna Tula Kumbha	Karka Vrishchika Meena
	y m d	y m d	y m d	y m d
0-00	Ket 7 0 0	Sun 4 6 0	Mar 3 6 0	Jup 4 0 0
1-00	6 5 21	4 0 18	2 11 21	2 9 18
2-00	5 11 12	3 7 6	2 5 12	1 7 6
3-00	5 5 3	3 1 24	1 11 3	0 4 24
3-20	5 3 0	3 0 0	1 9 0	Sat 19 0 0
4-00	4 10 24	2 8 12	1 4 24	18 0 18
5-00	4 4 15	2 3 0	0 10 15	16 7 15
6-00	3 10 6	1 9 18	0 4 6	15 2 12
6-40	3 6 0	1 6 0	Rah 18 0 0	14 3 0
7-00	3 3 27	1 4 6	17 6 18	13 9 9
8-00	2 9 18	0 10 24	16 2 12	12 4 6
9-00	2 3 9	0 5 12	14 10 6	10 11 3
10-00	1 9 0	Mon 10 0 0	13 6 0	9 6 0
11-00	1 2 21	9 3 0	12 1 24	8 1 27
12-00	0 8 12	8 6 0	10 9 18	6 7 24
13-00	0 2 3	7 9 0	9 5 12	5 2 21
13-20	Ven 20 0 0	7 6 0	9 0 0	4 9 0
14-00	19 0 0	7 0 0	8 1 6	3 9 18
15-00	17 6 0	6 3 0	6 9 0	2 4 15
16-00	16 0 0	5 6 0	5 4 24	0 11 12
16-40	15 0 0	5 0 0	4 6 0	Mer 17 0 0
17-00	14 6 0	4 9 0	4 0 18	16 6 27
18-00	13 0 0	4 0 0	2 8 12	15 3 18
19-00	11 6 0	3 3 0	1 4 6	14 0 9
20-00	10 0 0	2 6 0	Jup 16 0 0	12 9 0
21-00	8 6 0	1 9 0	14 9 18	11 5 21
22-00	7 0 0	1 0 0	13 7 6	10 2 12
23-00	5 6 0	0 3 0	12 4 24	8 11 3
23-20	5 0 0	Mar 7 0 0	12 0 0	8 6 0
24-00	4 0 0	6 7 24	11 2 12	7 7 24
25-00	2 6 0	6 1 15	10 0 0	6 4 15
26-00	1 0 0	5 7 6	8 9 18	5 1 6
26-40	Sun 6 0 0	5 3 0	8 0 0	4 3 0
27-00	5 10 6	5 0 27	7 7 6	3 9 27
28-00	5 4 24	4 6 18	6 4 24	2 6 18
29-00	4 11 12	4 0 9	5 2 12	1 3 9
30-00	4 6 0	3 6 0	4 0 0	0 0 0

124

Table XIV-3
Dashas proportionate to minutes of longitude of the Moon. Subtract these from the balance of dashas, for increase in the Moon's longitude.

Long.	Ket m d	Ven m d	Sun m d	Mon m d	Mar m d	Rah m d	Jup m d	Sat m d	Mer m d
5'	0 16	1 15	0 14	0 23	0 16	1 11	1 6	1 13	1 8
10'	1 1	3 0	0 27	1 15	1 1	2 21	2 12	2 26	2 17
15'	1 17	4 15	1 11	2 8	1 17	4 2	3 18	4 8	3 25
20'	2 3	6 0	1 24	3 0	2 3	5 12	4 24	5 21	5 3
25'	2 19	7 15	2 8	3 23	2 19	6 23	6 0	7 4	6 11
30'	3 4	9 0	2 21	4 15	3 4	8 3	7 6	8 17	7 20
35'	3 20	10 15	3 5	5 8	3 20	9 14	8 12	9 29	8 28
40'	4 6	12 0	3 18	6 0	4 6	10 24	9 18	11 12	10 6

Subperiods in Vimshottari Dasha

It will be noted that the planetary periods, as noted above, last for several years for each planet. It is difficult to use such broad time spans for timing day to day events. So as to narrow down the time when an event is likely to take place, the major planetary periods (also called as Mahadashas) mentioned above are further reduced into sub-divisions called sub-periods or Antardashas.

Under each Mahadasha (MD), the Antardasha (AD) of all the planets operate. The first AD in an MD belongs to the same planet and the remaining ones follow in order. The duration of the Antardashas of the various planets is in proportion to the duration of their major periods. The duration of an AD in a given MD can be easily calculated by the formula:

$$\frac{a}{120} \times b$$

where 'a' is the dasha period of the MD lord
and 'b' is the dasha period of the AD lord
according to Table XIV-1, vide supra.

For example, let us calculate the AD of Saturn in the MD of the Moon. According to the formula given above, we have

$$\frac{10 \text{ (Dasha period of Moon)}}{120} \times 19 \text{ (Dasha period of Saturn)}$$

$$= \frac{19}{12} \text{ years, or 1 year and 7 months.}$$

In this way, any AD can be calculated.

Sub-sub-periods or Pratyantardasha (PD)

Still finer divisions of time can be obtained by dividing a given Antardasha into sub-sub-periods (PD's) in the same proportions as the duration of their dasha periods mentioned above. The first PD in a given AD belongs to the AD lord itself while the remaining PD's follow in the usual order of the Vimshottari dasha.

A PD is calculated in an AD by the formula:

$$\frac{a}{120} \times \frac{b}{120} \times c \,,$$

where   'a' is the dasha duration of the MD lord;
          'b' is the dasha duration of the AD lord; and
          'c' is the dasha duration of the PD lord.

The result obtained in years is converted into months by multiplying by 12; and into days by further multiplying by 30.

Further finer divisions

The PD or sub-sub-period can be divided into *Sookshma dasha* which is subject to further subdivision into *Prana dasha*. The Sookshma dasha and the Prana dasha permit very accurate timing of events. However, their use demands an equally accurate recording of the birth time which may not be always possible.

THE YOGINI DASHA

The Yogini dasha cycle is a cycle of 36 years. There are eight Yoginis with a specific lord of each, as also a specific dasha period. This is given below in Table XIV-4.

Table XIV-4
Yogini Dasha

The Yogini Dasha	The Lord	Duration
1. Mangala	The Moon	1 year
2. Pingala	The Sun	2 years
3. Dhanya	Jupiter	3 years
4. Bhramari	Mars	4 years
5. Bhadrika	Mercury	5 years
6. Ulka	Saturn	6 years
7. Siddha	Venus	7 years
8. Sankata	Rahu/Ketu	8 years
Total		36 years

The Yogini dasha operating at the time of birth is obtained by adding 3 to the nakshatra of the Moon, and dividing by eight. The remainder gives the number of the Yogini dasha operating at the time of birth, according to the order given above. As in the Vimshottari dasha, the balance of Yogini dasha must be determined from the remaining part of the Moon's nakshatra. The lords of the various Yoginis are also to be used in a similar manner as the dasha lords of the Vimshottari are used. It would add to the success and accuracy of predictions by an astrologer if the two dashas, the Vimshottari and the Yogini, are simultaneously used in chart analysis. When both dasha systems indicate the same result, the event is most likely to happen. When there is any contradiction or discrepancy, a deeper analysis is called for.

Tables XIV-5, XIV-6, XIV-7 and XIV-8 give basic information about the Yogini dasha operating at birth, the duration of the AD's, and the nature of the AD's under various MD's. These are reproduced from *Applications of Yogini Dasha* by Jhanji and Sharma, to which the reader is referred for further information. This dasha is widely used by India's old and brilliant astrologers, particularly in the Himalayan belt, for fast and sure predictions. While the Vimshottari dasha is the one which is the most popular amongst astrologers and widely employed by them, there are those in some of the north Indian states who use the Yogini exclusively, with remarkable success.

Table XIV-5
Nakshatras and the Yogini Dasha

Yogini Dasha	Nakshatras
1. Mangala	Ardra, Chitra, Shravana
2. Pingala	Punarvasu, Swati, Dhanishtha
3. Dhanya	Pushya, Vishakha, Shatabhishaj
4. Bhramari	Ashlesha, Anuradha, P. Bhadrapad, Ashwini
5. Bhadrika	Magha, Jyeshtha, U. Bhadrapad, Bharani
6. Ulka	P. Phalguni, Moola, Revati, Krittika
7. Siddha	U. Phalguni, P. Ashadha, Rohini
8. Sankata	Hasta, U. Asadha, Mrigashira

Table XIV-6
Yogini Dasha by longitude of the Moon

Long of Moon	Rashi	Dasha	Rashi	Dasha	Rashi	Dasha
0°00' - 13°20'	Mesha	Bhramari	Simha	Bhadrika	Dhanu	Ulka
13°20' - 26°40'		Bhadrika		Ulka		Siddha
26°40' - 30°00'		Ulka		Siddha		Sankata
0°00' - 10°00'	Vrisha	Ulka	Kanya	Siddha	Makara	Sankata
10°00' - 23°20'		Siddha		Sankata		Mangala
23°20' - 30°00'		Sankata		Mangala		Pingala
0°00' - 6°40'	Mithuna	Sankata	Tula	Mangala	Kumbh.	Pingala
6°40' - 20°00'		Mangala		Pingala		Dhanya
20°00' - 30°00'		Pingala		Dhanya		Bhramari
0°00' - 3°20'	Karka	Pingala	Vrisch.	Dhanya	Meena	Bhramari
3°20' - 16°40'		Dhanya		Bhramari		Bhadrika
16°40' - 30°00'		Bhramari		Bhadrika		Ulka

Table XIV-7
Yogini Dasha Major and Sub Periods

Yogini	Mangala (1y)		Pingala (2 y)		Dhanya (3y)		Bhramari (4y)		Bhadrika (5y)		Ulka (6y)		Siddha (7y)		Sankata (8y)	
Sub periods	S.P. y–m–d	Total y–m–d	S.P. y–m–d	Total y–m–d	S.P. y–m–d	Total y–m–d	S.P. y–m–d	Total y–m–d	S.P. y–m–d	Total y–m–d	S.P. y–m–d	Total y–m–d	S.P. y–m–d	Total y–m–d	S.P. y–m–d	Total y–m–d
Mangala	0-0-10	0-0-10	–	–	–	–	–	–	–	–	–	–	–	–	–	–
Pingala	0-0-20	0-1-00	0-1-10	0-1-10	–	–	–	–	–	–	–	–	–	–	–	–
Dhanya	0-1-00	0-2-00	0-2-00	0-3-10	0-3-0	0-3-0	–	–	–	–	–	–	–	–	–	–
Bhramari	0-1-10	0-3-10	0-2-20	0-6-0	0-4-0	0-7-0	0-5-10	0-5-10	–	–	–	–	–	–	–	–
Bhadrika	0-1-20	0-5-00	0-3-10	0-9-10	0-5-0	1-0-0	0-6-20	1-0-0	0-8-10	0-8-10	–	–	–	–	–	–
Ulka	0-2-00	0-7-00	0-4-00	1-1-10	0-6-0	1-6-0	0-8-00	1-8-0	0-10-00	1-6-10	1-0-0	1-0-0	–	–	–	–
Siddha	0-2-10	0-9-10	0-4-20	1-6-0	0-7-0	2-1-0	0-9-10	2-5-10	0-11-20	2-6-0	1-2-0	2-2-0	1-4-10	1-4-10	–	–
Sankata	0-2-20	1-0-00	0-5-10	1-11-10	0-8-0	2-9-0	0-10-20	3-4-0	1-1-10	3-7-10	1-4-0	3-6-0	1-6-20	2-11-0	1-9-10	1-9-10
Mangala	–	–	0-0-20	2-0-0	0-1-0	2-10-0	0-1-10	3-5-10	0-1-20	3-9-0	0-2-0	3-8-0	0-2-10	3-1-10	0-2-20	2-0-0
Pingala	–	–	–	–	0-2-0	3-0-0	0-2-20	3-8-0	0-3-10	4-0-10	0-4-0	4-0-0	0-4-20	3-6-0	0-5-10	2-5-10
Dhanya	–	–	–	–	–	–	0-4-00	4-0-0	0-5-00	4-5-10	0-6-0	4-6-0	0-7-0	4-1-0	0-8-0	3-1-10
Bhramari	–	–	–	–	–	–	–	–	0-6-20	5-0-0	0-8-0	5-2-0	0-9-10	4-10-10	0-10-20	4-0-0
Bhadrika	–	–	–	–	–	–	–	–	–	–	0-10-0	6-0-0	0-11-20	5-10-0	1-1-10	5-1-10
Ulka	–	–	–	–	–	–	–	–	–	–	–	–	1-2-00	7-0-0	1-4-0	6-5-10
Siddha	–	–	–	–	–	–	–	–	–	–	–	–	–	–	1-6-20	8-0-0

Table XIV-8
Nature of various antardashas under the Yogini mahadashas

Mahadasha (MD)	Antardasha (AD)		
	Benefic	Malefic	Neutral
1. Mangala	Mangala, Dhanya Bhadrika, Siddha	Pingala, Bhramari, Ulka, Sankata	—
2. Pingala	Mangala, Pingala, Dhanya, Bhadrika	Bhramari, Ulka, Sankata	Siddha
3. Dhanya	Mangala, Dhanya, Bhadrika, Siddha	Pingala, Bhramari, Ulka, Sankata	—
4. Bhramari	Mangala, Dhanya, Siddha	Pingala, Bhramari, Ulka, Sankata	Bhadrika
5. Bhadrika	Mangala, Pingala, Dhanya, Bhadrika, Siddha	Ulka, Sankata	Bhramari
6. Ulka	—	Pingala, Dhanya, Bhramari, Bhadrika, Ulka, Siddha, Sankata	Mangala
7. Siddha	Mangala, Dhanya, Bhadrika, Siddha	Pingala, Bhramari, Ulka, Sankata	—
8. Sankata	Siddha	Mangala, Pingala, Dhanya, Bhramari, Ulka, Sankata	Bhadrika

...XV...
Interpretation of the Vimshottari Dasha

मयाध्यक्षेण प्रकृतिः सूयते सचराचरम् ।
हेतुनानेन कौन्तेय जगद्द्विपरिवर्तते ॥

Under My guidance, the nature brings forth all things, moving and unmoving; because of this, O Kaunteya, the world revolves in cycles.

Gita IX/10

Planets produce their results only when their dasha periods operate. Within the MD of a planet, the AD's of all the planets operate one after the other. Similarly, the PD's of different planets operated in each AD. The MD gives a broad timing which is narrowed by the use of the AD. The PD narrows it down further to within a few months. The Sookshma and the Prana dashas, if calculated accurately, help time an event extremely closely.
Planets produce their results :

1. According to their inherent nature, which includes their natural disposition toward other planets; and

2. According to their disposition in the horoscope, in the Rashi chart as well as the vargas.

MAHADASHAS

The principles that govern the results of dashas of planets are as follows :

1. *Favourable results* are produced by a dasha lord which is strong, exalted, in its own house, in its Moolatrikona, in a friend's house, under benefic association or aspect, and located in good houses like the kendras or the trines or the 11th or the 2nd house or associated with the 9th or the 10th lord.

2. *Adverse results* are produced by a dasha lord which is weak or debilitated, in the house of an enemy, combust, placed in houses 6, 8 or 12, and under malefic association or aspect.

3. *Timing of fructification of results* : A planet located in the first Drekkana of a sign produces its results during the beginning of its dasha. Located

in the middle Drekkana of a sign, the planet produces its results during the middle part of its dasha. When located in the third Drekkana, its results manifest during the concluding portion of its dasha.

For a retrograde planet, the above order gets reversed.

4. *Ownership of a house* : The ownership of a house by the dasha lord is extremely important. During the dasha of its lord, a house suddenly becomes active, and events pertaining to it manifest in varying ways depending upon the strength, the weakness and the extent of affliction of its lord.

The results of the Mahadashas of various planets are being, briefly, described below.

Dasha of the SUN

When favourable :

Gain in wealth, varied comforts, favours from the king, rise in status.
Associated with the 5th lord: child birth.
With the 2nd lord: prosperity, vehicles.
With the 4th lord: vehicles.

When adverse :

Miseries, loss of wealth, disfavour of the ruler, foreign residence, loss of status, punishment, opposition from friends and relatives, loss of father.

Dasha of the MOON

When favourable:

Wide renown, prosperity, auspicious events at home, association with the ruler, accomplishment of undertakings, favour from the king, rise in status, child birth, growth of cattle, acquisition of white clothes. *Particularly beneficial when located in the 2nd house.*

When adverse :

Loss of wealth, physical and mental torment, trouble from servants, worries in connection with the mother, opposition to the ruler.

Dasha of MARS

When favourable :

Rise in status, benefit from lands, gain of wealth, royal favours, acquisition of vehicles and clothes, gain in a foreign land, and generally good for siblings.

In a kendra or 3rd house : Gains through personal efforts, victory in war, royal favours and varied comforts in the beginning of the dasha, followed by some adverse results towards the end.

When adverse :

Loss of face, dominance by opponents, illness, accident- proneness.

Dasha of RAHU

When favourable :

Varied comforts, prosperity, religious inclinations, auspicious celebration, honour in foreign countries, recognition by a foreign ruler.

When adverse :

Displacement, mental anguish, loss of wife and child, unclean food, bodily suffering, loss of wealth. Relatively comfortable during the mid-portion of its dasha.

Dasha of JUPITER

When favourable :

Rise in status, several comforts, royal favour, acquisition of vehicles, worship of gods and Brahmins, comforts from wife and children, study of Vedic chants and hymns, accomplishment through king's grace and generally auspicious results.

When adverse :

Displacement, mental anguish, loss of cattle, pilgrimage. Begin-ning of the dasha is more hurtful but gradually becomes favourable as it concludes.

Dasha of SATURN

When favourable :

Favours from the ruler, religious pursuits, learning and wealth, rise in status, varied physical comforts.

When adverse :

Displacement, great fear, loss of parents, illness to wife and child, inauspicious happenings, imprisonment, etc.

Note : Saturn is particularly favourable when associated with or aspected by benefics, in a kendra, trine or the 11th house, and in the signs of Jupiter (Dhanu, Meena).

Dasha of MERCURY

When favourable :

Great comforts, wealth and prosperity, renown, gain of know-ledge and learn-ing, auspicious and virtuous deeds, good health, good food and earnings from business.

When adverse :

King's wrath, mental anguish, opposition from relatives, foreign travel, servility, urinary ailments, loss of pleasure and wealth, fear from thieves and fire, loss of cows and land. Generally favourable in the beginning of the dasha, ruler's favours in the middle of the dasha, followed by untoward results towards the concluding part of the dasha.

Dasha of KETU

When favourable :

Acquisition of objects of desire, lordship of a village or town or country, foreign travel, varied comforts.

When adverse :

Imprisonment, loss of dear ones, displacement, mental anguish, illness, association with low people.

Note : Ketu in 3rd, 6th or 11th house causes rise in status in the beginning of the dasha, fears during the middle of the dasha, and distant travel during the concluding portion of the dasha.

Dasha of VENUS

When favourable :

Royal status, vehicles, good clothes, ornaments, good food, favours from the ruler, good house, great prosperity, marriage, high status in army, gains from all directions.

When adverse :

Opposition from near and dear ones, troubles from womenfolk, loss in professional status, separation from near and dear ones. *Venus as the lord of the 2nd house or 7th house causes illness during its dasha.*

ANTARDASHAS OR SUB-PERIODS

The various planets run their Antardasha (AD) within the major period (MD) of each planet. Their good or bad results depend upon :

1. Favourable or adverse disposition of the MD lord; and

2. Favorable or adverse disposition of the AD lord.

The AD lord works within the overall limits imposed by the MD lord. The results promised by an MD lord manifest within an appropriate AD. Whether a particular AD would prove favourable or adverse depends upon the disposition of the AD lord. The following factors must be considered while deciding on the nature of a particular AD lord.

1. *Favourable* : An AD lord gives favourable results when it is:

    (a) Exalted, in its own house or in its Moolatrikona sign.

    (b) Placed in kendras or trikonas.

    (c) Placed in the 11th house.

    (d) Associated with or aspected by natural benefics.

    (e) Associated with the 9th or the 10th lord or with a Yogakaraka planet.

    (f) Placed in a kendra or trikona from the MD lord.

2. *Adverse* : This happens when the AD lord is :

    (a) Weak, debilitated, combust or placed in its enemy's house.

(b) Located in Trika houses.

(c) Influenced by natural malefics.

(d) Influenced by the Trika lords.

(e) Placed in an adverse house (6, 8 or 12) from the MD lord.

(f) Afflicted as above and, additionally, happens to be the lord of the 2nd or the 7th house. In this situation, it causes untimely death or physical illness. This is parti-cularly so when the AD lord is in one of the Trika houses.

The results of the various antardashas in the major periods of planets are being briefly described below. These are primarily based on the views of Parashara.

Antardashas in the Mahadasha of the SUN

Sun

Favourable :
Varied gains, prosperity, rise in professional status.

Adverse :
Excessive expenditure, bilious excess, misfortune to near and dear ones, untimely death.

Moon

Favourable :
Auspicious occasions (marriage, etc.), prosperity, favours from women, gain in wealth, accomplishment of desires through favours from the ruler, proliferation of such sources of wealth as houses, lands, cattle and vehicles, comforts fom wife and children, good fortune, glory, acquisition of clothes and ornaments, and reconciliation with enemies.

Adverse :
Troubles to wife and children, involvement in controversies, opposition to the ruler, mental anguish, fear of drowning, imprisonment, distress from the sons, unclean food, urinary ailments, untimely demise.

Mars

Favourable :
Auspicious ceremonies, gains from houses, lands and agriculture, gain of wealth, favours from the ruler, command of an army, stability of mind, destruction of enemies, acquisition of reddish robes and precious stones, general well being of the siblings.

Adverse :
Distorted discrimination, mental anguish, failure in undertakings, loss of wealth acquired from the ruler, physical illness, loss of near and dear ones, accident-proneness, incarceration, and generally adverse results.

Rahu

Favourable :

The first two months of the Rahu AD causes loss of wealth and general apprehensions. Thieves, serpents and accidents cause concern. Good results ensue after two months. Favours from the ruler and good fortune are other results.

Adverse :

Confinement, imprisonment, displacement, theft, accidents, fear from thieves, loss of lands, houses, etc., and danger of untimely death.

Jupiter

Favourable :

Auspicious ceremonies, king's favours, gain of wealth, child birth, attainment of objects of desire, inclination towards charities and religious pursuits, devotion to God and guru, mental peace and virtuous undertakings.

Adverse :

Physical illness to the native as well as to his wife and child, king's wrath, mental anguish, loss of desired objects.

Saturn

Favourable :

Loss of enemies, gain of wealth, auspicious ceremonies, royal favours.

Adverse :

Chronic and painful illness, imprisonment, loss of work and wealth, great apprehension, unexpected opposition, separation from parents.

Mercury

Favourable :

Gain in status, royal favours conferring vehicles, ornaments and good clothes, good health to wife and children, indulgence in religious pursuits, auspicious happenings like marriage or child birth, performance of prescribed religious rituals, renown, honours and awards.

Adverse :

Physical illness, mental anguish, ill health to wife and child, aimless wandering.

Ketu

Favourable :

Ketu produces favourable results in the MD of the Sun, if it is located in Upachaya (3, 6, 10 and 11) houses, associated with Yogakaraka planets and in the vargas of benefics. It leads to increase of friends, good fortune, mental satisfaction, rise in status and generally good results.

Adverse:

Physical illness, mental anguish, increased expenditure, king's wrath, disease of the oral cavity and teeth, urinary ailments, displacement from home, loss of father, inauspicious news, untimely death.

Venus

Favourable:

Fulfilment of objects of desire, association with the good and the powerful, royal favours, increase in status, good food, acquisition of precious stones and general prosperity.

Adverse :

Wrath of the ruler, mental torment, loss of child, wife and wealth, displacement, deprivation of physical comforts, untimely death. The beginning of the dasha produces mediocre results, the middle of the dasha causes benefic results, while the concluding portion of the dasha yields very adverse results.

Antardashas in the Mahadasha of the MOON

Moon

Favourable :

Acquisition of such objects of comfort as good clothes, horses, elephants and vehicles, devotion towards God and guru, recitation of sacred chants, rise in status, prosperity.

Adverse :

Loss of wealth, displacement from home, laziness and excessive somnolence, mental torment, illness to mother, incarceration and untimely death.

Mars

Favourable :

Great fortune, royal favours, acquisition of garments and ornaments, accomplishments through personal effort, gains from houses, lands and business.

Adverse :

Losses in business, physical illness, separation from dear ones, ruler's wrath, poor digestion.

Rahu

Favourable:

Success in all undertakings, favours from a ruler from a western country, acquisition of vehicles and garments, pilgrimage, religious undertakings.

Note : These results ensue when Rahu is in an Oopachaya house from the lagna, or in a benefic house (kendra, trikona, 3rd or 11th house) from the MD lord.

Adverse :

Displacement from place of work, mental anguish, unfounded fears, dominance and torture by enemies, fear from poisonous animals (snakes, scorpions, etc.), loss of face, and wrath of the ruler.

Note : Rahu produces adverse results even when located in a kendra or a trikona.

Jupiter

Favourable :

Enhanced status, royal favours, gain of wealth, child birth, auspicious occasions, acquisition of lands and vehicles, fulfilment of desires, courageous deeds, general prosperity.

Adverse :

Inauspicious events, displacement, loss of child and preceptor, loss of lands, vehicles and houses, unclean food, wandering in foreign countries, untimely death.

Saturn

Favourable :

Acquisition of wealth, gains from friends and children, royal favours, pilgrimage, favours from a Shudra king.

Adverse :

Troubles from enemies, bodily illness, unfounded fears, sad news.

Mercury

Favourable :

Enhanced income and status, study of scriptures, increased knowledge and learning, contentment, gains in business, marriage and child birth, religious rituals, association with scholars, acquisition of precious stones.

Adverse :

Physical illness, losses in agriculture and business, confinement, troubles to wife and child.

Ketu

Favourable :

Gain of wealth, religious pursuits, increased income from cattle.

Adverse :

Mental inconsistency, enmity with low people, sudden controversy, physical illness.

Venus

Favourable :

Rise in status, acquisition of garments, vehicles and ornaments through royal favours, benefits from cattle, residence in a new house, good food, good health, association with several charming women, birth of a daughter, general prosperity.

Adverse :

Foreign residence, painful illness, fear of theft, untimely death.

Sun

Favourable :

Acquisition of lost wealth and status, increased income, auspicious occasions at home, gains from lands, birth of a son, good health.

Adverse :

Fear from thief, serpent and the ruler, febrile illness, laziness, foreign residence.

Antardashas in the Mahadasha of MARS

Mars

Favourable :

Renown through the ruler's grace, proliferation of wealth, acquisition of lost wealth and status, gains from horses, lands and cattle.

Adverse :

Injury from weapon or fire, fear from thief, serpent and the king, urinary ailment, mental and physical torment.

Rahu

Favourable:

Honour by the ruler, gains from houses and lands, success in business, dips in holy rivers, foreign visits.

Adverse:

Fear of injury, thieves and serpents, loss of cattle, incarceration, loss of wealth and untimely death.

Jupiter

Favourable :

Enhanced status, royal favours, general prosperity, auspicious events, proliferation of lands and houses, good health, benefits from cattle, successful business, comforts from wife and children.

Adverse :

Fall in status, wrath of the ruler, loss of servants and siblings, fever, excess of Pitta or bile, untimely death.

Saturn

Favourable :

Rise in profession, gain in status, good fortune, honour by the ruler, comforts to children and grandchildren.

Adverse :

Fear from a mlechchha (belonging to an alien land) king, im-prisonment, physical illness, losses in travel, mental anguish, injuries from thieves and fire, loss of siblings, tragic events, sudden death.

Note : Saturn is bad when located in a kendra or trikona from the MD lord Mars. It is worse when in houses 8 or 12 from Mars.

Mercury

Favourable

Association with the virtuous, religious inclination, pious deeds, name and fame, pursuance of the prescribed path, good food, rise in status, acquisition of cattle, clothes and vehicles, gains from agriculture, command of an army, increased learning, general prosperity.

Adverse :

Loss of face, heart disease, incarceration, increase of enemies, foreign residence, lack of discriminative ability, fear from thieves and fire, bad speech, opposition from dear ones.

Ketu

Favourable :

Many comforts, increased income, service of the king, acquisition of horses, etc., gain in status, command of an army, religious pursuits, acquisition of garments and ornaments, etc.

Adverse :

Dental disease, fear of theft, physical illness, illness to wife and children, loss of face, and mental torment.

Venus

Favourable :

Rise in status, vehicles and physical comforts, gain in health and glory, excessive income, inclination towards music, song, dance and art, religious pursuits.

Adverse :

Physical illness, loss of wealth, fear from thieves and the ruler, injury from weapons, residence in a foreign land, discord at home and loss of cattle.

Sun

Favourable :

Acquisition of fame, vehicle and progeny, increased income and wealth, good health, stability of mind, royal favours, recognition in foreign countries.

Adverse :

Physical illness, mental anguish, losses at work, disease of the head, snakebite, febrile illness.

MOON

Favourable :

Rise in status, acquisition of wealth through the ruler, virtuous deeds, auspicious occasions at home, fulfilment of desires.

Adverse :

Illness to wife and child, loss of lands and cattle, fear from thieves, mental anguish, untimely death.

Antardashas in the Mahadasha of RAHU

RAHU

Favourable :

Royal honours, profits in business, westward journey, rise in professional status, courageous pursuits, gain in wealth.

Note : Rahu is particularly favourable in Karka, Vrishchika, Kanya and Dhanu.

Adverse :

Fear of injury, loss of near and dear ones, illness to wife and child, troubles from the ruler, loss of face.

Jupiter

Favourable :

Rise in status, stability of mind, loss of enemies, gain in wealth, travel and recognition in western countries, fulfilment of undertakings, return to one's native country, birth of child, good food, gain of houses and lands, religious inclinations.

Adverse :

Loss of wealth, obstruction in undertakings, mental turmoil, heart disease, illness to father and mother, loss of elder brother, untimely death.

Saturn

Favourable :

Service of the ruler, auspicious occasions in the house (marriage, etc.), founding of ponds and orchards, fulfilment of the objects of desire through a Shudra king, westward journey, return to one's native land.

Adverse :

General laziness, discord with wife and children, fear of enemies and the ruler, loss of face, heart disease, roaming in foreign countries, unclean food, untimely death.

Mercury

Favourable :

Enhancement of status, general well being, gains in business, higher education, good vehicle, marriage, comforts of the bed, good health, fulfilment of desires, recitation of sacred hymns, religious pursuits.

Adverse :

Loss of wealth and physical comforts, despising the gods and the Brahmins, resorting to falsehood, distorted wisdom, excessive expenditure, untimely demise.

Ketu

Favourable :

Fulfilment of desires, benefits from undertakings, gains from cattle, favours from the ruler, acquisition of wealth and ornaments.

Adverse :

Aimless wandering, physical and mental illness, fear from thieves, serpents and injuries, separation from mother and father.

Venus

Favourable :

Acquisition of wealth through Brahmins, auspicious happenings, honour and favours from the ruler, acquisition of a new house, good friends, good food, marriage, inclination towards song and music, charitable disposition.

Adverse:

Physical illness, sudden discord, separation from parents, danger from poisons, serpents, thieves and the ruler, imprisonment, punishment, loss of wife, child and the employer, blood disorders, diabetes.

Sun

Favourable :

Gain of wealth, favours from the ruler, name and fame, lordship over a village or a town or a country, great glory, foreign travel, fulfilment of desires.

Adverse :

Wrath of the ruler, increase of enemies, fear from thieves, fire and the ruler, serious illness.

Moon

Favourable :

Status of a king, honour from the king, gain of wealth, good health, comforts through wife, sons and vehicles, increase of houses and lands, success in all undertakings.

Adverse :

Unfounded fears and phobias, wastage of money, losses in journey, proneness to physical injury, abdominal disease, untimely death.

Mars

Favourable :

Acquisition of lost money and status, good food, good garments, comforts at home, beneficial journey, command of an army, material benefits through siblings.

Adverse :

Discord with wife and sons, displacement from home, fear of thieves, serpents and injury, general debility and laziness.

Antardashas in the Mahadasha of JUPITER

Jupiter

Favourable :

Attainment of rulership, worship by the ruler, acquisition of wealth, vehicles and physical comforts, gain of glory, name and fame.

Adverse :

Association with the low, illogical arguments, separation from wife and children, death of the employer, physical illness.

Saturn

Favourable :

Gain in professional status, acquisition of garments, ornaments and wealth, benefits from lands and houses, beneficial travel to the west, proliferation of cattle, benefits from the Shudras.

Adverse:

Loss of wealth and property, mental anguish, febrile illness, proneness to injury, inauspicious happenings, loss of cattle, obstruction to profession, physical disease, untimely death.

Mercury

Favourable:

Good health, gain in status, several comforts, fulfilment through king's favours, increased earnings in one's own land, comforts to father and mother.

Note : Despite a favourable placement of Mercury, its AD in the MD of Jupiter causes loss of money.

Adverse :

Losses in business, febrile illness, loss of wealth, foreign travel, losses in travel, eye disease, injury from weapon or fire, sudden discord, untimely death.

Ketu

Favourable :

Gain of wealth, earning through unfair means, acquisition of vehicles, fulfilment of desires, favours from a Yavana ruler.

Note : Even a favourably disposed Ketu during its AD in the MD of Jupiter provides little monetary benefit, unclean food and food belonging to others. May be good for spiritual pursuits.

Adverse :

Loss of wealth through the wrath of the ruler, physical illness, loss of vigour, mental anguish and discord with brother.

Venus

Favourable :

Much wealth and prosperity, excessive physical comforts, plenty of clothes and vehicles, gainful journey to the east, good for parents, devotion to God and guru, charitable disposition, marriage, association with learned people, inclination toward song and music.

Adverse :

Discord with dear ones, harm to wife and child, intense fear, troubles through women, loss of money, discord with the father-in-law, untimely death.

Sun

Favourable :

Gain of wealth and status, acquisition of vehicles and other wordly comforts, success in all undertakings.

Adverse :

Headache, fever, sinful acts, separation from dear ones, physical illness.

Moon

Favourable :

Gain of glory, comforts from wife and children, good food (consisting of milk products), pious deeds, well being of progeny, good income, charitable disposition.

Adverse :

Loss of face, wealth and dear ones, foreign travel, troubles from thieves, loss of mother's brother, illness to mother, illness to the native.

Mars

Favourable :

Gain in learning, marriage ceremony, gain of lands and houses, success in undertakings, good food, generally auspicious.

Adverse :

Loss of wealth, houses and lands, physical illness, eye disease, mental anguish.

Rahu

Favourable :

Inclination toward Yoga, gain of wealth (during the first five months of the

AD), leadership of a village or a country, favours from a Yavana king, distant travel, command of an army, religious inclinations.

Adverse :

Fear from thieves, serpents and weapons, opposition to the king, physical exertion, discord with brothers, inauspicious happenings, bad dreams, bodily disease.

Antardashas in the Mahadasha of SATURN

Saturn

Favourable :

Rise in status, benefits to wife and progeny, availability of vehicles, command of a king's army, acquisition of lordship over a village or a town.

Adverse :

Fear from the ruler, troubles arising from poisons and weapons, bleeding disorders, displacement from one's country, mental anguish, untimely death.

Mercury

Favourable :

Name and fame, learning, gain of wealth, mental and physical comforts, pilgrimage, bath in holy waters, gains in business, good food, charitable nature.

Adverse :

Physical illness, obstruction to undertakings, mental anguish, unfounded fears.

Note : The above adverse results occur during the middle and concluding portions of the AD of Mercury. During the early part of this AD, despite affliction, good results are experienced.

Ketu

Favourable :

Increased earnings, pilgrimages, religious inclinations, and association with the ruler.

Note : Good results only ensue if Ketu is associated with the lagna lord, or in houses 3 or 11 from the MD lord. In other situations generally held favourable (e.g., placement in a kendra or a trikona, or with a Yogakaraka planet), AD of Ketu only produces adverse results.

Adverse :

Displacement, penury, foreign travel, incarceration, unclean food, febrile illness, untimely death.

Venus

Favourable :

Accomplishment of desires, gain of wealth, wife and progeny, physical comforts, good health, auspicious ceremonies, name and fame, acquisition of imported garments, favours from the ruler, composing of poetry, study of sacred scriptures.

Adverse :

Loss of home, wife and friends, eye disease, febrile illness, toothache, heart disease, rectal disease, fear of drowning, fall from a tree, extreme mental anguish.

Sun

Favourable :

Favours from the employer, increased wealth, acquisition of vehicles, cows and comforts.

Adverse :

Heart disease, mental distress, loss of residential place, separation from dear ones, febrile illness.

Moon

Favourable :

Favours from the ruler, acquisition of vehicles, garments and ornaments, prosperity, comforts to mother, father and wife.

Adverse :

King's wrath, loss of wealth, separation from parents, illness to children, untimely food, necessity to take medicinal remedies, excessive somnolence, increase of opponents.

Mars

Favourable :

Gain of wealth, command of an army, favours from the ruler, benefits from lands and cattle, building of a new house, benefits from siblings.

Adverse :

Danger from thieves, serpents, accidents and weapons, joint pains, troubles to father and brother, loss of cattle, unclean food, untimely death.

Rahu

Favourable :

Gain of wealth, lands and houses, pilgrimage, auspicious celebrations, increased glory, favours from the ruler, physical comforts.

Note : Rahu here is particularly beneficial if located in Mesha, Vrisha, Karka, Simha, Kanya or Meena.

Adverse :

Discord with others, mental torment, physical illness, discord with children, foreign residence, loss of houses and lands.

Jupiter

Favourable :

Accomplishment of all undertakings, honour from the ruler, acquisition of wealth and jewellery, devotion toward God and guru, association with the learned, benefits to wife and son, study of scriptures, religious inclination, great renown and glory.

Adverse :

Loss of near and dear ones, loss of wealth, foreign travel, obstacles to profession, unclean food, physical and mental ailments, imprisonment, death of a near relative.

Antardashas in the Mahadasha of MERCURY

Mercury

Favourable :

Acquisition of precious stones, learning, high education, name and fame, honours from the ruler, comforts to wife, son, mother and father.

Adverse :

Loss of cattle and wealth, opposition from near and dear ones, abdominal pain, mental anguish, death of a near relative.

Ketu

Favourable :

Physical comforts, good health and wealth, gainful journey, acquisition of learning, spread of fame, favours from the ruler.

Adverse :

Fall off a vehicle, trouble from thieves and the king, sinful acts, scorpion stings, discord with low people, illness and misery.

Venus

Favourable :

Virtuous and religious pursuits, help from friends and the employer, gain of wealth, favours from the ruler, sudden and unexpected gains, profit in business, charitable inclination.

Adverse :

Heart disease, loss of face, febrile illness, separation from dear ones, mental torment, untimely death.

Sun

Favourable :

King's grace, gain of lands, increase in wealth, good food and clothes.

Adverse :

Troubles from thieves, fire, weapons and excess of Pitta, head-ache, mental torment, separation from a dear friend, untimely death.

Moon

Favourable :

Comforts from wife and children, acquisition of a new home, good food, inclination toward song and music, indulgence in sacred learning, southward journey, acquisition of clothes from a distant land, gain of pearls, pilgrimage, stability of mind, earnings from a foreign land.

Adverse :

Physical and mental torment, humiliation through association with women, fear from thieves, fire and the king, loss of wealth.

Mars

Favourable :

Peace at home, gain of wealth, recovery of lost wealth and status, acquisition of lands, houses and vehicles, comforts to wife and children, good health, name and fame.

Adverse :

Physical and mental illness, fall in status, loss of wealth, joint pains, fevers, injuries, accidents, king's displeasure, displacement from home, untimely death.

Rahu

Favourable :

Respect from others, excessive gain in wealth, bath in sacred waters, religious rituals.

Note : Rahu is particularly favourable in Vrisha, Karka, Kanya and Kumbha.

Adverse :

Loss of wealth, displacement from home, physical illness, mental anguish, imprisonment, heart disease, untimely death.

Jupiter

Favourable :

Gain of wealth, association with the ruler, marriage, good food, listening to sacred texts, devotion to gods and guru, charitable disposition.

Adverse :

Discord with the ruler, physical hurt from thieves, etc., death of parents, loss of wealth, punishment by the ruler, discord with wife and children, ill health and disease.

Saturn

Favourable :

Rise in status, great enthusiasm, good house, pilgrimages.

Adverse :

Intense trouble, loss of discriminative faculty, troubles to wife and child, fall in professional status, foreign travel, bad dreams, untimely death.

Antardashas in the Mahadasha of KETU

Ketu

Favourable :

Gain of wealth and cattle, king's favours, good for progeny, acquisition of lands, villages, houses, etc.

Note : Favourable disposition of Ketu notwithstanding, Ketu AD in its own MD causes some mental tension.

Adverse :

Heart disease, humiliation, loss of wealth and cattle, fickleness of mind, ill health and loss of dear ones.

Venus

Favourable :

King's favours, sudden gain in wealth, recovery of lost wealth and status, acquisition of vehicles, baths in holy waters, oceans, etc., lordship over lands and villages, good health, varied comforts.

Adverse :

Sudden quarrels, loss of wealth and cattle, head and eye disease, heart ailment, humiliation, physical and mental torment.

Sun

Favourable :

Gain of wealth, glory through the king, auspicious happenings, accomplishment of desired objects, good health, mental stability, lordship over small villages.

Adverse :

Fear from the ruler, loss of parents, foreign travel, fear of snakes and thieves, accidental injury, punishment from the ruler, loss of wealth, untimely death.

Moon

Favourable :

Favours from the king, great enthusiasm, gain of lands and houses, gains from profession, acquisition of vehicles, inclination towards virtuous deeds, visit by a dear friend, accomplishment of one's undertakings, foreign travel, good health.

Adverse :

Mental anguish, obstruction in undertakings, separation from parents, loss of cattle, unfounded apprehensions, untimely death.

Mars

Favourable :

Benefits from village, lands and cattle, rise in status through the king.

Adverse :

Fear of untimely death, misery in a foreign country, troubles from thieves and the ruler, urinary ailment, diabetes, fear of febrile illness and poisoning.

Rahu

Favourable :

Sudden excessive wealth gain, gains from a mlechchha ruler, acquisition of lands, houses and villages.

Adverse :

Excessive urination, physical debility, fever with chills and rigors, poisoning, sudden calamities.

Jupiter

Favourable :

Gain of wealth, enhanced enthusiasm, prosperity, grand celebration, foreign visits, help to near and dear ones.

Adverse :

Fear from thieves, serpents and accidental injuries, separation from wife and children, displacement, untimely death.

Saturn

Favourable :

Accomplishment of all undertakings, victory in war, many comforts.

Adverse :

Physical and mental torment, loss of wealth and cattle, unfounded fears, displacement from home, fear of theft in journey, laziness, humiliation, loss of parents, untimely death.

Mercury

Favourable :

Gain in status, listening to holy scriptures, undertaking charities, religious pursuits, acquisition of lands and progeny, desirable association, increased fortune, good health, good food, gains in business, pilgrimages.

Adverse :

Residence in others' houses, loss of wealth, vehicles and garments, illness to wife and child, fear from the king, untimely death.

Antardashas in the Mahadasha of VENUS

VENUS

Favourable :

Wealth gain through the help of Brahmins, son's marriage, favours from the king, building a new house, good and sweet food, indulgence in charities and religious pursuits, acquisition of cattle, vehicles and garments, westward journey, great enthusiasm.

Adverse :

Fear from thieves and injuries, loss of dear ones, illness to wife and child, death.

Sun

Favourable :

Gain of wealth, acquisition of wife, lordship and property, visit by a dear friend, comforts to mother, father and brother.

Adverse :

Febrile illness, mental anguish, discord with dear ones, trouble to father, injuries, snake bites, physical illness.

Moon

Favourable :

Varied gains, renown and glory, bath in sacred rivers, devotion to gods and Brahmins, indulgence in song and music, increase of cattle, lordship over village or town.

Adverse :

Loss of wealth, phobias, mental torment, foreign travel, discord in place of work, separation from dear ones.

Mars

Favourable :

Prosperity through the king, profits from vehicles, lands and precious stones.

Adverse :

Trouble to parents, febrile illness, excessive expenditure, loss in business.

Rahu

Favourable :

Great physical comforts, gain of wealth, fulfilment of under-takings, loss of enemies, great enthusiasm.

Adverse :

Obstacles to one's pursuits, mental anguish, ill health to parents, excessive laziness.

Jupiter

Favourable :

Recovery of lost status, gain of wealth, honour from the ruler, indulgence in the study of sacred texts, son's marriage, good for parents and siblings.

Adverse :

Troubles from thieves and the ruler, physical illness, mental torment, displacement leading to foreign residence.

Saturn

Favourable :

Association with friends and relatives, honour from the ruler, daughter's birth, pilgrimage, religious inclination, rise in pro-fessional status.

Adverse :

Excessive expenditure, bodily disease, illness to wife and child, aimless wandering, loss of cattle.

Mercury

Favourable :

King's favours, good fortune, birth of a son, earnings through legitimate means, listening to sacred scriptures, artistic pursuits, good and sweet food.

Adverse :

Loss of cattle, residence in other's house, mental torment, losses in undertakings, physical disease.

Ketu

Favourable :

Good food, excessive profit in business, increase of cattle, gain in wealth, victory in war.

Adverse :

Troubles from thieves, serpents and injury, loss of discriminative ability, headache, mental distress, quarrelsome nature, loss of wealth, opposition from wife and child, obstacle to profession, and physical disease.

INTERPRETATION OF THE PRATYANTARDASHA (PD)

An appropriate use of PD helps in making accurate predictions with a close timing. The good and the bad results of a PD depend on similar factors on which the results of AD depend. Thus the PD of an exalted or strong or beneficially disposed planet produces good results. A weak or afflicted planet on the other hand produces adverse results. The promise of an AD manifests in an appropriate PD. The results of various Praty-antardashas under the several Antardashas are being briefly presented below, chiefly based on Parashara's dicta. These results must be modified according to the disposition of the PD lord as well as its house-lordship.

I. PD's in the AD of the SUN

Sun   : Loss of wealth, headache, trouble to wife.
Moon   : Mental anguish, loss of wealth, quarrels.
Mars   : Fear from foes and fire, imprisonment.
Rahu   : Fear from foes, phobias, loss of wealth.
Jupiter : Annihilation of foes, great glory, acquisition of vehicles.
Saturn : Mental anguish, serious illness, loss of cattle.
Mercury : Acquisition of learning, gain of wealth, religious inclination.
Ketu   : Danger to life, substantial loss, torment through enemy.
Venus   : Ordinary gains, nothing extra-ordinary.

II. PD's in the AD of the MOON

Moon   : Prosperity, royal favours, pleasures from women.
Mars   : Gain of wealth and wisdom, fear from foes.
Rahu   : Gain of wealth, untimely death.
Jupiter : Great renown, higher learning, gain of wealth.
Saturn : Physical illness, loss of wealth, humiliation.
Mercury : Birth of a son, learning, great fame.
Ketu   : Discord with Brahmins, untimely death.
Venus   : Prosperity, birth of a daughter, good food.
Sun   : Loss of enemies, dominance all round.

III. PD's in the AD of MARS

Mars   : Fear from foes, frightening opposition, danger of death.
Rahu   : Loss of wealth, bad food, imprisonment.
Jupiter : Loss of discrimination, mental torment, failures.
Saturn : Quarrels, distress, loss of wealth.
Mercury : Loss of wisdom, loss of wealth, loss of friends.
Ketu   : Headache, bodily illness, untimely death.
Venus   : Trouble from 'Chandala' (the out-caste), risk of injury, gastroenteritis.
Sun   : Gain of lands and friends, mental peace.
Moon   : Gains from southern direction, acquisition of white clothes and ornaments.

IV. PD's in the AD of RAHU

Rahu   : Imprisonment, illness.
Jupiter : Name and fame, acquisition of wealth and vehicles.
Saturn : Incarceration, loss of physical comforts.
Mercury : Gain through wife, success in foreign lands.
Ketu   : Loss of discrimination, unnecessary obstacles.
Venus   : Unfounded fears (fears of the 'Yoginis'), tragic events.
Sun   : Bodily illness, carelessness, untimely death.
Moon   : Mental distress, phobias, illness to father.
Mars   : Peri-anal inflammation, mental anguish, blood disorders.

V. PD's in the AD of JUPITER

Jupiter : Much wealth, auspicious events.
Saturn : Gain of wealth and kine, means of comfort.
Mercury : Learning, wealth, visits by dear friends.
Ketu   : Fear of drowning or imprisonment, untimely death.
Venus   : Learning, several means of pleasure.
Sun   : Gains from father, mother, friend and the king.
Moon   : End of all miseries, success in undertakings.
Mars   : Injuries by weapons, indigestion.
Rahu   : Trouble from 'Chandala', loss of wealth, illness.

VI. PD's in the AD of SATURN

Saturn : Bodily illness, quarrels, miseries.
Mercury : Loss of discrimination, loss of wealth, fear from foes.
Ketu   : Confinement by the enemy, morbid fear, mental anguish.
Venus   : Acquisition of the object of desire.
Sun   : Rise in status, quarrel at home, illness.
Moon   : Great undertakings, excessive expenditure, sexual relations with several women.
Mars   : Injury to the son, fear from fire and foe.
Rahu   : Loss of wealth and lands, foreign travel, death.
Jupiter : Troubles at home, mental distress.

VII. PD's in the AD of MERCURY

Mercury : Learning, wealth and comforts.
Ketu   : Unclean food, abdominal and eye disease.
Venus   : Gains in the northern direction, rise in professional status, losses from cattle.
Sun   : Loss of health, loss of mental poise.

Moon : Gain of woman and wealth, birth of a daughter.

Mars : Gain of wealth and wisdom, fear from thieves, fire and weapons.

Rahu : Discord with women, sudden fears, injury from weapon.

Jupiter : Royal status, excessive learning.

Saturn : Bodily injury, loss of wealth.

VIII. PD's in the AD of KETU

Ketu : Sudden calamity, foreign travel, loss of wealth.

Venus : Fear from mlechchhas, eye disease, headache.

Sun : Opposition to friends, defeat, untimely death.

Moon : Loss of discrimination, humiliation, illness.

Mars : Injury from falls, fire or weapon.

Rahu : Trouble from women, dominance by enemies.

Jupiter : Loss of wealth, sudden calamity, varied losses.

Saturn : Death of friends, bodily disease.

Mercury : Loss of discrimnation, mental distress, morbid fears.

IX. PD's in the AD of VENUS

Venus : Gain of pearls, white clothes and pretty women.

Sun : Febrile illness, troubles from foes and the ruler.

Moon : Birth of a daughter, gain in wealth and status.

Mars : Injury in a brawl, blood disorders.

Rahu : Discord with women, sudden fear.

Jupiter : Gain of high status, vehicles and precious stones.

Saturn : Gain of beasts of burden (donkeys, camels, etc.), and of dark coloured objects (iron, black pulses, etc.).

Mercury : Gain of wealth and learning, rise in status.

Ketu : Displacement from one country to the other, fearful untimely death.

The results of PD's in the various AD's must be applied only judiciously. Where good results are described, they are modified favourably or adversely by benefic or malefic association or aspect. Similarly, bad results too get substantially modified. Planets also produce results according to the houses they own. This latter factor must obtain primary concern when the above mentioned results are being applied to individual charts.

...XVI...
Balarishta and Arishta Bhanga

भगवद्गीता किंचिदधीता गंगाजललवकणिका पीता।
सकृदपि येन मुरारिसमर्चा क्रियते तस्य यमेन न चर्चा॥

A little study of the Bhagvad Gita, drinking a drop of water of the Ganga, a casual worship of Murari (Lord Krishna) – these will save you from debate with Death.   Bhaja Govindam, Verse 20

By *Arishta* is meant a misery of any sort. *Balarishta* indicates misfortune that befalls a native during his infancy and childhood. Since the misfortune of a newborn baby can primarily be in terms of his physical health, the term Balarishta is used to indicate ill health soon after birth. Arishta is thus an affliction in the horoscopic chart. Classical astrologers stress that before pronouncing results of any benefic yogas or favourable dasha periods, an assessment must be made in respect of the presence or absence of combinations for Balarishta in a horoscope.

Balarishta: Death in Childhood?

Classical writers on astrology, while mentioning about Balarishta, almost invariably indicate that combinations for Balarishta lead to untimely death in childhood. Because of a literal application of the classical dicta, this term has come to mean a certain death in the presence of such combinations in the horoscopic chart. It has been repeatedly stressed here that a literal application of astrological dicta heralds failure in predictions, and is not called for. Balarishta must be understood to indicate an affliction in the horoscopic chart which can lead to ill health but not necessarily death. Recognition of a Balarishta combination calls for caution regarding the health of the native. Death occurs only if the affliction is intense and protective factors inadequate.

Uncertainity during the first twelve years

All classical writers, from Parashara downwards, are of the opinion that it is not generally possible to work out the span of life of a child upto the age of twelve years. During this time period, the child can suffer because of reasons that the horoscopic chart may not easily reveal. The newborn child can thus die anytime:

(a) *During the first four years* of his life, because of the Papa-karmas (or sinful deeds) of his mother.

(b) *From the fourth to the eighth year of life*, because of the Papa-karmas of his father.

(c) *From the eighth year to the twelfth year of life*, because of his own past Papa-karmas.

This concept stresses on the following factors:

(a) A law of cause and effect operates in our destinies. Our karmas, which broadly means the sum total of our physical and mental functions, provide the basis for our destiny. We all manufacture our own destinies through our karmas.

(b) A child birth is not a chance occurrence of a sporadic nature. It is a manifestation of a continuous process. The nature of birth, the circumstances where it occurs, and the benefic and malefic factors attendant upon it, all have their origin in past life or lives. The concept of re-incarnation or life after life is thus inherent in Vedic astrology.

(c) Vedic astrology also recognises the *law of inter-related destinies*. The actions of our near and dear ones too affect us considerably. Thus, the past actions of one's mother and father too influence one's survival in early childhood. Death during the first eight years of life may result from the karmas of one's parents. Only after the first eight years would this influence of parents wear off. Those who know astrology can appreciate how marvellously the destinies of people belonging to one group or family are inter-related.

It is because of the above-mentioned reasons that classical writers prohibit making any predictions about children under the age of twelve years. The chart can, however, be examined in respect of Balarishta so that appropriate remedial measures to neutralise Balarishta can be initiated.

Arishta-Bhanga

This means a cancellation of Balarishta or of the affliction. While Balarishta is like a lethal missile, Arishta-Bhanga acts as an anti-missile. In the presence of an Arishta-Bhanga, a Balarishta gets neutralised. It is thus important not to opine about a Balarishta in a horoscopic chart without at the same time recognising an Arishta-Bhanga.

It must, however, be appreciated that an Arishta-Bhanga presupposes the existence of an Arishta in the first place. There is an affliction in the chart along with its cancellation. The ultimate outcome will depend upon how complete is the cancel-lation. Very often there is only a qualitative improvement and not a complete neutralisation of the affliction. The classical texts sometimes attribute decidedly positive and favourable results to an Arishta-Bhanga combination. This may not hold true in actual practice.

Astrological Principles

Thousands of astrological combinations indicating Balarishta and Arishta-Bhanga are available in astrological texts. Instead of remembering all those combinations, it is important to understand the underlying astrological principles.

1. *The disposition of the Moon* : The disposition of the Moon in a horoscopic chart has important bearing on the health of a newborn. An afflicted or ill-placed Moon is a factor causing Balarishta and, unless adequately neutralised by benefic influences, may lead to early death of the child.

2. *The strength of the lagna* : A strong lagna, and a strong and well placed lagna lord, indicate sound health. When the lagna and the lagna lord are weak and under malefic influence, the health of the native suffers.

3. *The kendras* : Occupation of the four kendras (houses 1, 4, 7 and 10) by benefics is a strong factor indicating good health. When malefics occupy the kendras, the health suffers. Malefics particularly concentrating on the 1/7 axis from the lagna or the Moon cause early death after birth.

4. *The Eighth house* : Benefic influences on the eighth house or the eighth lord ensure good health. Malefic influences indicate the reverse. When malefics concentrate in the eighth house, longevity suffers. An exception to the general rule is the presence of Saturn in the eighth house which ensures good health and long life.

5. *Dashas and transits*: Several classical combinations of Balarishta categorically stress upon the actual time when death is supposed to befall a native having a particular adverse combination in his horoscope. That may be true in several instances. But it will be seen from actual horoscopes that the Balarishta combinations too follow the principles of dashas and transits. Often it is an adverse dasha, combined with an adverse transit, which precipitates the effects of an erstwhile quiescent adverse combination. Balarishta combinations thus indicate inherent weaknesses which manifest, sometimes later in life, when the appropriate dasha/transit come into play.

The classical combinations for Balarishta and Arishta-Bhanga are being reproduced here from the *Essentials of Medical Astrology* by the author.

Classical Combinations for Balarishta

As has been pointed out earlier, there are numerous combinations for Arishta as described in the astrological classics. Below are mentioned some of these, particularly taken from Parashara and Varahamihira, and a few from the generally not available *Sri Ranbir Jyotirmahanibandha*. The strong language of the combinations is retained, with a repeated warning to the reader that *'death'* in these combinations must be taken to mean *affliction* or *illness*.

1. The location of the Moon in houses 6, 8 or 12, aspected by malefics, causes death soon after birth.

Note:

(a) When only benefics aspect such a Moon, death occurs in eight years.

(b) Combined aspect of malefics and benefics causes death within four years.

(c) No affliction ensues if the Moon in the said houses is unaspected.

2. Retrograde benefics in houses 6, 8 or 12, aspected by malefics, cause death as does the Moon in such a situation.

Note:

(a) Benefics in houses 6 or 8 aspected by a retrograde malefic, unaspected by any benefics, are said to cause death within *one month of birth.*

(b) Lagna unaspected by any benefics also leads to death within *one month of birth.* This is a very general combination.

3. Birth at the time of sunrise or sunset in the Moon's Hora or in Gandanta (i.e., the end of the signs Karka, Vrishchika or Meena, or the beginning of the signs Mesha, Simha or Dhanu), with the Moon and malefics in quadrants indicates death of the newborn.

Note : Death ensues soon after birth in case of a birth in the evening, in the Moon's Hora, with malefics in Rashyanta (at the end – i.e., 29 degrees and more – of a sign) associated with the Moon in one of the kendras.

4. Lagna lord defeated in planetary warfare by a malefic, and posited in the 7th house, leads to death within a month of birth. Two planets are said to be at war when they are located within one degree; the one that is the farther advanced of the two is considered subjugated.

5. Placement of the Moon and all malefics in quadrants leads to death of the newborn.

Note :

(a) A weak Moon in lagna and malefics in quadrants and 8th house cause death soon after birth.

(b) The Moon associated with malefics, unaspected by benefics, in the lagna or in the houses 7, 8 or 12 leads to early death.

(c) Death also ensues soon after birth in the case of a weak Moon, in signs other than Mesha, Vrisha and Karka, posited in the ascendant and aspected by malefics.

6. One is bereft of any longevity in the case of Karka or Vrishchika rising, with all malefics placed in the eastern half (houses 10 to 4) and all benefics in the western half (houses 4 to 10) of the zodiac.

Note : This may be called as the *Vajra-Mushti Yoga.* According to one reading, this yoga arises in case of Vrishchika ascendant, when all malefics are located in houses 1 to 7, and all benefics in houses 7 to 1.

7. The Moon in houses 4, 7 or 8, or in lagna, hemmed between malefics, unaspected by strong benefics, leads to early death.

   Note :

   (a) Lagna hemmed between two malefics, and malefics placed in houses 12, 6, 8 or 2 lead to certain death. That is to say that malefics around the lagna and the seventh house – the ascendant and the descendant – are bad for longevity.

   (b) Malefics in houses 2 and 12 from lagna, or in 6 and 8 from lagna, unaspected by benefics, cause death in the 6th or 8th month of life.

8. The Moon in lagna, with malefics in the 7th house causes early death.

9. Retrograde Saturn in Mesha or Vrishchika in the 6th or the 8th house or in a quadrant, aspected by a strong Mars, leads to death within two years.

10. The Moon in lagna, Saturn in the 12th house, the Sun in the 9th house and Mars in the 8th house, with Jupiter bereft of power, leads to death soon after birth.

11. Mars, Saturn and the Sun together in the 6th or the 8th house lead to certain death within one month, even though Yama (the god of death) may attempt to protect the native.

12. A malefic in the sixth or the eighth house, aspected by another malefic, causes death within one year despite 'Amrita Paana' (i.e., consumption of the elixir of life).

    Note : This combination, as well as the preceding one, despite very strong assertion in the texts, should not be taken literally.

13. Venus in Karka or Simha, in the 6th or the 12th house, aspected by malefics causes death by the age of 6 years.

14. Mercury in Karka in the 6th or 8th house, aspected by the Moon leads to death by 4 years of age.

15. Rahu in a quadrant, aspected by malefics, causes death by 10 years or 16 years of age.

16. Any of the malefic Drekkanas rising in the lagna, associated with or aspected by malefics, unaspected by its own lord, leads to death within 7 years.

    Note: Malefic Drekkanas are:

    (a) Sarpa Drekkanas: the 2nd and 3rd of Karka, the 1st and second of Vrishchika, and the last of Meena.

    (b) Pasha Drekkanas: the 1st of Vrisha, Simha as well as Kumbha, the 2nd and 3rd of Tula, and the 1st and last of Makara.

17. Birth at the time of solar or lunar eclipse (i.e., the Rahu-Ketu axis on the Sun and the Moon), and lagna aspected by Saturn and Mars, causes death of the native within a fortnight.

18. All planets weak, in Apoklima rashis, lead to death by 6 months or by 2 months.

19. A waning Moon in twelfth house from the lagna, and all malefics in the lagna and the 8th house, with no benefics in kendras, lead to death soon after birth.

20. The Sun, Mars and Saturn in the lagna and a weak Moon in the 6th or the 7th house under Jupiter's aspect: Death in 7 years.

21. Malefic lagna lord in the Navamsha of the Moon, in the 12th house from the Moon, aspected by malefics: Death in 9 years.

22. Benefics in the visible half of the chart and malefics in the invisible half, with Rahu in the lagna: Death in 5 years.

    Note : See the Vajra-Mushti yoga under combination '6' mentioned above.

23. Rahu in the 7th house, aspected by the Sun and the Moon, unaspected by benefics: Death in 12 years.

Affliction to Mother

1. Saturn in the 10th house, the Moon in the 6th house and Mars in the 7th house, is a combination for the death of the newborn along with its mother.

2. The Moon hemmed between malefics, in the lagna, with malefics occupying the 7th or the 8th house causes death of the native along with its mother.

3. The Moon aspected by three malefics indicates death of the mother.

    Note : Benefic aspects relieve the affliction.

4. The Moon in the 7th or 8th house from a malefic, associated with a malefic, and aspected by a strong malefic: Death of mother.

5. Exalted or debilitated Sun in the 7th house: The child is deprived of its mother's milk and survives on goat milk.

6. Malefics in the lagna, the 2nd house, the 12th house and the 7th house, lead to destruction of the native's family.

7. Malefics in the 5th or the 9th from a weak Moon: Death of mother within 6 months of the birth of the native.

8. Birth at the time of eclipse, the Moon associated with malefics and posited in the lagna, and Mars located in the 8th house: Death of the native along with his mother, due to weapon (? surgical instrument!).

Affliction to Father

1. Saturn in lagna, Mars in the 7th house and the Moon in the 6th house: Death of father.

2. Jupiter in lagna, the Sun, Saturn, Mars and Mercury in second house: Father's death at the time of native's marriage.

3. The Sun associated with, or hemmed between, malefics, and malefic(s) in the 7th house from the Sun: Death of father.

4. Mars in the 10th house in an inimical sign indicates death of father.

5. The Sun in the Navamsha of Mars, aspected by Saturn: The father leaves home or dies before the birth of the native.

6. Rahu and Jupiter in the lagna or the 4th or the 6th house: Death of father in 23rd year of the native.

7. If the Sun is associated with or aspected by malefics, or hemmed between malefics, the father of the native undergoes suffering (and death!).

8. Affliction of the 6th and the 8th houses from the Sun by malefics, without benefic aspect: Affliction to father.

   Note: When the Moon is so affected, the mother of the native is subject to Arishta.

Time of Fructification of Arishta Yogas

In the several combinations causing Arishta to the newborn, the time of death (or suffering) has been indicated. Where such has not been indicated, the time of death may be ascertained from transit of the Moon over:

(a) The strongest of the planets causing affliction; or

(b) The natal Moon; or

(c) The ascendant.

When the transiting Moon is itself afflicted, the adverse event comes to pass. The sages say that death in these cases may be expected within one year.

Classical Combinations for Arishta Bhanga

Once again, the main sources for these classical combinations are Parashara and Varahamihira. In addition, some material has been taken from the *Sri Ranbir Jyotirmahanibandha* and the "Mansagari". All these combinations must be applied judiciously and not literally. It is best to integrate these combinations with the operating dashas in order to obtain the best results.

1. Jupiter alone, in strength, posited in lagna destroys all evil.

   Note : A strong Jupiter in the lagna is considered the most potent single factor in overcoming planetary afflictions. It has been said that Mercury in lagna overcomes one thousand defects; Venus in a similar situation overcomes ten thousand blemishes; Jupiter in lagna takes care of a hundred thousand afflictions in the horoscopic chart.

2. Any of the strong Mercury, Jupiter and Venus when located in one of the quadrants (houses 1, 4, 7 or 10) destroys all Arishta.

3. Strong lagna lord in a quadrant removes planetary afflictions.

4. A strong lagna lord unaspected by malefics, and aspected by benefics in quadrants, destroys all affliction and provides progressively increasing prosperity and long life.

5. The Moon in the 6th or the 8th house becomes a protector of the native born during daytime (from sunrise to sunset) in Krishna Paksha (the waning phase of the Moon), or during night time (from sunset to sunrise) in Shukla Paksha (the waxing phase of the Moon).

6. All planets located in Sheershodaya rashis (signs 3, 5, 6, 7, 8 and 11) at the time of birth remove affliction.

7. Rahu in the 3rd or the 6th or the 11th house aspected by a benefic removes affliction instantaneously. Arishtas also vanish if Rahu is located in signs Mesha, Vrisha or Karka coinciding with the lagna.

8. Malefics located in the vargas (signs in the divisional charts) of benefics, aspected by benefics which are themselves in benefic vargas: In this situation too, afflictions disappear.

9. When the rising sign belongs to a benefic, the benefics in the chart are strong, and the malefics are weak, Arishtas tend to disappear.

10. All Arishtas disappear when the Moon, though located in the 6th or the 8th house, is in the Drekkana of Mercury or Jupiter or Venus.

11. Afflictions get cancelled when malefics are surrounded by benefics, and the benefics are located in quadrants or trines.

12. Lagna lord in the lagna aspected by all other planets removes affliction. Similarly full Moon aspected by all the other planets neutralises affliction.

13. Benefics in houses 6, 7 and 8 unassociated with malefics remove affliction.

    Note : This forms a benefic Lagnadhi Yoga which is highly protective; it is comparable to a Chandradhi Yoga which too is beneficial.

14. A strong lagna lord in the 11th house or 3rd house or a quadrant removes affliction, ensures good health and promises long life.

15. Full Moon, hemmed between benefics, removes affliction. It becomes particularly beneficial if also aspected by Venus.

16. The Sun in the 12th house for Libra ascendant ensures a longevity for a hundred years.

17. Jupiter-Mars conjunction or the aspect of Jupiter on Mars cancels all affliction and is favourable for the native's mother.

Note : This is too general. It is important to keep in mind the houses involved in this combination and the houses owned by Jupiter and Mars in relation to a given lagna.

18. Malefics in houses 4 or 10, hemmed between benefics, and the benefics located in quadrants or trines: This situation proves auspicious for the father of the native.

19. Great afflictions vanish when a full Moon is exalted or in its own house, in the vargas of friendly planets or in its own varga, aspected by benefics and unaspected by malefics.

20. The location of Jupiter in Karka or Dhanu or in Meena, and in lagna or a quadrant or a trine, removes affliction.

21. When there are several benefic yogas in a horoscope, they remove affliction.

Examples

Chart XVI-1 shows a typical situation of Balarishta with the Moon located in the eighth house, associated with a malefic eighth lord. The lagna receives the aspects of an adverse sixth lord Saturn and a retrograde (hence adverse!) Jupiter. The lagna lord is afflicted by association with the twelfth lord, the Sun, although its condition improves in the Navamsha.

	Mars Moon	Jupiter (R)	
Rahu	**Chart XVI-1** January 15, 1989		
Sun Mercury			Ketu
Venus Saturn			Lagna

7 8		Lagna	Ketu 5 4
Venus Saturn	9	6 3 12	
10 Sun Mer	11 Rahu		2 Jup (R) 1 Mars Moon

Lagna	3°30'	Mars	4°18'	Venus	12°30'
Sun	1°50'	Mercury	18°10'	Saturn	13°38'
Moon	16°20'	Jupiter (R)	2°25'	Rahu	11°39'

		Mars	Mercury
Lagna	**Navamsha**		Venus Ketu
Sun Jupiter Rahu			Moon Saturn

		Lagna	Sun Jupiter Rahu 10
12 1			9
		11	
3 Mer	Mars 2	8	7
	4 Venus Ketu	Moon Saturn 5	6

It may be noted that the child was born during night time (Sun in the fifth house!) and in Shukla paksha (the Moon in the fourth house from the Sun!). This is a combination for Arishta-Bhanga. The child survived his affliction but is mentally retarded. The affliction has had its effect markedly reduced. Thus there has been a qualitative improvement but no complete cancellation of affliction.

The lagna in **Chart XVI-2** falls in a malefic Drekkana (second Drekkana of sign Karka), whose lord is debilitated and aspected by a malefic Saturn (see the Drekkana chart). The Drekkana lord does not aspect it (i.e., the Drekkana

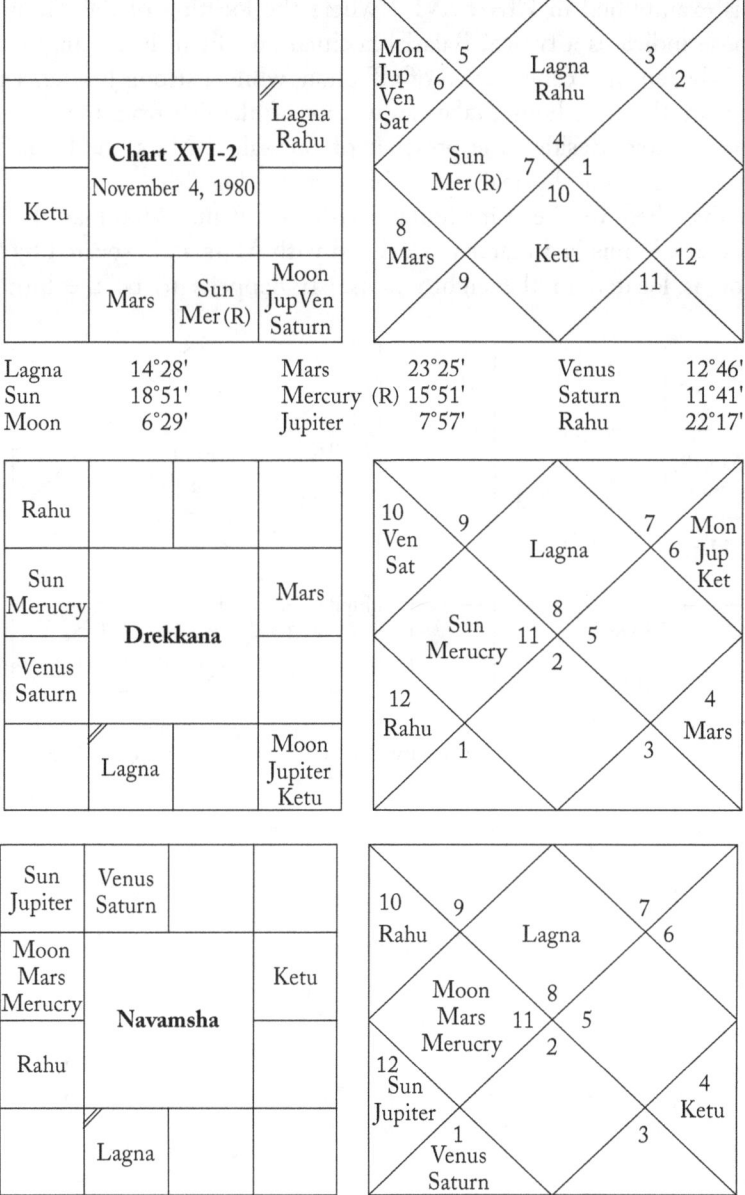

Lagna	14°28'	Mars	23°25'	Venus	12°46'
Sun	18°51'	Mercury (R)	15°51'	Saturn	11°41'
Moon	6°29'	Jupiter	7°57'	Rahu	22°17'

lagna). The child died within seven days of birth. It may be seen that in the Rashi chart, the Moon is afflicted by the sixth lord, the eighth lord, and a debilitated, functionally malefic, Venus. Malefics (except Saturn) occupy the kendras and the trikonas. The only benefic in a kendra (the fourth house) is a functionally malefic, retrograde and combust (hence weak) Mercury, who also happens to be the lord of the 22nd Drekkana. An exchange between the fourth and the sixth lords (indicating a proneness to accidents!) in the Navamsha ensured a surgical intervention before his death; the lagna lord in the fourth is associated with the eighth lord also.

That the principles of Balarishta can be applied to horoscopic charts, in later life also, is examplified in **Chart XVI-3** where the location of the Moon in the eighth house indicates a typical Balarishta situation. Birth during night time, in Shukla paksha, ensures cancellation of affliction, while a strong Jupiter, aspecting the lagna from the fifth house, takes away a lot of blemish from malefic occupation of the kendras. Besides, the presence of an exalted Mars, the lagna lord, in the third house is an additional favourable factor for health.

The native died in the Vimshottari dasha of Venus-Moon at the age of sixty-two years. Venus is a maraka associated with Mars and aspected by Saturn. The Moon is located in the eighth house. It happens to be the lord of the

Jupiter		Rahu	Moon
Mer (R) Sun	**Chart XVI-3** March 1, 1928		
Mars Venus			
	Lagna Saturn Ketu		

Lagna	5°28'	Mars	9°03'	Venus	17°04'
Sun	18°05'	Mercury (R)	5°50'	Saturn	25°41'
Moon	21°18'	Jupiter	15°11'	Rahu	21°38'

		Venus	Sun
Moon Merucry	**Drekkana**		Ketu Jupiter Saturn
Mars Rahu			
	Lagna		

Sun Mars	Moon		Venus
Saturn	**Navamsha**		Rahu
Ketu			Lagna
	Mercury Jupiter		

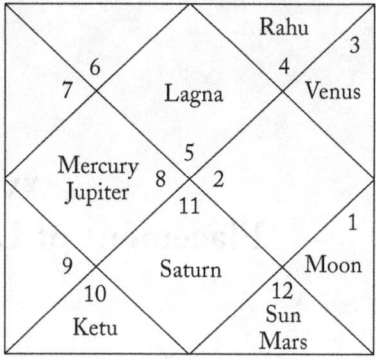

64th Navamsha and is associated with the lord of the 22nd Drekkana (Mercury) in the Drekkana chart. The birth here happens in an adverse Drekkana but the Drekkana lord is exalted and aspected by an exalted Jupiter. Natural benefics occupy the kendras in the Drekkana chart.

...XVII...

Placement of Lords of Houses

सर्वतः पाणिपादं तत्सर्वतोऽक्षिशिरोमुखम्।
सर्वतः श्रुतिमल्लोके सर्वमावृत्य तिष्ठति॥

With his hands and feet everywhere, with eyes, heads and faces on all sides, with ears on all sides, He dwells in the world, enveloping all.

Gita XIII/13

Just as different houses of a horoscope govern specific areas of an individual's life, so also do the various planets on account of their being the lords of those houses. For example, the first house or the lagna governs the body or the health of the individual. Various aspects relating to a person's body and health are, consequently, judged from the lord of the lagna. Similarly, matters pertaining to wealth are judged from the second house as well as its lord, or those pertaining to the siblings from the third house and the third lord, and so on.

Placement of the lord of a house in any of the twelve houses has specific relevance to matters pertaining to both houses (i.e., the house owned as well as the house occupied).

Given below, in accordance to the classical works of astrology, is a brief account of the results produced by the placement of the different house lords in various houses. These results must be applied to individual charts with appropriate flexibility. Additional factors that must be considered during an interpretation include:

(i)   The inherent nature of the involved planet (besides its lordship).

(ii) Its associations or aspects.

(iii) The state of the planet in the vargas or divisional charts.

(iv) The operating dasha to determine the time when a promise fructifies.

Lagna lord in different houses

The lord of the lagna, no matter whether a benefic or a malefic by nature, promotes the promise of the house it occupies.

First House: Of sound health; long-lived; valourous; thoughtful; very fickle; having two wives; adulterous; owns and benefits from landed property.

Second House: Learned; prosperous; religiously inclined; long-lived; sober; selfrespecting; having several wives; blessed with many virtues; earns from land and horses.

Third House: Very courageous; like a lion; prosperous; wise; selfrespecting; having two wives; blessed with brothers and relatives.

Fourth House: Derives comforts from mother; having several brothers; sensuous; virtuous; good in looks; long-lived; devoted to mother and father; small appetite.

Fifth House: Easily angered; proud; honoured by the ruler; ordinary comfort from children; his first born doesn't survive; long-lived; given to virtuous deeds.

Sixth House: Good health; destroys his opponents; frugal and rich; earns from lands. If afflicted, there occurs poor health and troubles from enemies.

Seventh House: Brilliant; good looking and good natured wife. If the lagna lord is malefic by nature: bereft of wife; detached; poor or a king; wandering in foreign lands.

Eighth House: Long-lived; accumulates wealth; ill-health; adulterous; thievish; a gambler; easily angered; good for spiritual pursuits. If the 8th lord is a malefic by nature, he suffers from eye diseases and if benefic then good looking.

Ninth House: Fortunate; learned; beloved of all; worships Lord Vishnu; benevolent talker; endowed with wife, sons and wealth; very famous.

Tenth House: Learned; honoured by the ruler; all comforts from father; attains fame and wealth through his own prowess.

Eleventh house: Manifold benefits; good qualities; multiple wives; famous; has long-lived sons; lives in comfort.

Twelfth House: Bereft of bodily comforts; engaged in unworthy pursuits; lives in a foreign land. If there is no benefic association or aspect on the 12th house: futile expenditure; easily angered. Benefic aspect/association reduces affliction.

Second Lord in Different Houses

Lord of the second house is a wealth-earner.

First House: Wealthy; thrifty; cruel; blessed with many comforts; endowed with sons; ever ready to help others but like a thorn in the flesh of his own family members.

Second House: Wealthy; earns well; enjoys comforts; proud; having two or three wives; son-less; inclined to oppose others.

Third House: Virtuous; wise; valourous; greedy; sensuous.

Note : Second lord malefic in nature: develops differences with his co-borns.

Second lord benefic by nature: opposed to the ruler.

Mars as 2nd lord in the 3rd house: a thief.

Second lord associated with malefics in the 3rd house: speaks ill of the gods ('devas' or virtuous beings).

Fourth House: Endowed with wealth; truthful; long-lived; benefits from father. If exalted, or associated with Jupiter or Venus, the native is equivalent to a king. Mars as 2nd lord here is a maraka.

Fifth House: Wealthy; famous for his efficiency; blessed with several sons; capable of earning wealth; sickly.

Sixth House: Accumulates wealth; destroys his enemies; earns wealth through his enemies.

If associated with malefics: loss of wealth, and disease of anal region and breast.

Seventh House: Sensuous and money earning wife. If afflicted by malefics, he becomes a physician. He and his wife indulge in adultery.

Eighth House: Income from lands and property; diminished comforts from wife; bereft of comforts from elder brother; harmful to others; lives on alms and charities; suicidal tendencies.

Ninth House: Wealthy; industrious; ill health in childhood; healthy and comfortable later, till his end; good speaker.

Tenth House: Sensuous; self-respecting; learned; blessed with several women; bereft of comforts from progeny; earns wealth through the ruler.

Eleventh House: Widely known; efficient; respectable; ever benefitting; wealthy; looks after the needs of the many.

Twelfth House: Courageous; laborious; devoid of comforts from his elder child; likely to lose his wealth. If the second lord is benefic in nature, he is a renowned trader.

Third Lord in Different Houses

The third lord indicates activity, including sexual activity

First House: Man of courage and self-effort; wealthy; valourous; wise but illiterate; inclined to adultery; a forger.

Second House: Covets others' wife and wealth; without valour; obese; disinterested in commencing a venture; devoid of comforts; short-lived; opposed to his own people.

Third House:	Healthy; valourous; comforts from brothers; blessed with sons, wealth and comforts; helpful family and friends; devoted to his preceptors and gods.
Fourth House:	Enjoys comforts; wealthy; wise; opposed to his mother; has a cruel wife.
Fifth House:	Virtuous; blessed with sons; long-lived; ever engaged in helping others. If malefics conjoin or aspect it, the wife is cruel.
Sixth House:	Enmity with brothers; very rich; little comfort from maternal uncle; desires his maternal aunt; eye diseases; sickly.
Seventh House:	Troubled in childhood, comfortable later; follower of a king; good natured wife.
Eighth House:	Thief; servile; capital punishment from the ruler; adverse for the siblings.
Ninth House:	Acquires fortune through women; no comfort from father; receives help from his children; learned.
Tenth House:	Earns wealth through his own efforts; varied comforts; looks after a wicked woman; honoured by the ruler.
Eleventh House:	Foolish; weak; sickly; servile; courageous; earns wealth through his own efforts; indulges in physical pleasures.
Twelfth House:	Wastes money in wicked pursuits; father is cruel; becomes fortunate through women; opposed to his relatives and friends; wanders in foreign countries.

Fourth Lord in Different Houses

The fourth lord deals with material possessions and comforts at home.

First House:	Comforts from mother; blessed with education, lands, vehicles, virtues, etc.
Second House:	Owns property; courageous; proud; has a big family; an enchanter; given to physical pleasures.
Third House:	Generous; talented; courageous; gives alms; blessed with servants; earns wealth through his own efforts; a source of trouble to his parents.
Fourth House:	Owns vast property; clever; sober; ever in comfort; a minister; well informed; proud; attached to his wife; a source of wealth and status to his father; given to religious pursuits.
Fifth House:	Enjoys physical comforts; loved by all; devoted to God; earns through his own efforts; long-lived; benefits from his father.
Sixth House:	Bereft of comforts from mother; short tempered; wicked; thoughful; an adulterer. If 4th lord is a malefic, he brings bad name to father; if a benefic, accumulates wealth.

Seventh House: Knows several subjects; gives up father's (ances- tral) property; unable to express in an assembly.

Eighth House: Lacks home comforts; impotent; little help from father and mother; cruel; sickly; wicked; born of a low woman.

Ninth House: Beloved of all; blessed with many comforts; proud; virtuous; no help from father; stays away from father; learned; worshipper of lord Vishnu.

Tenth House: Honoured by the ruler; very good health; many comforts; self-controlled; has knowledge of chemicals; father may have two wives.

Eleventh House: Generous; helpful to others; talented; given to charities; sickly; devoted to his father; performs virtuous deeds.

Twelfth House: Homeless; foolish; wicked; indolent; father resides in a foreign land.

Fifth Lord in Different Houses

Lord of the fifth house deals with the results of one's past karmas.

First House: Shrewd; learned; devoid of comforts of progeny; wastes the money of others; renowned.

Second House: Many sons; much wealth; renowned; liked by women; versed in song and music.

Third House: Liked by his siblings; an enchanter; back-biter; thrifty; selfish; sweet tongued; his children look after his brothers.

Fourth House: Comforts from mother; wealthy; wise; a minister or a precep-tor; follows his ancestral vocation; devoted to his mother.

Fifth House: Blessed with learning, pride and progeny; fore-most amongst the famous; virtuous.

Fifth lord under benefic influence: good for progeny; under malefic influence: childless.

Sixth House: Illness to child; opposed by his son; many enemies; sickly; poor; lacks respect.

Seventh House: Religiously inclined; proud; helpful to others; blessed with sons; devoted to gods and preceptors; virtuous wife.

Eighth House: Short tempered; cruel; miserable; bad for progeny; disease of the respiratory system.

Ninth House: High status for the son; renowned among his family members; writer of books; versed in poetry and music; good looking; honoured by the king.

Tenth House: Famous like a king; many physical pleasures; indulges in virtu-ous pursuits; good for mother.

Eleventh House: Very learned; wealthy; renowned; skilled in book writing; blessed with many sons; firm in friend-ship; brave; enjoys royal comforts.

Twelfth House: Deprived of comforts from his children (or childless!); wanders in foreign lands.

Sixth Lord in Different Houses

Lord of the sixth house signifies struggle and hostility.

First House: Ill-health; proud; renowned; wealthy by his own efforts; virtuous; courageous; opposed to his own relatives and siblings; overcomes his enemies; reliable; good health if under benefic influences.

Second House: Renowned in his family; courageous; an orator; lives in a foreign land; duty bound; ailing; earns and accumulates wealth.

Third House: Hostile to his brothers; easily angered; devoid of personal effort; suffers in battle; wicked servants.

Fourth House: No comforts from mother; thoughtful; hostile to others, and fickle, still rich; mutual hostility towards father; ailing father.

Fifth House: Inconstant friends and wealth; hostile to his own progeny; selfish; kind and happy; suffers at the hands of his children.

Sixth House: Hostile to his own fellowmen; friendly to outsiders; ordinary wealth; good health.

Seventh House: Bereft of pleasures from wife; blessed with wealth and virtues; courageous; hostile and short-tempered wife; incapable of bearing his progeny.

Eighth House: Ailing; hostile to the virtuous; ever eager to possess the wealth and woman of others; unclean.

Note : Cause of death depending upon the nature of 6th lord in the 8th house :

Saturn as 6L in 8H : Abdominal ailments.
Mars as 6L in 8H : Snake bite.
Mercury as 6L in 8H: Poisons (and septicaemia).
Moon as 6L in 8H : Hypothermia; watery diseases.
Sun as 6L in 8H : Lion (carnivorous animals).
Jupiter as 6L in 8H : Distorted wisdom (mental illness).
Venus as 6L in 8H : Eye disease.

Ninth House: Deals in wood; fluctuating income; a non- believer in scriptures; opposed to his brothers; lame.

Tenth House: Well known in his family; orator; not devoted to his father; opposed to his mother; lives in comfort in a foreign land.

Eleventh House: Courageous; proud; virtuous; gains from his opponents; dies at the hands of his enemies; suffers thefts; benefits from quadrupeds.

Twelfth House: Hostile to the learned; wastes money in wicked pursuits; killer of living beings; loses money through quadrupeds; a wanderer; a fatalist.

Seventh Lord in Different Houses

Lord of the seventh house signifies partnerships and relationships.

First House: Adulteror; wicked; very clever; good in looks; given to physical pleasures; attached to his own wife; suffers from Vaata-related ailments.

Second House: Associates with several women; abstains from women despite proximity; earns through women; slow in action.

Third House: Possesses spiritual strength; affectionate; wife suffers miscarriage.

Fourth House: Truthful and religious; wife resorts to adultery; dental illness; associates with the enemies of his father.

Fifth House: Wealthy; proud; virtuous; contented; his wife is looked after by his son.

Sixth House: Ailing wife; mutual hostility toward wife; easily angered, and miserable; suffers at the hands of his wife.

Seventh House: Good wife; learned; well known; suffers from Vaata-related diseases.

Eighth House: Ailing or wicked wife; bereft of wife; adulteror; miserable.

Ninth House: Ever inclined to associate with women; famous; good natured.

Tenth House: Religiously inclined; blessed with wealth and progeny; disobedient wife; given to physical pleasures.

Eleventh House: Earns through his wife; more daughters; beautiful and virtuous wife.

Twelfth House: Poor; a dealer in clothes; expenditure through wife; deceived by his wife.

Eighth Lord in Different Houses

Eighth lord stands for obstacles and deprivations.

First House: Bereft of physical comforts; speaks ill of gods and Brahmins; physical injuries; engaged in prohibited deeds.

Second House: Weak-armed; small wealth; loses his earnings; short-lived; thievish; many enemies; punished by the ruler.

Third House: Indolent; bereft of comforts from brothers; weak; opposed to friends and brothers; fickle.

Fourth House: Deceives his friends; bereft of comforts from mother, home, lands, etc.; opposed to his father.

Fifth House: Limited progeny; wealthy; long lived; poor intelligence; suffers after birth of child.

Sixth House: Ailing in childhood; overcomes his foes; fear from water and reptiles.

Note:

Sun as 8L in 6H : Opposed to the ruler.

Moon as 8L in 6H : Ailing.

Mars as 8L in 6H : Easily angered.

Mercury as 8L in 6H : Coward.

Jupiter as 8L in 6H : Diseased limbs.

Venus as 8L in 6H : Eye disease.

Saturn as 8L in 6H : Disease of the oral cavity.

Seventh House: Two wives; abdominal disease; wicked. When the 8th lord is associated with a malefic, there is loss in business and suffering at the hands of wife.

Eighth House: Long life; good health; deceitful; famous. If the 8th lord is weak, he has medium life span.

Ninth House: Atheist; a sinner; covets the wife and wealth of others; wicked wife; a killer of living beings; disease of the oral cavity.

Tenth House: Bereft of comforts from father; disinclined to put in effort; serves the ruler.

Eleventh House: Miserable in childhood; prosperous in late age; poor, if ill-associated; long-lived, if well-associated.

Twelfth House: Spends on wicked pursuits; cruel; sickly body; thievish.

Ninth Lord in Different Houses

The ninth lord denotes fortune and virtue.

First House: Learned; good looking; honoured by the king; fortunate; small appetite; devoted to gods and preceptors.

Second House: Sensuous; blessed with wife and sons; wealthy; learned; likeable; disease of oral cavity.

Third House: Very good looking; wealthy; virtuous; blessed with siblings, relatives and a beautiful wife.

Fourth House: Devoted to his mother; famous; possesses house, lands and vehicles.

Fifth House: Devoted to his preceptors; religiously inclined; learned; fortunate sons; virtuous.

Sixth House: Tormented by enemies; no comfort from maternal uncle; engaged in religious pursuits; sickly.

Seventh House: Blessed with a truthful, beautiful and devoted wife; virtuous.

Eighth House: Unfortunate; bereft of comforts from elder brother; killer of living beings; wicked; irreligious.

Ninth House: Very fortunate; good looking; virtuous; blessed with brothers; religiously inclined.

Tenth House: Virtuous; renowned; of a high status with the king; engaged in religious pursuits; devoted to parents.

Eleventh House: Virtuous; pious; continuous inflow of money; long-lived; engaged in religious pursuits; wealthy and famous.

Twelfth House: Unfortunate; loses wealth in religious deeds and charities; honoured in foreign lands; scholarly; good in looks.

Tenth Lord in Different Houses

The tenth lord indicates functions of the native.

First House: Learned; virtuous; sickly in childhood, healthy later; attains to progressively increasing wealth; devoted to father; hostile to mother.

Second House: Virtuous; wealthy; honoured by the ruler; given to charities; opposed to his mother; avaricious.

Third House: Valorous; virtuous; good speaker; righteous; blessed with brothers, servants, etc.; inclined to oppose his near and dear ones.

Fourth House: Prosperous; virtuous; blessed with lands, horses, vehicles and physical comforts; devoted to his mother and father.

Fifth House: Blessed with wealth, progeny and learning; healthful; engaged in pious deeds; favoured by the ruler; fond of song and music.

Sixth House: Tormented by foes; poor despite being skilled; no comfort from father; quarrelsome; healthful.

Seventh House: Good wife; virtuous; thoughtful; engaged in pious deeds.

Eighth House: Long-lived; talks ill of others; reluctant to undertake a venture; cruel; wickedly disposed.

Ninth House: Blessed with wealth and sons; a king or his equal; good-natured; worthy friends.

Tenth House: Truthful; valorous; very efficient, and blessed with comforts; benevolent towards his mother.

Eleventh House: Blessed with riches, sons and virtues; truthful; ever contented; long-lived; cared for by the mother.

Twelfth House: Clever; worrisome; frightened by opponents; suffers expenditure through the king. If the 10th lord is a malefic, native wanders or works in a foreign land.

Eleventh Lord in Different Houses

The eleventh lord is a multiplier.

First House: Wealthy; of Sattvika nature; writer of poetry; treats everyone equally; regular inflow of money; strong and brave; short-lived (according to some).

Second House: Very wealthy; blessed with comforts and spirituality; given to religious pursuits and charities; sickly; short-lived.

Third House: Very efficient; many brothers; destroys his enemies; afflicted by abdominal pains.

Fourth House: Wealthy through the mother; blessed with lands and houses; goes on pilgrimages; long-lived; devoted to his father; inclined to do the appropriate thing at the appropriate time.

Fifth House: Learned; engaged in religious pursuits; lives in comfort; virtuous sons; in mutual harmony with his father.

Sixth House: Sickly; cruel; tormented by foes; resides in a foreign land; powerful enemies. If the 11th lord is a malefic: native suffers death in a foreign land at the hands of a thief.

Seventh House: Virtuous; sensuous; generous; subservient to his wife; earns through women-folk; long-lived; high status.

Eighth House: A failure; long-lived; his wife dies before him; sickly.

Ninth House: Favoured by the ruler; wealthy; truthful; immersed in religious pursuits; very learned.

Tenth House: Honoured by the king; self-controlled; truthful; virtuous; follows his own religion; long-lived; devoted to his mother; hostile to father.

Eleventh House: Gains from all pursuits; renowned through his learning and worldly possessions; long-lived; blessed with many sons and grandsons; good in looks.

Twelfth House: Associates with mlechchhas (non-believers of other lands); sensuous; physical comforts from several women; spends on religious deeds; given to misdeeds; suffers chronic illness.

Twelfth Lord in Different Houses

The twelfth lord is a divider or a subtractor.

First House: Inclined to be spend-thrift; weak bodied; poor; stupid; resident in a foreign country; good in looks; unmarried or impotent; suffers from Kapha-related illnesses.

Second House: Religiously inclined; sweet tongued; spends on good deeds; comfortable; fear from thieves, fire and the king.

Third House: Bereft of brothers, or lives away from them; looking after himself alone; inimical to others; thrifty.

176

Fourth House: Devoid of lands, home, vehicles or comforts from mother; sickly; opposed by his own sons; miserable.

Fifth House: Spends for the sake of his son; bereft of sons and learning; inclined to go on pilgrimages.

Sixth House: Short tempered; miserable; a sinner; hostile to his own people; addicted to women other than his own; eye disease. Venus as the 12th lord in the 6th house leads to blindness.

Seventh House: Expenditure on wife; bereft of comforts from wife; weak and stupid; wicked; suffers at the hands of his own wife.

Eighth House: Sweet tongued; medium life span; blessed with good qualities; acquires wealth.

Ninth House: Selfish; hostile towards friends and preceptors; goes on pilgrimages.

Tenth House: Little comfort from father; loss of money through association with the ruler; averse to other's wives; accumulates wealth for his children.

Eleventh House: Rich; suffers losses even if there are combinations for wealth in the chart; long-lived; famous; truthful.

Twelfth House: Spend-thrift; easily angered; sickly; short-lived; looks after the cattle; well-known.

Points to Remember

The above mentioned results must be applied cautiously. The following points must be taken care of :

1. Planets which own two houses represent both the houses and, therefore, give results pertaining to both the houses.
2. When, because of the dual lordship, mutually contradictory results are indicated, they get cancelled.
3. When, because of the dual lordship, different results are indicated, they come to pass.
4. Strong planets produce full results. When the planets are weak, the results manifest weakly.
5. Any results indicated tend to occur when an appropriate dasha operates.

Note:

In the researches being published by our academic group in Delhi, we have been using the placements of different house lords in a very innovative way. For example, the 11th lord in the 12th house can mean an elder brother or sister settling in a foreign country, and also import or export business, etc. The new meanings in the context of changed times must not be lost sight of lest we commit mistakes in interpreting a chart.

...XVIII...

Planets in Different Houses

पश्य मे पार्थ रूपाणि शतशोऽथ सहस्रशः ।
नानाविधानि दिव्यानि नानावर्णांकृतीनि च ॥

*Behold, O Partha, My forms divine, hundreds and thousands of them,
various in kind, various in shapes and hues.* Gita XI/5

We have already discussed the results of placement of house lords in different houses. Here we give a brief account of the placement of various planets, irrespective of their lordship, in different houses. A proper understanding of this aspect is essential for correct predictions.

Placement of planets in different houses involves an inter-action between the inherent nature of the planet and the significations of the house concerned. The results of such planetary placements, as mentioned hereunder, have been taken from classical works on Vedic astrology. These results must be applied to individual horoscopes with the openness of a scientist along with suitable adjustments to make them coherent in the modern context.

The Sun

The Sun is favourable in the houses 3, 6, 10 and 11.

First House: Scanty body hair; indolent; cruel hearted; easily angered; of tall stature; arrogant; valiant; unfor-giving; dry eyes or defective vision.

    Note: (i) In Mesha lagna (exaltation) = poor vision.

        (ii) In Karka lagna = cataract.

        (iii) In Simha lagna (own house) = strong; night-blindness.

        (iv) In Tula lagna (debilitation) = Blind; poor; bad for progeny.

        (v) In Meena lagna = waited upon and served by women.

Second House: Loses wealth through the king; disease in the face or teeth; defective speech; immensely rich.

Third House: Valorous; wealthy; liberal and strong; bereft of brothers; learned; overcomes his opponents.

Fourth House: Bereft of home comforts; devoid of friends, relatives, land and house; heart disease.

Fifth House: Childless; short-lived; poor; worrisome; wise; a wanderer.

Note :

Sun in he fifth house is adverse for the first-born, particularly for a son.

Sixth House: Opulent; powerful; very rich; famous; victorious; a king or a judge; good appetite and digestion.

Seventh House: Poor; wicked; suffers humiliation; ill-looking; sickly; inimical to womenfolk; treads the forbidden path.

Eighth House: Devoid of wealth and comforts; few children; short-lived; deprived of near and dear ones; disease in the eye.

Ninth House: Blessed with wealth, friends, sons and happiness; devoted to gods and Brahmins; adverse for father.

Note :

The Sun is the significator for father. Ninth house indicates father. A significator in its relevant house generally damages the concerned signification.

Tenth House: Renowned, wise and powerful; very wealthy; blessed with sons and relatives; pursues his undertakings to completion; unconquerable; equal to a king.

Eleventh House: Wealthy; powerful and efficient; enjoys varied comforts.

Twelfth House: Physical ailment; eye disease; fallen from his prescribed pursuits; a wanderer; inimical to father.

The Moon

The Moon is adverse in houses 6, 8 and 12 where it causes Balarishta (or death in early childhood), unless under benefic influences.

First House: Insane; deaf; wicked; mute; mentally disturbed; dark complexioned; ill-looking. If such a Moon is under malefic influence, the native doesn't survive long. These results do not apply to the signs Mesha, Vrisha or Karka identical with the lagna.

Note: (i) In Mesha lagna : many children.

(ii) In Vrisha lagna (exaltation) : wealthy; famous; good in looks.

(iii) In Karka lagna (own house) : wealthy; famous; good in looks.

(iv) Full Moon in lagna : Fearless; wealthy; long-lived.

Second House: Sweet tongued; wealthy; physical comforts; fond of women; large family; a man of few words.

Third House: Virtuous; brave; blessed with brothers; educated.

Fourth House: Happy; detached; learned; sensuous; fond of water sports.

Fifth House: Blessed with children, wealth and learning; a coward.

Sixth House: Short-lived; soft skin; easily angered; troubled by opponents; abdominal disorders.

Seventh House: Good-looking; given to sexual excess; possesses a beautiful wife; a wanderer.

Eighth House: Wise and learned; fickle; diseased; short-lived.

Ninth House: Devoted to his duties; blessed with comforts, wealth, learning and children; adored by women.

Tenth House: Wealthy; pious; efficient; powerful and liberal; completes his undertakings to perfection.

Eleventh House: Wealthy and famous; brave; thoughtful; blessed with sons; long-lived.

Twelfth House: Indolent; humiliated; miserable; fallen; diseased in the eye; resides in a foreign country.

Mars

Mars is beneficial in houses 3, 6, 10 and 11. In houses 1, 4, 7, 8 and 12, it produces what is called as Kuja-dosha which is adverse for conjugal life.

First House: Cruel; dare-devilish; fickle and sickly; short-lived; injured in the body.

Second House: Bereft of learning, wealth, good food and good company; disease in the oral cavity; a wanderer.

Third House: Valorous; powerful; unconquerable, virtuous and upright; adverse for younger brother.

Fourth House: Bereft of house, lands, money, mother and friends; valiant.

Fifth House: Fickle; unrighteous and wicked; bereft of child-ren, wealth and friends; lacks peace of mind.

Sixth House: Lustful; powerful appetite and digestive capability; annihilation of his foes; a leader.

Seventh House: Wicked; sickly; loses his wife; slim-bodied; poor and quarrelsome.

Eighth House: Miserable; sickly; short-lived; indulges in prohi-bited deeds; injured body.

180

Ninth House: A traitor or a killer; irreligious; sinner; favoured by the ruler; adverse for parents.

Tenth House: Cruel; liberal; valorous; equal to a king; famous; held in high esteem.

Eleventh House: Wealthy; lustful; brave; attains to desired pleasures.

Twelfth House: Cruel, repulsive and wicked; bereft of wife; suffers incarceration, misery and eye disease.

Mercury

First House: Healthful; sweet-tongued; learned; a mathematician or a scholar; versed in scriptures; long-lived.

Second House: Good speech; learned; wealthy; enjoys good food.

Third House: Of wavering disposition; given to hard physical labour; deceitful; a sorcerer; good brothers and sisters.

Fourth House: Very learned and scholarly; blessed with wealth, vehicles, home, physical comforts and friends.

Fifth House: Gains eminence through learning; proficient in mantras (potent incantations); many sons; brave and happy.

Sixth House: Easily angered and quarrelsome; argumentative; conqueror of his opponents; indolent; sickly; unhelpful to his near ones.

Seventh House: Knowledgeable; wise and renowned; wealthy wife.

Eighth House: Famous; long-lived; equal to a king; a judge.

Ninth House: Opulent and learned; good speaker; very clever; virtuous and righteous.

Tenth House: Learned; powerful; given to righteous pursuits; famous and efficient.

Eleventh House: Long-lived; truthful; an intellectual; wealthy, famous and indulgent in physical pleasures.

Twelfth House: Indolent, repulsive and miserable; also learned and sweet tongued.

Jupiter

First House: Learned, fearless and long-lived; good in looks; balanced in outlook; wealthy.

Second House: Wealthy; eloquent speaker; good in looks; fond of good food; helpful to others; liberal in gifts.

Third House: Subdued by brother and wife; covetous; wicked and miserable; overcomes his foes; poor digestion; good for brothers and sisters.

Fourth House: Possessed of comforts, wealth, vehicle, wisdom, and near and dear ones; tormentor of foes; good in looks; happy.

Fifth House: Learned and famous; wealthy and virtuous; a minister; suffers because of sons.

Sixth House: Indolent; destroys his enemies; poor digestion; hen-pecked; very famous; physically weak and lustful.

Seventh House: Learned and famous; excels his father; blessed with good wife and sons.

Eighth House: Miserable; servile; earns from service; unclean; adulterous; long-lived.

Ninth House: Devout and learned; wealthy and famous; blessed with sons; a leader or minister.

Tenth House: Completes his undertakings to perfection; possesed of wisdom, wealth and virtue.

Eleventh House: Wealthy, steadfast and long-lived; few sons.

Twelfth House: Indolent, irresolute and wicked; servile; without progeny.

Venus

First House: Good-looking; amorous; learned; happy and long-lived.

Second House: Wealthy; graceful; good speaker; a poet.

Third House: Covetous, rich, controlled by his wife; disinclined toward physical venture.

Fourth House: Good house, ornaments, clothes and vehicles; good in looks; boastful; subdued by his wife.

Fifth House: Wealthy; sensuous; high status; blessed with comforts, sons and friends; good in looks.

Sixth House: Bereft of enemies; poor and miserable; associates with many women; little pleasure from wife; infamous.

Seventh House: Quarrelsome; lustful; lovely in looks; associates with beautiful and low women.

Eighth House: Long-lived; opulent; numerous physical comforts; equal to a king; ever contented.

Ninth House: Learned and wealthy; possesses wife, children, friends and other physical comforts; religiously inclined.

Tenth House: High status; powerful; wealthy and famous; helped by women.

Eleventh House: Wealthy; associates with women not his own; bereft of all pains and miseries.

Twelfth House: Indolent; fallen; skilled lover; debauched.

Saturn

First House: Miserable; indolent, lustful, ugly and sickly; defective limbs and mal-odorous body.

Note :

Very good results occur if Saturn is in the lagna identical with:

(i)   its exaltation sign (Tula),

(ii) own signs (Makara and Kumbha), and

(iii) signs of Jupiter (Dhanu and Meena)

In all these, Saturn in lagna makes one equal to a king, a headman of a village or town, long-lived, virtuous and scholarly.

Second House: Destitute; untruthful and indigent; suffers disease of oral cavity. In later years, he quits his place of residence and earns wealth, possessions and comforts.

Third House: Wickedly inclined; indolent; strong, liberal and full of wisdom; wealthy.

Fourth House: Adverse for mother; bereft of near and dear ones; wise and rich; sickly in early age.

Fifth House: Insane, fickle, unhappy; devoid of sons, comforts and wisdom; overcomes his opponents.

Sixth House: Wealthy; big appetite; very lustful; good in looks; tormented by his enemies.

Seventh House: Ever ailing; indigent; sickly wife; unclean and repulsive.

Eighth House: Heroic and aggressive in the beginning, he loses his strength and money later; perianal disease.

Note :

Saturn in the 8th house is generally favourable for good health and longevity.

Ninth House: Irreligious, unfortunate and penurious; adverse for father; hurtful to others.

Note :

Astrological prediction is an art of synthesis and should not be done on the basis of a single factor. For instance, Saturn in the 9th house has produced two of the greatest spiritual giants in recent times, Swami Ramakrishna Paramahamsa and Ma Anandamoyee.

See the horoscope of Swami Ramakrishna Paramahamsa.

Venus		Rahu	Jup (R)
Lagna SunMon Mer(R)	**Swami Ramakrishna Paramahamsa** February 18, 1836		
Mars			
	Ketu	Sat (R)	

Lagna	3°13'	Mars	22°15'	Venus	9°04'
Sun	6°53'	Mercury (R)	15°08'	Saturn (R)	13°41'
Moon	22°04'	Jupiter (R)	14°33'	Rahu	2°31'

Tenth House: Learned, wealthy and powerful; a judge or a leader; proud and heroic.

Eleventh House: Stable renown; good health; much wealth; voluptuous and long-lived.

Twelfth House: Defective vision; spendthrift; shameless and miserable; a leader.

Rahu

Rahu is beneficial in houses 3, 6, 10 and 11.

First House: Cruel, wealthy and short-lived; courageous but wicked; without compassion; ugly hair, nails and looks; disease in upper part of the body.

Note :

(i) Rahu in lagna, identical with Mesha, Karka and Simha : Pleasures and affluence.

(ii) Rahu in lagna, aspected by benefics : Productive of all comforts and enjoyments.

Second House: Quarrelsome; poor; thievish; earns money through favours from the king; unclear speech; disease in the oral cavity; speaks with hidden meanings; deals in animal skins or sale of fishes, etc.

Third House: Wealthy, valiant and proud; long-lived; opposed to his brothers; blessed with sons, wife, friends and physical enjoyments; if exalted it ensures vehicles and servants.

Note : Rahu gets exalted in Vrisha.

Fourth House: Destitute; foolish; short-lived; bereft of wealth and physical comforts; opposed to his wife.

Fifth House: Easily angered; harmful to children; compassionate; suffers from phobias; abdominal ailments.

Sixth House: Tormented by foes; annihilator of foes; blessed with wealth, children and varied physical com-forts; resorts to adultery; perianal disease; long-life.

Seventh House: Loses wealth through women; adulteror; bereft of wife; wicked; brave; ailing.

Eighth House: Short-lived; suffers from Vaata-related sickness; few children; wicked and miserable; fearless; perianal disease; indolent.

Ninth House: Leader of a group, village or town; opposed to his father; cruel; ugly dress; tormented by his opponents.

Tenth House: Fearless; helpful to others; famous; sensuous; engaged in unlawful pursuits; learned, wealthy and a minister; detached; a wanderer.

Eleventh House: Wealthy; long-lived; few children; eager for combat; keeps his senses under control; good looking; a man of few words; versed in scriptures; lives in a foreign land; suffers ear disease.

Twelfth House: Bereft of comfort, wealth and virtue; immoral; secretly sinful; fickle; sickly; suffers from water-related disease; lives in a foreign land.

Ketu

Like other malefics, Ketu too is good in houses 3, 6, 10 and 11.

First House: Sickly; avaricious; worrisome; displaced from residence and status; fear from wicked people; injured body; suffers from Vaata-related disorders.

Note :
(i) Ketu in lagna, aspected by benefics: princely pleasures.
(ii) In the lagna, in a sign of Saturn: wealthy and blessed with children.

Second House: Bereft of learning and wealth; disease of the eye or oral cavity; unclear speech; opposed to his near and dear ones; eats at others' houses.

Note :
Located in the sign of a natural benefic: physical comforts.

Third House: Virtuous; wealthy; eager for combat; destroys his enemies; sensuous; long-lived; lacks friends and brothers; pain in the upper limb.

Fourth House: Loses mother, wealth, ancestral lands, and house; lives in a distant land or in others' houses; fond of propagating malicious gossip.

Fifth House: Abdominal disease; phobias; scared of water; lacking in learning and progeny.

Sixth House: Annihilator of foes; good health; generous and erudite; humiliated by maternal uncle; gains through quadrupeds.

Seventh House: No comfort from wife; stupid; a wanderer; associates with wicked women; disease of the intestines and seminal fluid; loss of wealth; fear from water; suffers humiliation.

Note :

Ketu in the seventh house in Vrishchika (exaltation) : Multiple benefits.

Eighth House: Perianal ailments; separation from near and dear ones; accident or injury from weapons; avaricious; desirous of wealth and wives of others; sickly and immoral.

Note :

Ketu in the eighth house in Mesha, Vrisha, Mithuna, Kanya and Vrishchika : gain of wealth.

Ninth House: Short temper; eloquent; desirous of progeny; hostile to his father; bereft of brothers and sisters; arrogant; disease in the upper limb; becomes fortunate through the help of mlechchhas (outsider non-believers).

Tenth House: Powerful; renowned; cruel; destroys his opponents; knower of the Self; no comfort from father; not good in looks; ever a wanderer.

Note :

Ketu in the tenth house identical with Mesha, Vrisha, Kanya or Vrishchika : annihilates his foes.

Eleventh House: Valiant; powerful; renowned; virtuous; learned; good in looks; scared; wicked sons.

Twelfth House: Immoral; commits sins secretively; disease of legs, feet, anal region and eye; conqueror in war; spends on good deeds; fickle.

Planets in Different houses from The Moon

Manasagari, the classic on Vedic astrology, mentions specific results for placement of planets in relation to the Moon. This underscores the importance of the Moon in predictive astrology. The Moon has been considered as almost equal to the lagna or the ascendant in matters of prediction. The following is a brief account of the results of planets when located in different houses, as considered from the Moon.

Sun

1st House: Distant traveller; immersed in pleasures; inclined toward strife.

2nd House: Blessed with servants; commanding dignity; honoured by the ruler.

3rd House:	Desirous of riches (gold!); chaste; controlling many human beings (like kings).
4th House:	Mother's killer (causes harm to mother!).
5th House:	Troubles through daughters; many sons.
6th House:	Conqueror of foes; works for Kshatriyas.
7th House:	Association with beautiful wife; good character; honoured by kings; Tapasvi.
8th House:	Creates strife; numerous ailments.
9th House:	Inclined toward religion; truthful; suffers at the hands of relatives.
10th House:	Excessively rich; praised by the wealthy.
11th House:	Royal dignity; versed in several branches of knowledge, famous, heads his family.
12th House:	One-eyed.

Mars

1st House:	Red-eyed, reddish complexion; bleeding wounds.
2nd House:	Owns land; son takes to agriculture.
3rd House:	Has 4 brothers; good natured; ever comfortable.
4th House :	Bereft of comfort and wealth; loss of wife.
5th House :	Bereft of sons. If wife has Mars in lagna, he becomes childless certainly.
6th House:	Prone to Adharma, illness and enmity toward others.
7th House:	Ill-natured and ill-tempered wife.
8th House:	Sinner; killer; bereft of good nature and truth-fulness.
9th House:	Wealthy; begets a son in old age.
10th House:	Comforts, conveyances, money.
11th House:	Famous in king's court; dignified; handsome.
12th House:	Hurts all, including his mother.

Mercury

1st House:	Bereft of comforts and good appearance; harsh tongued; low thinking; ever on the move.
2nd House:	Wealthy, having house, relatives and money. Dies of ailments arising from cold.
3rd House:	Having wealth and property; benefits from association of great men and rulers.

4th House:	Ever comfortable; gains from maternal relations.
5th House:	Intelligent, learned, of good appearance, im-mersed in sensual pleasures; harsh of tongue.
6th House:	Miserly; coward; scared of conflicts; hairy body and big eyes.
7th House:	Dominated by women; miserly, wealthy; long lived.
8th House:	Coldness of constitution, famous among rulers, feared by foes.
9th House:	Opponent of his own religion; immersed in others' religion; opposes all, callous in nature.
10th House:	Blessed with 'Raja-Yoga'. If the Moon is in the tenth house, he is the leader in his family.
11th House:	Gains at each step; marries at 11 years.
12th House:	Ever miserly; his son never wins (always loses!).

Jupiter

1st House:	Long lived; free from ailments; powerful; ever wealthy.
2nd House:	Respected by rulers; lives a hundred years; quick in movements; valourous; endowed with virtue.
3rd House:	Loved by women; father gains wealth during the seventeenth year of the native.
4th House:	Bereft of comforts; trouble from maternal side; serves in other's house.
5th House:	Good eyesight; valorous; blessed with sons; wealthy and dominating.
6th House:	Indifferent; bereft of home; long life, but living on alms or through low deeds.
7th House:	Long lived; sweet tongued; healthy; impotent; jaundiced; leader in his family.
8th House:	Physical ailments and discomforts in plenty.
9th House:	Wealthy; virtuous; service to guru and gods.
10th House:	Leaves wife and sons to become a Tapasvi.
11th House:	Blessed sons; vehicles; dignified as a king.
12th House:	Opposes his near and dear ones. If Jupiter aspects the sixth house from lagna, the native is comfortable.

Venus

1st House:	Death in water; paralysis; violent death.
2nd House:	Wealthy; scholar; valorous like a king.
3rd House:	Religiously inclined; wise; earns from mlechchhas.

4th House:	Phlegmatic temperament; weak-bodied; bereft of money in old age.
5th House:	Many daughters; rich; no fame.
6th House:	Prodigal; loser in battle.
7th House:	Without 'Purushartha'; foolish, suspicious.
8th House:	Famed; fighter; generous; wealthy; gets various comforts.
9th House:	Many brothers; many sisters; many friends.
10th House:	Gives comfort to mother and father; long life.
11th House:	Long life; bereft of illness and opponents.
12th House:	Associatess with others' wives; lewd; foolish.

Saturn

1st House:	Adverse for health, friends and relatives.
2nd House:	Bad for mother; lives on goat milk.
3rd House:	Several daughters who die soon after birth.
4th House:	Shows 'Purushartha'; annihilates foes.
5th House:	Wife dark-complexioned and sweet-tongued.
6th House:	Alpayu (short-lived); many troubles.
7th House:	Religious; generous; marries many women.
8th House:	Bad for father; ill effects vanish by giving alms.
9th House:	Loss of wealth in Saturn dasha.
10th House:	Equivalent to a king; miserly; wealthy.
11th House:	Bad for health; irreligious.
12th House:	Poor; beggar; irreligious

Rahu

1st, 10th or 9th House:	King; by old age he only remains a wealthy man.
6th or 12th House:	King or minister; wealthy.
4th or 7th House:	Bad for parents; ever unhappy.
2nd or 11th House:	No comfort despite wealth and fame.
5th House:	Death by drowning; no comforts.

...XIX...
Planets in Different Signs

पश्यादित्यान्वसूनरुद्रानश्विनौ मरुतस्तथा।
बहून्यदृष्टपूर्वाणि पश्याश्चर्याणि भारत॥

*Behold the Adityas, the Vasus, the two Ashwins, and also the Maruts.
Behold, O Bharata, many wonders never seen before.*   Gita XI/6

Even as the placement of various house lords and planets in different houses
is important in predictions, so also are horoscopic indications consequent
upon an interaction of planets and signs. The inherent nature of a planet undergoes modi-fications depending upon the sign it is located in. The following
is a brief account of the indications given by planets when located in different
signs, according to the classical works on astrology. A literal application of the
results mentioned here-under must, however, be avoided.

The Sun in Different Signs

Mesha: Courageous, fighter, famous for book writing, wan-derer, aggressive,
of strong bones, afflicted by dis-orders of blood and Pitta, lacking
wealth, and earning his livelihood from the use of weapons. If the
Sun is *exalted*, his adverse influences are less marked.

Note :

The Sun is exalted at Mesha 10°. Mesha is a sign of Mars which
is an aggressive planet and also rules bone marrow. Mesha is also
a movable sign, hence 'wanderer'.

Vrisha: Tolerant, wise, skilful in dealing with others; earning through scents,
clothes as well as from sinful acts; dislikes feminine association;
skilled in instrumental music; suffers from diseases of the oral cavity
and the eye.

Mithuna: Good to look at, learned, wealthy, sweet-tongued; well-versed in
astrology; keen learner, famous, having two mothers.

Karka: Poor, ignorant, servile; opposed to his father and other near ones; tormented by hard labour; good speaker, religiously inclined, conceited; suffering from ailments of Kapha and Pitta; having royal bearing (if under benefic influence).

Note : The Sun is a royal planet. Karka is owned by the Moon which is also a royal planet.

Simha: Easily angered; destroyer of his enemies; frequents hills and jungles; full of strength and vigour; learned; versed in multiple arts; relishes animal food; rich; royal bearing; consistent, and suffering from ear trouble.

Kanya: Having a body like that of a woman; physically weak; skilled in writing, painting, poetry and mathematics; shy nature; linguist; respectful to elders; sweet tongued; capable of earning money.

Note : Kanya literally means a virgin. The Sun in this sign gives a delicate body.

Tula: Sinner; overcome by opponents; servile; quarrelsome; bereft of wealth; distiller of liquors, goldsmith, or a blacksmith; inconsistent; interested in others' wives; humiliated by the ruler; courageous (foolhardy!).

Note : The Sun is debilitated in Tula 10°.

Vrishchika: Quarrelsome, easily angered, keen to pick up fights, skilled in the use of weapons; cruel and daring; opposed to his parents; prone to be hurt by poison, weapon or fire; wastes his earnings; follows the prescribed norms of religious discipline.

Dhanu: Rich; liked by the ruler; scholar; devoted to gods and Brahmins; skilled in the use of weapons; worthy of reverence; intelligent; having knowledge of medicine; and strong of body.

Makara: Covetous; coward; wanderer; poor; bereft of comforts; indulgent in unworthy acts; adept; opposed to his dear ones and enjoying the wealth of others.

Kumbha: Bereft of comforts as well as children; strong of limb; indulgent in base and unworthy acts; short tempered; too fixed in his ideas; inconsistent in friendship; prone to heart disease.

Note : The Sun is uncomfortable in the signs of Saturn who happens to be his bitter enemy although also his son. The Sun also signifies the heart.

Meena: Blessed with friends and a loving wife; learned; destroyer of enemies; earning through the sale of articles procured from water, or through land and irrigation; respected by women; having many brothers; and suffering from some secret ailment.

Aspects on The Sun in Different Signs

1. In the signs of Mars (Mesha and Vrishchika)

   (a) *Moon* : Charitable; delicate body; good looking; many servants; fond of women.

   (b) *Mars* : Very strong; cruel; red-eyed; retains composure in war.

   (c) *Mercury* : Bereft of courage, comfort and wealth; servile; weak and ugly.

   Note : Mercury cannot aspect the Sun in a Rashi chart. Are these results to be applied to divisional charts?

   (d) *Jupiter* : Wealthy; minister or judge; charitable; respected among his family members.

   (e) *Venus* : Interested in women of ill-repute; opposed by many; poor; few friends; suffers from skin disease.

   Note : Venus too, like Mercury, cannot aspect the Sun in a Rashi chart.

   (f) Saturn: Devoid of courage; ailing; little intelligence; ugly.

2. In the signs of Venus (Vrisha and Tula)

   (a) *Moon* : Many wives; attached to women of ill-repute; earns through professions related to water.

   (b) *Mars* : Retains composure in war; strong and courageous; earns through his own efforts.

   (c) *Mercury* : Adept in music, poetry and book writing; good in looks.

   (d) *Jupiter* : Many friends and foes; minister; wealthy and satisfied.

   (e) *Venus* : Beautiful eyes; coward; minister to a king; wealthy.

   (f) *Saturn* : lazy; poor; ailing; cohabiting with old women.

3. In signs of Mercury (Mithuna and Kanya)

   (a) *Moon* : Tormented by friends and foes alike; always sad; troubled by foreign travel and residence.

   (b) *Mars* : Afraid of enemies; quarrelsome; conquered in war; sad and humiliated.

   (c) *Mercury* : Kingly qualities; famous; blessed with friends; devoid of foes; suffers from disease of the eye.

   (d) *Jupiter* : Very learned, knows secret mantras; aggressive, prone to lose mental poise; frequent foreign travel or residence.

   (e) *Venus* : Comforted by wife, children and wealth; good looking, healthy.

   (f) *Saturn* : Easily excited; foolish; tricky; with many servants.

4. In the Moon's sign (Karka)

    (a) *Moon* : Equivalent to a king; cruel; earns wealth through pursuits related to water.

    (b) *Mars* : Suffers from inflammations, perianal ailments etc.; devoid of friends; bereft of progeny.

    (c) *Mercury* : Famous for his learning and status; liked by the king; clever; without foes.

    (d) *Jupiter* : Ambassador; high status; very famous and versatile.

    (e) *Venus* : Earning through women; does good to others; brave; sweet tongued.

    (f) *Saturn* : Suffers from Kapha and Vaata ailments; covets others' wealth; distorted wisdom; back-biter.

5. In his own sign (Simha)

    (a) *Moon* : Tricky, wise, liked by the king; suffers from Kapha related ailments.

    (b) *Mars* : Brave and courageous; very clever; lover of several women; feared by others.

    (c) *Mercury* : Skilled in writing; fond of travel; lacks physical strength.

    (d) *Jupiter* : Builder of temples, orchards, ponds, etc.; strong; wise; loves solitude.

    (e) *Venus* : Cruel; shameless; disliked by his relatives; skin ailment.

    (f) *Saturn* : Torments his near and dear ones; spoils others' work; suffers impotence.

6. In the signs of Jupiter (Dhanu and Meena)

    (a) *Moon* : Blessed with sons, learning and fame; good to look at; equal to a king; contented.

    (b) *Mars* : Earns fame in war; aggressive; clear speech; wealthy and comfortable.

    (c) *Mercury* : Poet; linguist; sweet tongued; liked by others; possesses knowledge of minerals, metals etc.

    (d) *Jupiter* : Learned; wealthy; associates with the king.

    (e) *Venus* : Blessed with a virtuous and beautiful wife; good clothes.

    (f) *Saturn* : Unclean; serves the sinners; covets others' food; tends cattle.

7. In the signs of Saturn (Makara and Kumbha)

    (a) *Moon* : Trickster; unstable mind; loses money and comfort through association with women.

(b) *Mars* : Tormented by illness and enemy; physical injury.

(c) *Mercury*: Brave; of the nature of eunuchs; unclean body; covets the wealth of others.

(d) *Jupiter* : Wise; famous; provides refuge to many.

(e) *Venus* : Earns his living by dealing in conch shells and the like; gains from women of ill-repute.

(f) *Saturn* : Annihilator of foes; earns the confidence of the king; happy.

The Moon in Different Signs

Mesha: Easily angered; wealthy; without brothers (and sisters); blessed with sons; courageous; wanderer; inconsistent; lustful; pleasing to women; honoured by the ruler; scared of going into water; weak-kneed, having round and pretty eyes, disfigured nails and scarred head; scanty hair on the body.

Vrisha: Charitable; curly hair; sensuous; honoured; blessed with physical pleasures; very courageous; strong; father of many daughters; having prominent face, shoulders, thighs, knees and feet; deprived of money, family and progeny; forgiving in nature; stable in friendship. Moon in the first half of Vrisha is adverse for mother, in the second half for father.

Mithuna: Poet; blessed with physical pleasures, skillful in sexual act; good looking; highly intelligent; jovial; versed in scriptures, interprets hidden thoughts; pleasant eyes, sweet tongued.

Karka: Of fluctuating wealth; knower of astrology; fast in walking; blessed with houses, land, fortune and friends; indulgent in physical pleasures; liable to lose his cool; likes water sports, orchards and watery places.

Simha: Frequents hills and jungles; broad face, neck and bones; energetic; scanty hair on the head; hater of women; tormented by hunger, thirst, and abdominal and dental ailments; likes animal food; charitable; aggressive; few sons; devoted to his parents; indulges in physical pleasures.

Kanya: Fond of women and tormented by them; of pleasing looks; very learned; teacher; religiously inclined; sweet tongued, truthful, composed; does good to others; forgiving nature; many daughters and few sons; likes song, dance and music; enjoys the wealth of others; lives in a foreign land.

Tula: Prominent nose and eyes, slim-bodied; hen-pecked; devoted to gods, Brahmins and to the virtuous; skilled in trade; doesn't covet others' wealth; of fluctuating fortune; forgiving in nature; defective of some limb; ailing; helpful to relatives and abandoned by them.

Vrishchika:Sickly in early age; strong of body; covetous; atheist; pretty eyes; wealthy; fond of others' wives; cruel hearted; bereft of relatives; deprived of his wealth by the ruler; having prominent abdomen and forehead; indulges in secret sins.

Dhanu: Of a Sattvik nature; wealthy; haughty; versed in several arts; inherits property; charitable; strong; eloquent speaker; poet; religiously inclined; opposed to his own relatives; very courageous; yields only to love and kindness.

Makara: Versed in music; learned; subdued by women; charitable and forgiving; pleasing to his wife; religiously inclined; wanderer; lazy; intolerant of cold or chill; beautiful eyes and skin; beautiful and tall body.

Kumbha: Indolent; clever; attached to others' wives; sinful; sculptor; liked by friends; ill-natured; poor; enjoys the wealth of others.

Meena: Very talented; earning by dealing in produce of the ocean, like pearls, etc.; devoted to his wife and children; sculptor; overcomes his opponents; easily yields to women; good natured and charitable; has a beautiful and symmetrical body.

Aspects on the Moon in Different Signs

1. In Mesha

   (a) *Sun* : Short temper; poor; beggar.

   (b) *Mars* : Suffers from dental and eye ailments; injury from weapons; high status; ailments of the urinary system.

   (c) *Mercury* : Learned; good speaker and poet; famous.

   (d) *Jupiter* : Equal to a king in status; wealthy.

   (e) *Venus* : Very amiable; virtuous; good speaker.

   (f) *Saturn* : Sickly; liar; thief.

2. In Vrisha :

   (a) *Sun* : Devoted to agriculture; undergoes hard labour; servile.

   (b) *Mars* : Excessively indulgent in sex; liked by women; associates with good people; bereft of property.

   (c) *Mercury* : Learned; eloquent speaker; highly talented.

   (d) *Jupiter* : Virtuous; famous; adorable; blessed with good wife and children.

   (e) *Venus* : Blessed with numerous physical comforts; equivalent to a king.

   (f) *Saturn* : Wealthy; ill-natured; bad for mother.

3. In Mithuna

   (a) *Sun* : Poor; clever; good looking; suffers miseries.

(b) *Mars* : Very brave; learned; dealer in weapons; defective in some limb.

(c) *Mercury* : Equal to a king; confidant; overcomes his opponents.

(d) *Jupiter* : Sagacious; a teacher; learned.

(e) *Venus* : Bereft of fear; blessed with beautiful wife, conveyances and ornaments.

(f) *Saturn* : Bereft of wealth, wife, vehicle and progeny; a weaver.

4. In Karka

(a) *Sun* : Eye disease; looks after a king's fort; poor.

(b) *Mars* : Valiant; high status; weak body.

(c) *Mercury* : Learned; poet; a minister.

(d) *Jupiter* : Learned; famous; valiant; a king.

(e) *Venus* : Blessed with precious gems and ornaments; good to look at; associates with women of ill-repute.

(f) *Saturn* : Wanderer; hostile to mother; dealer in iron or weapons.

5. In Simha

(a) *Sun* : Blessed with good qualities; brave; equal to a king; delay or denial of progeny.

(b) *Mars* : Equal to a king; commander of an army; easily angered.

(c) *Mercury* : Devoted to wife; learned; astrologer.

(d) *Jupiter* : Wealthy; Virtuous; famous.

(e) *Venus* : Learned; sickly; devoted to wife; equal to a king.

(f) *Saturn* : Takes to agriculture; bereft of wealth and home comforts; sinner; a barber.

6. In Kanya

(a) *Sun* : Serves women; varied comforts.

(b) *Mars* : Sculptor; famous; wealthy; eager for battle.

(c) *Mercury* : A poet or astrologer; winner in a debate; equal to a king.

(d) *Jupiter* : Liked by the king; leader of an army; keeps his word.

(e) *Venus* : Many wives; wealthy; learned; highly talented.

(f) *Saturn* : Bereft of wealth and wisdom; dependant upon women; poor memory.

7. In Tula

(a) *Sun* : A wanderer; sickly; poor; humiliated; without any comforts.

(b) *Mars* : Ill-tempered; addicted to others' wives; a killer; suffers eye disease.

(c) *Mercury* : Possesses many talents; very wealthy; learned; good speaker.

(d) *Jupiter* : Highly respected; dealer in gold and precious stones.

(e) *Venus* : Healthy; good looking; wealthy; learned; a trader.

(f) *Saturn* : Cruel; wealthy; indulges in physical pleasures.

8. In Vrishchika

   (a) *Sun* : Learned; wanderer; devoid of comforts and wealth; disliked by others.

   (b) *Mars* : Famous; equal to a king; winner in a war; voracious eater.

   (c) *Mercury* : Crude in speech; father of twins; capable.

   (d) *Jupiter* : Adheres to norms; good looking.

   (e) *Venus* : Wealthy; pleasant; knower of others' weaknesses; a washerman.

   (f) *Saturn* : Sickly; defective of some limb; greedy.

9. In Dhanu

   (a) *Sun* : Wealthy; famous; equivalent to a king.

   (b) *Mars* : Leader of an army; wealthy; valorous; famous.

   (c) *Mercury* : Sculptor; astrologer; defends his near and dear ones.

   (d) *Jupiter* : Beautiful body; religiously inclined; a minister; high status; wealthy.

   (e) *Venus* : Good looking; several comforts; blessed with good friends and wife; offers refuge to many.

   (f) *Saturn*: Good speaker; possesses strength; inclined to philosophical learning; arrogant; addicted to courtesans.

10. In Makara

   (a) *Sun* : Poor; wanderer; ugly; helps others.

   (b) *Mars* : Famous; equal to a king; wealthy and fortunate.

   (c) *Mercury* : Equal to a king; shunned by wife and children.

   (d) *Jupiter* : Very valorous; a king; blessed with many wives, children and friends.

   (e) *Venus* : Learned; enjoys the wealth and women of others.

   (f) *Saturn* : Indolent; ugly; rich; addicted to others' wives.

11. In Kumbha

   (a) *Sun* : Ugly; immoral; takes to agriculture.

   (b) *Mars* : Truthful; lazy; servile; wicked.

   (c) *Mercury* : Blessed with physical comforts; good speaker; equal to a king.

(d) *Jupiter* : Equal to a king; blessed with status and possessions.

(e) *Venus* : Addicted to women not his own; devoid of physical pleasures; sinner; coward.

(f) *Saturn* : Addicted to others wives; irreligious. Benefic aspects ensure fame and prosperity.

12. In Meena

(a) *Sun* : Very sensuous (under the influence of Kamadeva, the god of sexual union!); rich; leader of an army; a sinner.

(b) *Mars* : Wicked; humiliated; bereft of comforts.

(c) *Mercury* : Very witty; wealthy and famous; enjoys others' wives.

(d) *Jupiter* : Good looking; very wealthy; enjoys many women; equal to a king.

(e) *Venus* : Learned; amiable; indulges in music, dance and singing.

(f) *Saturn* : Tormented by sexual urge; addicted to low and ugly women; a sinner.

Mars in Different Signs

Mesha: Truthful; bold; eager for battle; endowed with fame and wealth; good speech; liked by all; blessed with cattle and agricultural produce; easily angered; and associates with many women.

Vrisha: Many enemies; few comforts; foul-tongued; a sinner; singer; tends to corrupt virtuous women.

Mithuna: Big family; good looking; knows many subjects; poet, sculptor; religiously inclined; inclined to go abroad.

Karka: Lives and eats in the house of others; sickly; miserable; earns from land and water-related pursuits.

Simha: Valorous; poor; frequents forests; undertakes strenuous work; intolerant; likes hunting; irreligious tendancies; tends to lose his first wife.

Kanya: Wealthy; large family; sweet tongued; learned; spend-thrift; religiously inclined; frightened by enemies.

Tula: Wanderer; speaker; good looking; loves his wife, preceptors and friends; likely to lose his first wife.

Vrishchika: Conqueror; truthful; leader of a gang of thieves; tormentor of foes; sustains injury from poison, fire or weapon.

Dhanu: High status; weakened from injuries by weapons; bitter tongued; inclined towards hard labour; disrespectful to his preceptors and elders.

Makara: Leader of an army; a king; courageous in battle; earns through his personal efforts; resides in his own country.

198

Kumbha: Sickly; opposed to his own people; lacks humility; liar, jealous, unfortunate; having a hairy body.

Meena: Humiliated by his own people; disrespectful to Brahmins and preceptors; sickly; wicked; residing abroad; enjoys being praised.

Aspects on Mars in Different Signs

1. In its own signs
   (a) *Sun* : A minister or judge; good speaker; blessed with money, wife and sons.
   (b) *Moon* : Brave; addicted to others' wives; physical injuries; adverse for mother.
   (c) *Mercury* : Sensual; addicted to women of easy morals; covets others' wealth.
   (d) *Jupiter* : Learned; sweet tongued; devoted to his father; wealthy.
   (e) *Venus* : Voracious eater; suffers on account of women.
   (f) *Saturn* : Addicted to others' wives; shunned by his own people; weak-bodied.

2. In signs of Venus
   (a) *Sun* : Wanders in forests and mountains; easily angered; hates women.
   (b) *Moon* : Opposed to his mother; coward; addicted to several women.
   (c) *Mercury* : Learned; inclined to much talking; quarrelsome; good looking.
   (d) *Jupiter* : Fortunate; indulges in dance and music.
   (e) *Venus* : Worthy of praise; minister; commander; blessed with many comforts.
   (f) *Saturn* : Famous; amiable; wealthy; learned.

3. In signs of Mercury
   (a) *Sun* : Learned; wealthy; valorous; dweller of forests, mountains or forts.
   (b) *Moon* : Leader of women; amiable; wise; wealthy; takes to security of the ruler.
   (c) *Mercury* : Talks excessively; loves poetry; versed in mathematics; tells pleasing lies.
   (d) *Jupiter* : Ambassador or a king; very skilful; leader of men; quits his country.
   (e) *Venus* : Wealthy; enjoys good food and clothes; devoted to his wife.
   (f) *Saturn* : Takes to agriculture; lazy; brave; ugly.

4. In the Moon's sign

   (a) *Sun* : Suffers from excess of Pitta; a judge; capable of inflicting punishment.

   (b) *Moon* : Sickly; of low character; ordinary looks.

   (c) Mercury : Ugly; shameless; sinner; bereft of friends.

   (d) *Jupiter* : Famous; learned; high official status.

   (e) *Venus* : Tormented by association with women; suffers humiliation; loses money in wicked deeds.

   (f) *Saturn* : Travels, and earns, by sea; good looking; equivalent to a king.

5. In the Sun's sign

   (a) *Sun* : Wanders in woods and mountains; aggressive; protects his own people.

   (b) *Moon* : Tough body; cruel hearted; adverse for mother; skilful and intelligent.

   (c) *Mercury* : Sculptor or painter; poet; greedy; very clever.

   (d) *Jupiter* : Leader of an army; liked by the king; learned; fulfils the desires of many people.

   (e) *Venus* : Good looking; enjoys many women; famous; youthful.

   (f) *Saturn* : Looks older for his age; poor; worrisome; lives in others' houses.

6. In signs of Jupiter

   (a) *Sun* : Adored by men; lives in woods or mountains or forts; cruel nature.

   (b) *Moon* : Quarrelsome; learned; opposed to the king.

   (c) *Mercury* : Very clever; learned; sculptor; amiable.

   (d) *Jupiter* : Leaves his place of residence; bereft of wife and comforts; ever engaged in overcoming his foes.

   (e) *Venus* : Addicted to women; blessed with many comforts.

   (f) *Saturn* : Servile; ever wandering; poor looks; sinful.

7. In signs of Saturn

   (a) *Sun* : Aggressive; brave; blessed with wealth, wife and progeny.

   (b) *Moon* : Hostile to mother; inconsistent in friendship; displaced from his place of residence.

   (c) *Mercury* : Very sweet tongued; poor; weak; deceitful and irreligious.

   (d) *Jupiter* : Long-lived; good looking; liked by the king; and blessed with brothers.

(e) *Venus* : Quarrelsome; hen-pecked; blessed with numerous comforts.

(f) *Saturn* : Very wealthy; hates women; many children; learned; equal to a king, and valorous in battle.

Mercury in Different Signs

Mesha: Wicked; quarrelsome; cunning; slim-bodied; liar; of changing mind; versed in singing and dance; fond of sexual union; voracious eater; wastes money; suffers debts and imprisonment.

Vrisha: Wealthy; trustworthy; charitable; skilled in many arts; clever; sensual; famous; versed in music; witty.

Mithuna: Fine clothes; wealthy; good speaker or orator; proud; disinclined to-wards sex; brought up by two mothers; versed in Vedas and Shastras; and generally comfor-table.

Karka: Scholarly; residing in foreign country; addicted to pretty women; excessive talker; wickedly inclined; opposed to his friends and rela-tives; poet, singer, a dancer; earns through water-related pursuits.

Simha: Wanderer; devoid of learning; famous; liar; poor memory; bereft of wealth and property; disliked by women; and servile.

Kanya: Religiously inclined; learned; poet, writer, orator; honoured; fearless; arguementative; forgiving in nature.

Tula: Clever in speech; versed in several arts; keen to spend his money; devoted to gods, Brahmins and preceptors; trader; indulges in physi-cal pleasures.

Vrishchika: Industrious; irreligious; shameless; cruel; greedy; associates with wicked women; deceitful; covets the wealth and belongings of others.

Dhanu: Learned; scholarly; famous; forgiving; versed in scriptures; a renun-ciant; brave; wealthy; a teacher or preceptor, writer; clever speaker; associates with worthy women.

Makara: Servile; foolish; impotent; liar, back-biter; shunned by his relatives; very fickle; desirous of physical pleasures; ugly and coward.

Kumbha: Troubled by opponents; impotent; shuns the prescribed duties; un-clean; uncultured; defective speech; servile and coward.

Meena: Good natured; pious; lives in distant lands; capable; liked by friends; helps others while himself poor.

Aspects on Mercury in Different Signs

1. In signs of Mars

   (a) *Sun* : truthful; loved by his brothers; endowed with physical pleasures.

   (b) *Moon* : Lover of dance and music; fond of women; sensuous; wicked; blessed with servants and vehicles.

    (c) *Mars* : Resorts to falsehood; good speaker; quarrelsome; learned and very rich; suffers from thirst.

    (d) *Jupiter* : Wealthy; happy; endowed with soft skin and hair.

    (e) *Venus*: Clever speaker; polite; trustworthy; liked by women.

    (f) *Saturn* : Cruel; courageous; aggressive; and miserable.

2. In signs of Venus

    (a) *Sun* : Sickly; poor; servile; suffers humiliations.

    (b) *Moon* : Rich; trustworthy; healthy; famous; serves the ruler.

    (c) *Mars* : Humiliated by the ruler; tormented by disease and by opponents; deprived of physical pleasures.

    (d) *Jupiter* : Learned; trustworthy; leader of his town or village; famous.

    (e) *Venus* : Fortunate; good clothes and ornaments; young women fall for him.

    (f) *Saturn* : Devoid of comforts; tormented by wife, children or friends.

3. In its own signs

    (a) *Sun* : Truthful; good looking; liked by the ruler.

    (b) *Moon* : Fond of scriptures; sweet tongued but excessive talker; quarrelsome.

    (c) *Mars* : Liked by others; serves the ruler; back-biter.

    (d) *Jupiter* : High governmental status; good looking; wealthy; brave.

    (e) *Venus* : Scholarly; employed by the king; firm in friendship; addicted to wicked women.

    (f) *Saturn* : Kind hearted; pursues his undertakings to accomplishment; wealthy.

4. In the Moon's sign :

    (a) *Sun* : Washerman; gardner; builder; goldsmith; maker of garlands.

    (b) *Moon* : Suffers physical torments /ailments through women; weak-bodied; bereft of comforts.

    (c) *Mars* : Limited education; excessive talker; good in looks; tells likeable lies; thievish.

    (d) *Jupiter* : Wise; kind-hearted; fortunate; learned; honoured by the ruler.

    (e) *Venus* : Beautiful like Kamadeva (the god of Love); sweet tongued; versed in dance and music.

    (f) *Saturn* : Deceitful; wicked; thankless; suffers imprison-ment.

5. In the Sun's sign

    (a) *Sun* : Jealous; servile; cruel; fickle and shameless.

(b) *Moon* : Good in looks; capable; fond of poetry, dance and music; wealthy; well-dressed.

(c) *Mars* : Wicked; unwise; miserable; suffers physical injuries.

(d) *Jupiter* : Tender body; very learned; impressive speaker; high status with the king.

(e) *Venus* : Beautiful body; pleasure loving; wealthy.

(f) *Saturn* : Tall in stature; miserable; foul odour emits from his body.

6. In the signs of Jupiter

(a) *Sun* : Brave; cool-tempered; suffers from renal stones, diabetes, etc.

(b) *Moon* : Writer; good in looks; liked by all; company of friends.

(c) *Mars* : Writer; leader of thieves.

(d) *Jupiter* : Very learned; remarkable memory; pious; good looking; high status; treasurer to a king.

(e) *Venus* : Minister; youthful; brave; a thief.

(f) *Saturn* : Resides in a fort or a forest; voracious appetite; wicked; incompetent.

7. In the signs of Saturn :

(a) *Sun* : Large family; wicked nature; proficient wrestler; voracious appetite; famous.

(b) *Moon* : Earns through water-related pursuits; a trader in liquors; coward.

(c) *Mars*: Disinclined to activity; shy; good natured; wealthy.

(d) *Jupiter* : Very wealthy; famous; leader of his village or town.

(e) *Venus* : Many children; lacking in looks; very sensuous; husband of a wicked woman.

(f) *Saturn* : Sinner; poor; servile; miserable and destitute.

Jupiter in Different Signs

Mesha: Of a pious nature; argumentative; blessed with ornaments and precious stones; wealthy; famous; adorable; spender of money; opposed by many; cruel; body scarred by injuries.

Vrisha: Obese; healthy; devoted to gods, Brahmins and cows; good in looks; fortunate; devoted to his own wife; blessed with lands and cattle; wise and benevolent.

Mithuna: A minister; blessed with friends and sons; good looking; beautiful eyes; orator; religiously inclined.

Karka: Wealthy; learned; beautiful body; religiously inclined; strong; truthful; adorable; equal to a king.

Simha: Strong; learned; wealthy; pious; equivalent to a king; leader of an army; aggressive; resides in forts, forests and mountains.

Kanya: Learned; pious; efficient; fond of scents and flowers; tormentor of his opponents; versed in several branches of learning.

Tula: Wise, learned; earns from foreign lands; soft in speech; versed in scriptures; good in looks; a trader.

Vrishchika: Versed in several scriptures; commentator of books; clever; associates with worthy women; sickly; toilsome; easily angered; indulging in forbidden pursuits.

Dhanu: A religious preceptor; very wealthy; charitable; helpful to others; learned; of a high rank; frequents foreign lands as well as pilgrimages.

Makara: Servile and toilsome; bereft of physical pleasures; lacks strength; indulgent in forbidden deeds; irreligious; coward; lives in distant lands.

Kumbha: Sickly; greedy; loses money; lacks wisdom; attached to the wife of his preceptor; suffers from abdominal and dental diseases. According to Varahamihira, Jupiter in Kumbha gives the same results as in Karka.

Meena: Versed in Vedas and other scriptures; adorable; famous; hairy body.

Aspects on Jupiter in Different Signs

1. In the signs of Mars
   (a) *Sun* : Very pious, religious and truthful; famous; hairy body .
   (b) *Moon* : Soft-mannered; loved by his wife; religiously inclined; a scholar.
   (c) *Mars* : Brave; aggressive; destroys the pride of his opponents; leader of many.
   (d) *Mercury* : Sinner; a cheat; keen to notice the shortcomings of others; polite; resorts to falsehood.
   (e) *Venus* : A coward; blessed with good clothes, ornaments, women and other physical pleasures.
   (f) *Saturn* : Ugly; greedy; unstable in friendship.

2. In the signs of Venus
   (a) *Sun* : Wanderer; learned; serves the ruler; blessed with vehicles, cattle, etc.
   (b) *Moon* : Very rich; beautiful body; adored by women; indulges in pleasures.
   (c) *Mars* : Honoured by the ruler; liked by women and children; learned; wealthy.

(d) *Mercury* : Learned; clever; likeable; virtuous and good looking.

(e) *Venus* : Wealthy; famous; clean; enjoys comforts.

(f) *Saturn* : Scholarly; wealthy; head of a village or a town; unclean; shunned by women.

3. In the signs of Mercury

(a) *Sun* : Head of a village; large family; well known all around.

(b) *Moon* : Virtuous; very famous and wealthy; liked by his mother; good looking; unparalleled in good qualities.

(c) *Mars* : Ever indulgent in physical pleasures; ever victorious; wealthy; adorable; scars from injury to the body.

(d) *Mercury* : Proficient astrologer; sculptor; good speaker; blessed with wife and children.

(e) *Venus* : Blessed with wealth, wife, progeny, lands and houses; addicted to women of easy morals.

(f) *Saturn* : Head of a village or city; good in looks; honoured by the ruler.

4. In the Moon's sign

(a) *Sun* : Loss of wife's wealth and progeny, followed by the acquisition of them all; leader of men.

(b) *Moon* : Controls the king's treasure; wealthy; high status; many comforts.

(c) *Mars* : Takes young girl for a wife; wealthy; scholarly; marks of injury on the body.

(d) *Mercury* : Favours his brothers; wealthy; quarrelsome; trustworthy.

(e) *Venus* : Many wives; very famous; fortunate.

(f) *Saturn* : Head of a village, a town or an army; excessive talker; physical pleasures in old age.

5. In the Sun's sign

(a) *Sun*: Inclined to excessive spending; famous; kind-hearted; a king.

(b) *Moon* : Very fortunate; earns wealth through the help of his wife.

(c) *Mars* : Truthful to preceptors and friends; performs difficult tasks; pious; cruel; a leader.

(d) *Mercury* : Builder; scientist; good orator; minister; a scholar and a leader.

(e) *Venus* : Fond of women; obtains status from the king; strong.

(f) *Saturn* : Excessive talker; bereft of comforts; conquered in battle; fallen from status.

6. In its own signs

(a) *Sun* : Opposed to the ruler; shunned by friends and relatives.

(b) *Moon* : Several comforts; desired by women; arrogant from possession of wealth and status.

(c) *Mars* : Injured in battle; cruel; hurtful; helps others.

(d) *Mercury* : A minister or a king; pleases all; blessed with wealth, sons and good fortune.

(e) *Venus* : Wealthy; contented; famous; learned; long-lived.

(f) *Saturn* : Unclean; coward; fallen from status.

7. In the signs of Saturn

(a) *Sun* : Learned; a king; good looking; brave; blessed with several physical comforts.

(b) *Moon* : Sharp intellect; religiously inclned; proud; respectful to parents; wealthy and learned.

(c) *Mars* : Brave; fights for the king; arrogant; courageous; honoured.

(d) *Mercury* : Ever yielding to women; leader of a group; rich; religiously inclined; driver of a vehicle; many friends.

(e) *Venus* : Loved by women; blessed with numerous physical pleasures and possessions.

(f) *Saturn* : Of a high moral character; learned; famous; equal to a king; given to physical comforts.

Venus in Different Signs

Mesha: Leader of an army, a town or a group of people; addicted to women not his own; suffers imprisonment because of women; eager to go abroad; undependable; keen to oppose others; likely to suffer night blindness.

Vrisha: Blessed with many women and children; taken to agriculture and cattle rearing; fond of scents and flowers; bereft of enemies; good in looks.

Mithuna: Well versed in scriptures; very famous; beautiful body; engaged in writing; poet; friendly; earns from song and dance; devoted to God and Brahmins; sensuous.

Karka: Engaged in good deeds; learned; strong; religiously inclined; blessed with objects of desire; good looking; balanced in judgement; clever talker; two wives; suffers sickness from indulgence in women and liquor.

Simha: Monetary gains from women; few children; servile to women; destroyer of enemies; devoted to the preceptor and Brahmins; generally comfortable and wealthy.

206

Kanya: Very rich; clever in talking to women; simple natured; visits holy places; lacks physical comforts; learned.

Tula: Earns money through his efforts; fond of garlands and good clothes; likes foreign visits; learned; religiously inclined; lacks firmness in difficult situations.

Vrishchika:Quarrelsome; hated by others; irreligious; excessive talker; shunned by brothers; infamous; skilled in physical violence; poor; disease of private parts of the body.

Dhanu: Given to virtuous deeds; liked by others; wealthy; learned; high rank; obese and tall; adored by those around him.

Makara: Very sensuous; addicted to women older in age; spendthrift; lean body; indulges in prohibited deeds; suffers from heart disease; impotent; covets the wealth of others.

Kumbha: Addicted to other people's wives; irreligious; opposed to his own preceptors and children; ugly; bereft of good clothes; worrisome.

Meena: Very wealthy; overcomes his opponents; famous; given to charities; favoured by the ruler; fond of swimming; soft-spoken; learned.

Aspects on Venus in Different Signs

1. In the signs of Mars
   (a) *Sun* : Favoured by the ruler; tormented by his wife; scholarly.
   (b) *Moon* : Very fickle; suffers incarceration; tormented by excessive sexual urge.
   (c) *Mars* : Bereft of money and status; servile.
   (d) *Mercury* : Cruel hearted; wicked; shunned by relatives; earns through illegitimate means.
   (e) *Jupiter* : Good looking; given to charities; tall; good wife; pleasant in manners.
   (f) *Saturn* : Indolent; ugly; wanderer; thievish; has secret possessions.

2. In its own signs
   (a) *Sun* : Beautiful wife; associates with beautiful women; wealthy.
   (b) *Moon* : Son of a virtuous mother; blessed with sons, wealth and status; good looks; associates with women of easy morals.
   (c) *Mars* : Bereft of home and comforts; sensuous; subjugated in battle.
   (d) *Mercury* : Learned; good mannered; sensuous; virtuous and famous.
   (e) *Jupiter* : Obtains all objects of desire, like friends, women, children, vehicles, houses, etc.
   (f) *Saturn* : Poor; wicked; sickly; husband of a wicked woman.

3. In the signs of Mercury

   (a) *Sun* : Serves women; wise; rich; enjoys comforts.

   (b) *Moon* : Beautiful hair and eyes; youthful in looks; blessed with various comforts.

   (c) *Mars* : Fortunate; sensuous; skilful in sexual act; wastes money on women.

   (d) *Mercury* : Learned; good looking; wealthy; leader of a group of people.

   (e) *Jupiter* : Learned; preceptor; an artist or photographer; blessed with many comforts.

   (f) *Saturn* : Suffers humiliation; miserable; shunned by people in general.

4. In the Moon's sign

   (a) *Sun* : Easily angered; wealthy wife; troubled by opponents.

   (b) *Moon* : Daughter as the first issue, followed by sons; treats his mother and step-mother with equal regards.

   (c) *Mars* : Versed in various arts; wealthy; troubled by women; favourable to his relatives.

   (d) *Mercury* : Learned; husband of a learned wife; rich; wanderer.

   (e) *Jupiter* : Blessed with wealth, sons, servants, vehicles and friends; favoured by the king.

   (f) *Saturn* : Overcome by women; poor; fallen; bereft of comforts.

5. In the Sun's sign

   (a) *Sun* : Jealous; tormented by sexual urge; earns with the help of women.

   (b) *Moon* : Inconsistent; two mothers; famous; suffers because of women.

   (c) *Mars* : Favoured by the ruler; famous; fond of women; addicted to others' wives; wealthy.

   (d) *Mercury* : Hoards things; greedy; given to falsehood; excessive sexual urge.

   (e) *Jupiter* : High status; blessed with several women and children; rich.

   (f) *Saturn* : Equal to a king; good looking; husband of a widow.

6. In the signs of Jupiter

   (a) *Sun* : Short tempered; learned; wealthy; strong; visits foreign countries.

   (b) *Moon* : Famous; high status; very strong; blessed with numerous physical pleasures.

   (c) *Mars* : Hates women; blessed with varied comforts; leader by instinct.

   (d) *Mercury* : Enjoys ornaments, good dress, good food and good vehicles.

(e) *Jupiter* : Many wives and children; very wealthy; numerous physical pleasures.

(f) *Saturn* : Fortunate; rich; indulgent in physical pleasures; earns well.

7. In the signs of Saturn

(a) *Sun* : Consistent nature; famous; wealthy and powerful; truthful.

(b) *Moon* : Valorous; powerful; beautiful; wealthy.

(c) *Mars* : Sickly; exhausted by physical labour; suffers penury.

(d) *Mercury* : Learned; accumulates wealth; truthful; very scholarly.

(e) *Jupiter* : Youthful; versed in song and music; associates with worthy women; fond of good perfumes, garlands and fine clothes.

(f) *Saturn* : Dark complexion; blessed with servants and physical comforts.

Saturn in Different Signs

Mesha: Weak body; troubled by indulgence in excessive physical labour and pleasures; ill-tempered; deceitful; opposed to his near and dear ones; wicked; unclean; hated by others; a sinner.

Vrisha: Poor; servile; attached to elderly women; associates with wicked people; yielding to wives of others; versatile; follows socially prohibited norms in the selection of his mate.

Mithuna: Tormented by debts; imprisonment and physical labour; deceitful; inclined to sexual pleasures; lazy; wicked.

Karka: Weak constitution; bereft of mother; poor; sickly in childhood; learned; opposed to his relatives and friends; famous.

Simha: Skilful writer; quarrelsome; deviates from accepted social norms; miserable; servile; bereft of wife and friends; indulges in prohibited deeds; easily angered.

Kanya: Wicked; a failure; fickle; of the nature of a eunuch; addicted to women of easy morals; a sculptor; helpful to others; possesses wealth and progeny.

Tula: Equal to a king; excessively given to sexual pleasures; good speaker; honoured in an assembly; wanderer; associates with women who are given to dance or wickedness.

Vrishchika:Injury from fire, weapon or poison; ill-tempered; conceited; capable of aquiring others' wealth; indulges in prohibited deeds; insincere; suffers losses and illness.

Dhanu: Widely famous; contented; good earnings; well versed in several branches of knowledge; good children; man of a few words; honoured by all.

Makara: Devoted to the ruler; controls women and property belonging to others; learned; sculptor; adorable; famous; visits foreign countries; courageous.

Kumbha: Very rich; deceitful; given to drinking; addicted to other people's wives; wicked and fickle; irreligious.

Meena: Widely respected; helpful to others; wealthy; engaged in religious pursuits; mild mannered; cool tempered; possesses knowledge about precious stones.

Aspects on Saturn in Different Signs

1. In signs of Mars

   (a) *Sun* : Given to agriculture; rich; rears cattle.

   (b) *Moon* : Associates with low people; fickle; wicked; addicted to wicked and ugly women.

   (c) *Mars* : Wretched; cruel to animals; leader of thieves; indulges in meat, women and wine.

   (d) *Mercury* : Quarrelsome; irreligious; voracious eater; a famous thief.

   (e) *Jupiter* : Religiously inclined; fortunate; high status with the king; a minister; wealthy.

   (f) *Venus* : Ever changeable nature; ill-looking; addicted to others' wives; destitute.

2. In the signs of Venus

   (a) *Sun* : Lacks wealth; learned; weak of body; speaks clearly.

   (b) *Moon* : High status with the ruler; liked and helped by women; good clothes and ornaments.

   (c) *Mars* : Skilled in warfare; kind-hearted; excessive talker; rich.

   (d) *Mercury* : Very witty; keen to please women; liked by the king.

   (e) *Jupiter* : Helpful to others; given to charities; skilful.

   (f) *Venus* : Liked by the ruler; benefits from precious stones; indulges in wine and women.

3. In the signs of Mercury

   (a) *Sun* : Bereft of wealth, pleasures and anger; religiously inclined; contented.

   (b) *Moon* : Equal to a king; soft skin; loved and respected by women.

   (c) *Mars* : A fighter or wrestler; wise; defective of limb; well known.

   (d) *Mercury* : Wealthy; skilled in fighting and dancing; talented singer, painter or sculptor.

   (e) *Jupiter* : Favoured by the ruler; virtuous; liked by his friends.

(f) *Venus* : Fond of women; versed in Yoga Shastra; skilful in serving women.

4. In the Moon's sign

   (a) *Sun* : Loses his father in early age; bereft of money, wife and comforts; a sinner.

   (b) *Moon* : Wealthy; hurtful to mother and brothers.

   (c) *Mars* : Lacks strength; favoured by the ruler; worrisome.

   (d) *Mercury* : Wanderer; deceitful; cruel; orator.

   (e) *Jupiter* : Possesses friends, sons, lands and houses; wealthy.

   (f) *Venus* : Bereft of comforts, despite being born in a good family.

5. In the Sun's sign

   (a) *Sun* : Without money, comforts and good qualities; resorts to falsehood; fond of drinking; slim body; miserable.

   (b) *Moon* : Blessed with fame, wealth, women, and precious stones; favoured by the ruler.

   (c) *Mars* : Wanderer; resides in a fort or on a mountain; cruel and fighter.

   (d) *Mercury* : Deceitful; indolent; poor and ugly.

   (e) *Jupiter* : Leader of a village, town or a group of people; wealthy; virtuous.

   (f) *Venus* : Good looking; wealthy; troubles from women.

6. In the signs of Jupiter

   (a) *Sun* : Famous; fond of others' children.

   (b) *Moon* : Deprived of mother; blessed with wife, sons and riches.

   (c) *Mars* : Suffers from Vaata-related illnesses; lives in foreign lands.

   (d) *Mercury* : Equal to a king; respectable; rich; good in looks.

   (e) *Jupiter* : Equivalent to a king; commander of an army; powerful.

   (f) *Venus* : Resides in a foreign land; two mothers or two fathers; follows several pursuits at a time.

7. In its own sign

   (a) *Sun* : Sickly; husband of an ugly woman; wanderer; miserable; carries loads.

   (b) *Moon* : Possesses wealth and wife; opposed to mother; given to sexual excess.

   (c) *Mars* : Courageous; famous; powerful; a leader of multitudes; cruel.

   (d) *Mercury* : Powerful; easily angered; famous; possesses limited amounts of money.

(e) *Jupiter* : Famous; virtuous; long lived and healthy; beautiful body.

(f) *Venus* : Very wealthy; sensuous; addicted to women not his own; follows no norms.

Rahu

Rahu is particularly favourable in Karka, Kanya, Dhanu and Vrishchika.

Rahu owns Kumbha (or Kanya, according to some) and is exalted in Vrisha. Its Moolatrikona sign is Mithuna.

In the above mentioned signs, Rahu gives favourable results like increase in wealth, help from friends and the ruler, varied physical comforts, religious inclinations, new house and clothes, and foreign travel with honours.

Ketu

Ketu owns Vrishchika (or Meena, according to some) and is also exalted in Vrishchika. Its Moolatrikona is Dhanu.

In these signs Ketu gives favourable results.

In general, Rahu and Ketu give benefic results in the signs of Jupiter and Mercury or when they are associated with or aspected by Jupiter or Mercury.

The results of various planets in different signs, and of aspects on these planets, have been taken from standard classical texts. These must not be applied literally, but only with caution and scientific openness. For example, 'favours from the ruler', in the present day context, may only mean a promotion in a government job. Similarly, 'death of wife' may only signify a separation or a divorce. The classical dicta must only be applied after proper consideration of various other factors which are likely to influence the results in a given chart.

...XX...
Nabhasa Yogas

नैनमूर्ध्वं न तिर्यंच न मध्ये परिजग्रभत्।
न तस्य प्रतिमा अस्ति यस्य नाम महद् यशः॥

None can grasp Him from above, nor obliquely, nor in the middle. There exists no likeness of Him whose name is Great Fame.

Shvetashvatara Upanishad IV/19

N abhasa yogas are planetary configurations which give an overall view of a person's life pattern. They are not dependent upon planetary lordships, conjunctions or aspects. These yogas must be examined before the horoscope is subjected to a detailed analysis. The influence of these yogas is felt throughout the life of a native. In other words, these yogas do not depend on any dashas to manifest their results. Rahu and Ketu are not included in the formation of these yogas.

There are four major categories of these yogas. Under each major category are further divisions, which total to thirty-two yogas. Still finer divisions give us 1800 varieties of these yogas. A resume of these yogas is being given here.

Major categories of Nabhasa Yogas

The four categories of Nabhasa Yogas are as under :

1. *Aashraya* (i.e., 'refuge') : There are three Aashraya yogas. They depend upon the placement of planets in the Chara, the Sthira or the Dwiswabhava rashis.

2. *Dala* (i.e., 'side') : There are two of them.

3. *Aakriti* (i.e., 'appearance') : Their number is twenty. They are formed by the placement of planets in specific arcs of the horoscope or in the specific areas of the horoscope.

4. *Sankhya* (i.e., 'number') : There are seven of these. They depend upon the number of houses over which the seven planets are distributed.

The Aashraya Yogas

The three Aashraya yogas are:

1. *Rajju* : All planets in Chara rashis (movable signs). One born in this yoga is fond of travel, good to look at, visits alien countries and has a cruel nature.

2. *Musala* : All planets in Sthira rashis (fixed signs). One born in Musala yoga is learned, wealthy, proud, famous and of a stable nature.

3. *Nala* : All planets in Dwiswabhava rashis (mixed signs). The native with Nala yoga is defective of a limb, very clever, good to look at and fond of his near and dear ones.

Comments : Planets represent life force. Their accumulation in movable, fixed or mixed signs brings appropriate nature of these signs into manifestation. When several planets accumulate in movable signs, the person acquires a changeable nature, ambition, liking for travel, quick decisions and greater adaptability. **Chart XX-1** has no planets in fixed signs. If the lagna is also a movable sign, the capacity for mobility is greater. On a negative side, predominance of planets in movable signs indicates an ever changing nature, untrustworthiness, fickle mind, inability to persist with one thing, and continuous struggle.

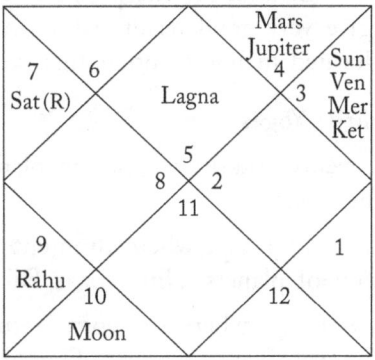

Several planets accumulating in fixed signs lead to stability, fixity, durability, determination and trustworthiness. **Chart XX-2** shows no planets in movable

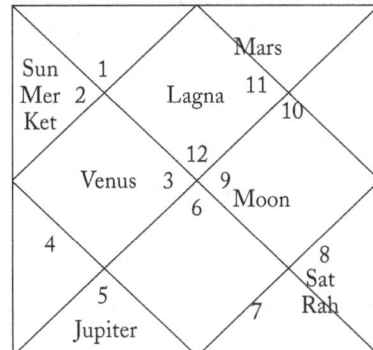

214

signs and a predominant concentration in fixed signs. There is a tendancy to stay longer in one place, and to develop contacts or acquire property. The negative aspect of this yoga indicates obstinacy, inability to take quick decisions and difficulty in adjusting to change.

As far as dual signs are concerned, their first half (0°-15°) must be considered as fixed (being adjacent to a fixed sign) and the second half (15°-30°) as movable (being adjacent to a movable sign).

The Dala Yogas

They are :

1. *Maala* or *Srak* : All benefics in three kendras and malefics not in kendras. Maala yoga ensures constant enjoyment, vehicles, good food and association with pretty women.

2. *Sarpa* : All malefics in three kendras and benefics elsewhere. This leads to miseries, dependence, penury and wickedness.

   Comments :

   (i) The Moon should be left out of the formation of Dala yogas. In other words, it should neither be treated as a benefic nor a malefic.

   (ii) The kendras are the pillars of a horoscope. Benefics located in kendras give very good results while malefics produce adverse results. Benefics located in houses other than kendras and trikonas are wasted benefics.

The Aakriti Yogas

Of the twenty Aakriti yogas, the planetary dispositions can be divided into two main groups :

I. *The angular group*, where different yogas result from specific angular disposition of planets. Nine yogas fall under this group.

II. *The arc group*, where the yogas result from planets occupying specific arcs (of houses) in a horoscope. This group consists of eleven yogas.

I. The Angular Group

This group may be further sub-divided into three subgroups as follows :

A. *The Kendra (quadrangular) disposition* : The yogas falling under this group are :

   1. *Gada* : All planets in two adjacent kendras. The native is wealthy, learned and ever engaged in earning money.

   2. *Shakata* : All planets in houses one and seven. This leads to ill health, penury and earning only through hard labour.

   3. *Pakshi (or Vihaga)* : All planets located in houses four and ten. The native with this yoga is servile, vagrant, quarrelsome and a message-bearer.

4. *Vajra* : Benefics in houses one and seven; malefics in houses four and ten. One born in this yoga is good in looks, brave, and happy during early life and old age.

5. *Yava* : Malefics in houses one and seven, benefics in houses four and ten. Such a native is consistent in nature, wealthy, charitable, and happy in the middle portion of his life.

6. *Kamala* : All planets occupying the four kendras. The native with this yoga acquires wide renown, long life, virtuous qualities and royal status.

Comments : Strong kendras elevate the status of an individual. In **Chart XX-3**, an exalted Venus has strayed into the ninth house; the remaining planets occupy three kendras. Rahu and Ketu are not considered in these yogas. In the actual analysis of the chart, the nature of planets, their ownership and such other qualities as debilitation, exaltation, etc., will have to be considered.

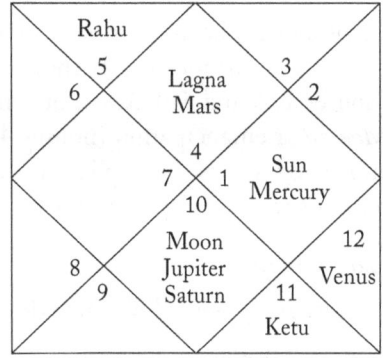

B. *The Non-kendra disposition* :

7. *Vaapi* : All planets falling in houses other than the four kendras. Such a native is engaged in accumulating wealth, has small but lasting comforts, tends to hoard his wealth and possessions.

Comments : In **Chart XX-4**, all the kendras are un-occupied. There is an accumulation of planets (as well as planetary aspects) on the second house. The stress here is on accumulation and hoarding.

According to several authors, Vaapi yoga has two variants:

(i)   All planets falling in Panaphara (successant) houses; and

(ii) All planets falling in Apoklima (cadent) houses.

C. *The Trikona (Trinal) disposition* : This includes :

8. *Shringataka* : All planets located in trikonas (i.e., houses 1, 5 and 9). The native is blessed with comforts, fond of combat, and wealthy.

9. *Hala* : All planets located in trinal houses

    (a) 2, 6 and 10; or

    (b) 3, 7 and 11; or

    (c) 4, 8 and 12.

    The native is servile, poor, engaged in agriculture, and miserable.

    Comments : The four trinal groups of houses have specific functions of *Dharma* or virtuous deeds (houses 1, 5 and 9), *Artha* or material pursuits (houses 2, 6 and 10), *Kama* or sensual pleasures (houses 3, 7 and 11), and *Moksha* or emancipation (houses 4, 8 and 12). The results attributed to the above yogas must be applied in the light of inherent characteristics of the relevant trinal group of houses.

II. The Arc Group

A. *The Short Arc group* : This includes :

1. *Yoopa* : All planets located in houses one to four. The native is engaged in sacrificial rituals, blessed with home comforts, valorous, and pursues his worldly duties.

    Comments : The first four houses are concerned with the self, wealth and possessions, courage, and home. The stress here is on stability at home, prosperity, and personal efforts toward material and spiritual pursuits.

2. *Shara* : All planets in houses four to seven. The result is a native who is cruel, wicked, a hunter, a jailor, and engaged in making arrows.

    Comments : The four houses involved in this yoga are concerned with home, investment, intellect, crime, theft, sex, etc. There is earning of wealth through a greater movement away from home as compared to the preceding yoga.

3. *Shakti* : All planets occupying the houses seven to ten. The native with this yoga is poor, wicked, lazy, long-lived, stable, good to look at, and tormented by failures.

    Comments : This yoga involves the houses concerned with sex, obstacles, virtue and activity. The involvement of the eighth house involves obstacles, failures, transgression of norms, hidden talents and ill-health. Being part of the visible zodiac (houses 7 to 1), it involves public exposure, fame, recognition, notoriety, and a non-conformist attitude. Such natives are more outgoing.

4. *Danda* : All planets located in houses ten to one. Such a native is bereft of all comforts, devoid of near and dear ones, poor, servile and rejected.

Comments : The houses involved in this yoga involve work, earnings, spending, emancipation, distant residence, spiritual activity, etc. This yoga is considered adverse for material possessions and comforts.

B. *The Long Arc Group* : This includes :

5. *Nauka* : Planets continuously occupying houses one to seven. This makes the native famous, miserly, greedy, ambitious, earning through water-related pursuits.

Comments : Involves the invisible half of the zodiac. Not all qualities and deficiencies of the native receive recog-nition.

6. *Koota* : Planets continuously occupying the houses four to ten. The result is an untruthful native, a jailor, cruel, inclined to live in a fort or on hilly areas.

7. *Chhatra* : Planets continuously occupying houses seven to one. Such a native looks after his dependents, is kind hearted, wise, long-lived, and comfortable in the early and concluding portions of his life.

Comments : This involves the complete visible half of the horoscope.

8. *Dhanusha (Chaapa)* : Planets continuously occupying houses ten to four. The native is brave, a jailor, a thief, a wanderer, and happy in the middle portion of his life.

9. *Ardha-Chandra* : This yoga is formed when the seven planets occupy seven contiguous houses starting from houses other than the kendras. Eight such yogas are formed as the planets occupy the seven houses starting from the 2nd, the 3rd, the 5th, the 6th, the 8th, the 9th, the 11th or the 12th house. The native is a commander of an army, good in looks, wealthy, brave, and honoured by the ruler.

Comments : In all the above yogas, the interaction of planets, houses, house lords, and signs is of essence.

C. *The Interrupted Arc Group* : This consists of :

10. *Chakra* : Planets in six alternate houses starting from the lagna (i.e., the six odd houses). The native is a king or his equivalent.

11. *Samudra* : Planets in six alternate houses starting from the second house (i.e., the six even houses). The native is wealthy, blessed with physical pleasures, likeable, virtuous and stable of mind.

218

Comments : The preceding two yogas stress the impor-tance of planets placed in alternate houses, mutually 3/11 or 5/9 in position. **Chart XX-5** shows a disposition of most of the planets in alternate houses. Although it is not forming an exact Chakra yoga, such a disposition of planets is considered highly favourable.. The native of this chart is a high ranking administrative official.

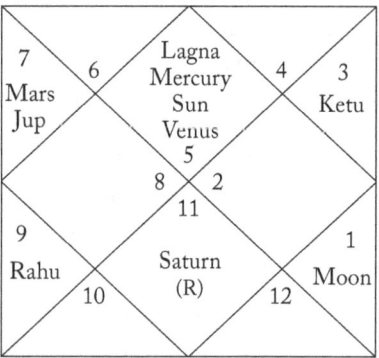

The Sankhya Yogas

There are seven of these yogas which depend upon the number of rashis the seven planets occupy in a horoscope.

1. *Veena* : The seven planets occupying seven different rashis in a chart. The native is fond of music and dance, skillful, wealthy, a leader.

2. *Daama (or Daamani)* : Planets distributed over six rashis. The native is liberal, renowned, wealthy, learned, and earns through legitimate means.

3. *Paasha* : Planets distributed over five rashis. The native has a large family, is adept in work, skillful in earning wealth, impolite, crafty.

4. *Kedaara* : Planets located in four rashis in a chart. Such a native does good to many, is truthful and wealthy, and resorts to agriculture.

5. *Shoola* : All planets restricted to three rashis only. The native is lazy, cruel, socially rejected, injured and scarred, a fighter.

6. *Yuga* : Planets restricted to two rashis only. The native is poor, heretic, socially rejected, devoid of mother, father and virtue.

7. *Gola* : Planets confined to one rashi. The native with such a yoga is a destitute, illiterate, wicked, miserable, ever wandering.

Commments : The Sankhya yogas are concerned with the distribution of planets in the horoscope. When the planets are distributed over a larger number of houses, there is greater balance and a wider range of interests that a native pursues.

As the planets get restricted to fewer and fewer houses, the life force signified by the planets is concentrated in specific areas. This causes strengthening of certain houses but an overall imbalance and weakness.

Summary

The Nabhasa yogas indicate a native's pattern of life, his inclinations, strong points and weaknesses. They give results all through his life and do not depend on any dashas.

By definition, yogas belonging to one group may coincide with yogas of another group. In such situations certain rules must be followed. These are hinted at below.

1. Sankhya yogas are applicable only if other yogas mentioned herein do not obtain simultaneously in a horoscopic chart. For example, if there are seven planets distributed in seven contiguous or alternate houses, one of the Aakriti yogas will be formed as also the Sankhya yoga. In such a situation, the results as described for the particular Aakriti yoga will manifest.

2. When Aashraya yogas coincide with an Aakriti yoga, again the Aakriti yoga takes precedence.

3. The Sankhya yogas called Kedaara, Shoola and Yuga become inoperative if they coincide at the same time with an Aashraya yoga. However, if Gola yoga coincides with an Aashraya yoga, the former remains operative and the latter becomes inoperative.

The formation and the order of the Nabhasa Yogas as mentioned in the classical works is briefly shown in Table XX-1.

Table XX-1
Formation and order of the Nabhasa Yogas as mentioned in the classical texts

Major Category	Yogas	Formation
I. **Aashraya**	1. Rajju	All planets in Chara rashis.
	2. Musala	All planets in Sthira rashis.
	3. Nala	All planets in Dwiswabhava rashis.
II. **Dala**	1. Maala (Srak)	All benefics in three kendras; malefics not in kendras.
	2. Sarpa	All malefics in three kendras; benefics not in kendras.
III. **Aakriti**	1. Gada	All planets in two adjacent kendras.
	2. Shakata	All planets in houses 1 and 7.
	3. Pakshi (Vihaga)	All planets in houses 4 and 10.
	4. Shringataka	All planets in trikonas (1, 5, 9).
	5. Hala	All planets in houses: (a) 2, 6 and 10; or (b) 3, 7 and 11; or (c) 4, 8 and 12.

Table XX-1 Contd.

Major Category	Yogas	Formation
	6. Vajra	Benefics in houses 1 and 7; malefics in 4 and 10.
	7. Yava	Malefics in houses 1 and 7; benefics in 4 and 10.
	8. Kamala	All planets in four kendras.
	9. Vaapi	All planets in houses other than kendras.
	10. Yoopa	All planets in houses 1 to 4.
	11. Shara	All planets in houses 4 to 7.
	12. Shakti	All planets in houses 7 to 10.
	13. Danda	All planets in houses 10 to 1.
	14. Nauka	Planets occupying houses 1 to 7 in continuity.
	15. Koota	Planets occupying houses 4 to 10 in continuity.
	16. Chhatra	All planets occupying houses 7 to 1 in continuity.
	17. Dhanusha (Chaapa)	All planets occupying houses 10 to 4 in continuity.
	18. Ardhachandra	The seven planets occupying seven houses starting from other than a kendra (8 types).
	19. Chakra	Planets in six alternate houses from lagna onwards (i.e., houses 1, 3, 5, 7, 9 and 11).
	20. Samudra	Planets in six alternate houses starting from 2nd house onwards (i.e., houses 2, 4, 6, 8, 10 and 12).
IV. **Sankhya**	1. Veena	All planets distributed over 7 rashis.
	2. Daama	All planets distributed over 6 rashis.
	3. Paasha	All planets distributed over 5 rashis.
	4. Kedaara	All planets distributed over 4 rashis.
	5. Shoola	All planets restricted to 3 rashis.
	6. Yuga	All planets restricted to 2 rashis.
	7. Gola	All planets restricted to 1 rashi.

...XXI...
Yogas Based on Ownership of Houses

इहैकस्थं जगत्कृत्स्नं पश्याद्य सचराचरम्।
मम देहे गुडाकेश यच्चान्यद्द्रष्टुमिच्छसि॥

Behold today the whole universe, moving and unmoving and whatever else you desire to see, O Gudakesha, all unified in My body. Gita XI/7

It has already been explained that planets behave as benefics or malefics depending upon the houses they own in a horoscope. This naturally varies with the lagna. The lordship of houses by the planets is an extremely important factor in deciding the results that accrue from varied planetary dispositions. It is the inter-action of different planets, as different house lords, that results in the formation of various yogas so often referred to in astrology.

A yoga is a specific disposition of a planet or planets which is productive of specific results. There are hundreds, nay thousands, of yogas described in astrological texts. Their presence or absence in a horoscope, as also their strength and placement, determines the nature and stature of a native.

It is not possible to discuss all the various yogas mentioned in the classical texts. Some principles underlying the formation of the yogas, depending upon the ownership of the houses by the planets, will be discussed here. It is proposed to discuss these yogas under four heads.

I.   Raja yogas
II. Dhana yogas
III. Arishta yogas
IV. Parivartana yogas

I. Raja Yogas

These yogas are so called because they elevate the status of an individual. When they are formed by planets which are strong and located in benefic houses, they manifest fully. When formed by weak planets or those located in adverse houses, they do not manifest fully and lead to numerous obstacles and struggles.

Formation of Raja Yogas

It has already been pointed out that planets get related to each other by: (i) conjunction; (ii) mutual aspect; (iii) exchange of houses; and (iv) by one planet being placed in the other's house and aspected by that planet. Raja yogas form when the lords of the kendras are related to the lords of the trikonas in any of the above manner.

It has been said that the kendras (houses 1, 4, 7 and 10) belong to lord Vishnu, the Preserver, while the trikonas (houses 1, 5 and 9) belong to His consort Laxmi, the goddess of Prosperity. The union of the two (kendra and trikona) lords forms a Raja yoga. The lagna is to be treated as both a kendra and a trikona. Raja yogas will thus result from a mutual relationship between:

(a) The lagna lord on the one side and the lord of the 4th or the 5th or the 7th or the 9th or the 10th house on the other (5 combinations).

(b) The lord of the fourth house on the one side and the lord of the 5th or the 9th on the other (two combinations).

(c) The lord of the fifth house on the one side and lords of the 7th or the 10th on the other (two combinations).

(d) The lord of the seventh house on the one side and that of the ninth on the other (one combination).

(e) The lord of the ninth house on the one side and the lord of the tenth on the other (one combination).

Thus eleven different types of Raja yogas are formed by relationship between appropriate house lords. It may be pointed out that yogas formed between the 9th and the 10th lords, and those between the lagna lord on one side and the lords of the 9th or the 10th or the 4th or the 5th on the other, are particularly productive of favourable results.

Some other Raja Yogas

Parashara mentions several other Raja yogas some of which are as follows :

1. A conjunction or mutual aspect between the lord of the fifth and the lord of the ninth leads to kingship or royal status.

   Note : The ninth lord is a minister; the fifth is a chief minister. By kingship is meant a high governmental status in the modern context.

2. Exchange between lords of the fourth and the tenth houses, aspected by or associated with the fifth or the ninth lords, is another combination for high official status.

   Note : The tenth house indicates the government, the fourth house also stands for the Parliament in a democracy.

3. Lords of the fourth and the tenth associating with the lords of the fifth or the ninth produce a Raja yoga.

4. Lord of the fifth house associated with the lagna lord or the ninth lord, and located in houses one, four or ten, brings forth a king.

5. Jupiter-Venus conjunction occurring in the ninth house or associated with the fifth lord produces a king.

6. Venus in the lagna aspected by the Moon and Jupiter causes a Raja yoga.

7. Debilitated lords of the third, the sixth, the eighth or the twelfth, in the presence of a strong lord of the lagna which aspects or associates with the lagna, produce a Raja yoga during their dasha.

8. Tenth lord exalted or in its own house, aspecting the lagna at the same time, produces a Raja yoga.

Examples

Chart XXI-1 belongs to a late Prime Minister of India. The lords of the 9th and the 10th houses are combined in the tenth house producing a powerful Raja yoga. A close association of the eighth and the ninth lords in the tenth house leads to the Raja yoga materialising suddenly and unexpectedly because of the death of his predecessor. The same combination resulted in a sudden and unexpected fall. The Sun in the tenth house gains directional strength and ensures high status in government.

In the Navamsha too, a Raja yoga is formed in the lagna by the association of the lagna lord and the tenth lord. This combination too is joined by the lord of the eighth house, confirming the indications of the Rashi chart.

In the Dashamamsha, a powerful Raja yoga again forms in the tenth house by the conjunction of the fifth and the ninth lords, along with the Sun.

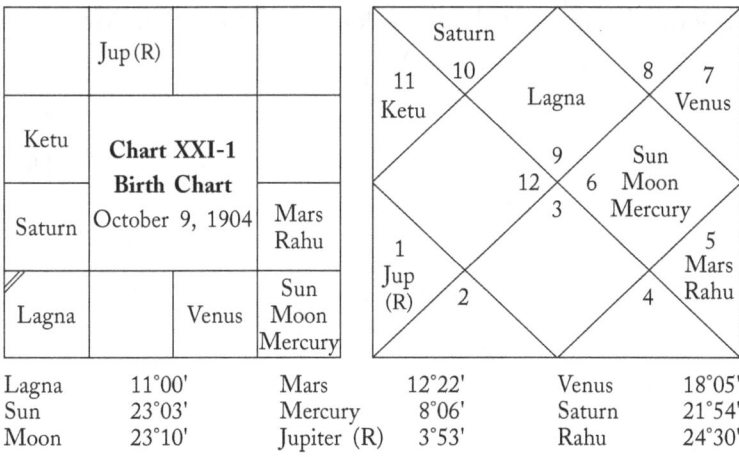

Lagna	11°00'	Mars	12°22'	Venus	18°05'
Sun	23°03'	Mercury	8°06'	Saturn	21°54'
Moon	23°10'	Jupiter (R)	3°53'	Rahu	24°30'

224

Navamsha (chart)

Mercury Venus	Jupiter Ketu	
		Lagna SunMon SatMar
	Navamsha	
	Rahu	

(South Indian chart)

```
      5 / Lagna \ 3
    6 /  Sun Moon \ 2  Jup
      \  Saturn   /    Ketu
       \  Mars   /
        \   4   /
      7 / \   / \ 1
          10
   8                12
 Rahu              Mer
      9        11  Venus
```

Dashamamsha (chart)

Lagna	Rahu Venus Saturn	Jupiter
		Mercury
	Dashamamsha	
Sun Moon Mars	Ketu	

(South Indian chart)

```
   Rahu Venus Saturn
   2 \  1  / 11
 Jupiter \ Lagna / 10
          \    /
       12 /    \ Sun
     3 /  9     \ Mon
       \    6   / Mars
    4   \      /   8
   Mer   \ 5  /  7
              Ketu
```

Vipareeta Raja Yoga

An odd Raja yoga results when :

(a) The sixth lord is in the eighth or the twelfth house (Harsha yoga);
(b) The eighth lord is in the sixth or the twelfth house (Sarala yoga); or
(c) The twelfth lord is in the sixth or the eighth house (Vimala yoga).

This leads to rise in status, fame and financial gain during the concerned dasha.

In **Chart XXI-2**, a powerful Raja yoga results from a mutual aspect between the ninth lord Mercury and the tenth lord, the Moon. The Moon as the 10th

	Rahu	Mars	Jupiter
Moon	**Chart XXI-2**		Sun
	Birth Chart		
	August 12, 1930		Mercury
Sat (R)		Lagna Ketu	Venus

(South Indian chart)

```
                      Venus
     9 \  8  / Lagna \  6  / 5
  Sat(R) \  /  Ketu   \   / Mer
          \            \ /
           \    7      / \
       10 / \ 4      /    \
         /  1      / Sun   \
    11 /         /          \  3
  Moon \   12  / Rahu   \ 2 / Jupiter
        \     /          \ /
                    Mars
```

Lagna	14°16'	Mars	26°40'	Venus	9°35'
Sun	25°56'	Mercury	19°44'	Saturn (R)	13°01'
Moon	26°39'	Jupiter	17°15'	Rahu	4°14'

Navamsha chart:

Jupiter Venus	Moon Rahu		
Lagna Sun	**Navamsha**		Saturn
	Ketu		Mars Mercury

North Indian chart (Rashi):

Jupiter Venus — 12 / 1	Lagna Sun	10 / 9
Moon Rahu — 2 / 5	11 / 8	Ketu
3 / 4 — Saturn		6 / 7 — Mars Mercury

Dashamamsha chart:

	Saturn	Rahu	
Lagna Mercury	**Dashamamsha**		
			Venus
	Sun Jupiter Ketu	Moon	Mars

North Indian chart (Dashamamsha):

1 Saturn / 12	Lagna Mercury	10 / 9
Rahu — 2 / 5	11 / 8	Sun Jupiter Ketu
3 / 4 — Venus		6 / 7 — Mars / Moon

lord also receives the aspects of the fourth and fifth lord, Saturn, as also the natural benefic Jupiter. This powerful combination involves the 5/11 axis which is an axis for earnings and wealth, a Dhana yoga which will be described soon.

The native, a senior bureaucrat in the Government of India, enjoyed status and enhanced income particularly in the dasha periods of Ketu as well as Venus. This is a combination of a Raja yoga and a Dhana yoga occurring simultaneously. Ketu is aspected by Jupiter in both the Rashi chart and the Navamsha chart. Venus is the debilitated lord of the eighth house which is capable of causing a Raja yoga, as has been mentioned above; it is exalted in the Navamsha. These indications can be confirmed in the Dashamamsha too where Ketu in the 10th house is assocoiated with Jupiter, and Venus happens to be a yogakaraka located in the seventh house.

II. Dhana Yogas

The Dhana yogas are astrological combinations for wealth and prosperity. These combinations prove fruitful in the presence of a strong lagna and a strong lagna lord. Any benefic combinations, whether Raja yogas or Dhana yogas, manifest fully only when the lagna is strong.

The second and the eleventh houses are the ones which are concerned with the earning and accumulation of wealth. Besides these, the trines are considered as the abodes of Laxmi, the goddess of Wealth. Thus, any relationship among these various lords ensures wealth and prosperity. The Dhana yogas, in their simplest form, may thus occur when there is a mutual relationship between :

(a) The lagna lord on one side and the second, or the fifth, or the ninth, or the eleventh lord on the other (four combinations).

(b) The second lord on one side and the fifth, or the ninth, or the eleventh lord on the other (three combinations).

(c) The fifth lord on one side and the ninth, or the eleventh lord on the other (two combinations).

(d) The ninth lord on the one side and the eleventh lord on the other (one combination).

   This leads to ten different combinations. There are numerous other combinations mentioned in several texts. All such combinations must be examined in the light of strength of the constituent planets, their lordship, their placement in specific houses and the influence of benefic and malefic planets on them.

Some other Dhana Yogas

Parashara makes a mention of several other Dhana yogas. Some of these are enumerated here.

A. *Significance of the 5/11 axis*

1. Venus occupying the fifth house identical with its own rashi (Vrisha/Tula), and Mars placed in the eleventh house.

2. Mercury occupying the fifth house identical with its own rashi (Mithuna/Kanya), with the Moon, Mars and Jupiter in the eleventh house.

3. The Sun occupying the fifth house identical with its own rashi (Simha), and the Moon, Jupiter and Saturn in the eleventh house.

4. Saturn occupying the fifth house identical with its own rashi (Makara/Kumbha), and the Sun and the Moon in the eleventh house.

5. Jupiter occupying the fifth house identical with its own rashi (Dhanu/Meena), and Mercury in the eleventh house.

6. Mars occupying the fifth house identical with its own rashi (Mesha/Vrishchika), and Venus in the eleventh house.

7. The Moon in Karka in the fifth house, and Saturn in the eleventh house.

B. *Significance of the lagna and its lord*

1. The Sun in Simha lagna, under the influence (aspect or association) of Mars and Jupiter.

2. The Moon in Karka lagna, under the influence of Mercury and Jupiter.

3. Mars in its own rashi (Mesha/Vrishchika) in the lagna, under the influence of Mercury, Venus and Saturn.

4. Mercury in its own rashi (Mithuna/Kanya) in the lagna, under the influence of Jupiter and Saturn.

5. Jupiter in its own rashi (Dhanu/Meena) in the lagna, under the influence of Mars and Mercury.

6. Venus in its own rashi (Vrisha/Tula) in the lagna, under the influence of Mercury and Saturn.

7. Saturn in its own rashi (Makara/Kumbha) in the lagna, under the influence of Mars and Jupiter.

C. *Houses five and nine*

Houses five and nine are particularly wealth-giving houses. Planets associated with these houses or their lords ensure acquisition of wealth.

Examples

In **Chart XXI-3**, six of the nine planets occupy the 5/11 axis, the axis of wealth. The fifth house contains several Raja yogas and Dhana yogas. They are:

1. Lagna lord with the fourth lord.

2. Lagna lord with the fifth lord.

Rahu		Lagna	
Jup (R)	**Chart XXI-3** **Birth Chart** October 15, 1950		
			Sun Ven Sat Ket Mer
	Moon Mars		

	3 4	Lagna 1	12 Rahu
		2 5 11 8	Jup (R)
Sun Ven Sat Ket Mer 6 7		Moon Mars	10 9

Lagna	27°01'	Mars	20°54'	Venus	21°06'
Sun	28°33'	Mercury	16°46'	Saturn	3°08'
Moon	25°29'	Jupiter (R)	4°33'	Rahu	4°54'

			Mercury
Moon Ketu	**Navamsha**		Venus
Sat Mars			Rahu
	Jupiter		Lagna Sun

8 Jupiter 7	Lagna Sun	Rahu 5 4 Venus
9 12	6	3 Mercury 2
10 Sat Mars 11 Moon Ketu		1

3. Lagna lord with the ninth lord.
4. Lagna lord with the tenth lord.
5. Fourth lord with the fifth lord.
6. Fourth lord with the ninth lord.
7. Fifth lord with the ninth lord.
8. Fifth lord with the tenth lord.
9. Lagna lord with the second lord.
10. Second lord with the ninth lord.
11. Mars and the Moon joining together in a house is an additional combination for wealth.

No wonder the native is very prosperous and enjoys a high status in the U.S.A. In the Navamsha also, the second and the ninth lord Venus, located in the eleventh house, is aspected by the fifth lord Saturn occupying its own house.

Chart XXI-4 shows a conjunction of the lagna lord, the second lord and the tenth lord in the fourth house. This chart also shows a special Dhana yoga of Parashara which is obtained when a single planet owning the second and the seventh houses simultaneously, occupies the fourth house. This can only happen

Sun Mercury	Ketu		
	Chart XXI-4 **Birth Chart** March 16, 1958		
Moon Mars Venus			
Saturn	Lagna Jup (R) Rahu		

9 Saturn	8	Lagna Jup (R) Rahu	6
			5
Moon Mars Venus	10	7	4
			1
11	Ketu		3
12 Sun Mercury			2

Lagna	25°46'	Mars	6°19'	Venus	18°36'
Sun	2°20'	Mercury	14°26'	Saturn	2°09'
Moon	21°49'	Jupiter (R)	7°07'	Rahu	8°25'

	Saturn	Lagna	Venus Ketu
Mars			Sun Moon
	Navamsha		
Jupiter Rahu	Mercury		

4 Sun Moon	Venus Ketu 3	Lagna	Saturn 1 12
		2	
	5	11	Mars
	8		
6	7	Mercury	10
		9 Jupiter Rahu	

in the case of Mesha and Tula lagnas. For Mesha lagna, Venus as the lord of the second and the seventh houses, causes a Dhana yoga when located in the fourth house. For Tula lagna, as in this case, Mars as the lord of the second and the seventh houses, occupies the fourth house. An additional factor for riches is the association of the Moon and Mars which goes under the name of Chandra-Mangala yoga. It is present in Chart XXI-3 also.

Chart XXI-5 shows a very close conjunction of the ninth and the tenth lords, a potent Raja yoga, obtaining in the second house of prosperity, while the lagna lord and the second lord Saturn occupies the eleventh house. The lagna lord and the eleventh lord mutually aspect each other along the 5/11 axis. Powerful Raja yogas and Dhana yogas are thus formed. The combination in the second house is also associated with the Sun which is the eighth lord indicating obstacles as well as interruptions. The native changed many jobs, each successive break virtually causing further rise in his status and eminence, as also proving financially more benefic (the effect of the second house!).

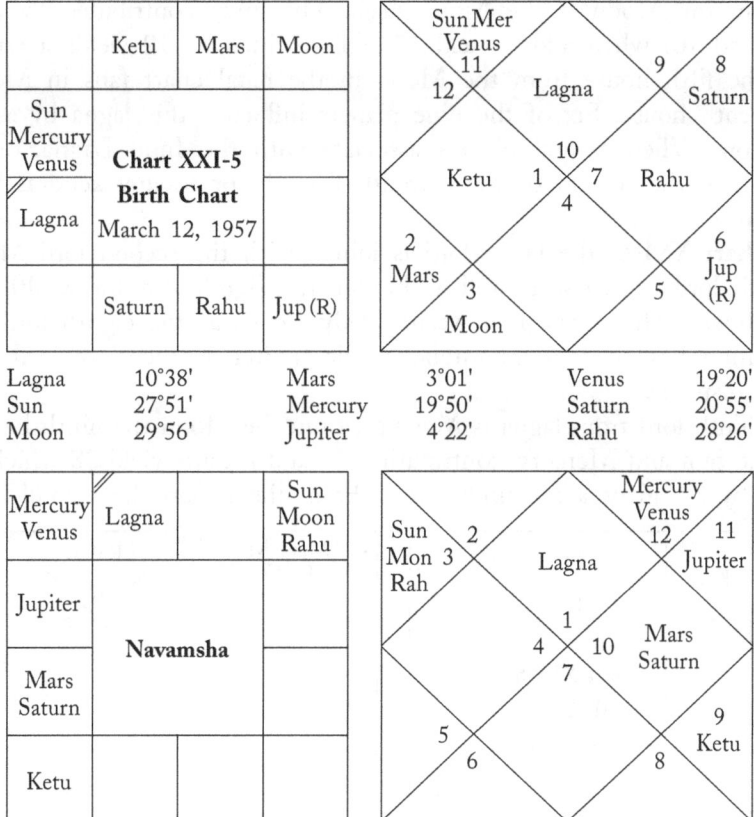

Lagna	10°38'	Mars	3°01'	Venus	19°20'
Sun	27°51'	Mercury	19°50'	Saturn	20°55'
Moon	29°56'	Jupiter	4°22'	Rahu	28°26'

The Indu Lagna

A method of working out the extent of prosperity of a person is to determine the Indu lagna in his chart and see the disposition of planets from it.

Method of casting the Indu Lagna

The seven planets, from the Sun to the Saturn, contribute 30, 16, 6, 8, 10, 12 and 1 Kalas or units respectively.

(a) Note the ninth lord from the lagna and the ninth lord from the Moon.

(b) Add the units contributed by the two lords.

(c) Divide by 12 to remove multiples of 12.

(d) See which house is indicated by the remainder, when counted from the position of the Moon.

(e) That house becomes the Indu Lagna.

An unblemished benefic or an exalted malefic in the Indu Lagna makes one a multi-millionaire according to the classical texts. Ordinary malefic influence on this lagna leads to ordinary financial status.

In Chart XXI-3, the ninth lord from the lagna is Saturn, and the ninth lord from the Moon is the Moon itself. The units contributed by the two (i.e., 1 and 16) when added yield 17. This divided by 12 yields a remainder of 5. The fifth house from the Moon in the natal chart falls in Meena, in the eleventh house. Six of the nine planets influence this lagna by aspect or occupation. When several planets associate with the Indu Lagna, or aspect it, or fall in the second or the eleventh from it, or occupy kendras from it, riches are ensured.

In **Chart XXI-6**, the lagna lord is joined with the second lord Mars and the ninth lord Mercury, as well as Jupiter, the significator for wealth, in the second house. The native is a wealthy lady. Venus as the eighth lord in this combination has ensured inheritence while Jupiter as the sixth lord has led to legal disputes.

The ninth lord from lagna is Mercury; from the Moon the ninth lord is the Sun. The Sun and Mercury, contributing 30 and 8 units yield 38 which, when divided by 12, gives a remainder of 2. From the Moon the second house is

Lagna	18°54'	Mars	25°29'	Venus	2°35'
Sun	14°08'	Mercury	28°33'	Saturn	15°55'
Moon	15°36'	Jupiter	24°59'	Rahu	5°05'

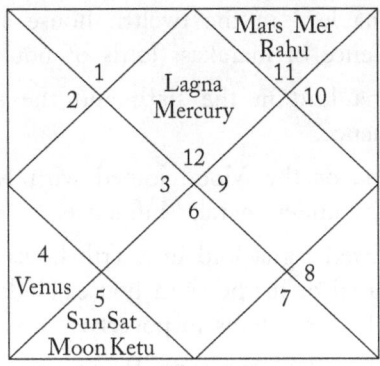

Makara. This becomes the Indu lagna. Fom here, the eleventh house has four planets and powerful Dhana yogas. This chart suffers the blemish of having all planets concentrated in only two houses (the second and the third) of the horoscope forming the 'Yuga' variety of Sankhya yogas, under the main head of Nabhasa yogas. It will be seen that the presence of the 'Yuga' yoga has not caused poverty, as a literal application of this yoga might suggest.

III. Arishta Yogas

These yogas lead to ill health. The results of Raja yogas and Dhana yogas get adversely modified in the presence of potent Arishta yogas. Detailed description of these yogas leads one into medical astrology which is a complete subject in itself. Here it is only pertinent to touch on the basic principles as relevant to the lordship of planets over various houses.

The highly malefic houses are the Trik houses, viz., the sixth, the eighth and the twelfth. Their lords produce adverse results. Further association of these lords with maraka planets enhances their virulence. In their simplest form, the Arishta yogas may be formed when there is a relationship between :

(a) The lagna lord on the one side and the sixth or the eighth or the twelfth lord on the other (three combinations).

(b) The sixth lord on the one side and the eighth or the twelfth lord on the other (two combinations).

(c) The eighth lord on the one side and the twelfth lord on the other (one combination).

The above six combinations become worse when associated or aspected by the maraka planets.

The Daridrya Yogas

The Daridrya yogas of Parashara cause penury and sufferring. It will be seen that when the lagna lord is weak and afflicted, along with combinations for 'daridrya', there occurs ill health. Some of the Daridrya yogas of Parashara are defined below :

232

1. Lagna lord in the twelfth house and the twelfth lord in the lagna, and influence of marakas (lords of houses 2 or 7) on either or both of them.

2. Lagna lord in the sixth and the sixth lord in the lagna, under maraka influence.

3. Lagna or the Moon joined with Ketu, and the lagna lord in the eighth house, under maraka influence.

4. Afflicted lagna lord in a Trik house, and the lord of the second house debilitated or in the sixth house. Under such a yoga, a person born to a royal family also attains to poverty.

5. Fifth lord in the sixth house, and the ninth lord under maraka influence located in the twelfth house.

6. Malefics in benefic houses and benefics located in adverse houses.

7. The dasha of planets associated with the Trik lords leads to excessive loss of wealth if unaspected by the lords of the fifth or the ninth.

8. Location of Mars and Saturn in the second house.

   Note: If Mercury aspects this combination, the native is very wealthy.

9. Saturn in the second house aspected by the Sun.

10. The Sun in the second house aspected by Saturn.

    Note: If Saturn does not aspect the Sun in the second house, the native is wealthy.

Example

Several Arishta yogas manifest in **Chart XXI-7**.

1. Three planets are debilitated in the Rashi chart and two in the Navamsha chart.

2. Lagna lord associates with a retrograde sixth lord and the Sun, and is aspected by Saturn.

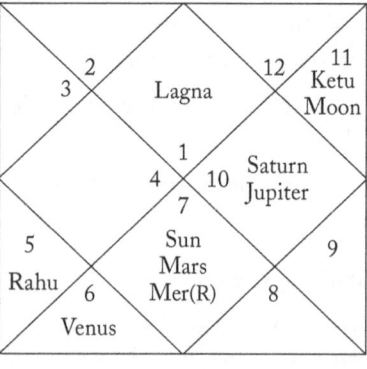

Lagna	29°35'	Mars	18°49'	Venus	8°28'
Sun	2°37'	Mercury (R)	9°44'	Saturn	0°18'
Moon	4°02'	Jupiter	5°04'	Rahu	2°06'

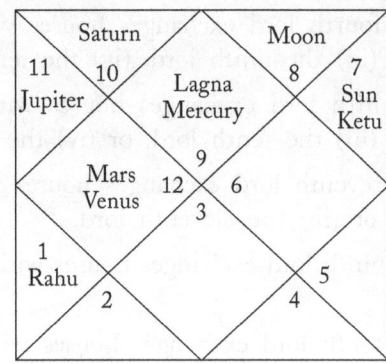

Mars Venus	Rahu		
Jupiter	**Navamsha**		
Saturn			
Lagna Mercury	Moon	Sun Ketu	

3. The Moon is involved in the Rahu-Ketu axis and gets debilitated in the Navamsha.

4. A retrograde, functionally malefic, Mercury aspects the lagna. Retrograde planets lose their beneficence as far as health is concerned.

The native suffers from a chronic incurable disease of the muscular system. He is, however, not poor monetarily. Some of the combinations promising financial stability here are :

1. A mutual aspect between the lagna lord and the eleventh lord.

2. The lagna lord and the fifth lord together, aspecting the lagna.

3. A debilitated lord of the twelfth. It has been mentioned already that the debilitated lords of the third, the sixth, the eighth and the twelfth prove beneficial.

4. A debilitated planet in the sixth house!

5. Some Dhana yogas obtain in the Navamsha too.

IV. Parivartana Yogas

These yogas are characterised by exchange of house lords. When two planets exchange houses, they gain some strength and behave as if they are located each in his own house. By an exchange, they get linked to each other. Obviously, if the lord of a good house establishes an exchange with a benefic house, good results are produced. However, when adverse houses are involved, the results too are adverse.

Mantreshwara gives three categories of Parivartana yogas.

A. *Maha Yogas* (or great combinations): These result when :

1. The lagna lord exchanges houses with (i) the second lord, (ii) the fourth lord, (iii) the fifth lord, (iv) the seventh lord, (v) the ninth lord, (vi) the tenth lord, or (vii) the eleventh lord.

2. The second lord exchanges houses with (i)the fourth lord, (ii) the fifth lord, (iii) the seventh lord, (iv) the ninth lord, (v) the tenth lord, or (vi) the eleventh lord.

3. The fourth lord exchanges houses with (i) the fifth lord, (ii) the seventh lord, (iii) the ninth lord, (iv) the tenth lord, or (v) the eleventh lord.

4. The fifth lord exchanges houses with (i) the seventh lord, (ii) the ninth lord, (iii) the tenth lord, or (iv) the eleventh lord.

5. The seventh lord exchanges houses with (i) the ninth lord, (ii) the tenth lord, or (iii) the eleventh lord.

6. The ninth lord exchanges houses with (i) the tenth lord, or (ii) the eleventh lord.

7. The tenth lord exchanges houses with the eleventh lord.

Note :

Mutual exchanges between the lords of the second house, the eleventh house, the kendras and the trikonas give rise to the above mentioned twenty-eight yogas which promise wealth, status and physical enjoyments.

B. *Dainya Yogas* (or combinations for misery): These result when:

1. The sixth lord exchanges houses with (i) the lagna lord, (ii) the second lord, (iii) the third lord, (iv) the fourth lord, (v) the fifth lord, (vi) the seventh lord, (vii) the eighth lord, (viii) the ninth lord, (ix) the tenth lord, (x) the eleventh lord, or (xi) the twelfth lord.

2. The eighth lord exchanges houses with (i) the lagna lord, (ii) the second lord, (iii) the third lord, (iv) the fourth lord, (v) the fifth lord, (vi) the seventh lord, (vii) the ninth lord, (viii) the tenth lord, (ix) the eleventh lord, or (x) the twelfth lord.

3. The twelfth lord exchanges houses with (i) the lagna lord, (ii) the second lord, (iii) the third lord, (iv) the fourth lord, (v) the fifth lord, (vi) the seventh lord, (vii) the ninth lord, (viii) the tenth lord, or (ix) the eleventh lord.

Note :

1. The above thirty yogas result from exchanges of various house lords with the lords of the sixth, the eighth and the twelfth houses. These Trika lords spoil the houses whose lords they associate with. These combinations lead to a wicked nature, persistent trouble from opponents, and ill health.

2. Exchanges between lords of the Trika houses are specially referred to as Vipareeta Raja Yogas. The results attributed to a Vipareeta Raja yoga are financial prosperity and rise in status. This is an additional area where results given by yogas do not permit a literal application.

C. *Khala Yogas* (or combinations for wickedness):

These are obtained when the lord of the third house exchanges places with the house lords other than the lords of the Trika houses. That is, the third lord establishes an exchange with (i) the lagna lord, (ii) the second lord, (iii) the fourth lord, (iv) the fifth lord, (v) the seventh lord, (vi) the ninth lord, (vii) the tenth lord, or (viii) the eleventh lord.

Note :

1. These eight yogas are characterised by a fickle and a wicked nature, fluctuating fortunes and fluctuating temperament.

2. A literal application of these yogas is again not warranted. Some of the very interesting results are obtained when these combinations are applied judiciously.

...XXII...
Specific and Miscellaneous Yogas

न तु मां शक्यसे द्रष्टुमनेनैव स्वचक्षुषा।
दिव्यं ददामि ते चक्षुः पश्य मे योगमैश्वरम्॥

*But you cannot see Me with this (human) eye of yours; I bestow on you
the supernatural eye. Behold My divine yoga.* Gita XI/8

The Nabhasa yogas, and the yogas dependant upon the ownership of
houses by the planets, have been described already. Besides these there
are numerous other yogas mentioned in the classical texts, by authors from
Parashara downwards, which deserve special mention. As usual, these yogas
are also specific planetary dispositions which usually, though not invariably,
involve two or more planets to effect their formation. They give their specific
results which are subject to modifications depending upon such conditions as :

(a) The nature of planets forming a particular yoga.

(b) Ownership of houses by the planets constituting the yoga.

(c) The house or houses occupied by the yoga-forming planets.

(d) Strength of the constituents of a yoga.

(e) Modifications as are appropriate to the ancient dicta, keeping in view the
modern context.

Since there is no limit to the number of yogas mentioned in the classical texts,
only some important ones will be mentioned here. For a similar reason, it is
also not easy to classify them though a crude attempt is being made to group
them into some categories. There is some overlap amongst the categories; for
example, the Gajekesari yoga, involving the Moon, has been described under a
category separate from that concerned with the yogas associated with the Moon.

We now proceed to discuss some of these miscellaneous yogas.

I. Pancha-Mahapurusha Yogas

They are not yogas in the strictest sense since they depend only on one planet.

They are thus single-planet 'combinations'. Five different yogas arise, based on the strength and location of the five planets, viz., Mars, Mercury, Jupiter, Venus and Saturn, in a horoscope. These five yogas are :

1. *Ruchaka yoga* : Formed when Mars, exalted or in its own house, is located in a kendra from the lagna.

2. *Bhadra yoga* : When Mercury, exalted or in its own house, is located in a kendra.

3. *Hamsa yoga* : When Jupiter, exalted or in its own house, is located in a kendra.

4. *Malavya yoga* : When Venus, exalted or in its own house, is located in a kendra.

5. *Shasha yoga* : When Saturn, exalted or in its own house, is located in a kendra.

1. Ruchaka yoga

The native born under this yoga is bold and courageous, good looking, having a prominent face, full of strength and vigour, dark haired, with beautiful eyebrows, eager for battle, cruel, annihilator of opponents, kingly, discriminating, with slim lower limbs, versed in the sacred hymns as well as magic spells, commander of an army or a leader of a gang of thieves. He is keen on all adventurous pursuits, suffers scars (or death) from fire and weapons, and lives happily to an age of seventy years.

2. Bhadra yoga

This yoga brings forth a native with the face of a tiger, the majestic gait of an elephant, large chest and shoulders, a commanding stature, skilled in the technique of 'yoga', very learned, intelligent, of beautiful body parts, dark haired, sensuous, of a 'Sattvika' nature, knower of the sacred scriptures, blessed with friends wife, children and physical comforts, enjoying high status, and lives to an age of eighty years.

3. Hamsa yoga

One born under this yoga is fair-complexioned, with the voice like that of a swan. He has beautiful limbs and face, a phlegmatic ('Kapha') disposition, fondness for water sports, a thirst for the knowledge of sacred scriptures, a virtuous nature, an intense sexual urge, and comforts of all sorts at his disposal. He is blessed with a beautiful wife, a lovely physical form, and lives to a ripe age of a hundred years.

4. Malavya yoga

One born under Malavya yoga has a graceful appearance, slim waist, handsome body, beautiful lips, long arms, deep voice and sparkling teeth. He is

238

blessed with children, wife, wealth and physical comforts, indulges in extra-marital relationships, is well versed in sacred scriptures and attains an age of seventy years.

5. Shasha yoga

This yoga confers on the native a cruel nature, leadership over an army, a group or a village, acquisition of wealth, courage and valour. He is competent, learned and finds fault in others. He roams around in jungles, mountains, forts and other odd places. He takes to metallurgy, acquires the wealth and women of others and is devoted to his mother. Of medium height and slim waist, he lives upto an age of seventy years.

Note :

(a) The Pancha-Mahapurusha yogas indicate five different natives depending upon the predominent influence of each of the five planets, from Mars to Saturn. Mars signifies strength and aggression; Mercury signifies learning and intelligence; Jupiter signifies oratory and wisdom; Venus stands for grace and pleasures; Saturn indicates mass appeal.

(b) The Pancha-Mahapurusha yogas yield results only when the Sun and the Moon are also strong. Else, they produce ordinarily good results during their relevant dashas.

(c) The disposition of the yoga-causing planets must also be seen in the divisional charts to assess the extent to which the results indicated by yoga would fructify.

II. The Chandra Yogas

Yogas arising primarily from the Moon, the Lunar yogas, are as follows:

1. Sunapha Yoga

When the second house from the Moon is occupied by a planet, other than the Sun, the Sunapha yoga arises. This yoga bestows upon the native status, huge wealth, capacity to earn his fortune, religious inclination, virtuous pursuits and a quiet nature.

Note : The exact nature of this yoga will depend upon the nature of planet or planets causing this yoga. Several varieties of this yoga thus arise depending upon which planet occupies the second house from the Moon, and whether it is a single occupant or has other associates.

2. Anapha Yoga

This arises when there is a planet, other than the Sun, occupying the twelfth house from the Moon. This yoga makes a native healthy, amiable, famous and renowned, an orator, virtuous, capable, wealthy, given to varied comforts, and happy.

Note : Whereas the stress in the Sunapha yoga is on accumulation and possession, in the Anapha yoga it is on spending and enjoyment. As in the case of Sunapha yoga, there are numerous varieties of the Anapha yoga also, depending upon the nature and the number of the occupants of the twelfth house from the Moon.

3. Durudhara Yoga

Presence of planets in both the second and the twelfth from the Moon causes this yoga. Here again, the Sun is not to be considered. One born in this yoga earns renown through good speech, learning, valour and virtue. This yoga confers upon the native wealth, vehicles, servants, physical comforts and freedom from enemies.

Note :

(a) In Durudhara yoga, the stress is both on possession and enjoyment. When a Durudhara is formed by benefics, it is very auspicious. When malefics form this yoga, it has a constricting influence on the Moon and yields adverse results.

(b) The same principles can be extended to medical astrology also. When benefics surround the lagna or the lagna lord, they prove good for health. When malefics do so, they produce adverse results.

(c) The strength of these yogas depends upon the strength of the Moon.

4. Kemadruma Yoga

When the second and the twelfth houses from the Moon are unoccupied, it leads to the adverse Kemadruma yoga. The presence of the Sun in these houses does not make any difference.

When the Kemadruma yoga exists in any chart, the native is bereft of wife, progeny, learning and mental peace. He suffers misery, penury, physical illness and humiliation. A Kemadruma yoga destroys the benefic effects of Raja yogas.

Cancellation of the Kemadruma

A Kemadruma is said to attain cancellation under the following circumstances :

(a) Presence of planets in kendras from the lagna.

(b) Presence of planets in kendras from the Moon.

(c) All planets aspecting the Moon.

(d) Strong Moon in a kendra aspected by or associated with benefics (Mercury, Jupiter or Venus).

Note : The Moon needs a support on either side; else it proves adverse.

5. Adhi Yoga

This yoga is produced by the occupation of the sixth, seventh and eighth houses from the Moon by benefics (Mercury, Jupiter and Venus). This gives rise to high status, the command of an army, kingship and governmental recognition. This yoga further ensures good health, long life and prosperity.

Note : This yoga demands that the three benefics must occupy the three houses (6, 7 and 8) from the Moon jointly or singly (in whatever combination!). The presence of malefics in these houses spoils this yoga.

6. Dhana yoga from the Moon

All the three benefics occupying Upachaya houses (i.e., houses 3, 6, 10 or 11) from the Moon produce a very wealthy individual; two of the benefics placed in such houses give medium wealth, and only one benefic planet in any of these houses from the Moon ensures only ordinary wealth.

Note :

(a) Upachaya houses are houses of expansion.

(b) Depending upon the location of the Moon being in a kendra or a panaphara or an apoklima house as reckoned from the Sun, the wealth and learning of the individual is ordinary, medium or plenteous.

(c) The results indicated by the Chandra yogas take precedence over the results indicated by other yogas.

III. The Ravi Yogas

Yogas arising from the Sun, the Solar yogas, are as follows:

1. Veshi Yoga

Caused by the occupation of the second house from the Sun by a planet other than the Moon. Such a native is truthful, lazy, having a long stature and a balanced outlook, and has only ordinary wealth. When benefics cause this yoga, the native is eloquent and wealthy. When malefics cause it, the native is destitute and associates with wicked people.

2. Voshi Yoga

Caused by the occupation of the twelfth house from the Sun by a planet other than the Moon. This yoga bestows upon the native good learning, eloquence, charitable nature, sharp memory and generally virtuous disposition. When benefics cause this yoga, the native is intelligent, learned, strong, wealthy and engaged in scientific pursuits. Malefics causing this yoga lead to cruel nature, ugly looks, lack of intelligence and excessive lust.

3. Ubhayachari Yoga

Caused by planets other than the Moon occupying the second and the twelfth houses from the Sun. This produces a native with strong physique, capability to shoulder great responsibility, learning, good looks, wealth, and numerous objects of pleasure. When malefics cause this yoga, the native is destitute, servile and ailing.

Note : No adverse yoga results if the Sun is not associated with a planet on either side of it.

IV. Diverse Yogas

Some of the very important yogas are included in this section. They are being briefly described below in a random order.

1. Gaja-Kesari Yoga

This yoga is produced when Jupiter occupies a kendra from the Moon. One born in this yoga is wealthy, famous, learned, virtuous and honoured by the king.

Note :

(a) This is an important yoga. It occurs frequently in horoscopes and, therefore, must be studied judiciously.

(b) The yoga fructifies only if Jupiter is not combust, and is associated with or aspected by benefics. The Moon too should not be combust or debilitated, and must be under benefic influence.

(c) The exact nature of the yoga, and the extent to which it yields results, will depend upon such factors as:

    (i) Exaltation or debilitation, i.e., strength or weakness, of both Jupiter and the Moon;

    (ii) Placement of Jupiter in the first, fourth, seventh or tenth house from the Moon;

    (iii) The houses occupied by Jupiter and the Moon, when reckoned from the lagna;

    (iv) The signs or rashis in which the two planets are located;

    (v) Concurrent planetary influences on either or both of them;

    (vi) The dasha pattern.

(d) A strong Gaja-Kesari yoga leads to lasting fame.

Chart XXII-1 shows an exalted Jupiter in the tenth house from the Moon, producing a powerful Gaja-Kesari yoga. There are several planets in the twelfth house from the Moon producing an Anapha yoga. Accumulation of planets in the eighth house has its own special meaning as this house gains prominence in the horoscope. Of course, it is important to go into consideration of the vargas for finer analysis. The chart belongs to a prominent cinema artiste who dominated the screen world for several years in the recent past.

It will be appreciated that the best Gaja-kesari can occur only if the Moon and Jupiter occupy Karka, which is the own house for the Moon and the exaltation sign for Jupiter. It cannot form with both planets exalted or both in their own houses.

242

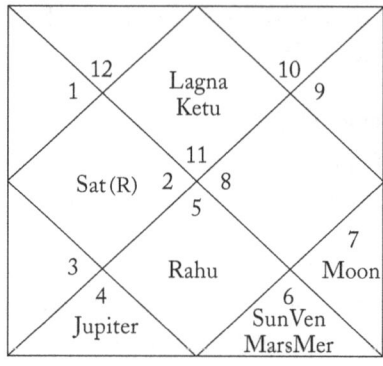

		Sat (R)	
Lagna Ketu	**Chart XXII-1** **Birth Chart** October 13, 1942	Jupiter	
		Rahu	
		Moon	Sun Ven Mars Mercury

2. Amalaa (or Amala-Kirti) Yoga

This yoga is said to exist when a natural benefic occupies the tenth house from the lagna or the Moon. Such a person is revered by the ruler, enjoys physical pleasures, is charitably disposed, likeable and helpful.

Note : The tenth house is an extremely important house of the horoscope. When benefics influence this house, one pursues legitimate and honourable means of earning, and enjoys fame as a consequence. A strong Amalaa yoga ensures lasting fame for the native.

3. Kartari Yogas

These are of two types:

(a) *Shubha-Kartari*, when natural benefics occupy houses 2 and 12 from the lagna. This yoga ensures health, wealth and fame for the native.

(b) *Papa-Kartari*, when natural malefics occupy houses 2 and 12 from the lagna. This yoga leads to criminal tendencies, ill health and impure food.

Note : This yoga is equivalent to the Durudhara yoga which forms around the Moon. The reader is referred to Chart XXIV-1 where the lagna is surrounded by the Sun in the twelfth house, and Mars and Rahu in the second house. When malefics surround the lagna or the lagna lord, health suffers.

4. Parvata Yoga

It has two variants :

(a) The seventh and the eighth houses being vacant, or occupied only by benefics, and benefics occupying the kendras; or

(b) The lord of the lagna and that of the twelfth house placed in mutual kendras, and aspected by benefics.

A native with this yoga in his horoscope is famous, wealthy, charitable, fortunate, orator, a leader, learned and lustful.

5. Chaamara Yoga

This also has two variants:

(a) Exalted lagna lord placed in a kendra and aspected by Jupiter; or

(b) Two benefics conjoined in the lagna, the seventh house, the ninth house or the tenth house.

Such a native is a king or honoured by a king, an orator, skillful, wise, and versed in sacred scriptures.

6. Shankha Yoga

This again has two variants :

(a) The fifth lord and the sixth lord are in mutual kendras, and the lagna lord is strong; or

(b) Lords of the lagna and the tenth house occupy Chara rashis (movable signs), and the ninth lord is strong.

A native with either of the above combinations in his chart is kind, virtuous, learned, long-lived, morally sound, blessed with wife and children, owns lands and enjoys prosperity.

Note : This yoga confers on the native the authority to discipline or punish.

7. Lakshmi Yoga

This yoga arises when the lagna lord is strong, and the ninth lord is in a kendra identical with its own house, Moolatrikona or exaltation.

One born in this yoga is good in looks, virtuous, very wealthy, widely renowned, honoured by the king, blessed with wives and children.

8. Lagnadhi Yoga

When benefics occupy houses seven and eight from the lagna, bereft of malefic association or aspect, this yoga is said to arise. This gives rise to a native who is learned and comfortable.

Note : Lagnadhi yoga is an equivalent of the (Chandra) Adhi yoga already mentioned. Perhaps here, the sixth house from the lagna must also be considered for occupation by benefics as in case of the Chandradhi yoga. It confers on the native virtue, high status, learning and capability of compilation or writing.

9. Maha-Bhagya Yoga

The formation of this yoga involves the following:

A. *In the horoscope of a male* :

   (a) Birth during daytime;
   (b) Odd sign rising in the lagna;
   (c) The Sun in an odd sign;
   (d) The Moon also in an odd sign.

B. *In the horoscope of a female* :

    (a) Birth during night time;

    (b) Even sign rising in the lagna;

    (c) The Sun in an even sign;

    (d) The Moon also in an even sign.

One born in Maha-Bhagya yoga is pleasant to look at, liberal, renowned, of good character, owner of lands and equivalent to a king. Women having this yoga in their chart are blessed with all feminine qualities and virtues, good fortune, good character and lots of wealth.

Note : Odd signs are masculine signs and even signs are feminine signs. It is desirable to have the lagna, the Moon and the Sun in odd signs in the horoscopes of males, and in even signs in the horoscope of females.

Chart XXII-2 belongs to the late Indian Prime Minister, Mr. Morarji Desai. The lagna, the Sun and the Moon are all situated in odd or masculine signs. Even the Navamsha lagna (Dhanu in this case) happens to be odd. The birth occurred during daytime. There is a Vipreeta Raja yoga occurring in the eighth house.

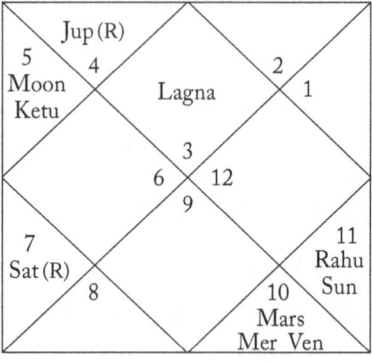

Mrs. Indira Gandhi, another late Prime Minister of India, has her birth occurring at night time, and the lagna, the Moon and the Sun all falling in even signs (**Chart XXII-3**). Even the Navamsha lagna (Meena) falls in an even sign.

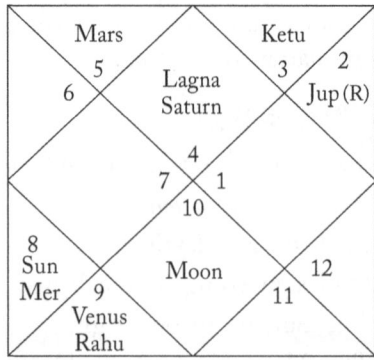

245

The chart is characterised by three sets of exchanges :

(a) Between the lagna lord and the seventh lord;

(b) Between the second lord and the fifth lord; and

(c) Between the sixth lord and the eleventh lord.

A Maha-Bhagya yoga is a highly fortunate combination.

10. Vipareeta Raja Yoga

This yoga has been discussed in the preceding chapter. It arises from the lords of the sixth or the eighth or the twelfth houses occupying one of these houses (other than their own).

11. Chandra Mangala Yoga

This too finds mention in the previous chapter. It is a combination for financial prosperity.

12. Shakata Yoga

This results when Jupiter, located in a house other than a kendra, occupies the sixth, the eighth or the twelfth from the Moon. This yoga produces a native who is destitute, ever toiling, disliked by all, with ever fluctuating fortunes.

Note :

(a) Jupiter and the Moon in mutually adverse (six/eight or two/twelve) relationship are not supposed to augur well for the native. It must, however, be realised that Jupiter's location in the 6th, the 7th or the 8th house from the Moon is also a constituent of the Chandradhi yoga. This placement, thus, cannot be considered adverse in all circumstances.

(b) Another important aspect to be considered is whether the Moon and Jupiter are strong or weak. In **Chart XXII-4**, Jupiter is located in the sixth house from the Moon, thus producing a typical Shakata yoga. However, both the planets occupy their own houses, and Jupiter additionally happens to be in its Moolatrikona sign. The lagna is strong because of the placement of the lagna lord in the lagna itself. This chart belongs to Mr Jawaharlal Nehru, the first Prime Minister of India.

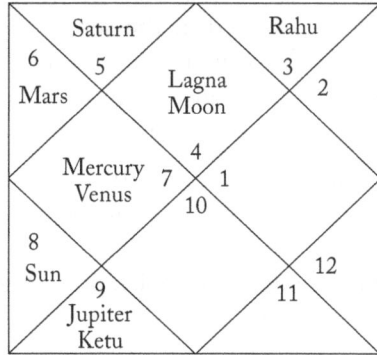

13. Chatussaagara yoga

This combination arises when :

(a) All planets occupy the four kendras; or

(b) All planets occupy the Chara rashis (i.e., signs 1, 4, 7 and 10).

This yoga destroys numerous Arishta yogas and ensures wealth and high status to the native.

Note : According to one view, this yoga is said to exist when all four kendras are occupied. See the horoscope of Lord Rama, **Chart XXII-5**, in this connection. Four planets are exalted and one is located in its own house. A strong Gaja-Kesari yoga is obtained in the lagna while three Pancha-Mahapurusha yogas, involving the lagna., the fourth house and the seventh house are also there. All four kendras are occupied by planets. The kendras are the pillars of a horoscope and their occupation bestows immense strength upon them. A malefic in the fourth house deprived lord Rama of comforts at home; another malefic in the seventh house led to separation from wife.

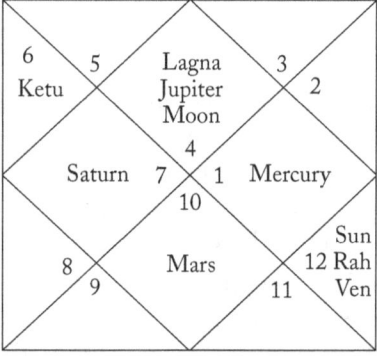

14. Daridra Yoga

A special Daridra yoga has been described to obtain when the seven planets from the Sun to Saturn are placed in contiguous houses in such a manner that a planet next in natural order is placed in the preceding house. In other words, Venus is placed in the second house from Saturn, Jupiter in the second from Venus, Mercury in the second from Jupiter, Mars in the second from Mercury, the Moon in the second from Mars, and the Sun in the second from the Moon. This yoga is said to cause extreme penury and destitution.

Note : It will be appreciated that such a yoga cannot exist in the Rashi chart. It is perhaps intended to be examined in the Navamsha chart. Classical writers have given us certain peculiar combinations without giving any hints about their application. A great field exists for a serious researcher of astrology.

15. Hatha-Hantaa Yoga

This yoga arises when the Moon is located in the eleventh house and the Sun in the Moon's sign (Karka). The native with this yoga in the horoscope suffers humiliation (or death!) as a consequence of some stupid action of his.

16. Neecha-Bhanga Raja Yoga

This yoga indicates cancellation of debilitation of a planet. Cancellation of debilitation is supposed to produce benefic results or give rise to a Raja yoga. A planet achieves Neecha-Bhanga when :

(a) The lord of the house where a planet is debilitated (i.e., the debilitation lord of the planet) is in a kendra from the lagna or the Moon.

(b) The exaltation lord of the debilitated planet is in a kendra from the lagna or the Moon.

(c) The debilitated planet is associated with or aspected by its debilitation lord.

(d) The debilitated planet is associated with or aspected by its exaltation lord.

(e) The debilitated planet exchanges houses with its debilitation lord.

(f) Two debilitated planets aspect each other.

Note : Neecha planets, because of their inherent weakness, generally give adverse results during their dashas. When a Neecha-Bhanga yoga is present, the debilitation yields place to a benefic situation.

Chart XX-3 (see Nabhasa yogas) shows two planets, Mars and Jupiter, debilitated in the lagna and the seventh house. A typical Neecha-Bhanga obtains here as Mars recieves the aspect of its Uchcha-naatha (lord of exaltation sign) and Jupiter associates with its Uchcha-naatha, the Moon, as well as its Neecha-naatha (lord of debilitation sign) Saturn.

V. Pravrajya Yogas

These yogas, also known as *Sanyasa yogas*, lead to a renunciation or giving up of worldly attachments. There are several combinations which lead to detachment from woldly things. Some of these are being mentioned here.

1. When the lord of the tenth house associates with four planets in a kendra or in a trikona, the native achieves emancipation after death.

   Note : It is desirable that such a combination does not occur in adverse houses, and no planet participating in this yoga formation should be combust. Else it leads to a fall from the state of final emancipation, the Yoga-Bhrashta of the Gita.

   Chart XXII-6 belongs to Acharya Rajneesh. Five planets, including the lord of the tenth house, are posited together. But the combination occurs in the eighth house of inter-ruptions, obstacles, intrigues and uncertainties.

248

Rahu		Lagna	
	Chart XXII-6 **Birth Chart** December 11, 1931		Jup (R)
MonSat MarVen Mer	Sun		Ketu

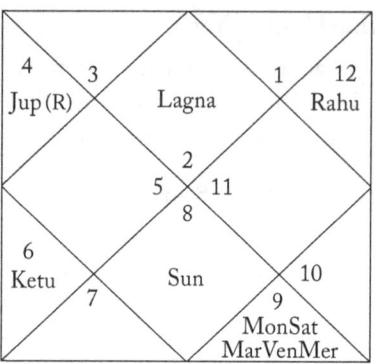

If the Gita is to be believed, such a native must return with considerable yogic merit in his karmic balance.

2. The Moon in the Drekkana of Saturn aspected by Mars and Saturn, or in the Navamsha of Mars aspected by Saturn.

3. Lord of the Moon sign aspected by Saturn alone and by no other planet.

4. Lord of the Moon sign aspected by the remaining planets situated together in one house.

5. Jupiter occupying the ninth house, and the lagna, the Moon and Jupiter all aspected by Saturn: Such a native attains recognition because of founding a system of philosophy.

...XXIII...
Mathematical Calculation of Longevity

पश्येम शरदःशतं जीवेम शरदःशतं शृणुयाम शरदःशतम्।
प्रब्रवाम शरदःशतमदीनाः स्याम शरदःशतम्॥

May I see for a hundred years, live for a hundred years, hear for a hundred years. May I speak for a hundred years, live in comfort and freedom for a hundred years.   Yajurveda XXVI/24

Sages opine that good and bad results on the basis of planetary combinations in a horoscope must only be pronounced after determining the length of life. It is fruitless to make any prediction if the native is not going to live long enough for the prediction to materialise. For general purposes of astrology, the life of a native may fall under one of the following categories.

1. *Balarishta* or age upto 8 years. During this period, the survival of a child is subject to combinations of Balarishta and Arishta-Bhanga.

2. *Yogarishta*, from 8 to 20 years. This is a difficult area and an exact length of survival during this period is a matter of very fine judgement on the part of an astrologer.

3. *Alpayu* or short span, upto 32 years of life.

4. *Madhyayu* or medium life span, from 32 to 70 years (or 66 years according to some).

5. *Poornayu* or full length of life, from 70 to 100 years (or more).

Determination of span of Life

Determination of longevity is a difficult area of astrology. The availability of numerous methods of longevity determination only indicates that no one method is totally reliable. A general method of deciding on short, medium or full life span involves the consideration of three groups of factors :

Group I.   (a) Lagna lord, and   (b) the eighth lord.

Group II.   (a) Lagna, and   (b) the Moon.

Group III.   (a) Lagna, and   (b) the Hora lagna.

In each of the three groups above, there are two components. See which rashis these two components (a) and (b) fall into. The placement of each of the two factors (a) and (b) provides the life span indicated by the concerned group thus :

1. If both (a) and (b) fall in Chara rashis: Poornayu
2. Both in Sthira rashis: Alpayu
3. Both in Dwiswabhava rashis: Madhyayu
4. One in Chara and the other in Sthira: Madhyayu
5. One in Chara and the other in Dwiswabhava: Alpayu
6. One in Sthira and the other in Dwiswabhava: Poornayu

If all three groups or any two of these indicate the same life span, that must be considered as final. In case the three groups indicate three different life spans, consider the one indicated by Group III (i.e., lagna and the Hora lagna).

In case the three groups indicate three different life spans, but there is the Moon located in the lagna or the seventh house, consider the life span indicated by Group II (i.e., lagna and the Moon).

Determination of the Hora lagna

The Hora lagna for the purposes of longevity demands some elucidation. It may be determined as below.

Step I   Find out the number of hours and minutes that have elapsed from the time of sunrise to the time of birth.

Step II   Consider the hours as rashis (divide by 12 if their number exceeds 12, and accept the remainder). Divide the minutes by 2 and consider them as degrees. These rashis and degrees may be called as the Ishta-Kaala.

Step III   Obtain the Hora lagna thus:

(a) If the lagna is even, add the Ishta-Kaala to the cusp of the lagna.

(b) If the lagna is odd, add the Ishta-Kaala to the longitude of the Sun.

Example

Native born at 4:30am (IST) on March 12, 1957 at Lat. 32°N43', Long. 074°E52'.

Lagna: Makara 10°38'; Sun: Kumbha 27°51'; Moon: Mithuna 29°56'; Mars: Vrisha 3°01'; Mercury: Kumbha 19°50'; Jupiter (R): Kanya 4°22'; Venus: Kumbha 19°20'; Saturn: Vrishchika 20°55'; Rahu: Tula 28°26'; Ketu: Mesha 28°26'.

This is the same as **Chart XXI-5** under Dhana yogas (q.v.).

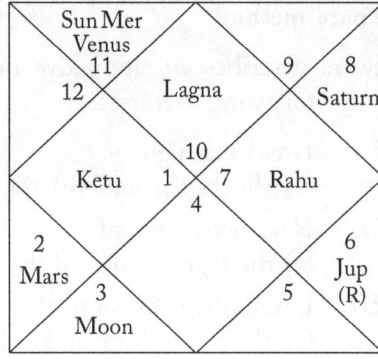

	Ketu	Mars	Moon
Sun Mercury Venus	**Chart XXI-5** **Birth Chart** March 12, 1957		
Lagna			
	Saturn	Rahu	Jup (R)

Sunrise (on March 11, 1957) = 6:49 a.m.

No. of hours elapsed from sunrise to time of birth =
     28 hours 30 minutes (i.e., the time of birth) *minus*
     6 hours 49 minutes (sunrise),

or   21 hours 41 minutes.

Ishta-Kaala, converted to signs, degrees, etc.,

     $21^s20.5°$

or $9^s20°30'$

Since the birth lagna is even, the Hora lagna is obtained by adding the Ishta-Kaala to the cusp of the birth lagna.

	s	°	'
Thus,			
the lagna	9	10	38
Ishta-Kaala	9	20	30
Hora lagna	19	1	8

or (removing multiples of 12 signs)
     $7^s1°8'$, i.e., Vrishchika 1°8'.

Considering the above three groups of longevity, we have :

Group I	Lagna lord (Saturn)	Sthira (Vrishchika)
	Eighth lord	Sthira (Simha)
	Longevity	Alpayu (short span)
Group II	Lagna	Chara (Makara)
	Moon	Dwiswabhava (Mithuna)
	Longevity	Alpayu (short span)
Group III	Lagna	Chara (Makara)
	Hora lagna	Sthira (Vrishchika)
	Longevity	Madhyayu (medium span)

Since two of the above groups indicate Alpayu (short life span), that must be accepted.

An alternate method

Mantreswara describes an alternative method of finding the life span by considering the following factors :

Group I: Drekkana sign of
           (a) the lagna, and (b) the Moon

Group II: Navamsha sign of
           (a) the lagna lord, and (b) lord of the Moon sign

Group III: Dwadashamsha sign of
           (a) the lagna lord and (b) the eighth lord.

Applying these principles to the example chart above, we have:

Group I   Lagna Drekkana sign   Sthira (Vrisha)
            Moon's Drekkana sign   Sthira (Kumbha)
            Longevity   Alpayu (short span)

           Note : Construct a Drekkana chart for this.

Group II   Sign occupied by the lagna lord
            (Saturn) in the Navamsha chart: Chara (Makara)
            Sign occupied by the lord of the Moon sign
            (Mercury) in the Navamsha chart: Dwiswabhava (Meena)
            Longevity   Alpayu (short span)

           Note : See the Navamsha chart for this.

Group III   Sign occupied by the lagna lord
            (Saturn) in the Dwadashamsha chart: Chara (Karka)
            Sign occupied by the eighth lord
            (Sun) in the Dwadashamsha chart: Chara (Makara)
            Longevity   Poornayu (Full span)

           Note : Construct a Dwadashamsha chart for this purpose.

Since two of the above groups indicate Alpayu, that must be accepted.

It may be noted here that this method of Mantreshwara deserves to be researched on. It has been applied less often in actual horoscopes.

Other combinations that indicate the length of life are as follows :

1. All benefics in kendras: Poornayu

2. All benefics in panapharas: Madhyayu

3. All benefics in apoklimas: Alpayu

4. Eighth lord and all malefics in kendras: Alpayu

5. Eighth lord and all malefics in panapharas: Madhyayu

6. Eighth lord and all malefics in apoklimas: Poornayu

7. Strong lagna lord, benefics in kendras, and malefics in
   houses 3, 6, 11:   Poornayu

8. Stronger of the lagna lord and the eighth lord in a
   kendra indicates Poornayu, in a panaphara Madhyayu,
   and in an apoklima   Alpayu.

9. Lagna lord and the eighth lord located in their own
   houses ensure Poornayu, in the houses of neutrals
   Madhyayu, and in inimical houses   Alpayu.

10. Weak lagna lord in the houses 6, 8 or 12, bereft of
    benefic aspect: Alpayu

11. Malefics in kendras, bereft of benefic aspect, and the
    lagna lord being weak: Alpayu

12. Malefics in houses 2 and 12, sans benefic aspect: Alpayu

Methods of Mathematical Calculation of Longevity

It may be pointed out at the outset that mathematical methods of calculation of longevity do not always prove accurate in actual horoscopes. The actual length of life appears to be a divine secret not to be deciphered too easily. There are several methods available some of which are being described below.

I. PINDAYU

According to this method of calculation of longevity, the seven planets, from the Sun to Saturn, contribute 19, 25, 15, 12, 15, 21 and 20 years respectively, when at their points of exaltation. They each contribute half this period (i.e., 9.5, 12.5, 7.5, 6, 7.5, 10.5 and 10 years respectively) at their points of debilitation. Between deep exaltation and deep debilitation, they contribute proportional amounts.

Step I :   Find out the distance of a planet from its point of debilitation by subtracting this latter point from the longitude of the planet. This gives the 'arc' of longevity.

Note: The same 'arc' of longevity is obtained by subtracting either of the planet's longitude and its debilitation point from the other. In case the result exceeds 180 degrees (six signs), this must be subtracted from 360 degrees (or 12 signs).

Step II :   Since 180 degrees (between exaltation and debi-litation) corresponds to half the age contributed by the planet, find the actual age contributed by the arc of longevity, from the number of degrees the planet is removed from its debilitation point.

Step III :   Add the above value to half the age contributed by the planet (since this amount is contributed by the planet anyway, even at deep debilitation).

Let us apply this information to the example chart being considered in this chapter.

SUN

	s	°	'
Debilitation point	6	10	0
Sun's present position	10	27	51
Arc of longevity	4	17	51

or 137° 51'

Sun's contribution = 9.5 (i.e., half the Sun's contribution)

$$+ \frac{9.5 \times 137°51'}{180}$$

= 16.775 years.

MOON

	s	°	'
Debilitation point	7	3	0
Moon's present position	2	29	56
Arc of longevity	4	3	4

or 123° 4'

Moon's contribution $= 12.5 + \dfrac{12.5 \times 123°4'}{180}$

= 21.046 years.

MARS

	s	°	'
Debilitation point	3	28	0
Mar's present position	1	3	1
Arc of longevity	2	24	59

or 84° 59'

Mar's contribution $= 7.5 + \dfrac{7.5 \times 84°59'}{180}$

= 11.041 years.

MERCURY

	s	°	'
Debilitation point	11	15	0
Mercury's present position	10	19	50
Arc of longevity	0	25	10

or 25° 10'

Mercury's contribution $= 6 + \dfrac{6 \times 25°10'}{180}$

= 6.839 years.

JUPITER

	s	°	'
Debilitation point	9	5	0
Jupiter's present position	5	4	22
Arc of longevity	4	0	38

or 120° 38'

$$\text{Jupiter's contribution} \quad = \quad 7.5 + \frac{7.5 \times 120°38'}{180}$$

$$= 12.526 \text{ years.}$$

VENUS

	s	°	′
Debilitation point	5	27	0
Venus's present position	10	19	20
Arc of longevity	4	22	20

or   142° 22′

$$\text{Venus's contribution} \quad = \quad 10.5 + \frac{10.5 \times 142°22'}{180}$$

$$= 18.803 \text{ years.}$$

SATURN

	s	°	′
Debilitation point	0	20	0
Saturn's present position	7	20	55
Arc of longevity	4	29	5

or   149° 05′

$$\text{Saturn's contribution} \quad = \quad 10 + \frac{10 \times 149°05'}{180}$$

$$= 18.282 \text{ years.}$$

Note: Detailed steps in actual determination of the arc of longevity have been omitted in the above calculations. See 'Note' to Step I, wide supra, for details.

Thus the years contributed by the seven planets are as follows:

Sun	16.775
Moon	21.046
Mars	11.041
Mercury	6.839
Jupiter	12.526
Venus	18.803
Saturn	18.282

Haranas or Reductions

The above values of longevity contributed by the seven planets are subjected to four stages of Haranas or reductions. These are as follows :

A. *Astangata Harana* (a reduction consequent upon combustion)

Planets become combust when close to the Sun. Their limits are as follows :

Moon	within 12° of the Sun.
Mars	within 17° of the Sun.
Mercury	within 14° of the Sun.
	(within 12° if retrograde)
Jupiter	within 11° of the Sun.
Venus	within 10° of the Sun.
	(within 8° if retrograde)
Saturn	within 15° of the Sun.

A combust planet loses half his contributed years.

Exceptions : Saturn and Venus. They are not subject to reduction due to combustion.

The example chart shows conjunction of Venus and Mercury with the Sun. Both are combust but only Mercury loses half its contributed years.

The years contributed by the seven planets after Astangata Harana would thus be :

Sun	16.775
Moon	21.046
Mars	11.041
Mercury	3.419 (reduced by half)
Jupiter	12.526
Venus	18.803
Saturn	18.282

B. *Shatru-Kshetra Harana* (or reduction consequent upon occupation of an enemy's house): One-third of the contributed age (after Astangata Harana stage) is lost if a planet is in an enemy's house.

Exceptions :

(i) Retrograde planets.

(ii) Mars, according to some.

In the example chart, the Sun, Jupiter and Saturn occupy the houses of their natural enemies. Of these, Jupiter is retrograde and falls under exceptions. The Sun and Saturn, however, lose their contributed age by one-third.

Thus, the years contributed by the seven planets after Shatru-Kshetra Harana are :

Sun	11.183
Moon	21.046
Mars	11.041
Mercury	3.419
Jupiter	12.526
Venus	18.803
Saturn	12.188

C. *Chakrapaata Harana* (or reduction consequent upon the placement of planets in the six houses, from the seventh house to the twelfth house). This reduction is more if the planets are in the twelfth house, and progressively less as they occupy houses 11, 10, 9, 8 and 7. Benefics cause half the loss as compared to malefics.

House occupied	Loss from malefics	Loss from benefics
12	whole	one half
11	one half	one-fourth
10	one-third	one-sixth
9	one-fourth	one-eighth
8	one-fifth	one-tenth
7	one-sixth	one-twelfth

Note:

(a) When there are multiple planets in one house, only the strongest planet causes reduction in the contributed age.

(b) Weak Moon is not to be considered a malefic in longevity calculation.

In the example chart: Saturn, a malefic, in the eleventh house loses half its contribution. Jupiter, a benefic, in the ninth house loses one-eighth of its contribution.

The years contributed by the seven planets after the Chakrapata reduction are:

Sun	11.183
Moon	21.046
Mars	11.041
Mercury	3.419
Jupiter	10.960
Venus	18.803
Saturn	6.094
Total	82.546 years

D. *Krurodaya Harana* (or reduction consequent upon the occupation of the lagna by a malefic): This reduction is applied if the lagna is occupied by a malefic (Sun, Mars or Saturn). The procedure here is thus :

(a) Convert the degrees, etc., of the lagna into minutes.

(b) Multiply the above minutes by the age contributed by *each planet*.

(c) Divide the value obtained by *Chakraliptaa* (i.e., 21,600 minutes; i.e., the total number of minutes in the zodiac).

(d) The quotient is reduced from the total Ayu or span of life obtained earlier. This gives the span of life according to the Pindayu calculation.

Note :

(i)   If the malefics occupy the lagna but there is also a benefic aspect, only half the reduction is to be applied.

(ii) If the lagna is occupied by both malefics and benefics, the planet nearest to the degree of the lagna must be considered. For example, if a benefic lies closer to the degree of the lagna compared to a malefic, this reduction is not applied.

(iii) Another method to obtain the Krurodaya reduction is thus:

The number of the Navamsha rising in the lagna, multiplied by the age contributed by each planet, and divided by 108 (the total number of Navamshas in the zodiac). The quotient is reduced from the total span of life. The maximum reduction to be effected could reach upto one-twelfth of the total longevity in case the lagna happens to be at the very end of a sign.

In the example chart, the lagna is not occupied by malefics. The Krurodaya reduction is thus not applicable here.

Contribution from the lagna

Some authorities suggest that age contributed by the lagna should be added to the total Pindayu obtained from the above method. This is calculated as follows :

(a)   *If the lord of the lagna is stronger:* The completed signs indicating the lagna represent the number of years, while the degrees and minutes of the lagna represent the equivalent months and days (i.e., one sign or 30 degrees represent one year).

(b)   *If the lord of the navamsha lagna is stronger:* The navamsha rising in the lagna represents the number of years, months and days to be contributed. The method for this is the same as that for finding out the contribution of lagna in Amshayu (Vide infra).

(c)   *If the lagna lord and the navamsha lord are equally strong:* Add the total contribution from both to the Pindayu already obtained.

II. AMSHAYU

The procedure for this method of longevity determination involves the following steps.

Step 1   Convert the signs, degrees and minutes of a planet's longitude, as well as the lagna into minutes.

Step 2   Divide each of the above separately by 200.

Step 3   If the quotient is more than twelve, divide it by 12 to obtain the number of years.

Step 4   The remainder obtained from step 2 gives the fraction of the year (in months, days, etc.).

Step 5   The total life span contributed by the lagna as well as the various planets is subjected to the Bharanas (additions) and Haranas (reductions) to obtain the actual age.

Let us apply this method to the example chart.

	Planet	Longitude	Minutes	Contributed years Divided by 200
1.	Sun	327° 51'	19671	98.355
2.	Moon	89° 56'	5396	26.980
3.	Mars	33° 01'	1981	9.995
4.	Mercury	319° 50'	19190	95.950
5.	Jupiter	154° 22'	9262	46.310
6.	Venus	319° 20'	19160	95.800
7.	Saturn	230° 55'	13855	69.275
8.	Lagna	280° 38'	16838	84.190

The actual years of Amshayu contributed by the different planets and the lagna are as follows :

Sun	2.355	(obtained by removing multiples of 12 from contributed years, i.e., 98.355)
Moon	2.980	
Mars	9.995	
Mercury	11.950	
Jupiter	10.310	
Venus	11.800	
Saturn	9.275	
Lagna	0.190	

The Bharanas (or additions)

(a) Exaltation, retrogression: treble the contributed age.
(b) Vargottama, own house, own Navamsha, or own Drekkana: Double the contributed age.
(c) Where several multiplications crop up, apply only one which is the highest.

In the example chart, the *Moon* is Vargottama; *Mercury* is in its own Drekkana; *Jupiter* is retrograde and *Saturn* is in its own Navamsha. Jupiter's contribution is trebled while that of the others is doubled. The Amshayu, in years, after the Bharanas, would be:

Sun	2.355
Moon	5.960
Mars	9.995
Mercury	23.900
Jupiter	30.930
Venus	11.800
Saturn	18.550
Lagna	0.190

The Haranas (or reductions)

These are similar to those in Pindayu calculation except that the Krurodaya reduction is not applied here. In addition, if several reductions are applicable to a planet, only the larger reduction must be applied.

We have already seen in the example chart that :

1. Astangata reduction (one-half) applies to Mercury;

2. Shatru-Kshetra reduction (one-third) applies to the Sun and Saturn (Jupiter being retrograde is an exception); and

3. Chakrapaata reduction applies to Saturn (one-half) and Jupiter (one-eighth).

Note : Since Saturn is subject to two reductions, Shatru-Kshetra and Chakrapaata, only the larger one, i.e., the Chakrapaata, is applicable.

The contributed Amshayu will thus be:

Sun	1.177
Moon	5.960
Mars	9.995
Mercury	11.950
Jupiter	27.064
Venus	11.800
Saturn	9.275
Lagna	0.190
Total	77.411 years

III. NISARGAYU

From birth onwards, the various planets contribute a fixed number of years in a fixed order, as follows:

Moon	1	year
Mars	2	years
Mercury	9	years
Venus	20	years
Jupiter	18	years
Sun	20	years
Saturn	50	years

Principles of Pindayu apply to the determination of Nisargayu also.

Note:

(i) It has been said that of the Sun, the Moon and the lagna:

    (a) If the lagna is the strongest, apply Amshayu.

    (b) If the Sun is the strongest, apply Pindayu.

    (c) If the Moon is the strongest, apply Nisargayu

(ii) It may be pointed out that methods of calculation of longevity by mathematical means are generally unsatisfactory. Dependance on the determination of the life-span (e.g., Alpayu, Madhyayu and Poornayu) as mentioned earlier, co-ordinated with appropriate maraka or adverse dasha periods, gives more reliable results.

Death-inflicting Dashas

Mention has been made of the role of marakas elsewhere. A few additional points are made here:

1. If in the order of the Vimshottari main dasha, the fourth dasha belongs to Saturn, or the fifth to Mars, or the sixth to Jupiter, or the seventh to Rahu, these dashas can prove fatal (or adverse for health).

2. If the Vimshottari dasha of a combust or debilitated or otherwise weak planet happens to be the third or the fifth or the seventh in order, it is again to be watched.

3. The dashas of Chhidra grahas or vulnerable planets can also cause death or disease. The Chhidra grahas are:

    (a) The eighth house lord.

    (b) Occupant of the eighth house.

    (c) Planet aspecting the eighth house.

    (d) Owner of the 22nd Drekkana (from the lagna).

    (e) Associate of the eighth house lord.

    (f) Owner of the 64th Navamsha (from the Moon).

    (g) The bitter enemy (Adhi-shatru) of the eighth lord.

Note : Since determination of longevity is a difficult subject, and the mathematical formulae unreliable in this regard, a great caution must be exercised in making predictions about longevity and time of death.

...XXIV...

Astrology of Health and Disease

न तस्य रोगो न जरा न मृत्युः
प्राप्तस्य योगाग्निमयं शरीरम् ॥

For the one who has attained a body made of the fire of Yoga, there exists neither disease nor senescence nor death.

Shvetashvatara Upanishad II/12

Analysis of an astrological chart in respect of health and disease is often a matter of fine judgement. It requires a judicious balancing of the often conflicting factors which tend to cause ill-health on the one hand, and protect the native on the other. This means that a horoscope has to be judged:

(a) For inherent strength, which ensures good health and re-covery from disease; and

(b) For inherent weakness which manifests as illness at times indicated by the dasha pattern.

Status of Health

The folowing factors must be considered in order to determine the soundness, or otherwise, of health.

1. *The lagna*: The single most important factor for sound health is the sound-ness of the lagna (and its lord). A lagna is strong and ensures good health if it is :

   (a) Occupied by its own lord;

   (b) Aspected by its own lord;

   (c) Occupied by natural benefics;

   (d) Aspected by natural benefics;

   (e) Occupied by strong or exalted planets;

   (f) Occupied or aspected by fuctional benefics;

   (g) Unaspected or un-occupied by natural or functional malefics.

Note : The nearer a benefic planet is to the cusp of the lagna, the stronger does the lagna become. Conjunctions within one degree have a very profound influence.

A lagna becomes weak if it is:

(a) Neither occupied nor aspected by its own lord;

(b) Neither occupied nor aspected by natural benefics;

(c) Neither occupied nor aspected by functional benefics;

(d) Occupied or aspected by natural malefics and functional malefics;

(e) Occupied by debilitated or weak planets.

Note : If a debilitated or a weak planet is placed within one degree of the cusp of the lagna, it has an adverse influence on the soundness of health.

2. *The lagna lord*: For a sound health, the lagna lord must be:

(a) Strong or exalted in the Rashi chart as well as the vargas;

(b) Associated with benefics;

(c) Aspected by benefics;

(d) Placed in benefic houses.

A lagna lord behaves adversely if it is :

(a) Weak or debilitated in the Rashi chart and the vargas;

(b) Associated with malefics;

(c) Aspected by malefics;

(d) Placed in adverse houses, e.g., houses 6, 8 or 12.

Note :

(a) Here again, a close association of the lagna lord with a benefic or a malefic is important. Planets located within one degree of the lagna lord exert a more intense influence.

(b) When the lagna or the lagna lord are Vargottama (falling in the same sign in the Rashi as well as the Navamsha charts), they become particularly strong and capable of withstanding several adverse influences.

3. *Status of the Moon*: Strength of the Moon is important for maintenance of sound health. Adverse placement (in the sixth, eighth or twelfth) of the Moon leads to ill health in childhood (Balarishta). Association or aspect of malefics or opposition by malefics is equally adverse. If there are combinations in the horoscope which protect the native in childhood, ill health is likely to occur later when the cycle of dashas gets involved in the 'Balarishta' combination. In other words, a Balarishta acts as a weakness in the horoscope which may manifest in later years during an appropriate dasha.

4. *The role of Kendras and Trikonas*: The kendras are like four pillars of a horoscope. Along with the trikonas, they form the most important houses of a horoscopic chart. Benefics located in the kendras and the trikonas go a long way to ensure sound health for the native. When malefics are placed in these houses, they indicate disease.

   Note : Retrograde benefics do not protect against disease. Instead they cause ill health during their dasha or antardasha. Retrograde malefics are worse. Retrograde benefics aspected by natural malefics, as also direct benefics aspected by retrograde natural malefics, also behave adversely.

5. *The Tri-shadayas*: Houses 3, 6 and 11 are considered bad houses. Their lords too behave adversely. When natural malefics are located in these houses, they indicate sound health. It may, however, be pointed out that while the presence of malefics in these houses protects the native against ill health in general, the dashas and antardashas of these planets do disturb health. The lords of these houses also cause ill health during their dashas.

6. *The eighth house/eighth lord*: The eighth house is the house of longevity. Malefics in the eighth house cause chronic or incurable ailments. Saturn, though a malefic, is an exception; it ensures sound health and long life by its occupation of the eighth house.

   For good health and long life, the eighth lord must be strong and under benefic influences.

   Note : If the lagna and the eighth house are strong in the Sarvashtakavarga, it is good for health. When these two houses are weak in the Sarvashta-kavarga, they indicate poor health.

7. *Role of the Yogas*: When strong and benefic yogas form in relation to the lagna or the lagna lord, they are good for health. One must carefully look for :

   (a) Formation of Raja yogas in the lagna.

   (b) Involvement of the lagna lord in the formation of the Raja yogas.

   (c) Benefic Durudhara formation around the lagna or the lagna lord.

   Note : A Durudhara is generally described in relation to the Moon when planets other than the Sun occupy the second and the twelfth places from it. When benefics occupy the second and the twelfth places from the lagna or the lagna lord, it forms a benefic Durudhara, or a 'Shubha-kartari yoga'. When malefics form a Durudhara around the lagna or the lagna lord, they indicate adverse health. A direct malefic in the twelfth house from the lagna/lagna lord, and a retrograde one in the second from it, is a particularly adverse combination since two malefics approach the lagna/lagna lord from the two sides and tend to strangulate it.

8. *Appropriate Dasha*: It must be realised that planetary dis-position in a chart indicates a fixed promise. This needs the operation of a dynamic component, in the form of an appropriate dasha, to manifest itself. Thus, ill health will only accrue if the relevant adverse dasha comes into operation. Thus, both the promise of ill health and the relevant dasha are important. The dasha results can be more accurately deciphered if planetary transits are combined with the dashas.

Houses, Signs and Parts of the Body

In order to locate the site of disease, one must be aware of the parts of the body indicated by each house of the horoscope or the sign of the zodiac. They are as follows:

House	*Sign*	*Part of the body*
First house	Mesha	Head
Second house	Vrisha	Face; right eye
Third house	Mithuna	Shoulders; upper limb; right ear
Fourth house	Karka	Chest
Fifth house	Simha	Heart; stomach
Sixth house	Kanya	Intestines
Seventh house	Tula	Umbilical region
Eighth house	Vrishchika	Generative organs
Ninth house	Dhanu	Hips; thighs
Tenth house	Makara	Knees
Eleventh house	Kumbha	Legs; left ear
Twelfth house	Meena	Feet; left eye

The Role of Drekkanas

Drekkanas are supposed to have a special relevance to medical astrology. Depending upon which Drekkana is rising in the lagna, it may be possible to locate the site of disease in the body.

The three Drekkanas represent three divisions of the body :

(a) From the head to the mouth;

(b) From the neck to the navel; and

(c) From the pelvis to the feet.

The various parts of the body depending upon the rising Drekkana, are indicated in Table XXIV-1.

266

Table XXIV-1
Drekkanas and Body Parts Based on the Drekkana rising in the lagna.

House	Ist Drekkana	2nd Drekkana	3rd Drekkana
1st	Head	Neck	Pelvis
2nd	Right eye	Right shoulder	Organ of generation
3rd	Right ear	Right arm	Right testicle
4th	Right nostril	Right side of body	Right thigh
5th	Right cheek	Right side (atrium & ventricle) of the heart.	Right knee
6th	Right jaw	Right lung & breast	Right calf
7th	Mouth	Naval	Legs and feet
8th	Left jaw	Left lung & breast	Left calf
9th	Left cheek	Left side of the heart	Left knee
10th	Left nostril	Left arm	Left thigh
11th	Left ear	Left arm	Left testicle
12th	Left eye	Left shoulder	Anus

The Planets

Success in making any predictions depends on an understanding of the inter-action among the planets, the houses as well as the signs. Different planets provide specific indications relevant to medical astrology. Very briefly, they are given below.

Sun   Pitta (the bile element); heart and eye disease; gall bladder disease; burns.

Moon   Kapha (the phlegm element); mental stability; menstrual disorders; diseases of the breast.

Mars   Pitta; accidents and surgical operations; burns; menstrual disorders; the bone marrow.

Mercury   All the three doshas, i.e., Vaata (the wind element), Pitta and Ka-pha; discrimination; nervous breakdown; temperament; skin disease.

Jupiter   Kapha; liver; gall bladder; diabetes; obesity.

Venus   Vaata and Kapha; sexual perversions; venereal disease; eye sight; urinary system; intestines; appendix.

Saturn   Vaata; chronic or incurable disease; paralysis; diseases of legs and feet.

Rahu/Ketu Chronic and incurable diseases; poisoning; snake bite; worm infes-tations; viral diseases; eruptive fevers.

Diagnosis of an Illness

It may be pointed out here that making a diagnosis on the basis of a horoscopic chart is a difficult area. The modern allopathic diagnosis demands an elaborate understanding of the pathogenesis of a disease and requires long years of training. The astrological methods could not be any simpler. To make any coherent diagnosis on astrological grounds, without understanding the process of disease, is not at all possible. Some self-styled astro-diagnosticians may resent these strong remarks. However, at best, they can only indicate that a given native is suffering from a heart disease or a kidney ailment or some intestinal trouble. This information is often provided by the patient himself and the astrologer need not go into the rigours of his techniques. An astrologer can only be helpful if he is able to provide an elaborate scientific diagnosis, and guide the physician in his treatment process.

Unfortunately, the allopathic system has not strived to understand the basis of the erstwhile vastly prevalent, and far more efficient, system of Ayurveda. It is much easier to use astrology to indicate the basis of an illness according to the Ayurvedic principles. Some method of translating the ancient Ayurveda into modern allopathy, and vice versa, has to be evolved for the benefit not only of astrology but of allopathy and Ayurveda as well. Until then, the actual diagnosis of disease is best left to the physician or the researching astro-physician.

Timing an Illness

Far less tedious than making an astrological diagnosis is the area of timing a likely illness and determining its outcome. This needs the application of some standard principles of astrology. They are briefly discussed below.

1. *Dasha of functional malefics*: Elsewhere, while discussing the nature of planets, mention has been made of planets which behave as malefics depending upon the lordship of houses in a horoscopic chart. Natural benefics can behave as malefics if they own adverse houses. It is the lagna which decides the nature of various planets.

   Since the lagna stands for the body of the native, planets adversely disposed toward a particular lagna can indicate ill health. It is important to carefully study the nature of planets whose dasha is operating at a given time.

2. *Role of the Trika houses/Trika lords*: Particularly important in causing ill health are the dashas and antaradashas of the lords of the Trika houses, or houses 6, 8 and 12. Lords of these houses transmit their maleficence to other planets whom they aspect or associate with. Planets placed in Trika houses are also adverse and cause chronic ailments.

3. *Retrograde planets*: Dashas of rerograde planets, more so when they are located in the kendras or in association with the lagna lord, produce ill health during their dasha periods.

4. *Weak planets*: Dashas of planets which are combust, ill-placed or debilitated, particularly if they do not regain strength in the Navamsha or other divi-

268

sional charts, are also adverse for health. If the dasha lord is weak, there is poor resistance against disease and general lack of strength.

5. *The Rahu-Ketu Axis (RKA)*: The RKA falling on the lagna or the dasha lords tends to afflict them and ensures ill health, if other indications for ill health exist in the chart.

6. *Lords of 22nd Drekkana/64th Navamsha*: These are additional adverse factors for health.

7. *Protective influences* : Whenever a chart is being examined for health and disease, particular attention should be paid toward factors that protect against illness. When there are strong influences protecting a native, mild fluctuations in dasha sequence do not disturb health. In this connection, favourble transits must also be taken note of. Unfavourable transits have contrary influence.

8. *The dasha sequence*: This is important in deciding the outcome of disease. In general, the dasha sequence has the following influence :

    (a) Favourable dasha followed by an unfavourable dasha : Occurrence of disease

    (b) Unfavourable dasha followed by a favourable dasha : Recovery.

    (c) Unfavourable dasha followed by another unfavourable dasha : Prolongation of disease; complications.

    (d) Unfavourable dasha, followed by an unfavourable dasha, followed by another unfavourable dasha : Non-recovery or death. The native may not survive until the third unfavourable dasha.

Pre-requisites for chart analysis

Medical astrology is a very specialised area. In order to obtain sound results, the data must be very accurate and the chart must be subjected to a thorough analysis using several methods at any given time. At least the following data must be worked out :

1. The Rashi chart along with accurate calculation of the cusp of the lagna and the longitudes of houses.

2. The Drekkana, the Navamsha, the Dwadashamsha and, preferably, the Trimshamsha charts.

3. The Vimshottari dasha worked from Mahadasha (MD) through Antaradasha (AD) to Pratyantaradasha (PD). Particular attention must be paid to work out the dasha operating at the time of birth.

4. Additional tools for confirmation :

    (a) At least one additional dasha, e.g., the Yogini, or the Chara dasha of Jaimini.

(b) Ashtakavarga.

(c) Varshaphala or the annual chart for the relevant year(s).

(d) Transits.

(e) Prashna or the Horary system, where appropriate.

Illustrations

Chart XXIV-1 shows the presence of the eighth lord in the lagna. The lagna lord is located in an inimical sign and aspected by the sixth lord, the Moon. The lagna is variously afflicted in the Navamsha, the Drekkana as well as the Dwadashamsha chart. Some relief is provided by Jupiter aspecting the lagna lord in the Rashi, Navamsha and the Drekkana charts, and additionally the lagna in the Navamsha.

The native was born in Mars-Jupiter. In Mars-Saturn he was detected to have developed allergy to milk and egg proteins. This worsened during the AD of Mercury. Mercury is particularly bad as the lord of the eighth house and also of the 22nd Drekkana. Mars is a functional malefic. Jupiter owns the 64th Navamsha. The child also suffers from Autism.

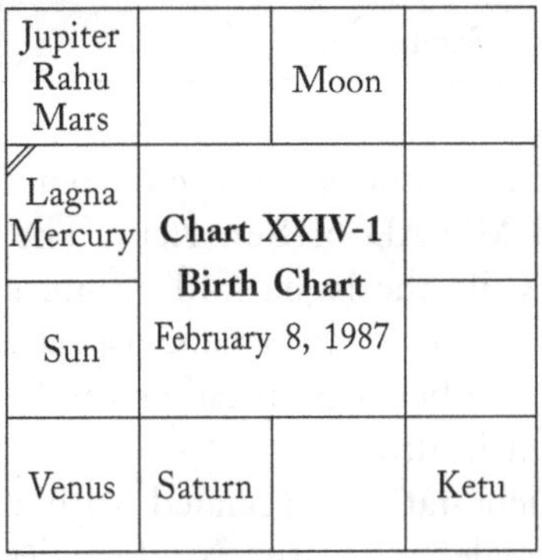

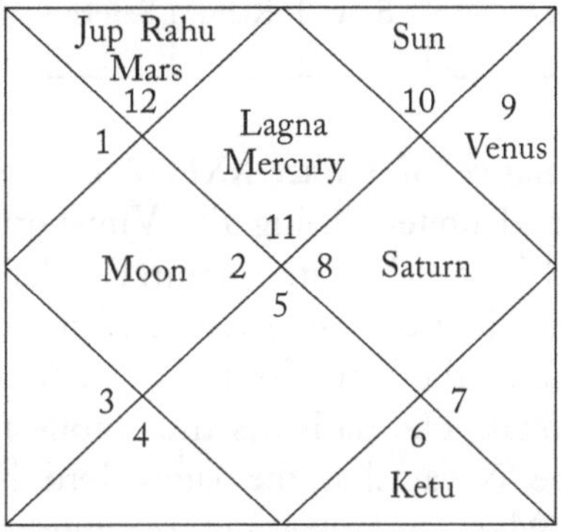

Chart XXIV-1 Birth Chart February 8, 1987

Lagna	5°46'	Mars 27°59'	Venus 10°11'
Sun	25°35'	Mercury 13°04'	Saturn 25°26'
Moon	27°13'	Jupiter 1°15'	Rahu 19°31'

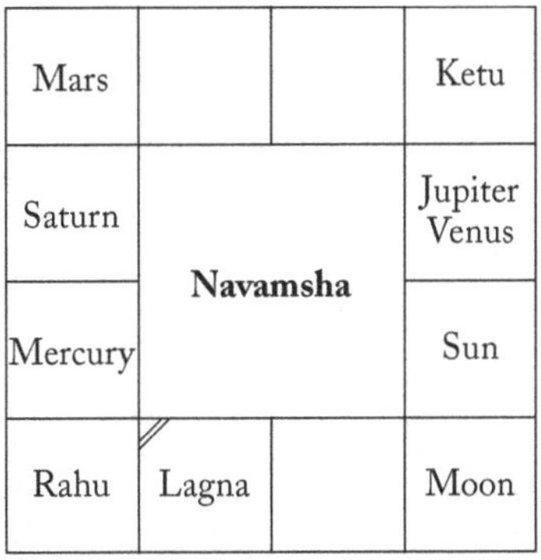

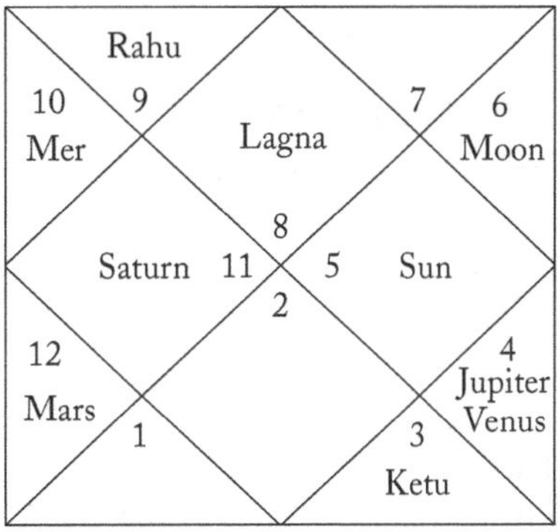

Navamsha

Drekkana

Jupiter	Venus		Mercury
Lagna			Saturn Rahu
Moon Ketu			
	Mars		Sun

(North Indian chart)
1 — 12 Jupiter / Venus; Lagna; Moon Ketu 10 — 9; 11; 2 — 8 Mars; 5; 3 Mer; 4 Saturn Rahu; 7; 6; Sun

Dwadashamsha

Moon Jupiter	Lagna Venus Ketu		
Mars			Mercury
	Sun	Rahu	Saturn

(North Indian chart)
2; 3; Lagna Venus Ketu; Moon Jupiter 12 — 11; Mars; 1; Mercury 4 — 10; 7; 5 — 6; Rahu; 9 — 8; Saturn; Sun

The native of **Chart XXIV-2** had multiple stones removed from his right kidney and ureter during the Vimshottari MD/AD of Sun-Ketu. The lagna is occupied by a debilitated natural malefic while the lagna lord occupies the adverse sixth house in association with Ketu. There is no benefic aspect either on the lagna or the lagna lord. Also there are no benefics in either the kendras or the trikonas. The native is thus prone to ill health.

In the Navamsha, the lagna lord is debilitated, associated with a natural malefic Mars and aspected by another malefic Saturn. No benefics occupy

	Jup (R)	Rahu
Sat (R)	**Chart XXIV-2** **Birth Chart** October 12, 1964	Lagna Mars
		Venus
Moon Ketu		Sun Mercury

(North Indian chart)
Venus; Rahu; 6 Sun Mer; 5; Lagna Mars; 3 — 2 Jup (R); 4; 7 — 1; 10; 8 — 9 Moon Ketu; 11; 12; Sat (R)

Lagna	26°41'	Mars	22°40'	Venus	13°35'
Sun	25°09'	Mercury	22°16'	Saturn (R)	5°21'
Moon	4°42'	Jupiter (R)	1°34'	Rahu	2°18'

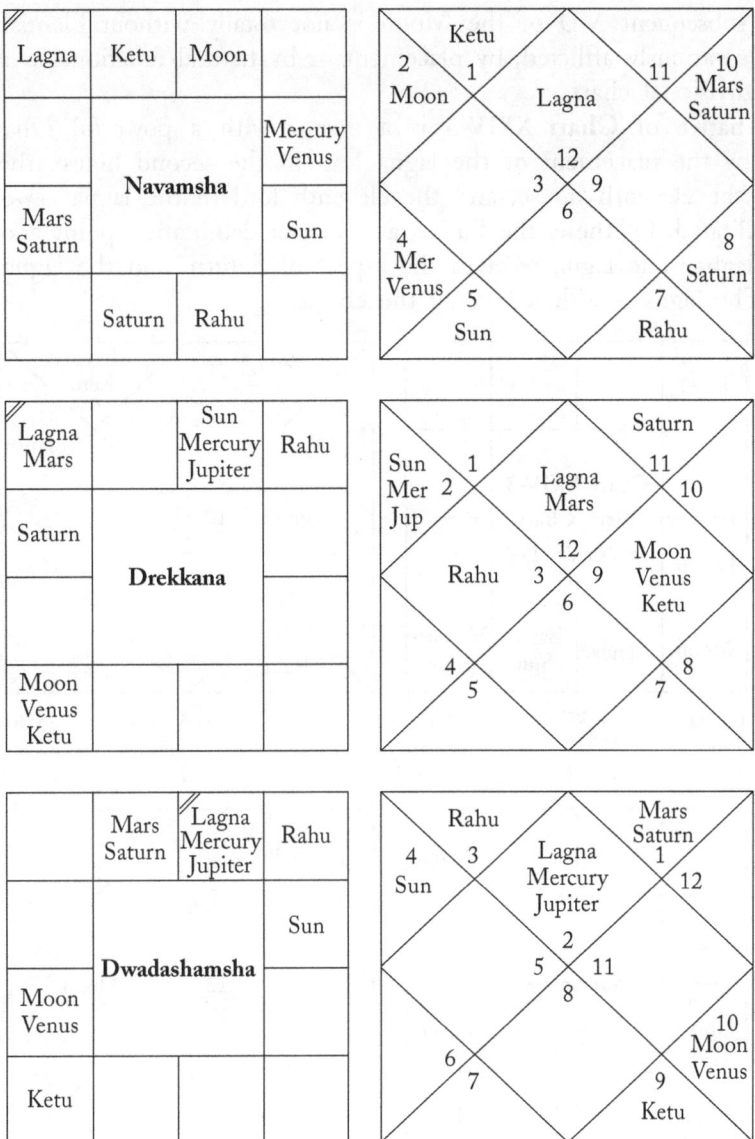

Navamsha

Lagna	Ketu	Moon	
			Mercury Venus
Mars Saturn			Sun
	Saturn	Rahu	

Drekkana

Lagna Mars	Sun Mercury Jupiter	Rahu	
Saturn			
Moon Venus Ketu			

Dwadashamsha

	Mars Saturn	Lagna Mercury Jupiter	Rahu
			Sun
Moon Venus			
Ketu			

the kendras although three benefics lie along the 5/11 axis which may be considered as favourable.

The MD of the Sun coincided with ill health. The Sun is associated with a functional malefic for Karka lagna and is aspected by a retrograde sixth lord. The Sun also owns and occupies the 64th Navamsha. Ketu the AD lord is located in the sixth house along with the lagna lord. In the Drekkana, Ketu is associated with the eighth lord, and in the Dwadashamsha it occupies the eighth house.

It may also be noted that both the lagna and the Moon fall in the Gandanta (q.v.).

The subsequent MD of the Moon is not totally without blemish as the Moon is variously afflicted, by placement or by natural/functional malefics, in all the divisional charts.

The native of **Chart XXIV-3** is a doctor with a powerful Dhana yoga caused by the placement of the lagna lord in the second house, the second lord in the eleventh house, and the eleventh lord in the lagna. Two planets are debilitated. Of these, the Sun is at its exact debilitation point and located in the lagna. The lagna receives the aspect of Saturn, and the lagna lord of Mars. The lagna is afflicted in all the charts.

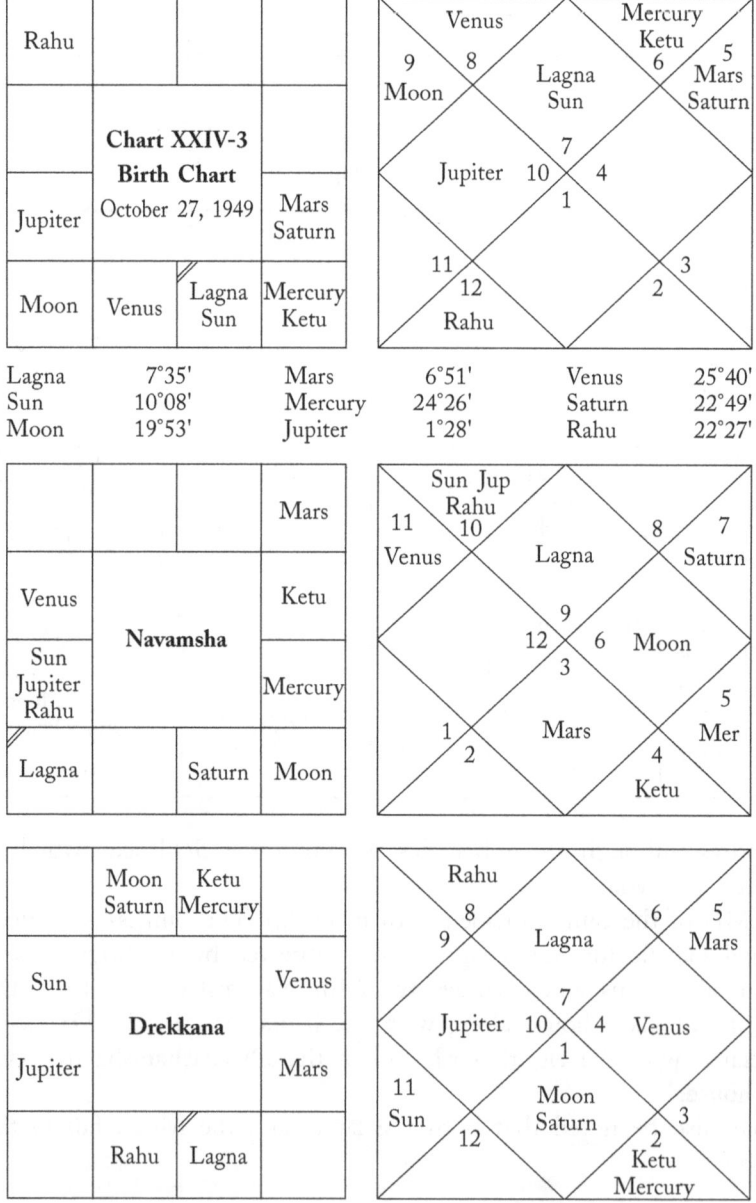

Lagna	7°35'	Mars	6°51'	Venus	25°40'
Sun	10°08'	Mercury	24°26'	Saturn	22°49'
Moon	19°53'	Jupiter	1°28'	Rahu	22°27'

		Saturn Ketu	Mercury
Sun			Moon
Lagna Jupiter	**Dwadashamsha**		
	Rahu	Mars	Venus

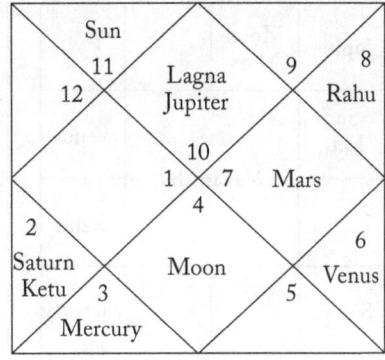

Since the onset of the Rahu dasha, the native has been suffering from progressive rheumatoid polyarthritis, with joint deformities. Rahu (a malefic) in the sixth house should normally indicate sound health. However, it must give the results of the sixth house (disease) during its own dasha particularly when the lagna is so weak and afflicted. In the Rashi, Navamsha as well as the Drekkana, Rahu is aspected by Mars; in the Dwadashamsha it is aspected by Saturn.

Chart XXIV-4 shows the placement of the eighth lord, the Sun, in the lagna, and the Moon in the eighth house, in a typical Balarishta combination. The Moon is also in Gandanta (q.v.), falls in the 22nd Drekkana, and owns the 64th Navamsha. It receives the adverse aspect of Saturn which also aspects the Sun and the lagna. Malefics alone occupy the kendras. The only benefic aspect on the lagna is that of Jupiter, which is retrograde.

The Balarishta manifested in the MD of the Moon and AD of Saturn (operative from Feb 19, 1994 to Sept 20, 1995). Mercury is the retrograde sixth lord located in the twelfth house. It is thus the MD of the seventh lord (a maraka) placed in the eighth house, and the AD of the sixth lord (disease) located in the twelfth house (hospitalisation, etc). The native has developed an incurable serious illness, a particular type of a lymphoma. The important point here is the

	Mars	Ketu	
	Chart XXIV-4		
Lagna Sun	**Birth Chart** January 18, 1957		Moon
Mer (R) Venus	Saturn Rahu	Jup (R)	

Lagna	0°30'	Mars	0°24'
Sun	4°28'	Mercury (R)	19°02'
Moon	0°18'	Jupiter (R)	8°32'

Venus	13°16'
Saturn	17°46'
Rahu	3°46'

274

Navamsha

Jupiter	Moon Mars		
Sun Ketu			Venus
Lagna			Rahu
Saturn			Mercury

North Indian chart:
12 Jupiter — Sun Ketu 11 — Saturn 9 — 8 — Lagna — 10 — 1 Moon Mars — 7 — 4 — 6 — 2 — 3 Venus — 5 Rahu — Mer

Drekkana

Saturn	Mars Venus Mercury	Ketu	
Lagna Sun			Moon
	Rahu		Jupiter

North Indian chart:
12 Saturn — 11 — Lagna Sun — 9 — 8 Rahu — Mars Venus Mercury 1 — 10 — 7 — 4 — 2 Ketu — 6 — 3 — 5 Moon — Jupiter

Dwadashamsha

	Mars	Venus	Saturn Ketu
Sun			Mercury
Lagna			Moon
Jupiter Rahu			

North Indian chart:
Sun — Jupiter Rahu 9 — 11 — Lagna — 12 — 8 — Mars 1 — 10 — 7 — 4 — 2 Venus — Mercury — 6 — 3 Saturn Ketu — 5 Moon

existence of a Balarishta which manifests at a time when the appropriate dasha operates. There is no Arishta-Bhanga as the birth is at night time (Sun's longitude greater than the cusp of the lagna!) while the lunar phase is Krishna-paksha.

For greater details regarding astrological aspects of health and disease, the reader is referred to the *Essentials of Medical Astrology* by the author.

...XXV...
Varshaphala or Annual Horoscopy

संवत्सरो वै प्रजापतिस्तस्यायने दक्षिणं चोत्तरं च।

The year is verily the lord of all creatures. Of him there are two courses, the Southern and the Northern.

Prashna Upanishad I/9

Vedic astrology abounds in techniques. The Vedic method of casting annual horoscopes, also called as Varshaphala or the Tajika system, is a brilliant method of applying the transit of planets for a particular year of life of a native. By this is signified that the *Varshaphala is essentially a system of transit.* It must be applied in association with the natal chart. The promise indicated in a natal chart attains fruition during the year indi-cated by an appropriate annual chart. The annual chart also provides more detailed information about an event. This branch of astrology, therefore, provides an additional predictive tool in the hands of an astrologer.

Basis of Vedic Annual Chart

The Varshaphala is Sun-based. That is to say that it considers the position of the Sun in the zodiac as of prime importance. The annual chart for a given year of the native is cast for a time when the Sun attains the same longitude as it had at the time of his birth. After each sidereal year, the Sun would return to its original position. This time of *solar return* is thus important. An annual horoscopic chart is also known as *the solar return chart.*

Solar cycle

We are aware that a sidereal year consists of three hundred and sixty five days, six hours, nine minutes and some ten seconds. This means that the Sun, after this duration of time, attains its original longitude in the zodiac. If we add the above time duration to the time of birth of a native, we get a time next year when the Sun would regain its original longitude. Adding the same time duration each year, we get successive moments of solar return for successive years of life of a native. The moment of solar return is also called as *Varsha-pravesha*. A horoscope cast for Varsha-pravesha derived for a particular year of life of the native is called an annual chart or a *Varsha-kundali*.

If we remove the completed (i.e., fifty two) weeks from the time duration of a sidereal year (i.e., 365 days 6 hours 9 minutes 10 seconds), we get a remainder of 1 day 6 hours 9 minutes and 10 seconds. If this is added to the weekday of birth of a native, we get the week day next year when the solar return occurs. Multiples of this value, added to the day and time of birth, help us obtain the weekday of the solar return or Varsha-pravesha for any specified year of life. This value of 1d 6h 9m 10s is a constant for one year and is called as *Dhruvanka*.

When the Dhruvanka for one year is added to the day and time of birth, it yields the Varshapravesha for the second year. When Dhruvanka for two years is added instead, it yields the Varshapravesha for the third year. Thus, the Dhruvanka for any number of completed years of life, when added to the day and time of birth, yields the Varshapravesha for a subsequent year of life. The weekday of Varshapravesha as obtained above generally falls on the calendar birthday of the native, or may fall a day before or a day after the actual birthday.

A horoscope cast for the weekday as worked out above, falling on or around a native's natural birthday, yields the annual chart.

Casting an Annual Chart

Constructing an annual chart involves the following steps :

1. Note down the birth details: Name, time of birth, date of birth, place of birth and the day of birth.

2. Cast a birth chart for the native and work out the dashas as required. Particularly work out the dasha, Antaradasha and Pratyantaradasha for the year for which the annual chart is being considered.

3. Decide on the particular calender year for which the annual chart is to be constructed. This may be considered as the current year.

4. Find the *completed years* of life by subtracting the year of birth from the current year.

5. Add the Dhruvanka for the completed years (see Table XXV-1) to the weekday (consider '0' for Sunday, '1' for Monday, etc.) and time of birth. This gives the Varshapravesha.

6. Cast a horoscope (ascendant, planets, etc.) in the usual manner for the Varshapravesha obtained above. This is the annual horoscope for the current year.

Note : It will be noted that the longitude of the Sun as obtained for the above Varshapravesha may differ from the Sun's longitude in the birth chart by a few minutes. This difference is due to the disturbance of the longitude of the Sun by the planets and must be ignored.

Table XXV-1

Completed years	Dhruvanka d	h	m	s	Completed years	Dhruvanka d	h	m	s
1	1	6	9	10	20	4	3	3	14
2	2	12	18	19	25	3	9	49	3
3	3	18	27	29	30	2	16	34	52
4	5	0	36	39	35	1	23	20	40
5	6	6	45	49	40	1	6	6	29
6	0	12	54	58	45	0	12	52	17
7	1	19	4	8	50	6	19	38	6
8	3	1	13	18	55	6	2	23	55
9	4	7	22	27	60	5	9	9	43
10	5	13	31	37	65	4	15	55	32
11	6	19	40	47	70	3	22	41	20
12	1	1	49	57	75	3	5	27	9
13	2	7	59	6	80	2	12	12	58
14	3	14	8	16	90	1	1	44	35
15	4	20	17	26	100	6	15	16	12

An Example

Annual chart for the year commencing February 1993, for a native born on Thursday, February 14, 1957 at 10:25am (IST) at Delhi (Lat. 28°N39'; Long. 077°E13').

1. *Completed years* :

      1993 - 1957 = 36 years

The annual chart will thus be for the 37th year of the native.

2. *Day and time of birth* :

      4d (i.e., Thursday) 10h 25m 0s (IST)

3. *Dhruvanka* for 36 years = 3d 5h 29m 50s

      This value is obtained from the Dhruvanka table   (Table XXV-1) by adding Dhruvankas for one year   to those for 35 years.

4. *Varshapravesha*

	d	h	m	s
Birth day and time	4	10	25	0
plus Dhruvanka for 36 years	3	5	29	50
	7	15	54	50

Removing the multiple(s) of seven, we get   0d 15h 54m 50s

This gives us the Varshapravesha for the 37th year of the native as falling on Sunday at 15h 54m 50s (IST).

For the year 1993, Sunday nearest to the native's calender birthday falls on Feb 14, i.e., his original date of birth. Thus, the Varshapravesha for the native's 37th year of life falls on Feb 14, 1993 (Sunday) at 15h 54m 50s (IST) for Delhi.

5. A chart (**Chart XXV-1**) cast for this time would be thus:

Lagna	:	Karka	3°	54'
Sun	:	Kumbha	1°	59'
Moon	:	Vrishchika	11°	52'
Mars (R)	:	Mithuna	14°	55'
Mercury	:	Kumbha	17°	47'
Jupiter (R)	:	Kanya	20°	30'
Venus	:	Meena	15°	57'
Saturn	:	Makara	27°	44'
Rahu	:	Vrishchika	25°	22'
Ketu	:	Vrisha	25°	22'

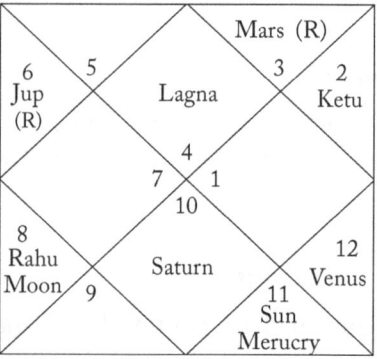

The Muntha

A special feature of the annual horoscope is the location of the Muntha in the chart. The Muntha is essentially the birth lagna in transit. At the time of birth, the Muntha is at the lagna. Every year it moves by one sign. When the second year of life begins, the Muntha shifts to the sign identical with the second house of the birth chart. During the third year, it moves to the sign falling in the third house of the birth chart. After twelve years it again returns to the sign it occupied at birth.

The position of Muntha is obtained thus :

(No. of completed years + lagna sign in birth chart) ÷ 12

The remainder gives the sign in which the Muntha is placed in the relevant annual chart.

In case of the native, whose annual chart has been calculated above, the lagna in the birth chart is Mesha. In his case the Muntha for the 37th year would be calculated thus:

36 (i.e., completed years) + 1 (i.e., Mesha), divided by 12 gives us 37 ÷ 12. This yields a remainder of one. The Muntha thus falls in Mesha, the first sign.

In the annual chart, the sign Mesha falls in the tenth house. The Muntha is thus marked in the 10th house of the annual chart.

The Muntha is supposed to be particularly auspicious in houses 9, 10 and 11. In the houses 1, 2, 3 and 5 it yields good results during the year through the personal efforts of the native. The Muntha is particularly inauspicious in houses 4, 6, 7, 8 and 12 of the annual chart. The lord of the Muntha (i.e., the lord of the sign in which Muntha is located) too yields adverse results in houses 4, 6, 7, 8 and 12. Elsewhere it proves beneficial.

Other special features of the Annual Chart

The annual chart has some distinct features when compared with the natal chart. These may be briefly mentioned below.

1. *Planetary aspects and relations* : There are three types of aspects in an annual chart. They are:

    (a) *Friendly*, between planets placed mutually in houses 3, 5, 9 and 11 from each other.

    (b) *Inimical*, between planets placed mutually in houses 1 (conjunction), 4, 7 (opposition) and 10 from each other.

    (c) *Neutral* (or no aspect), between planets placed mutually in houses 2, 6, 8 and 12 from each other.

    Depending upon the above aspects, the planets become friends, enemies and neutrals (or equals) of each other.

2. *Dashas* : There are several dasha systems which are employed in the annual chart. Of these, the Vimshotttari Mudda dasha (equivalent to the Vimshottari dasha of the natal chart) and the Yogini dasha (equivalent to the Yogini dasha of the natal chart) are popular. The natural cycles of these dashas (120 years in case of the Vimshottari and 36 years in case of the Yogini) are reduced each to a period of one year to render them applicable to the annual chart.

3. *The year lord* : The lord of the year, also known as the *Varshesha*, is chosen from amongst the planets according to the standard rules of annual horoscopy. The Varshesha is generally the strongest planet which influences the lagna by association or aspect.

    The system of Varshaphala has an elaborate method of deter-mining the strength of planets. The various results accrue from an annual chart depending upon the inherent strength of the planets.

4. *Yogas* : Annual horoscopy employs sixteen different yogas. All major predictions from the annual chart are primarily based on an understanding and application of the various Tajika yogas. The important ones among these make use of the actual degrees of longitude of planets, their relative motions, their orbs of influence as well as the presence or absence of mutual aspects.

5. *Sahams* : Another important feature of the Varshaphala is the determination of Sahams. A Saham is a mathematical point obtained by a manipulation of the longitudes of planets and the cusps of houses (esp. the ascendant). There is a Saham for each particular aspect of a person, like his brothers, mother, father, children, educatiuon, marriage, illness, travel, profession, business, death and the like. Sahams produce their results depending upon their strength, weakness and disposition.

Clues to Interpretation of an Annual Chart

It must be stressed at the outset that an anual chart must be judged conjointly with the birth chart. *It is the promise of the birth chart that is confirmed in the annual chart.* The latter in itself cannot give what the natal chart does not promise. The annual chart must be employed to have a more comprehensive view of the events indicated by the natal chart.

1. *Position of the birth lagna* : The sign identical with the lagna in the birth chart must be observed for its placement in the annual chart. The house in which the birth lagna falls in the annual chart gets activated.

2. *Varsha lagna and the birth chart* : The house in the birth chart which becomes the lagna in the annual chart also gets activated.

3. *Dwijanma year* : The year when the birth lagna recurs in the annual chart has a special significance. Such a year is called the Dwijanma year and is considered particularly adverse. It turns more malignant as :

   (a) The cusp of the annual chart lagna falls within one degree of the cusp of the birth lagna; or

   (b) The birth nakshatra too recurs in the annual chart (i.e., the nakshatra of the Moon in the birth chart and the natal chart is identical); or

   (c) The Moon and Jupiter respectively occupy the 6th and the 8th houses in the annual chart.

   The malefic influence of the Dwijanma year wanes as :

   (a) The cusp of the annual ascendant is further removed from the cusp of the birth chart; or

   (b) The lagna lord, the Muntha lord and the lord of the year happen to be strong; or

   (c) Both the Moon and Jupiter are strong and well placed; or

(d) The natural benefics occupy kendras and trikonas, and natural malefics occupy houses 3, 6 and 11.

4. *Importance of the 6th and 8th houses* : When the sign identical with the 6th or the 8th house of the birth chart becomes the ascendant in the annual chart, it proves inauspicious, and particularly adverse for health.

5. *Natal lagna lord in the annual chart* : A benefic position of the natal lagna lord in the annual chart ensures a comfortable year. An adverse location indicates otherwise.

6. *Malefics in the birth chart* : A malefic occupying a kendra in the birth chart, happening to be occupying the lagna in the annual chart causes adverse results. Benefics in such situations produce good results.

7. *Income and loss* : Malefics in the second house, particularly when the lagna happens to be a movable sign, lead to loss of money. A weak planet in the eleventh house causes loss of wealth.

8. *Progeny* : Jupiter as lord of the year occupying the fifth or the eleventh house causes childbirth during the year. The sign occupied by Jupiter in the natal chart, happening to become the lagna in the annual chart, also promises childbirth under a favourable dasha in the birth chart.

Strong lagna lord and the fifth lord together in the fifth house indicate childbirth. Retrograde Mars in the fifth house is adverse for progeny.

9. *Ill health* : Some combinations for ill health during a given year, besides those already mentioned, are :

(a) A direct malefic in the twelfth house from the lagna and a retrograde malefic in the second house.

(b) The sign occupied by Saturn in the birth chart happening to become the lagna of the annual chart, and under inimical aspect of Saturn.

(c) Lagna lord of the annual chart having a direct malefic in its twelfth house and a retrograde one in its second house.

(d) Placement of the lord of the year in the eighth house, in association with Mars.

(e) A malefic in the birth lagna falling in the eighth house in the annual chart.

(f) A combust lagna lord of the birth chart placed in the eighth house in the annual chart.

(g) Afflicted Mars or Saturn in the tenth house.

10. *Marriage* : Involvement of the lagna lord with the seventh lord, or that of Venus with Mars, in appropriate Tajika yogas indicate marriage if the same event is indicated also in the birth chart. Placement of a strong fifth lord in the seventh house of the annual chart also indicates similar results.

11. *Profession* : Placement of the Sun in the tenth house of the annual chart is a highly auspicious factor in relation to profession. If the Sun is strong, it leads to regaining of the lost status. A strong Sun in the eleventh house gives a promise for royal favours.

    Malefics in general produce benefic results when placed in the tenth house, particularly when they are strong and under benefic influence.

12. *Relative importance of the birth chart and the annual chart* : The birth chart always takes precedence over the annual chart. The annual chart acts as a very superior transit chart which holds sway over a given year of life of a native. It explains more clearly or vividly what the natal chart indi-cates, remaining always within the confines of the natal chart.

    For a more elaborate account of annual horoscopy, the reader is referred to the *A Textbook of Varshaphala* by the author.

...XXVI...
Muhurta or the Astrology of Election

न कर्मणामनारम्भान्नैष्कर्म्यं पुरुषोऽश्नुते।
न च संन्यसनादेव सिद्धिं समधिगच्छति॥

Not by abstention from work does a man achieve freedom from action;
nor even by renunciation does he attain to perfection. Gita III/4.

The word *Muhurta* means a moment of time, or a time duration of two Ghatis (forty-eight minutes). In astrology, the muhurta deals with picking up the most appropriate moment for accomplishment of a purpose, while avoiding the less appropriate moments.

Importance of time

All astrology is based on time. The disposition of the lagna and the planets at a given time determines all that pertains to a native's life. Just as individuals have a birth time, so also all work and actions have their times of birth. A horoscope cast for the moment when a work is commenced indicates the turn of events during the accomplishment of that work, very much like the natal horoscope indicating the various events taking place during the life of a native. Since we generally have control over the moment of commencing an action, it is but appropriate that we chose the most appropriate moment to do so. In this way, the difficulties that one might encounter in the fulfilment of a job can be avoided or minimised.

Muhurta thus is a practical application of the knowledge of astrology. In India, this aspect of astrology is so much ingrained in day to day life that even a lay and illiterate villager uses it in his varied pursuits of life like travel, marriage, building a house, shifting into a new house, sowing and reaping a harvest, digging of wells and ponds, naming or christening of a child, returning home, meeting or bidding farewell to a friend or a relative, and the like. The kings employed it in wars and conquests. The present day educated man employs this know-ledge in selecting appropriate moments for joining or quitting a job, sending in job applications, filing of nominations for elections, taking oath of office, procurement of a vehicle, shifting into a new house, etc. People have lately used this knowledge in choosing the birth time of their child in case of a cesarean birth. Muhurta thus finds a wide use in day to day life in India. The slavish neo-scientist, with his imported learning and natural ignorance of the rich Vedic culture, gives the belief in this brilliant branch of practical astrology the name of superstition.

Difficulty in choosing the best Muhurta

It must be appreciated that no given horoscope can be considered as perfect in all possible respects. The best of planetary dispositions available will have a flaw. Similarly, the best and the most auspicious moment selected for commencing an undertaking will not be perfect in all respects.

The selection of an appropriate Muhurta aims at selecting the best moment available. The modern day man does not have enough time at his disposal. He may have to undertake a journey at short notice or to join a job within a stipulated period. Or a child in the womb, eager to come out, may only give a limited time frame within which to plan a cesarean. Under such circumstances, the moment that best suits one's purpose is to be chosen.

The underlying principles

Muhurta uses the same basic principles as are applicable to the predictive aspect of astrology. The stress is, however, shifted to certain specific areas which constitute the five limbs of the Panchanga or the Indian almanac. These five limbs, already hinted at elsewhere, are the Tithi, Vaara, Nakshatra, Yoga and Karana. The Panchanga is specifically suited to the Indian way of life where astrology finds its practical use.

The importance of the Sun and the Moon in Vedic astrology cannot be overemphasised. The five limbs of the Panchanga depend on the disposition of these two luminaries only. The Muhurta also makes use of the lagna (or even the Navamsha) rising at the time of commencing an act. It can be individualised, for best results, when combined with Ashtakavarga worked out on the natal horoscope of an individual.

Muhurta is a vast subject demanding a very thorough treatment which is beyond the scope of this work. Here it is proposed to present the very basic concepts of this branch of astrology. For detailed information, the reader is referred to the book on Muhurta by K.K. Joshi.

Tithi or the Lunar Date

Fifteen Tithis constitute the *Shukla-paksha* or the brighter half of the lunar cycle, while another fifteen constitute the *Krishna-paksha* or the darker half of the lunar cycle. These Tithis are numbered from 1 to 30; or they are numbered from 1 to 15 (from the Pratipada to the Poornima) for the Shukla-paksha, and 1 to 14 (Pratipada to Chaturdashi) and 30 (Amavasya) for the Krishna-paksha.

Tithis are very important in Muhurta. All Hindu festivals depend upon the Tithis. Even the birthdays are celebrated according to the Tithis.

Five sub-divisions of the Tithis

The Tithis are sub-divided into five groups :

(a) Nanda	Tithis 1, 6 and 11.
(b) Bhadra	Tithis 2, 7 and 12.
(c) Jaya	Tithis 3, 8 and 13.
(d) Rikta	Tithis 4, 9 and 14.
(e) Poorna	Tithis 5, 10, 15 and 30.

In general, Tithis 1 to 5 of the Krishna-paksha and 10 to 15 of the Shukla-paksha are favourable. Tithis 5 to 10 of both the pakshas are average. Tithis 10 to 15 (i.e., 10 to 14, and 30) of the Krishna-paksha and 1 to 5 of the Shukla-paksha are unfavourable. This is because the Moon is relatively weak for five days on either side of the Amavasya (New Moon) due to its proximity to the Sun. Similarly, it is strong for five days on either side of the Poornima (Full Moon).

Prescribed acts for various Tithis :

1. *Pratipada* (Tithi 1) : Writing, drawing, agriculture, extraction of liquor, felling trees, sculpting, bed or seat. Avoid auspicious events like marriage, etc.

2. *Dwiteeya* (Tithi 2) : Marriage, travel, royal duties, house building, acquisition of ornaments.

3. *Triteeya* (Tithi 3) : Sculpting, transactions related to cattle, elephants, etc., travel through water, feeding the infant, entering a new house, and other auspicious pursuits mentioned under the 'Dwiteeya' above.

4. *Chaturthi, Navami and Chaturdashi* (Tithis 4, 9 and 14; the Rikta group) : Cruel deeds, study of mantras, confinement, use of fire, poison and weapons, causing injury or death, killing of an opponent. Avoid all auspicious pursuits.

5. *Panchami* (Tithi 5) : Riding, marriage, propitiation of planets, all auspicious pursuits. Avoid lending money.

6. *Shashthi* (Tithi 6) : Buying and selling, transactions of cattle and land, war-related pursuits, ornaments and garments, house building.

7. *Saptami* (Tithi 7) : Travel, vehicle, service to the king, marriage, house building.

8. *Ashtami* (Tithi 8) : War-related pursuits, house building, sculpting, farming and agriculture, writing, digging, work related with water, ornaments.

9. *Dashami* (Tithi 10) : Worship in a temple, journey, marriage and all the pursuits mentioned under Tithis 2, 3, 5 and 7.

10. *Ekadashi* (Tithi 11) : Religious pursuits, festivals, house building, sculpting, agriculture, marriage, dancing, war-related pursuits.

11. *Dwadashi* (Tithi 12) : All Chara and Sthira (i.e., change-oriented and fixity-oriented) pursuits, religious and auspicious deeds.

12. *Trayodashi* (Tithi 13) : Marriage, rituals related to fire, travel, all auspicious deeds.

13. *Poornima* (Tithi 15; Full Moon) : Sacrificial rituals ('yajnas'), war-related pursuits, house building, marriage, sculpting, ornaments.

14. *Amavasya* (Tithi 30; New Moon) : Rituals related to the Pitras (the Manes).

Prescribed acts for sub-divisions of Tithis

(a) *Nanda* : Dance, music, agriculture, festivals, house building, garments, ornaments, sculpting.

(b) *Bhadra* : Marriage, the sacred thread ceremony, travel, ornaments, sculpting, artistic pursuits, vehicles.

(c) *Jaya* : War-related pursuits, house building, medication, agriculture, work related to weapons, etc.

(d) *Rikta* : Already mentioned above.

(e) *Poorna* : The sacred thread ceremony, marriage, travel, propitiation of planets, sitting on the royal throne.

Vaara or the Week Day

The seven days of the week have the seven Grahas from the Sun to Saturn as their lords. Specific jobs are prescribed for the seven days.

(a) *Sunday* : Coronation, festivities, fire-related rituals, com-mencing medical treatment, making weapons, travelling, cattle rearing, fighting, work related with wood, wool, gold, copper, etc.

(b) *Monday* : Work related with silver, pearls, ornaments and precious stones, sexual indulgence, planting trees, water related deeds, agricultural pursuits, food and eatables, flowers, song and music, garments, milk and curd, yajnas, etc.

(c) *Tuesday* : Deeds of cruelty, theft, killing, work related with fire, weapons and poisons, injury, surgery, arrogance, imprisonment, coral, treasure, etc.

(d) *Wednesday* : Dance, sculpting, music, writing, compilation, learning, marriage, warfare, etc.

(e) *Thursday* : Religious pursuits, nutrition, auspicious deeds, house building, acquiring vehicles, travel, medication, wearing ornaments, trees, vines, etc.

(f) *Friday* : Dance, music, sexual indulgence, decoration, land deals, constructing or decorating a bed, garments, shopping, festivals, etc.

(g) *Saturday* : House building, shifting into a new house, spiritual initiation, weapons, poisons, hoarding, sinful acts, servility, work which has long lasting effect, etc.

Use of the Hora

Whatever has been prescribed for a particular day can also be pursued during the Hora relevant to the lord of that day.

Travel and Week day

Travel must be avoided in certain directions on certain days. This is shown below :

Direction to be avoided	Week day(s)
1. East	Monday, Saturday
2. South	Thursday
3. West	Friday, Sunday
4. North	Tuesday, Wednesday

Tithi-Vaara combinations

A combination of Tithis and Vaaras (weekdays) gives rise to the following types of Tithis.

(a) *Siddha Tithis* : Nanda (1, 6, 11) on Friday; Bhadra (2, 7, 12) on Wednesday; Jaya (3, 8, 13) on Tuesday; Rikta (4, 9, 14) on Saturday; and Poorna (5, 10, 15) on Thursday are auspicious and may be considered when other blemishes exist in the elected moment.

(b) *Dagdha Tithi* : Nanda on Sunday, Bhadra on Monday, Nanda on Tuesday, Jaya on Wednesday, Rikta on Thursday, Bhadra on Friday, and Poorna on Saturday are inauspicious.

(c) *Krakacha Tithi (or Vaara-Dagdha)* : A combination of Tithi and Vaara totalling to 13 is considered inauspicious. Thus, Sunday (the first day) and Dwadashi (the 12th Tithi), when co-existing, are bad. Similarly Monday (the 2nd day) and Ekadashi (the 11th Tithi) are bad. Equally so, Tuesday and the 10th, Wednesday and the 9th, Thursday and the 8th, Friday and the 7th, and Saturday and the 6th, when coinciding are inauspicious.

Nakshatras or the Constellations

The twenty-seven nakshatras constitute another important limb of the Panchanga which is essential in electional astrology. The various functions or aspects appropriate to these Nakshatras are mentioned below.

1. *Ashwini* : Garments, the sacred thread, shaving, riding, agri-culture, studying, dealings with women.

2. *Bharani* : Digging a well or a pond, poisons, weapons, entering a cave, mathematics, cruel deeds.

3. *Krittika* : Fire-related pursuits, weapons, war, medication, truce, deeds of cruelty.

4. *Rohini* : All stable deeds (Sthira-karma), marriage, clothes, ornaments, horses and elephants, house building.

5. *Mrigashira* : House building, travel, elephants, horses, camels, marriage, ornaments.

6. *Ardra* : Flag, war, fort, weaponry, skill in arms, truce, an archway.

7. *Punarvasu* : House building, shaving, dealing with weapons, ornaments, exit, riding.

8. *Pushya* : A special Nakshatra which is suitable for all auspicious deeds other than marriage.

9. *Ashlesha* : Gambling, base acts, lies, quarrels, medication, business.

10. *Magha* : Agriculture, business, cattle, fighting, hoarding, singing, dancing.

11. *The three Poorvas* (Poorvaphalguni, P. Ashadha and P. Bhadrapad; Nakshatras 11, 20, and 25) : Quarrels, poisons, weapons, fire, fighting, cruel deeds, sale of meat.

12. *The three Uttaras* (Uttara-phalguni, U. Ashadha, U. Bhadra-pad; Nakshatras 12, 21 and 26): Coronation, house building, marriage, the sacred thread, entry.

13. *Hasta* : Marriage, riding, house building, garments, orna-ments, shaving, coronation.

14. *Chitraa* : Entry, clothes, the sacred thread, house building, ornaments

15. *Swati* : Marriage, clothes, ornaments, disagreement, agri-culture, shaving, entry, the sacred thread ceremony.

16. *Vishakha* : Clothes, ornaments, hoarding, song, dance, sculpting, writing.

17. *Anuradha* : Entry, marriage, garments, ornaments, house building, truce, discord, auspicious deeds.

18. *Jyeshtha* : Shaving, weapons, business, cattle, water, music, sculpting, writing.

19. *Moola* : Marriage, agriculture, business, deeds of cruelty, fighting, medication, dance, sculpting, weapons, writing.

20. *Shravana* (Nakshatra 22) : Shaving, riding, the sacred thread ceremony, medication, travel, entry into a house, repair of an old house.

21. *Dhanishtha* (Nakshatra 23) : The sacred thread ceremony, medication, house building, entry into a new house, ornaments, riding.

22. *Shatabhisha* (Nakshatra 24) : Entry into a new house, shaving, medication, riding, house building.

23. *Revati* (Nakshatra 27) : Marriage, ornaments, garments, riding, entry, shaving, medication.

Categories of Nakshatras

The Nakshatras can be put under several categories as under :

1. *Dhruva (Sthira) or fixed* : Rohini, the three Uttaras (Nak-shatras 4, 12, 21, 26), as well as Sunday.

   These are suitable for such deeds as sowing seeds, pursuit of peace, and deeds prescribed under the 'Mridu', vide infra. The intention here is to achieve a lasting result.

2. *Chara (chala) or movable* : Punarvasu, Swati, Shravana, Dhanishtha, Satabhisha (Nakshatras 7, 15, 22, 23, 24) and Monday.

   These are suitable for riding, travel, and deeds prescribed under the 'Laghu', vide infra.

3. *Krura (Ugra) or cruel* : Bharani, Magha, the three Poorvas (Naskshatras 2, 10, 11, 20, 25), and Tuesday.

   Suitable for killing, dealing with weapons, poison, fire related pursuits, cruelty, and deeds prescribed under the 'Teekshna', vide infra.

4. *Mishra or ordinary* : Krittika, Vishakha (Nakshatras 3 and 16), and Wednesday.

   Suitable for rituals of fire, pursuits of mixed nature, as well as deeds prescribed under the 'Krura', vide supra.

5. *Kshipra (Laghu) or agile* : Ashwini, Pushya, Hasta, Abhijit (nakshatras 1, 8, 13 and 22; when Abhijit is considered, the total number of nakshatras goes up to 28), and Thursday.

   Pursuits such as shopping, , sexual act, learning of scriptures, ornaments, sculpting, dance, artistic pursuits, and prescriptions for the 'Chara', vide supra.

6. *Mridu (Maitra) or amiable* : Mrigashira, Chitraa, Anuradha, Revati (Nakshatras 5, 14, 17 and 27), and Friday.

   Suitable for singing, garments, sexual indulgence, friendly acts, ornaments and pursuits prescribed under the 'Dhruva', vide supra.

7. *Teekshna (Daruna) or aggressive* : Ardra, Ashlesha, Jyeshtha, Moola (nakshatras 6, 9, 18 and 19), and Saturday.

   Suitable for magic, killing, aggression, taming of animals, and deeds prescribed under the 'Krura', vide supra.

Directions of Nakshatras

Nakshatras have the following three categories depending upon the direction they face.

1. *Adho-mukha* (facing downwards) : Bharani, Krittika, Ashlesha, Magha, Moola, Vishakha and the three Poorvas (i.e., Ashlesha, Moola, 'Krura' and 'Mishra' Nakshatras).

   Suitable for such acts as digging, work on the ground, fighting, and cruel deeds.

2. *Urdhva-mukha* (facing upwards) : Rohini, Ardra, Pushya, Shravana, Dhanishtha, Shatabhisha and the three Uttaras (i.e., Ardra, Pushya, Shravana, Dhanishtha, Shatabhisha and the 'Dhruva' Nakshatras).

   Suitable for coronation, high rise buildings, flag hoisting, riding.

3. *Tiryang-mukha* (facing forwards) : Ashwini, Mrigashira, Punarvasu, Hasta, Chitra, Swati, Anuradha, Jyeshtha and Revati (i.e., Ashwini, Punarvasu, Hasta, Swati, Jyeshtha, and the 'Mridu' Nakshatras).

   Suitable for travel, ploughing, planting trees, vehicles, business, dealing in cattle.

The Panchaka

This is a special category of Nakshatras extending from the second half of Dhanishtha to the end of Revati. This coincides with the position of the Moon in the signs Kumbha and Meena. During the Panchaka, such pursuits as cremating the dead, travel to the south, making of cots, accumulation of grass and wood, and thatching a roof are prohibited.

Some important combinations involving Nakshatras

Specific nakshatras falling on specific days give rise to certain combinations some of which are mentioned below.

1. *Siddha Yoga* : Moola on Sunday, Shravana on Monday, U. Bhadrapada on Tuesday, Krittika on Wednesday, Punarvasu on Thursday, P. Phalguni on Friday and Swati on Saturday produce this. This combination is good for all pursuits.

2. *Amrita Siddhi Yoga* : Hasta, Shravana, Ashwini, Anuradha, Pushya, Revati, and Rohini falling each on the seven days starting from Sunday give rise to this yoga. It ensures accomplishments.

3. *Sarvartha Siddhi Yoga* : *Sunday* coinciding with Ashwini, Pushya, Hasta, Moola and the three Uttaras; *Monday* coinciding with Rohini, Mrigashira, Pushya, Anuradha and Shravana; *Tuesday* coinciding with Ashwini, Krittika, Ashlesha and U. Bhadrapada; *Wednesday* coinciding with Krittika, Rohini, Mrigashira, Hasta and Anuradha; *Thursday* coinciding with Ashwini, Punarvasu, Pushya, Anuradha and Revati; *Friday* coinciding with Ashwini, Punarvasu, Anuradha, Shravana and Revati; *Saturday* coinciding with Rohini, Swati and Shravana.

   These combinations are good for all pursuits.

4. *Mrityu Yoga* : Anuradha, U. Ashadha, Shatabhisha, Ashwini, Mrigashira, Ashlesha and Hasta each falling respectively on seven days from Sunday onwards produce this yoga. It is an adverse combination, and must be particularly avoided in travel.

The Taara

Count from the birth nakshatra of a native to the nakshatra falling on a particular day. Divide by nine. The result is (1) Janma, (2) Sampata, (3) Vipat, (4) Kshema, (5) Pratyari, (6) Sadhaka, (7) Vadha, (8) Maitra, and (9) Ati-maitra, respectively depending on the remainder being one to nine.

Taaras 1, 2, 4, 6, 8 and 9 are auspicious; 3, 5 and 7 are adverse. Taara must be considered during the Krishna-paksha, and the Moon during the Shukla-paksha.

The Yogas

The 27 yogas are either (a) *auspicious*, when all good undertakings are permitted, or (b) *in-auspicious*, when all important pursuits must be avoided.

Vyatipaata and *Vaidhriti* (yogas 17 and 27) must be completely avoided.

Of *Parigha yoga* (yoga 19), the first half is to be avoided in all pursuits.

Of *Vishkumbha* and *Vajra* (yogas 1 and 15), avoid the beginning three Ghatis (1 hour and 12 minutes).

Of *Ati-Ganda* and *Ganda* (yogas 6 and 10), avoid the first six Ghatis (2 hours and 24 minutes).

THE KARANAS

Bhadra

The Vishti Karana is called as Bhadra. This coincides with :

(a) The first half of the Tithis 8 and 15 of the Shukla-paksha.

(b) The second half of the Tithis 4 and 11 of the Shukla-paksha.

(c) The first half of the Tithis 7 aand 14 of the Krishna-paksha.

(d) The second half of the Tithis 3 and 10 of the Krishna-paksha.

Bhadra must be generally avoided in all auspicious pursuits.

The Sthira Karanas

The four sthira or fixed Karanas have their specific application.

(a) *Kimstughna* :   Suited for all auspicious deeds.

(b) *Shakuni* :   For medication and propitiation of planets.

(c) *Chatushpada* : For all pursuits pertaining to cow, Brahmin, king and father.

(d) *Naga* :   For benign pursuits, study, battle.

The Lagna

In all Muhurta, the lagna is extremely important. One should ensure an appropriate lagna for an appropriate objective. In general, the kendras and trikonas must be occupied by benefics, while the malefics should occupy houses 3, 6, and 11. Specific pursuits appropriate to different lagnas are briefly hinted at below.

1. *Mesha* :   Riding, truce, discord, treasure, ornaments, battle.
2. *Vrisha* :   Auspicious deeds, work of a lasting nature, entry into a new house, agriculture, cattle, business.
3. *Mithuna* :   Art, science, learning, accomplishment, battle, marriage, seeking refuge, coronation, purchase and sale of elephants.
4. *Karka* :   Pond, lake, well, canal, bridge, nutrition, writing.
5. *Simha* :   Business, food grains, shop, agriculture, coura-geous acts, battle, royal pursuits.
6. *Kanya* :   Learning, sculpting, medicine, ornament, auspicious deeds.
7. *Tula* :   Agriculture, business, vehicle, marriage, cattle, utensils.
8. *Vrishchika*: Pursuits of a lasting nature, service to the king, coronation, theft.
9. *Dhanu* :   Restraint, marriage, sculpting, weapons, acts of a fixed nature
10. *Makara* :   Bridges, canals, weapons, exit, cattle, servility.
11. *Kumbha* :   Agriculture, trade, sculpting, work related to water, sea travel, weapons.
12. *Meena* :   Marriage, coronation, entry, ornaments, water reservoir.

Note : While considering a lagna, an appropriate Navamsha lagna must also be considered.

GANDANTA

Gandanta is a junctional area. It is considered adverse. A child born in Gandanta is likely to undergo physical suffering. Marriage or other auspicious acts, performed during Gandanta are likely to end in disaster. The Gandanta may be of the following types :

(a) *Nakshatra Gandanta* : Nakshatras of Ketu and Mercury (Ashwini, Ashlesha, Magha, Jyeshtha, Moola and Revati) constitute the Nakshatra gandanta.

(b) *Lagna Gandanta* : The last half Ghati (12minutes) of Karka, Vrishchika and Meena lagnas, and the first half a Ghati of Mesha, Simha and Dhanu lagnas constitute the lagna gandanta.

(c) *Tithi Gandanta* : The last one Ghati (24 minutes) of the Poorna (Tithis 5, 10, 15/30) and the first one Ghati of the Nanda (Tithis 1, 6, 11) constitute the Tithi gandanta.

The Abhijita Muhurta

One Ghati (24 minutes) on either side of the local noon (or local midnight!) is called as the Abhijita muhurta. This time is favourable for beginning any work, and must be considered when an appropriate Muhurta is not available.

Ashtakavarga in Muhurta

For individualised results, a native's Ashtakavarga (see Chapter XXX) may be considered for selecting a suitable Muhurta. A simple method of this is to decide on the relevant house, in the horoscope of the native, to which the required pursuit belongs. Choose a lagna from which the relevant house is strong in Sarvashtakavarga. For example, one wants to purchase a vehicle, which is to be seen from the fourth house. Choose a lagna from which the fourth house has the maximum benefic points in the Sarvashtakavarga. Similarly choose a strong fifth house for education, seventh house for partnership, tenth house for profession, etc.

Note : It will be appreciated that the classical Muhurta is particularly applicable to the ancient Indian way of life. Suitable modifications are essential if the Muhurta has to be applied in modern context.

...XXVII...
Matching of Charts:
The Traditional Method

मम योनिर्महद्ब्रह्म तस्मिन्गर्भं दधाम्यहम्।
संभवः सर्वभूतानां ततो भवति भारत॥

The great brahma (the Maya with the three qualitites of Sattva, Rajas
and Tamas) is My womb; in that I establish the seed. From that results
the birth of all beings, O' Bharata (Arjuna).   *Gita XIV-3.*

Marriage has been considered a very sacred duty of human beings in India. It involves an intimate link between two different individuals. Generally in India, amongst the traditional people, the two individuals involved in the act of marriage are strangers to each other, their union often having been arranged by their parents. There has been some change lately, particularly amongst the urban populace, so that the marrying couple meet, or often select, each other before being tied in wedlock.

The traditional Indian marriage being between two strangers, the ancient seers devised astrological methods to choose the right partner. This involves a process of matching of the horoscopes of the prospective bride and groom before getting them united in wedlock. The methods of horoscopic matching involve different factors which aim to ensure a physical as well as a mental matching of the prospective partners, keeping in view the social system of those times. While the traditional techniques need to be applied in a modified manner in the changed social ambience of today, they are still valid in a general sense. It will be no exaggeration to state that, even today, more than ninety percent of Hindus have their horoscopes matched before getting married. In fact, the natal astrology in ancient India was primarily directed at marriage, progeny and Muhurta.

Personal Selection

Even in the traditional India of ancient times, couples have fallen in love and united in wedlock. The scriptures deem that a relationship based on true mutual love needs no further matching of horoscopic charts of the couple.

The Blemish of Mars

The disposition of Mars in a chart is considered to be of special significance while considering a marital relationship. The location of Mars in the houses 1, 4, 7, 8 and 12 is labelled as 'Mangala Dosha' or the blemish of Mars. If Mars is located in any of these houses, in the chart of the girl, it is said to lead to widowhood by causing death of her husband. Similar disposition of Mars in the chart of the boy can cause death of his wife. It is said that such disposition of Mars in a horoscope must be considered both from the lagna as well as the Moon. When the horoscopes of the bride and the groom both are free from *Mangala Dosha,* when considered both from the lagna and the Moon, the situation is favourable and needs further study.

The blemish of Mars may be considered nullified in the following circumstances:

(a) When the blemish exists in the horoscopes of both the boy and the girl.
(b) When one chart has the blemish of Mars while the other chart shows its neutralisation by the placement of another malefic (Sun, Saturn, Rahu or Ketu) in one of the houses mentioned above.

From the above it is apparent that any malefic located in the houses 1, 4, 7, 8 or 12 from the lagna as well as the Moon in a given chart is not good for marital harmony unless equally matched by a similar disposition of malefics in the chart of the spouse. Preferably, the number of malefics influencing these houses must also be matched. Sometimes, remedial measures are prescribed to neutralise the *Mangala Dosha.*

Matching the Traditional Way

Eight different 'Kootas' (the *Ashtakoota!*) or 'factors of matching' are taken into consideration while matching the charts of the prospective bride and bridegroom. These are based on the sign and the nakshatra of the natal Moon in the charts of
the couple.

These eight factors, which are successively stronger in effect and considered to be possessive of successively increasing 'gunas' or benefic qualities, are as follows:

1. Varna
2. Vashya
3. Taara
4. Yoni
5. Graha-maitri
6. Gana
7. Bhakoota
8. Naadi

With *Varna* having one *guna* and the successive *Kootas* possessing the number of *gunas* progressively increasing by one until *Naadi* possesses eight *gunas,* a maximum of thirty-six *gunas* are possible. When a horoscopic pair shows anything from 24 to 36 *gunas,* it is considered an excellent match. When the match shows 12 to 24 *gunas,* it is considered only mediocre; less than 12 is adverse and generally not recommended for marriage. Very strict adherence to these rules may not be necessary when the planetary disposition in both charts is otherwise favourable.

1. Varna

The twelve Moon signs, in four groups of three each, indicate the four castes as follows:

(i)   Brahmins (the literate!)   : signs   4, 8, 12

(ii)   Kshatriyas (the warriors!)   : signs   1, 5, 9

(iii) Vaishyas (the traders!)   : signs   2, 6, 10

(iv)   Shudras (the unskilled!)   : signs   3, 7, 11

The first Varna (Brahmin) is the superior most and the subsequent ones are inferior in that order so that the Shudra is the inferior most. The *Varna* of the bridegroom should be the same as that of the bride, or superior to that of the bride. This earns the couple one *guna* or benefic point. This Koota ensures that the woman may only be raised higher in status.

Table XXVII -1: Gunas from matching of Varna

Groom / Bride	Brahmin	Kshatriya	Vaishya	Shudra
Brahmin	1	0	0	0
Kshatriya	1	1	0	0
Vaishya	1	1	1	0
Shudra	1	1	1	1

2. Vashya

The word 'Vashya' means 'controllable'. The Moon signs of the bride and the bridegroom must fall in the same group, to earn two benefic points; or the bride's sign should be in the groom's 'Vashya' for the same benefic score. The signs are classified as follows:

(i)   Chatushpada (quadruped) : Mesha, Vrisha, second half of Dhanu, first half of Makara.

(ii) Manava/Nara (biped)   : Mithuna, Kanya, Tula, first half of Dhanu, Kumbha.

(iii) Jalachara (aquatic)   : Karka, Meena, second half of Makara.

(iv) Vanachara (wild)   : Simha (not included amongst the quadrupeds above).

(v)   Keeta (insect)   : Vrishchika. (Karka has been included under Jalachara, vide supra).

All signs except Vrishchika (the Keeta) are Vashya for Simha (the Vanachara sign). Except Simha, all signs are Vashya for Manava (the biped signs). The Jalachara serves as food for Manava as does Chatushpada for Vanachara, and these combinations are not favoured. The following table (Table XXVII-2) shows the points gained from Vashya matching of the couple's charts.

Table XXVII - 2 : Gunas from Vashya matching

Groom / Bride	Chatush-pada	Manava	Jalachara	Vanachara	Keeta
Chatushpada	2	1	1	½	1
Manava	1	2	½	0	1
Jalachara	1	½	2	1	1
Vanachara	0	0	0	2	0
Keeta	1	1	1	0	2

3. Taara

Count from the bride's nakshatra to the groom's (both inclusive) and divide by nine. A remainder of 3, 5 or 7 is considered malefic and yields '0' gunas. Else, it is benefic and merits 1½ points. Similarly count from the groom's nakshatra to the bride's and divide by nine. A remainder of 3, 5 or 7 is again malefic ('0' gunas), while anything else is benefic and merits 1½ points. A fully benefic Taara (favourable countings in both cases) thus yields three benefic points. Table XXVII-3 gives the benefic points yielded by Taara in a couple's charts depending upon the remainder obtained after dividing by nine the number obtained by (i) counting the nakshatras from the groom's nakshatra to the bride's (horizontal), and (ii) from the bride's to the groom's (vertical).

Table XXVII - 3 : Gunas from Taara

		Remainder, from Groom's nakshatra								
		1	2	3	4	5	6	7	8	9
Remainder, from Bride's nakshatra	1	3	3	1½	3	1½	3	1½	3	3
	2	3	3	1½	3	1½	3	1½	3	3
	3	1½	1½	0	1½	0	1½	0	1½	1½
	4	3	3	1½	3	1½	3	1½	3	3
	5	1½	1½	0	1½	0	1½	0	1½	1½
	6	3	3	1½	3	1½	3	1½	3	3
	7	1½	1½	0	1½	0	1½	0	1½	1½
	8	3	3	1½	3	1½	3	1½	3	3
	9	3	3	1½	3	1½	3	1½	3	3

4. Yoni

The different nakshatras are said to possess the 'Yonis' of different animals. The birth nakshatras of the bride and the groom should indicate the *Yonis* of animals that are not mutually hostile. If they indicate the same *Yoni* or a neutral *Yoni*, it is considered desirable. Fourteen categories of *Yonis*, each indicated by two nakshatras, are described. For this purpose, the Abhijit nakshatra (extending from 6°40'00" to 10°53'20" in the Makara rashi) is also to be considered, raising the total number of nakshatras to twenty-eight.

The nakshatra pairs, their relevant Yonis and the intensely inimical Yoni are indicated below:

Nakshatras and Yonis

Nakshatras		*Yoni*	*Intense Enemy*
1. Ashwini,	Shatabhishaj	Ashwa (Horse)	Mahisha (Buffalo)
2. Bharani,	Revati	Gaja (Elephant)	Simha (Lion)
3. Krittika,	Pushya	Mesha (Ram)	Vanara (Monkey)
4. Rohini,	Mrigashira	Sarpa (Serpent)	Nakula (Mangoose)
5. Ardra,	Moola	Shwana (Dog)	Mriga (Deer)
6. Punarvasu,	Ashlesha	Marjara (Cat)	Mushaka (Rat)
7. Magha,	P. Phalguni	Mushaka (Rat)	Marjara (Cat)
8. U. Phalguni,	U. Bhadrapada	Gau (Cow)	Vyaghra (Tiger)
9. Hasta,	Swati	Mahisha (Buffalo)	Ashwa (Horse)
10. Chitra,	Vishakha	Vyaghra (Tiger)	Gau (Cow)
11. Anuradha,	Jyeshtha	Mriga (Deer)	Shwana (Dog)
12. P. Asadha,	Shravana	Vanara (Monkey)	Mesha (Ram)
13. U. Asadha,	Abhijit	Nakula (Mongoose)	Sarpa (Serpent)
14. Dhanishtha,	P. Bhadrapada	Simha (Lion)	Gaja (Elephant)

When the groom and the bride belong to the same Yoni, they earn 4 points. If they belong to the intensely inimical Yonis, they get no points. In case of mutually friendly Yonis, they get 3 points, for neutral Yonis 2 points, and for simply inimical Yonis only 1 point. Table XXVII-4 indicates the gunas earned by the couple on the basis of their Yonis.

Table XXVII - 4: Gunas from Yoni-matching

Bride \ Groom	Ashwa	Gaja	Mesha	Sarpa	Shwana	Marjara	Mushaka	Gau	Mahisha	Vyaghra	Mriga	Vanara	Nakula	Simha
Ashwa	4	2	3	2	2	3	3	2	0	1	3	2	2	1
Gaja	2	4	3	2	2	3	2	3	3	1	3	2	2	0
Mesha	3	3	4	2	2	3	2	3	3	1	3	0	2	1
Sarpa	2	2	2	4	2	1	1	2	2	2	2	1	0	2
Shwana	2	2	2	2	4	1	1	2	2	2	0	2	2	2
Marjara	3	3	3	1	1	4	0	3	3	2	3	2	2	2
Mushaka	3	2	2	1	1	0	4	3	3	2	3	2	1	2
Gau	2	3	3	2	2	3	3	4	3	0	3	2	2	1
Mahisha	0	3	3	2	2	3	3	3	4	1	3	2	2	1
Vyaghra	1	1	1	2	2	2	2	0	1	4	1	2	2	3
Mriga	3	3	3	2	0	3	3	3	3	1	4	2	2	1
Vanara	2	2	0	1	2	2	2	2	2	2	2	4	2	2
Nakula	2	2	2	0	2	2	1	2	2	2	2	2	4	2
Simha	1	0	1	2	2	2	2	1	1	3	1	2	2	4

5. Graha-maitri

This is based on mutual inclination of the lords of the Moon signs of the bridegroom and the bride. When the two lords are friends or are the same, full 5 points are granted. When the lord of the Moon sign of the one is friendly towards the other while the other's lord is neutral, 4 points are given. When both rashi lords are neutral to each other, 3 points are given. When one is friendly to the other and the other is inimical to it, only 1 point is allotted. Half a point is given where one planet is neutral to the other while the other is inimical. No gunas are earned if both the Moon-sign lords are mutually inimical. See Table XXVII-5 for Graha-maitri gunas.

Table XXVII-5 : Gunas from Graha-maitri

Moon-sign lord of the Bride	Moon-sign lord of the Groom						
		Sun	Moon	Mars	Mer	Jup	Ven	Sat
	Sun	5	5	5	4	5	0	0
	Moon	5	5	4	1	4	½	½
	Mars	5	4	5	½	5	3	½
	Mer	4	1	½	5	½	5	4
	Jupiter	5	4	5	½	5	½	3
	Venus	0	½	3	5	½	5	5
	Saturn	0	½	½	4	3	5	5

6. Gana

The twenty-seven nakshatras are divided into three categories of nine nakshatras each. Each category of nine nakshatras indicates one of the three *Ganas*, viz., *Deva-gana*, *Manushya-gana* and *Rakshasa-gana*. The nakshatras indicating these Ganas are as follows:

(a) **Deva-gana**: Ashwini, Mrigashira, Punarvasu, Pushya, Hasta, Swati, Anuradha, Shravana, Revati.

(b) **Manushya-gana**: Bharani, Rohini, Ardra, the three Purvas (P. Phalguni, P. Asadha, P. Bhadrapada), the three Uttaras (U. Phalguni, U. Asadha, U. Bhadrapada).

(c) **Rakshasa-gana**: Krittika, Ashlesha, Magha, Chitra, Vishakha, Jyeshtha, Moola, Dhanishtha, Shatabhishaj.

The benefic points earned by the couple depending upon their *Gana* based on their Moon's nakshatras are indicated in Table XXVII-6.

Table XXVII-6: Gunas earned from Gana matching

Bride \ Groom	Deva	Manushya	Rakshasa
Deva	6	5	1
Manushya	6	6	0
Rakshasa	0	0	6

7. Bhakoota

Here, the mutual disposition of the natal Moon signs of the couple is considered. When the Moon signs of the couple happen to fall mutually in positions 2/12, 6/8 or 5/9, no *gunas* are earned. Under other situations, seven points are allotted. Table XXVII-7 indicates the Bhakoota-gunas for various combinations of the Moon signs of the couple.

Table XXVII-7: Bhakoota Gunas

Rashis (Bride)	Bridegroom 1	2	3	4	5	6	7	8	9	10	11	12
1	7	0	7	7	0	0	7	0	0	7	7	0
2	0	7	0	7	7	0	0	7	0	0	7	7
3	7	0	7	0	7	7	0	0	7	0	0	7
4	7	7	0	7	0	7	7	0	0	7	0	0
5	0	7	7	0	7	0	7	7	0	0	7	0
6	0	0	7	7	0	7	0	7	7	0	0	7
7	7	0	0	7	7	0	7	0	7	7	0	0
8	0	7	0	0	7	7	0	7	0	7	7	0
9	0	0	7	0	0	7	7	0	7	0	7	7
10	7	0	0	7	0	0	7	7	0	7	0	7
11	7	7	0	0	7	0	0	7	7	0	7	0
12	0	7	7	0	0	7	0	0	7	7	0	7

While considering Bhakoota gunas, a few points need to be taken note of. These are as follows:

(a) 6/8 position: The sixth rashi from an odd sign and the eighth from an even sign form malefic mutual 6/8 positions since the lords of such signs are mutually hostile. On the other hand, the sixth rashi from an even sign and the eighth from an odd sign form favourable mutual 6/8 positions since the lords of such signs are mutually not hostile but friendly. A favourable 6/8 disposition of the Moon signs of the couple is not too bad.

(b) An adverse 6/8 position is supposed to lead to death of a marital partner. A mutual 2/12 position of the Moon signs of the couple leads to penury while a mutual 5/9 disposition causes childlessness.

(c) When the two marital partners have the same Moon sign in their natal charts, it in considered favourable provided that the nakshatras of the two Moons are different.

(d) When the rashi lords of the two Moons in mutual 2/12 positions are friendly, the blemish of the 2/12 disposition is greatly diminished. It is further desirable to have the bride's Moon sign identical with the 12th house of the groom's Moon instead of vice versa.

8. Naadi

The twenty-seven nakshatras fall into three Naadis as follows:

(a) *Adya*: Ashwini, Ardra, Punarvasu, Uttara Phalguni, Hasta, Jyeshtha Moola, Shatabhishaj, P. Bhadrapada.

(b) *Madhya*: Bharani, Marigashira, Pushya, Purva Phalguni, Chitra, Anuradha, P. Asadha, Dhanishtha, U. Bhadrapada.

(c) *Antya*: Krittika, Rohini, Ashlesha, Magha, Swati, Vishakha, U. Asadha, Shravana, Revati

The Nakshatras of the groom and the bride should not fall in the same Naadi. The *gunas* are considered as shown in Table XXVII-8.

Table XXVII-8: Naadi-gunas

Bride \ Groom	Adya	Madhya	Antya
Adya	0	8	8
Madhya	8	0	8
Antya	8	8	0

The following points need consideration while judging the Naadi-gunas:

(a) When both the bride and the groom have the same Rashi but different nakshatras, the blemish of the same Naadi does not apply.

(b) When both the bride and the groom have the same nakshatra but different rashis, again the blemish of the Naadi does not apply.

(c) When both the bride and the groom fall in the Adya Naadi, the groom suffers. When they both have Antya Naadi, the bride suffers. When both have Madhya Naadi, both bride as well as groom suffer adverse effects, including death.

The process of chart matching in respect of a couple, considering the eight Kootas or gunas, is being shown here (**Charts XXVII-1** and **2**). The nakshatra of the male is Moola (19th nakshatra) and that of the female is Uttara Bhadrapada (26th nakshatra). Their rashis are Dhanu and Meena respectively.

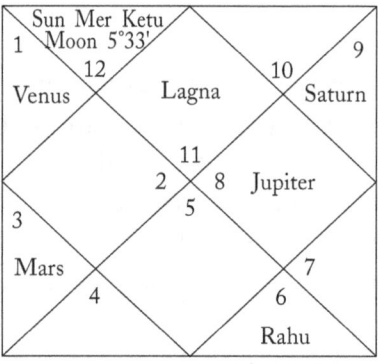

	Groom	Bride	
Kootas	*Groom*	*Bride*	*Gunas*
1. Varna	Kshatriya	Brahmin	0
2. Vashya	Manava	Jalachara	½
3. Taara	8 (÷9; R=8)	21 (÷9; R=3)	1½
4. Yoni	Shwana	Gau	2
5. Graha-maitri	Jupiter	Jupiter	5
6. Gana	Rakshasa	Manushya	0
7. Bhakoota	Dhanu	Meena	7
8. Naadi	Adya	Madhya	8
		Total	24

A total of twenty four gunas as available here falls in the range of acceptability. It will also be seen that the chart of the male has Mars in the twelfth house and, therefore, indicates the *Mangala Dosha*. This finds neutralisation in the chart of the female because of the placement of Rahu in the eighth. It might be preferable to have a horoscope where the *Mangala Dosha* is neutralised by a malefic occuping the same house in the chart of one spouse as occupied by Mars in that of the other.

More About Naadi

A more detailed method of reckoning Naadi has been suggested depending upon the nature of the nakshtras. According to this method, three different consider-ations are employed as follows:

(a) *Tri-Naadi (three Naadis)*: This is considered in cases where the girl's nakshatra belongs to the group of nakshatras that completely fall in a given sign. Such nakshatras include Ashwini, Bharani, Rohini, Ardra, Pushya, Ashlesha, Magha, P. Phalguni, Hasta, Swati, Anuradha, Jyestha, Moola, P. Asadha, Shravana, Shatabhishaj, U. Bhadrapada, Revati. The Naadis for matching to be considered here are the same as shown above (Table XXVII-8).

(b) *Chatur-Naadi (four Naadis)*: When the girl's nakshatra belongs to one of the nakshatras that has three of its quarters in one sign (and one quarter in another), four Naadis are to be considered. The relevant nakshatras here are Krittika, Punarvasu, U. Phalguni, Vishakha, U. Asadha, P. Bhadrapada, i.e., the nakshatras of the Sun and Jupiter.

The four Naadis are as follows:
(i)   First Naadi   : Krittika, Magha, P. Phalguni, Jyeshtha, Moola, U. Bhadrapada, Revati.
(ii) Second Naadi : Rohini, Ashlesha, U. Phalguni, Anuradha, P. Ashadha, P. Bhadrapada, Ashwini.
(iii) Third Naadi : Mrigashira, Pushya, Hasta, Vishakha, U. Ashadha, Shatabhishaj, Bharani.
(iv) Fourth Naadi : Ardra, Punarvasu, Chitra, Swati, Shravarna, Dhan-ishtha.

(c) *Pancha-Naadi (five Naadis)*: This is to be applied where the girl's nakshatra happens to occupy two adjacent nakshatras equally (i.e., it has its two quarters falling in two adjacent signs). These nakshatras are Mrigashira, Chitra and Dhanishtha, i.e., the nakshatras of Mars. The five Naadis to be considered are as given below:
(i)   First Naadi   : Mrigashira, Chitra, Swati, Shatabhishaj, P. Bhadra-pada.
(ii) Second Naadi : Ardra, Hasta, Vishakha, Dhanishtha, U. Bhadrapada.
(iii) Third Naadi : Punarvasu, U. Phalguni, Anuradha, Shravana, Revati.

(iv) Fourth Naadi : Pushya, P. Phalguni, Jyeshtha, U. Ashadha, Ashwini, Rohini.

(v) Fifth Naadi : Ashlesha, Magha, Moola, P. Ashadha, Bharani, Krittika.

According to this method too, the nakshatras of the bridegroom and the bride should fall in different Naadis to earn the eight benefic points. Naadi matching ensures a long marital life and protection against dangers.

The Ashta-Kootas mentioned here for matching the horoscopes of prospective bride and bridegroom indicate the traditional method of horoscope matching. This method lays great stress on a mental match for the couple, hence its almost total reliance on the rashi or the Moon signs of the marital partners. When two horoscopes secure a score of 18 or above, out of a possible total of 36, they are considered acceptable for marriage. The greater the score, the higher is the compatibility.

It may, however, be pointed out that this is only one of the methods of matching the horoscopic charts. In actual matching, several additional factors need to be considered. These include a thorough study of each of the two horoscopes separately, consideration of the longevity of the partners, the promise of a reasonably good marital life and of progeny, and the dasha pattern. Also to be considered are the vargas like the navamsha and the Saptamsha. In the modern times, it also needs to be considered whether the partners want marriage primarily for progeny or for such other aspects of life as financial stability, excessive earning and professional excellence for one or both of them. In a way, the process of matching of charts for marriage has become more difficult and time consuming today than it used to be in the ancient times.

...XXVIII...
Prashna or Horary Astrology

व्यामिश्रेणेव वाक्येन बुद्धि मोहयसीव मे।
तदेकं वद निश्चित्य येन श्रेयोऽहमाप्नुयाम्॥

With an apparently confused utterance you virtually bewilder my intelligence. Spell out decisively the one thing which leads me to the highest good. Gita III/2.

Prashna is a unique system of Vedic astrology which does not involve the necessity to possess a birth chart. The important factor here is the actual moment of making a query. Generally, it involves the erection of a horoscopic chart for the moment of the query. The predictions also are generally related to the question made, and to the answers derived astrologically.

Prashna seems to have the blessings of the ancient sage Parshurama. The system of Prashna is very elaborately developed in the southern Indian state of Kerala, and the principles of this system are briefly available in the classic known as the *Prashna Marga*. According to this highly evolved system, almost any query pertaining to a querist, or his relatives, etc., can be answered. In the rest of India, the Prashna method is mainly based on the *Shatapanchashika* of Prithuyashas, son of the celebrated Varahamihira. Lately, the methods of the Tajika system or Varshaphala were incorporated into it. It is thus a common practice to use the Tajika yogas in the Prashna chart. Except for the elaborate system practised in Kerala, the Prashna system in general throws light only on a limited area and primarily concerns itself with the question put by a querist. Long range predictions or widely ranging predictions can generally not be made on this basis. However, Prashna is a quick and reliable method for finding answers to specific questions especially when the birth time of the native is not known.

The astrologer notes down the time when a querist approaches him with a question, or rings him up about his question. A question can also be asked on behalf of someone else. Questions regarding theft, litigation, success or failure, disease, treatment, missing persons, survival in accidents, etc., can be answered easily on the basis of Prashna. A horoscope is cast for the moment a query is made, and this is subjected to standard astrological principles applicable to horary charts.

Planets, houses and signs

The significations of the planets, houses and signs in a Prashna chart remain the same as for natal astrology. Thus, kendras and trikonas associated with natural benefics prove to be beneficial. Placement of malefics in houses 3, 6 and 11, and their absence from the kendras, trikonas and the eighth house also prove beneficial in respect of the query made.

Importance of the Lagna

The lagna is of utmost importance in a Prashna chart. The nature of the lagna indicates the turn of events pertaining to a query.

(a) *Lagna in a Chara rashi* (movable sign) : A Chara rashi rising in the lagna indicates change. In a query regarding the health of a patient, the condition will change for better or worse. In case of a job, there will be a change of place or status. If it concerns a missing person, such a person is unable to settle or attain a position or appointment at his existing place which he is likely to change.

(b) *Lagna in a Sthira rashi* (fixed sign) : A Sthira rashi rising in the lagna indicates that a change is unlikely. Depending upon the nature of query, the condition of the patient remains static, or there is no transfer or change in status in a job, or the missing person remains and settles in his existing position, etc.

(c) *Lagna in a Dwiswabhava rashi* (mixed sign) : The first half of a Dwiswabhava rashi, being adjacent to a Sthira rashi, produces results like a Sthira rashi. The second half of a Dwiswabhava rashi, being closer to a Chara rashi, produces results like a Chara rashi.

Multiple Queries

When a person puts several questions at the same time, the following rule must be observed :

First question:	Judge from the lagna
Second question:	Judge from the position of the Moon
Third question:	From the position of the Sun
Fourth question:	From Jupiter
Fifth question:	From the stronger of the two, viz., Mercury and Venus.

The role of kendras

The kendras are very important in the Prashna system.

The *first house* (the lagna) concerns itself with change or disturbance of one's existing position. The *fourth house* indicates success or prosperity. The *seventh house* indicates return (to his home or native country) while the *tenth house* indicates absence from one's home or country.

In a question about health, the physician is represented by the lagna, disease by the seventh house, patient by the tenth house and the medicine by the fourth.

In a query about a traveller or a missing person, the lagna stands for the traveller, the seventh for the path or for return, the tenth for absence (from home, etc.) and the fourth for the well being of the traveller.

In a query about theft, the lagna indicates the querist while the seventh house indicates the thief. The tenth house indicates the authority (police, etc.) and the fourth indicates the property stolen.

In a query about litigation, the lagna indicates the litigant while the seventh house indicates the opponent. The tenth house indicates authority, and the fourth house judgement.

Favourable indications

1. A house aspected or occupied by its lord or by benefics tends to prosper.

2. When a benefic occupies the lagna, or the rising Navamsha belongs to a benefic, or when the lagna as well as the rising Navamsha fall in Sheershodaya signs (Mithuna, Simha, Kanya, Tula, Vrishchika, Kumbha), success in business is favoured.

3. Take note of the nature of query. If the question pertains to such fixed things as house, lands, marriage, etc., a fixed or Sthira lagna is favourable. When a question is concerned with transfer, recovery from disease, return of the traveller, etc., a movable or Chara lagna is better.

4. Note the house to which the query pertains. If the lagna lord (lagnesha!) and the lord of the concerned house (karyesha) (a) occupy their own houses, (b) occupy each other's houses, (c) aspect their own houses, or (d) aspect each other's houses, then the query pertaining to that house has a favourable outcome.

At the time of a question pertaining to a pursuit of a highly creative nature, the following chart (**Chart XXVIII-1**) was obtained. Venus, the lagna lord as well as the planet of art and sophistication, occupies the fifth house of creativity, along with the fifth lord. Venus gets exalted in the Navamsha. Some important Tajika yogas too form in this chart indicating success and monetary gains from this venture. The Navamsha and the Dashamamsha charts are favourable too. Rahu is on the exact degree of the lagna indicating a somewhat unorthodox undertaking, perhaps also making the intentions of the querist suspect.

Sun Mercury	Ketu		Moon
Venus Saturn	**Chart XXVIII-1**		Mars
	April 6, 1995		
	Jup (R)	Lagna Rahu	

Lagna	11°42'	Mars	20°20'	Venus	17°28'
Sun	22°32'	Mercury	14°19'	Saturn	25°00'
Moon	4°42'	Jupiter	21°33'	Rahu	11°55'

5. Placement of benefics in kendras and trikonas, and malefics in houses 3, 6 and 11 is considered highly favourable.

Nature of Signs

Biped signs (Mithuna, Kanya, Tula, Kumbha, first half of Dhanu) are strong in the lagna. Quadruped signs (Mesha, Vrisha, Simha, latter half of Dhanu and first half of Makara) are strong in the tenth house. Watery signs (Karka, Meena, latter half of Makara) find strength in the fourth house. Vrishchika finds strength in the seventh house.

Some diverse combinations in a Prashna chart

1. Jupiter and Venus occupying the second and third houses from the ascendant indicate the return of a traveller who has gone abroad. In the fourth house, they indicate immediate return. Mercury and Venus in the second and twelfth from the lagna or the Moon indicate non-return of the traveller.

2. A Kartari yoga forming around the lagna, the Moon or the seventh house indicates that a person intending to undertake a journey will not do so.

3. A Prishtodaya sign (Mesha, Vrisha, Karka, Dhanu and Makara) rising in the ascendant, aspected by malefics and unaspected by benefics, with the sixth house occupied by malefics, does not augur well for the safety of the traveller or the missing person.

4. A Shubha Kartari yoga around the seventh house indicates non-return of the traveller because of his friends and masters; a Paapa Kartari, because of such compulsions as illness or enemies.

5. A benefic occupying the lagna, and benefics located in houses 3, 6, 9 and 11 contribute to the cure of disease in the case of an ailing person.

6. If Jupiter and Venus occupy kendras in a Prashna chart, the ailing man recovers.

7. The patient gets cured when the benefics occupy kendras and trikonas, the Moon occupies an Upachaya house and the benefics aspect the lagna.

8. Placement of the Moon in the eighth house from the lagna, particularly when aspected by malefics and unaspected by benefics, does not augur well for the health or survival of a patient.

9. In cases of theft, a Sthira lagna or a Sthira Navamsha or a Vargottama lagna indicates that the thief is a member of the family. A Chara lagna indicates that the thief is a stranger.

10. If the first Drekkana of the lagna rises at the time of a query, the missing article has been left (or dropped) at the gate of the house; if the middle Drekkana rises, the article is within the house; if the last Drekkana rises, it will be found in the backyard of the house.

11. Mars or the second lord located in the seventh or the eighth house indicates that the property will not be recovered.

12. Malefics in the lagna indicate quarrel or physical injury involving the querist. Malefics in the fourth house indicate discord at home, and loss of happiness and unity in the family.

Intentions of the querist

It often so happens that the querist is not sincere in his query and only intends to test the knowledge of the astrologer, or wants to subject him to ridicule. In such cases it is necessary to ensure whether or not the querist is sincere and straightforward. Some clues are given here.

1. When Saturn occupies a kendra, Mercury is combust, and the Moon in the ascendant is aspected by Mercury and Mars, the querist is insincere and has ill intentions.

2. A benefic located in the ascendant indicates that the querist is sincere, a malefic that he is crooked.

3. If either Jupiter or Mercury or an inimical planet aspects the lord of the seventh house, the querist is insincere.

4. In the foregoing situation, if the seventh lord and the planet aspecting it are in turn aspected by benefics, the querist is trustworthy.

5. When the seventh house receives the aspects of Mercury or Jupiter or the Moon (jointly or separately), the querist is sincere and honest.

6. The Moon in the lagna, and the Sun, Mercury and Saturn, together in a kendra, do not speak well of the intentions of the querist.

Note : This chapter on Prashna has been dealt with very briefly and superficially. For a detailed account, the reader is referred to appropriate works available on the subject.

...XXIX...
Gochara or Planetary Transits

तदेजति तन्नैजति तद्दूरे तद्वन्तिके।
तदन्तरस्य सर्वस्य तदु सर्वस्यास्य बाह्यतः ॥

That moves, That moves not; That is far off, That is very near; That is within all this (manifestation), (and) That is without all this

Ishavasyopanishad, Sl 5.

A horoscopic chart is like a still picture of the zodiac and the planets which are otherwise in a state of flux. The horoscopic chart indicates the position of planets at the time of birth. The constant movement of planets, however, continues, and in this process the various planets transit over sensitive areas of the horoscope. This makes occurrence of specific events possible. The sequence of dashas indicates the sequence of events that happen in an individual's life at appropriate moments. Transit of planets helps us clinch the moment of occurrence of events very accurately.

By the foregoing it is meant that the horoscopic chart carries a promise which the dasha pattern unfolds in time. The transits confirm the unfolding of that promise at a given time. The transits are thus subservient to the natal chart and its dasha pattern. They confirm the promise in the chart and indicate its fructification.

Gochara from the lagna or the Moon?

Classically, the transit of planets in different houses is considered from the position of the Moon in the natal chart. The sign occupied by the Moon in the natal chart is known as the Janma Rashi of the native. Different planets are said to produce different results when they transit the various houses considering the Janma Rashi as the lagna. In north India, astrologers make a separate Chandra Kundali, or the lunar chart, marking the Moon sign as the lagna. This is used as an alternate horoscope as well as a chart for reckoning transits.

It may, however, be pointed out that transits considered from the lagna appear to be working as well in actual horoscopes. They must, therefore, be applied to the natal chart also. Their results are perhaps more individualised when they are considered from the lagna, than from the Moon.

Since classical works mention the results of transits in relation to the Moon, they will be briefly described here a such. They can be equally well applied to the lagna.

Transits over Houses

Different planets produce benefic or malefic results when they transit various houses considered from the house occupied by the Moon in the natal chart. Good results produced by the planets transiting certain houses are obstructed by other planets occu-pying certain other specific houses. These obstructing planets are said to produce what is called 'Vedha'. Hereunder, the houses of benefic transits and the corresponding Vedha positions for each planet are being given.

Sun

Benefic transits:	3,	6,	10,	11	
Vedha positions:	9,	12,	4,	5	

Note : This means that the Sun produces benefic results when transiting the third house, unless there is an obstructing planet in the ninth house, from the Moon (or lagna!). Similarly, its sixth house transit is good unless obstructed from the twelfth house, and so on.

Moon

Benefic transits:	1,	3,	6,	7,	10,	11
Vedha positions:	5,	9,	12,	2,	4,	8

Mars

Benefic transits:	3,	6,	11
Vedha positions:	12	9,	5

Mercury

Benefic transits:	2,	4,	6,	8,	10,	11
Vedha positions:	5,	3,	9,	1,	8,	12

Jupiter

Benefic transits:	2,	5,	7,	9,	11
Vedha positions:	12	4,	3,	10,	8

Venus

Benefic transits:	1,	2,	3,	4,	5,	8,	9,	11,	12
Vedha positions:	8,	7,	1,	10,	9,	5,	11,	3,	6

Saturn and Rahu

Benefic transits and Vedha positions are the same as in the case of Mars.

Note :

(a) The father-son duo (Sun and Saturn, or Moon and Mercury) do not cause Vedha to each other.

(b) While a planet gives benefic results when transiting benefic houses, its transit over the corresponding Vedha positions gives adverse results. For example, the Sun transiting the third house gives benefic results, but its transit over the ninth house produces bad results. These bad results are obstructed (or get subjected to Vedha) if another planet, other than Saturn, transits the third house at the same time. Thus Vedha obstructs benefic results as also adverse results.

Results of Transits

The various planets transiting the twelve houses from the Moon (or the lagna) produce varying results as listed below.

The Sun

The effects of the Sun's transit in the twelve houses are: (1) Ill health, travel; (2) Loss of wealth; (3) Health and wealth; (4) Illness, worries; (5) Mental anguish; (6) Annihilation of foes; (7) Travel, illness to wife; (8) Humiliation, disease; (9) Humiliation, mental anguish; (10) Success in undertakings; (11) High status; and (12) Losses and ill health.

The Moon

The results of the transit of the Moon in the several houses are: (1) Good fortune; (2) Loss of wealth; (3) Victory; (4) Apprehensions; (5) Depression; (6) Freedom from illness; (7) Varied comforts; (8) Unexpected adverse events; (9) Ill health; (10) Success in undertakings; (11) Gains, happiness; and (12) Expenditure.

Mars

The results of Mars' transit in the twelve houses are: (1) Mental torment; (2) Loss of wealth; (3) Victory; (4) Displacement from place of work or residence; (5) Mental anguish; (6) Victory over enemy and disease; (7) Discord with wife; (8) Unexpected tragedy, accident, etc.; (9) Loss of health and wealth; (10) Obstacles, physical exertion; (11) Gain of health and wealth; and (12) Loss of wealth.

Mercury

The results of Mercury's transit are: (1) Loss of wealth; (2) Gain of wealth; (3) Fear from foes; (4) Multiple gains; (5) Discord with wife and children; (6) Dominance over opponents; (7) Quarrels; (8) Gain of wealth, loss of health; (9) Obstacles to undertakings; (10) All comforts; (11) Multiple gains; (12) Dominance by opponents.

Jupiter

The transit of Jupiter produces the following results: (1) Displacement and expenditure; (2) Gain of wealth; (3) Ill health; (4) Discord at home, increase of opponents; (5) Happiness, birth of a child; (6) Troubles from enemies; (7) Comforts from wife and children, auspicious journey; (8) Unwanted travel, loss of wealth; (9) Virtuous pursuits, many gains; (10) Apprehensions about career; (11) Acquisition of wealth and status; (12) Loss of wealth.

Venus

The results of transit of Venus are: (1) Physical pleasures; (2) Inflow of wealth; (3) Varied gains; (4) Increase in the number of friends; (5) Birth of a son; (6) Misfortunes; (7) Troubles to or from wife; (8) Gain of health and wealth; (9) Varied comforts; (10) Quarrels; (11) Gain of wealth, apprehensions, etc; (12) Acquisition of wealth.

Saturn

Saturn's transit over the twelve houses causes: (1) Ill health; (2) Loss of wealth; (3) Rise in status; (4) Discord at home; (5) Illness to chidren, and mental anguish; (6) Dominance over opponents; (7) Troublesome journey, and illness to wife; (8) Varied misfortunes; (9) Base acts, harm to father; (10) Obstacles to career; (11) Inflow of wealth, varied comforts; (12) Wastage of effort and money.

Rahu

Rahu's transit in the twelve houses leads to: (1) Illness; (2) Loss of wealth; (3) Varied pleasures; (4) Miseries; (5) Loss of wealth; (6) Comforts; (7) Humiliation; (8) Serious illness; (9) Losses; (10) Comforts; (11) Good fortune; (12) Excessive expenditure.

Points to Remember

1. When a planet transits a benefic house identical with its debilitation sign or enemy's house, its benefits are fore-shortened. Debilitation coinciding with bad transits leads to adverse results.

2. Transits coinciding with exaltation or own house are favourable.

3. Transits of malefics over the natal malefics are particularly harmful.

4. The Sun and Mars produce results, immediately after entering a sign; Jupiter and Venus produce results in the middle of a sign; the Moon and Saturn produce their results when in the concluding one-third of a sign; Mercury and Rahu produce their results throughout the transit of a sign.

5. All transits are subservient to the static promise in the horoscope and the sequence of dashas.

Transits over Nakshatras

Transit of malefics over the following nakshatras is considered adverse:

1. Birth nakshatra (Janma), and its trinal nakshatras, i.e., the tenth (Karma) and the nineteenth (Adhana) from it.
2. Third (Vipat) from the birth nakshatra.
3. Fifth (Pratyari) from the birth nakshatra.
4. Seventh (Vadha) from the birth nakshatra.
5. Twenty-second (Vainashaka) from the birth nakshatra.

The Sade-Sati of Saturn

Saturn takes approximately two and a half years to transit a sign. Its transit in the three houses, falling in the twelfth, first and second from the Moon, and lasting a period of seven and a half years (Sade-Sati: seven and a half!), is considered particularly adverse. This period coincides with varied troubles, apprehensions, losses, tragedies, wanderings and physical ailments.

Sade-sati recurs roughly after a cycle of thirty years. A person may have a maximum of three cycles of Sade-Sati. It is said that the first cycle of the Sade-Sati proves adverse for the parents of the native, the second for the native himself, and the third for his progeny.

While this transit of Saturn over the Moon and its two surrounding houses has been widely condemned, it is important not to apply these results blindly. One must consider the location of the Moon in the natal chart, the sign occupied by the Moon, as also the planetary period (MD, AD, PD, etc.,) in operation. Only after considering all these factors should the results of Sade-Sati be announced.

Examples

The native of **Chart XXIX-1** was running the MD/AD of Jupiter-Rahu from April 2, 1992 to August 26, 1994. Jupiter is the retrograde eighth and eleventh

Lagna	25°01'	Mars	29°30'	Venus	7°30'
Sun	21°12'	Mercury	14°13'	Saturn (R)	3°30'
Moon	1°33'	Jupiter (R)	6°20'	Rahu	5°25'

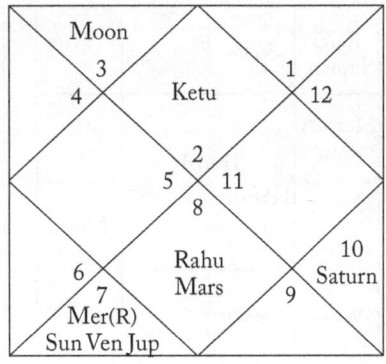

		Ketu	Moon
	Transit November 5, 1993		
Saturn			
	Rahu Mars	Mer(R) SunVen Jupiter	

lord in the eleventh house, whereas Rahu is located in the sixth house along with a debilitated Sun. The MD/AD lords are placed 6/8 from each other.

On November 5, 1993 the native was compulsorily retired by official orders. Mars in transit aspects the tenth house from the natal Moon; Jupiter too does the same; Saturn, the debilitated retrograde lord of the tenth in the natal chart, occupies the fifth house (eighth from the tenth!) from the natal Moon. The Moon occupies the tenth house from the natal Moon on the day the retirement orders were received by the native.

Transits in effect sensitise or activate specific houses so that events pertaining to those houses take place. Jupiter transiting the second house from the natal Moon and aspecting the second house from the lagna ensured good amount of money as terminal benefits.

The native of **Chart XXIX-2** was running the MD/AD/PD of Rahu-Mars-Sun from February 5, 1987 to February 24, 1987 during which he sustained a serious car accident (on February 15, 1987). Rahu involves the 3/9 axis of movement, Mars is the planet of accidents aspecting the third lord, whereas the Sun is debilitated, associated with Mars and aspected by Saturn.

In transit, the Sun was in the third house from the lagna (hence the importance of lagna in transit), on natal Ketu (watch for malefics transiting

		Moon	
Ketu	**Chart XXIX-2** **Birth Chart** October 27, 1961		
Saturn Jupiter			Rahu
Lagna		Mer(R) Sun Mars	Venus

Lagna	17°45'	Mars	24°09'
Sun	10°13'	Mercury	0°53'
Moon	24°46'	Jupiter	5°46'

Venus	17°57'
Saturn	0°37'
Rahu	1°22'

Rahu Jupiter	Mars		
Mercury Sun	**Transit** February 15, 1987		
			Moon
Venus	Saturn		Ketu

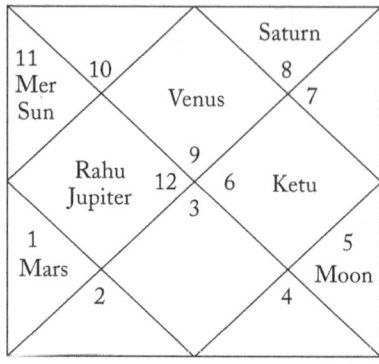

the malefics in natal chart!). Saturn in transit occupied the twelfth from the lagna, and the seventh from the Moon (both adverse), and aspected the lord of the third house. Mars transited the twelfth from the Moon. The Moon was in the ninth house aspecting the third house and transiting the RKA. The Moon's transit in effect clinches the day an event occurs. Transit of the eleventh house from the Moon by Jupiter and Rahu acts as a protective factor.

The native of **Chart XXIX-3** had her marriage fixed for a day when five planets were located in the eighth house from her natal Moon. Three of these,

Jupiter	Moon		Rahu
Venus	**Chart XXIX-3** **Birth Chart** January 22, 1964		
Saturn Mars Sun			
Ketu Mercury			Lagna

Lagna	29°08'	Mars	13°21'	Venus	12°20'
Sun	7°24'	Mercury	13°30'	Saturn	29°20'
Moon	1°30'	Jupiter	19°49'	Rahu	16°54'

		Ketu	
Saturn	**Transit** December 7, 1993		
			Moon
	RahSun MarVen Mercury	Jupiter	

the Sun, Mars, and Rahu, are natural malefics while Mercury is a functionally bad planet considered from the Moon. The marriage party came to her house, insulted her as well as her parents, and left without going through the marriage ceremony. There are too many malefics in the eighth house from the Moon. The transit Moon, in the fifth from the natal Moon, and the twelfth from the lagna, is no good. While fixing a Muhurta for marriage, it is esential to ensure that the eighth house from the lagna as well as the Moon is free from affliction.

...XXX...

Ashtakavarga

भूमिरापोऽनलो वायुः खं मनो बुद्धिरेव च।
अहंकार इतीयं मे भिन्ना प्रकृतिरष्टधा॥

Earth, water, fire, air, ether, mind and reason and ego – thus is My nature divided eightfold.   *Gita VII/4*

A shtakavarga is a unique system of prediction in Vedic astrology. It is primarily used to decipher the results of planetary transits. Combined with the dasha system, it helps in making remarkably accurate predictions. The whole system of Ashtakavarga is quite elaborate and, therefore, beyond the scope of this work. Here, only the elementary concepts of this technique of prediction are being presented. For greater details, the reader is referred to the *Ashtakavarga: The Dots of Destiny* by Vinay Aditya.

Basis of Ashtakavarga

1. Each chart has seven planets (from the Sun to Saturn) and the lagna from where all good or bad results ensue. The Ashtakavarga (i.e., eight-fold) system considers these eight points as of special relevance. Rahu and Ketu are not considered in Ashtakavarga calculations, though there is some controversy in this regard.

2. Each of the seven planets influences certain houses beneficially when considered from the above-mentioned eight points. The remaining houses are influenced adversely. The houses beneficially influenced are marked by a rod or a dot (called henceforth as the benefic point).

3. Seven different charts are thus possible for the seven different planets. These are called as *Bhinnashtakavargas*. The position of each planet in the natal chart is of primary consideration.

4. Any given house can have a maximum of eight benefic points contributed by the planet in respect of seven planets and the lagna. The greater the number of benefic points in a house, the stronger and more benefic it is.

5. When the benefic points contributed by each planet in different signs are added, we get a *Sarvashtakavarga*. The Sun contributes a total of 48 benefic points, the Moon contributes 49 points, Mars contributes 39 points, Mercury contributes 54 points, Jupiter contributes 56 points, Venus contributes 52 points, and Saturn contributes 39 benefic points. A total of 337 benefic points are contributed, by the seven planets, to various houses in relation to seven planets and the lagna.

6. In general, good results accrue when planets transit strong houses (i.e., houses containing greater number of benefic points) and bad results follow when they transit weak houses (with fewer benefic points).

Below are given the specific houses where each of the seven planets proves auspicious when considered from each of the eight cardinal points (the seven planets and the lagna). This gives the Bhinnashtaka of the seven planets.

The Sun

The Sun is beneficial in the houses indicated against each of the eight cardinal points, as follows:

(1)	Sun	1,	2,	4,	7,	8,	9,	10,	11,
(2)	Moon	3,	6,	10,	11,				
(3)	Mars	1,	2,	4,	7,	8,	9,	10,	11,
(4)	Mercury	3,	5,	6,	9,	10,	11,	12,	
(5)	Jupiter	5,	6,	9,	11,				
(6)	Venus	6,	7,	12,					
(7)	Saturn	1,	2,	4,	7,	8,	9,	10,	11,
(8)	Lagna	3,	4,	6,	10,	11,	12,		

Total : 48 benefic points.

The Moon

The Moon is beneficial in the houses indicated against each of the eight cardinal points, as follows:

(1)	Sun	3,	6,	7,	8,	10,	11,		
(2)	Moon	1,	3,	6,	7,	10,	11,		
(3)	Mars	2,	3,	5,	6,	9,	10,	11,	
(4)	Mercury	1,	3,	4,	5,	7,	8,	10,	11,
(5)	Jupiter	1,	4,	7,	8,	10,	11,	12,	
(6)	Venus	3,	4,	5,	7,	9,	10,	11,	
(7)	Saturn	3,	5,	6,	11,				
(8)	Lagna	3,	6,	10,	11,				

Total : 49 benefic points.

Mars

Mars is beneficial in the houses indicated against each of the eight cardinal points, as follows:

(1) Sun   3,   5,   6,   10,   11,
(2) Moon   3,   6,   11,
(3) Mars   1,   2,   4,   7,   8,   10,   11,
(4) Mercury   3,   5,   6,   11,
(5) Jupiter   6,   10,   11,   12,
(6) Venus   6,   8,   11,   12,
(7) Saturn   1,   4,   7,   8,   9,   10,   11,
(8) Lagna   1,   3,   6,   10,   11,

Total : 39 benefic points.

Mercury

Mercury is beneficial in the houses indicated against each of the eight cardinal points, as follows:

(1) Sun   5,   6,   9,   11,   12,
(2) Moon   2,   4,   6,   8,   10,   11,
(3) Mars   1,   2,   4,   7,   8,   9,   10,   11,
(4) Mercury   1,   3,   5,   6,   9,   10,   11,   12,
(5) Jupiter   6,   8,   11,   12,
(6) Venus   1,   2,   3,   4,   5,   8,   9,   11,
(7) Saturn   1,   2,   4,   7,   8,   9,   10,   11,
(8) Lagna   1,   2,   4,   6,   8,   10,   11,

Total : 54 benefic points.

Jupiter

Jupiter is beneficial in the houses indicated against each of the eight cardinal, points as follows:

(1) Sun   1,   2,   3,   4,   7,   8,   9,   10,   11,
(2) Moon   2,   5,   7,   9,   11,
(3) Mars   1,   2,   4,   7,   8,   10,   11,
(4) Mercury   1,   2,   4,   5,   6,   9,   10,   11,
(5) Jupiter   1,   2,   3,   4,   7,   8,   10,   11,
(6) Venus   2,   5,   6,   9,   10,   11,
(7) Saturn   3,   5,   6,   12,
(8) Lagna   1,   2,   4,   5,   6,   7,   9,   10,   11,

Total : 56 benefic points.

Venus

Venus is beneficial in the houses indicated against each of the eight cardinal points, as follows:

(1)	Sun	8,	11,	12,						
(2)	Moon	1,	2,	3,	4,	5,	8,	9,	11,	12,
(3)	Mars	3,	5,	6,	9,	11,	12,			
(4)	Mercury	3,	5,	6,	9,	11,				
(5)	Jupiter	5,	8,	9,	10,	11,				
(6)	Venus	1,	2,	3,	4,	5,	8,	9,	10,	11,
(7)	Saturn	3,	4,	5,	8,	9,	10,	11,		
(8)	Lagna	1,	2,	3,	4,	5,	8,	9,	11,	

Total : 52 benefic points.

Saturn

Saturn is beneficial in the houses indicated against each of the eight cardinal points, as follows:

(1)	Sun	1,	2,	4,	7,	8,	10,	11,
(2)	Moon	3,	6,	11,				
(3)	Mars	3,	5,	6,	10,	11,	12,	
(4)	Mercury	6,	8,	9,	10,	11,	12,	
(5)	Jupiter	5,	6,	11,	12,			
(6)	Venus	6,	11,	12,				
(7)	Saturn	3,	5,	6,	11,			
(8)	Lagna	1,	3,	4,	6,	10,	11,	

Total : 39 benefic points.

EXAMPLE

It is now possible to tabulate the above information in respect of each planet. This would give us a 'scattered' picture known as the "Prastaraka Ashtakavarga". From this can be derived the Bhinnashtaka varga of each planet.

Let us work out the Bhinnashtaka charts for a native (John F. Kennedy) born on May 29, 1917 at 3:15:28 hours (LMT), Long. 071W08', Lat. 42N20' (USA). The horoscopic chart (**Chart XXX-1**) is as under.

Lagna	27°37'	Mars 25°43'
Sun	15°03'	Mercury 27°53'
Moon	24°30'	Jupiter 0°20'

Venus 24°02'
Saturn 4°27'
Rahu 18°32'

Prastaraka of the Sun

Signs	1 Mar Mer	2 Sun Ven Jup	3	4 Sat	5 Mon	6 Asc	7	8	9	10	11	12	Total
Sun		0	0		0			0	0	0	0	0	8
Moon		0	0				0			0			4
Mars	0	0		0			0	0	0	0	0		8
Mercury			0		0	0			0	0	0	0	7
Jupiter						0	0			0		0	4
Venus	0						0	0					3
Saturn	0	0		0	0		0			0	0	0	8
Lagna			0	0	0				0	0		0	6
Bhinna-Ashtaka	3	4	4	3	4	2	5	4	4	6	5	4	48

Bhinnashtaka Chart SUN:

4	3	Sun 4	4
5	Bhinnashtaka Chart SUN		3
6			4
4	4	5	Lagna 2

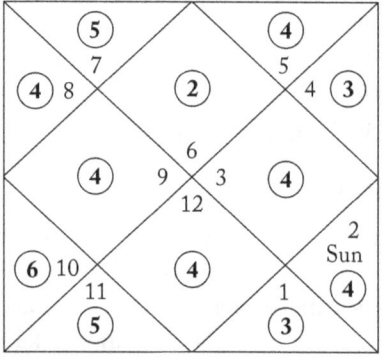

Similarly Prastaraka and Bhinnashtaka charts are prepared for all the planets. The Bhinnashtaka charts for the remaining planets are given below. Prastaraka charts for the remaining planets are not being given for reasons of constraints of space.

Bhinnashtaka Chart MOON:

3	2	4	4
7	Bhinnashtaka Chart MOON		4
4			Moon 5
4	6	3	Lagna 3

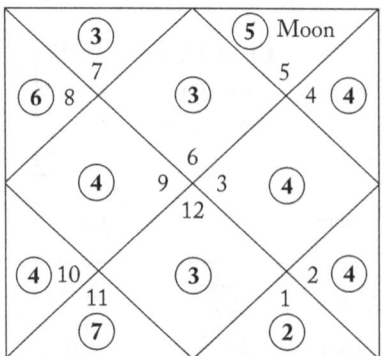

4	Mars 4	2	3
6	**Bhinnashtaka Chart** **MARS**		4
3			1
1	2	6	⁄Lagna 3

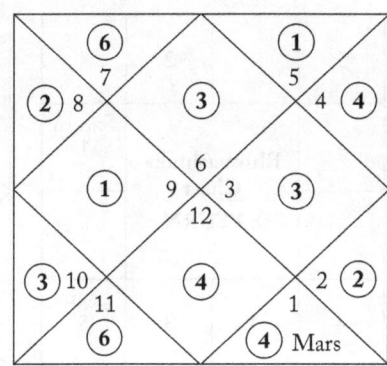

6	Mercury 6	4	4
4	**Bhinnashtaka Chart** **MERCURY**		4
6			3
5	2	5	⁄Lagna 5

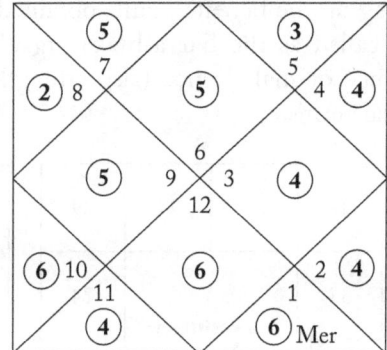

4	3	Jupiter 5	6
7	**Bhinnashtaka Chart** **JUPITER**		5
5			3
6	4	3	⁄Lagna 5

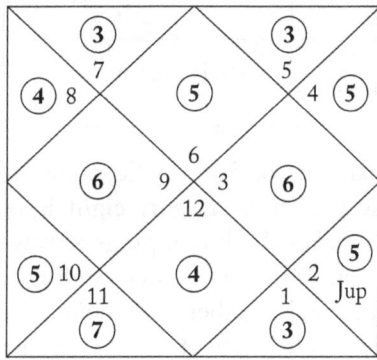

6	4	Venus 3	4
5	**Bhinnashtaka Chart** **VENUS**		3
3			4
7	3	3	⁄Lagna 7

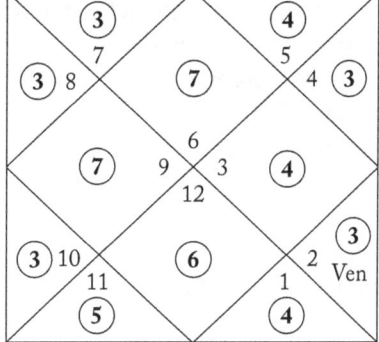

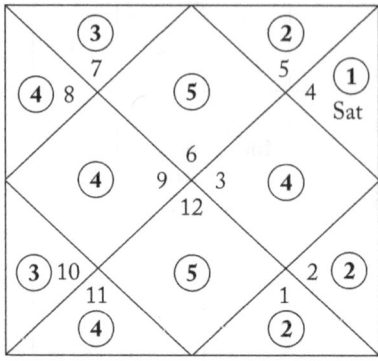

5	2	2	4
4	Bhinnashtaka Chart		Saturn 1
3	SATURN		2
4	4	3	Lagna 5

Adding up the benefic points obtained by different signs (and houses), we get what is called as the Sarvashtakavarga. This gives a ready view of the relative beneficence or maleficence (also strength and weakness) of different houses in numerical terms.

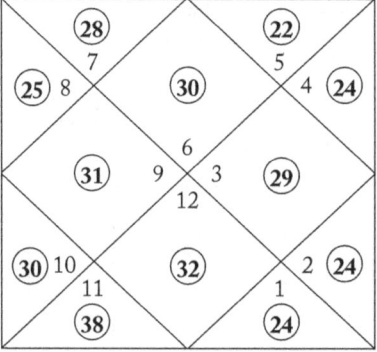

32	24	24	29
38	Sarvashtaka-Varga		24
30			22
31	25	28	Lagna 30

A maximum of 56 benefic points are possible in a given sign in the Sarvashtakavarga chart. Twenty-eight is considered as the average strength; more than this makes the house progressively strong; less than this progressively weak.

Based on the above understanding, it is possible to construct a table which shows the total number of benefic points in the twelve different houses when considered from each of the seven planets and the lagna. Table XXX-1 given here indicates benefic points contributed to the various houses as considered from each of the seven planets and the lagna. These may be used to make a Sarvashtakavarga chart without making any Bhinnashtaka chart. This applies to any given horoscope.

Table XXX-2 shows the application of this information to chart XXX-1. It may be noted here that this information is for constructing a Sarvashtakavarga chart directly, without going into the construction of the different Bhinnashtakavarga charts. The numbers under the different rashis or houses, and against the seven planets and the lagna, have nothing to do with the Bhinnashtakavarga values.

Table XXX-1:
Benefic points from the lagna and the planets for making a Sarvashtakavarga chart.

Houses Planets/ Lagna	1	2	3	4	5	6	7	8	9	10	11	12	Total
Sun	3	3	3	3	2	3	4	5	3	5	7	2	43
Moon	2	3	5	2	2	5	2	2	2	3	7	1	36
Mars	4	5	3	4	3	3	4	4	4	6	7	2	49
Mercury	3	1	5	2	6	6	1	2	5	5	7	3	46
Jupiter	2	1	1	2	3	4	2	4	2	4	7	4	36
Venus	2	3	3	3	4	4	2	3	4	3	6	3	40
Saturn	3	2	4	4	4	3	3	4	4	4	6	1	42
Lagna	5	3	5	5	2	6	1	2	2	6	7	1	45
											337		

Table XXX-2:
Sarvashtakavarga making the use of table XXX-1

Signs Planets/ Lagna	1 Mar Mer	2 Sun Ven Jup	3	4 Sat	5 Mon	6 Asc	7	8	9	10	11	12	Total
Sun	2	3	3	3	3	2	3	4	5	3	5	7	43
Moon	2	3	7	1	2	3	5	2	2	5	2	2	36
Mars	4	5	3	4	3	3	4	4	4	6	7	2	49
Mercury	3	1	5	2	6	6	1	2	5	5	7	3	46
Jupiter	4	2	1	1	2	3	4	2	4	2	4	7	36
Venus	3	2	3	3	3	4	4	2	3	4	3	6	40
Saturn	4	6	1	3	2	4	4	4	3	3	4	4	42
Lagna	2	2	6	7	1	5	3	5	5	2	6	1	45
Savrash-takvarga	24	24	29	24	22	30	28	25	31	30	38	32	337

Ashtakavarga for Daily Use: The Concept of Kakshya

The Prastaraka charts for different planets can be represented in a different manner to make use of the concept of Kakshyas. Each rashi or sign is divided into eight equal parts or Kakshyas, each of an extent of 3°45'. They are owned by the seven planets and the lagna in the following manner:

Kakshya number	Kakshya lord	Extent of Kakshya from	to
1	Saturn	0°00'	3°45'
2	Jupiter	3°45'	7°30'
3	Mars	7°30'	11°15'
4	Sun	11°15'	15°00'
5	Venus	15°00'	18°45'
6	Mercury	18°45'	22°30'
7	Moon	22°30'	26°15'
8	Lagna (Ascendant)	26°15'	30°00'

The Prastaraka chart for each planet can thus be readjusted to bring in the concept of the Kakshyas. The Prastaraka chart for the Sun for the chart XXX-1 would thus appear as given below:

Prastaraka of the Sun (in the order of Kakshyas)

Signs / Planets/Lagna	1	2	3	4	5	6	7	8	9	10	11	12	Total
(lords)	Mar Mer Jup	Sun Ven		Sat	Mon	Asc							
Saturn	0	0		0	0		0			0	0	0	8
Jupiter						0	0			0		0	4
Mars	0	0		0			0	0	0	0	0		8
Sun		0	0		0			0	0	0	0	0	8
Venus	0						0	0					3
Mercury			0		0	0				0	0	0	7
Moon		0	0				0			0			4
Lagna			0	0	0			0	0		0		6
Total	3	4	4	3	4	2	5	4	4	6	5	4	48

Prastarakas for the different planets can be made in a similar manner. When a planet in transit happens to be within the first 3°45' of a sign, it is considered to be in the Kakshya of Saturn. Between 3°45' and 7°30' of a sign, the planet in transit is considered to be in the Kakshya of Jupiter. Similarly, a planet's transit in various Kakshyas in the Prastaraka of a given planet can be ascertained. A planet is considered to be productive of benefic results when it transits a Kakshya where there is a benefic point.

Kakshyas for daily use: The concept of Kakshyas can be employed for daily use. The method of this application is simple. Prepare the Prastaraka charts for the seven planets. Then find out the longitudes of each of the seven planets

on a given day. In the Prastaraka of the Sun, see if the transiting Sun is passing through a Kakshya with a benefic point. For the Moon's transit, consider
the Prastaraka of the Moon. See for all the planets. When several planets
are transiting the Kakshyas where the natal planets have contributed benefic
points, that day is auspicious. When several planets transit the Kakshyas where
there are no benefic points, it is adverse time for the native. Depending upon
the number of planets transiting Kakshyas with benefic points, the results in
general will be as follows:

1. All seven planets transiting Kakshya with a benefic point:
                         Excellent; day of achievements.

2. Six planets   :   Excellent.

3. Five planets   :   Very good.

4. Four planets   :   Good results; this is the borderline.

5. Three planets   :   Average; some difficulties.

6. Two planets   :   Very bad.

7. One planet   :   Extremely bad; set backs, accidents.

8. No planet transiting a Kakshya with a benefic point:
                         Extremely bad, accidents, even death.

The above mentioned results must only be applied with caution. The Kakshyas are not the final word in Ashtakavarga. It must also be remembered
that Ashtakavarga is only a system of transits and, therefore, subservient to
the natal chart as well as the dasha system.

General Principles Applicable to Ashtakavarga

As is true of all horoscopic study, Ashtakavarga also sheds light on the two
basic aspects of a chart :

A. *The static aspect*, by the number of benefic points in different houses. This
   shows the promise inherent in a horoscopic chart.

B. *The dynamic aspect*, when dashas and transits are applied to the Ashtakavarga charts. It involves certain subtle calculations which, meticulously done,
   yield extra-ordinary results. This indicates the time of fructification of the
   promise inherent in a chart.

Some very general principles governing the use of Ashtakavarga are described
below.

1. Ashtakavrga must be calculated on the basis of the Rashi position of the
    planets and not the Bhava position which may differ from the natal chart.

2. Ashtakavarga is subservient to the dashas as well as the inherent promise
    in the horoscope. It will not take precedence over the natal chart but is a
    most substantial complimentary aid. In any given chart, a particular dasha
    indicates happenings of a particular nature. The extent and nature of such

a promise fructifying during the relevant dasha must be judged from the Ashtakavarga.

3. Primarily, the results of Ashtakavarga are determined from Gochara or transit of planets over different houses as reckoned from the lagna or the Moon.

4. The nature of results produced by a planet depend upon the house it owns or occupies, as well as the natural significations of this planet.

5. In a Bhinnashtakavarga, the maximum number of benefic points is eight and the minimum is zero. Four points in a house indicates average or mixed results. As the number of benefic points increases to 5, 6 or 7, the beneficence of the house increases. With 8 points in a house, excellent results are expected.

   Houses with 3, 2 or 1 benefic points become progressively inauspicious. Houses with no benefic points in them are extremely bad. Transits of malefics through these houses prove decidedly harmful.

6. The results produced by the varying number of benefic points in a house have been described thus in the classics:

   No benefic point : Humiliation, disease and danger.

1 point	:	Disease, misery, hardships, aimless wandering.
2 points	:	Mental anguish, censure by the ruler, deprivation by the thieves.
3 points	:	Mental and physical discomforts.
4 points	:	Both good and bad results in equal measure.
5 points	:	Learning, wealth, children, good clothes.
6 points	:	Good character, victory over opponents, wealth, vehicles, renown.
7 points	:	Honours, awards, extremely good fortune.
8 points	:	Regal grace and glory.

7. Planets which are strong, exalted or placed in their own houses lose much effect if they are associated with fewer benefic points in their Bhinnashtakavarga charts.

8. Weak, debilitated or combust planets retain much of their efficacy if associated with greater than average number of benefic points in their Ashtakavarga charts.

9. Sarvashtakavarga chart provides an overall view of the strength and weakness of different houses. It is the most elaborate and the most scientific of all transits as it contains a cumulative planetary influence of all the seven planets in relation to all the seven planets and the lagna. Such observations, and several others, can be made on its basis as are given hereunder:

(a) When the lagna and the eighth house have more than average number (28 is the average number!) of benefic points, the native possesses good health. Less than average number of benefic points in these houses indicates proneness to disease. In the chart of J.F. Kennedy, the eighth house is relatively weak.

(b) Larger number of benefic points in the eleventh house compared to the tenth indicates greater achievements (or earnings) through less labour.

(c) Larger number of benefic points in the twelfth house compared to the eleventh indicates excessive spending compared to the earnings. Or it may mean benefits or earnings from foreign countries.

(d) More benefic points in the second house compared to the twelfth stresses on greater accumulation and less spending or enjoyments.

(e) A strong sixth house may indicate struggles and a proneness to illness.

10. A *quantum jump* between any two houses indicates a significant rise or fall as the planets transit from one house to the next.

11. An observation of the late Col. Gaur (see *Professions* by Col. A.K. Gaur) is that when the fifth house has greater number of benefic points compared to the tenth house, the career of the native suffers, unless a strong eleventh house acts as an antidote. Whether this principle can be extended to other houses of the chart is a matter of research.

12. Transits of Jupiter through strong houses confer dignity on the native; those of Saturn confer power and leadership.

13. When the MD, AD and PD lords transit strong houses, they produce benefic results. When they transit weak houses, the results produced are adverse.

14. For daily application, the consideration of transit of planets through Kakshyas yields reasonably dependable results, especially when considered along with the dasha-antardasha.

15. Ashtakavarga has been advocated to be used in Muhurta also. A simple method of using Ashtakavarga for Muhurta is to choose a lagna from which a particular house, which happens to signify the intended undertaking, has greater number of benefic points. The significator for the intended undertaking should also be transiting a strong house. For example, the Sun is the karaka for official matters or government jobs, Mars stands for land deals and houses, Venus for marriage or vehicles, Jupiter for children or education, etc. These planets must be transiting strong houses at the time of such pursuits as pertain to these significators.

16. Accuracy in results demands the use of subtler techniques of Ashtakavarga, integrated with dashas and transits.

Sudarshana Chakra

अनादिमध्यान्तमनन्तवीर्यमनन्तबाहुं शशिसूर्यनेत्रम् ।
पश्यामि त्वां दीप्तहुताशवक्त्रं स्वतेजसा विश्वमिदं तपन्तम् ॥

I behold Thee as one without beginning, middle or end, of infinite power,
of numberless arms, with the Moon and the Sun as Thine eyes, with Thy
face as a flaming fire, whose radiance burns up this universe.

Gita XI/19

The Sudarshana Chakra is the discus that lord Krishna carries on his right index finger in the battlefield. It is used selectively, to annihilate the most dreaded opponent, and is supposed to be unfailing in its effect. The Sudarshana Chakra of Parashara is likewise supposed to yield the most dependable results in horoscopic analysis. It makes a composite use of three lagnas: the natal lagna, the Chandra lagna and the Surya lagna.

While teaching Jyotish to his disciple Maitreya, sage Parashara spoke thus of the Sudarshana Chakra: "Now, O' Brahmin, I shall talk of that confidential and superlative piece of wisdom which lord Brahma Himself spoke of, with the good of the world in mind. This is about the Chakra, named as Sudarshana, by the use of which the wise are able to decipher the auspicious and the inauspicious events of human beings, pertaining to the twelve houses from the lagna onwards, from birth till their death, every year, every month and every day. May you, therefore, listen about that carefully".

Sage Parashara then goes on to describe how to make use of the Sudarshana Chakra in order to obtain accuracy in making predictions.

Constructing the Sudarshana Chakra

Make three circles, one outside the other, on a common centre. Draw lines across as well as tangentially to divide it into twelve parts. Within the minor circle, mark the twelve rashis in an anticlockwise direction, starting from the natal lagna. Locate the planets in the appropriate signs according to their placement in the natal chart.

In the middle circle, start from the Moon-sign instead of the natal lagna and place the planets in the houses as considered from the Moon in the natal chart.

In the outermost circle, start from the Sun-sign as in the natal chart and mark the signs and planets in an anticlockwise direction accordingly.

We shall use here the example of Smt. Indira Gandhi, the late Prime Minister of India, born on November 19, 1917, at 23:11 hours IST, at Allahabad 25°N27', 81°E51' (**Chart XXXI-1**). The Sudarshana Chakra appropriate to this chart is depicted as Figure 1.

		Jupiter (R)	Ketu
	Chart XXXI-1		Lagna Saturn
Moon	November 19, 1917	Mars	
Venus Rahu	Sun Mercury		

North Indian chart:
- 5 / 6: Mars
- Lagna Saturn (center top)
- 3 / 2: Ketu
- Jupiter (R)
- 7 / 1 / 4 / 10
- 8 / 9: Sun Mercury, Venus Rahu
- Moon
- 11 / 12

Lagna	27°22'	Mars	16°22'	Venus	21°00'
Sun	04°08'	Mercury	13°14'	Saturn	21°47'
Moon	05°35'	Jupiter (R)	15°00'	Rahu	09°12'

It will now be seen that the first house is represented by the natal lagna, the Moon lagna and the Sun lagna. It will be affected by all the planets that in the natal chart occupy the lagna as well as those that are in association with the Moon and the Sun. The distribution of planets in the remaining houses of the chart will vary accordingly. It is in essence a composite view of the lagna chart, the Moon chart and the Sun chart lying one over the other.

Applicability

The Sudarshana Chakra gives an authentic view of all the houses of the horoscope and its use is highly recommended. This is because it comprises the study of all the twelve houses from three cardinal points of the horoscope: the lagna, the Moon and the Sun. However, its application is to be restricted to those cases only where the lagna, the Moon and the Sun fall in different houses of the chart. When any two or all three fall in the same house, this method should not be used. In such cases, predictions must be done from the natal lagna only.

Guidelines for prediction

The first house of the Sudarshana Chakra contains the lagna, the Sun and the Moon (as well as any other planets that associate with these three lagnas). This house is to be treated as the (composite) lagna. The next one is to be considered the (composite) second house; and so on in case of the remaining houses.

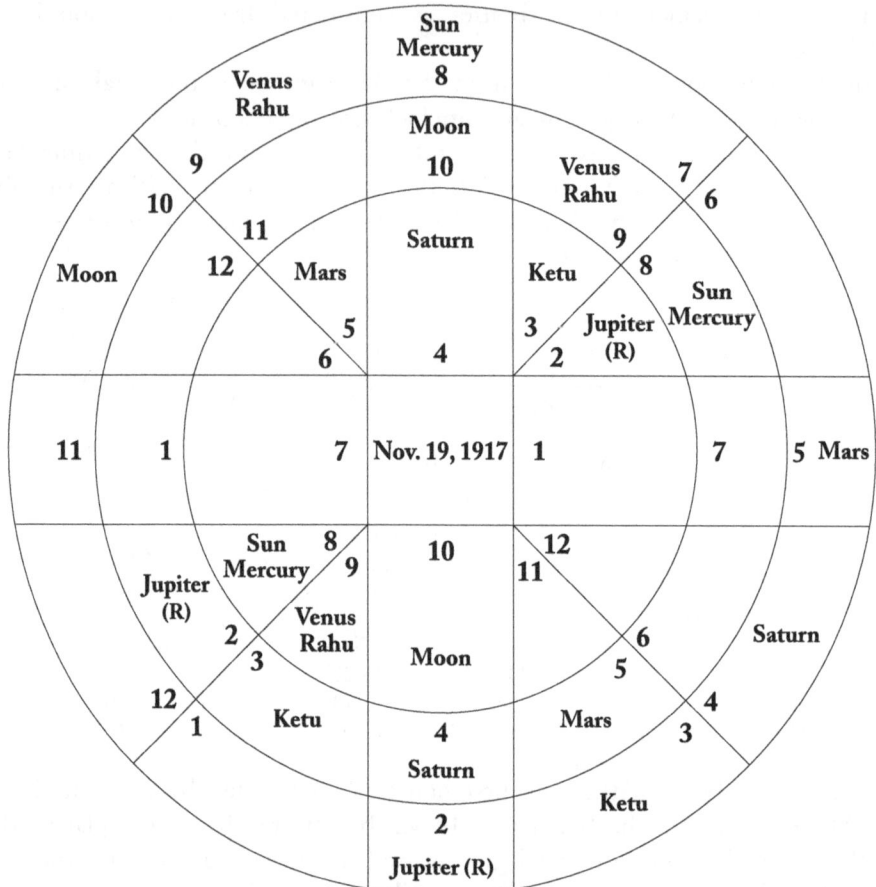

Figure 1: Sudarshana Chakra:
Planetary disposition in the twelve houses of the chart

- The Sun in the lagna is not to be considered as a malefic in the Sudarshana Chakra system. In fact, it is to be considered as a benefic here.

- Natural malefics in exaltation or in their own signs are also to be considered as benefic.

- Natural benefics would behave adversely if they are debilitated or in inimical signs.

- The house that harbours its own lord or a benefic planet tends to prosper. Benefic aspect on the house also ensures its well-being.

- A house that is associated with or aspected by malefics tends to suffer.

- A house that has an occupant yields results according the effects of the occupant of the house.

- An unoccupied house yields results according to the planet or planets aspecting it.

- A house occupied or aspected only by benefics yields benefic results.
- The one occupied or aspected only by malefics yields malefic results.
- When there are both benefic and malefic influences on a house, the nature of results yielded by the house would depend on whether the benefics or the malefics predominate.
- When both benefic and malefic influences are equal on a given house, the nature of results would depend on the relative strengths of the benefics and the malefics that influence it. The stronger of the two influences is likely to prevail.
- When a house is neither occupied nor aspected, the results must be judged from the disposition of its lord.

Deciding on the Benefic and Malefic Nature of Planets

It is important to understand about what is a benefic and what is a malefic. Any planet, benefic or malefic by nature, would acquire beneficence if it occupies benefic vargas. On the other hand, a planet acquires maleficence if it falls in malefic vargas. Here, the vargas of natural benefics as well as own and exaltation signs confer beneficence. Contrarily, the vargas of natural malefics as well as signs of inimical planets and debilitation confer maleficence. It is customary to use the Saptavargas, viz., Rashi, Hora, Drekkana, Saptamsha, Navamsha, Dwadashamsha and Trimshamsha. We tabulate the disposition of the planets in different vargas as appropriate to our example chart, to decide about their relative beneficence or maleficence (Table XXXI-1). We also consider here the inherent nature of each planet as a factor, besides its disposition in the seven vargas.

Table XXXI-1: Lords of Saptavargas of planets and their nature

Planet →	Sun	Moon	Mars	Merc.	Jupiter	Venus	Saturn	Rahu	Ketu
Rashi	Mars	Saturn	Sun	Mars	Venus	Jupiter	Moon	Jupiter	Merc.
Hora	Moon	Moon	Moon	Moon	Sun	Moon	Sun	Sun	Sun
Drekkana	Mars	Saturn	Jupiter	Jupiter	Merc.	Sun	Jupiter	Jupiter	Merc.
Saptamsha	Venus	Sun	Mars	Sun	Saturn	Mars	Merc.	Saturn	Sun
Navamsha	Sun	Saturn	Sun	Venus	Venus	Venus	Saturn	Merc.	Jupiter
Dwadashamsha	Jupiter	Jupiter	Saturn	Mars	Mars	Sun	Jupiter	Jupiter	Merc.
Trimshamsha	Venus	Merc.	Jupiter	Jupiter	Jupiter	Merc.	Saturn	Saturn	Saturn
Nature of Planet	Benefic	Neutral	Neutral	Benefic	Benefic	Benefic	Benefic	Neutral	Neutral

Note: The inherent nature of each planet has also been considered as a factor in deciding the nature of the planet, besides its disposition in the seven vargas.

It may be noted that the nature of planets based on their disposition in the Saptavargas is not specific to the Sudarshana Chakra. However, this information can be used in the Sudarshana Chakra to decide about the nature of results one would expect from the different houses in the Sudarshana Chakra.

Results from the Different Houses

After deciding on the nature of planets, it is required to decipher whether the different houses in the Sudarshana Chakra would yield benefic or malefic results. This is determined from the number of benefic and malefic influences (by association or aspect) on each house. This has been shown in Table XXXI-2.

Table XXXI-2: Benefic and malefic nature of houses based on the Saptavarga

Houses ↓	No. of occupants	Aspects (in case unoccupied)	Benefic	Malefic	Neutral	Nature of the house
1st House	4	–	3	–	1	Benefic
2nd House	3	–	1	–	2	Benefic
3rd House	1	–	–	–	1	Neutral
4th House	–	1	–	–	1	Neutral
5th House	3	–	3	–	–	Benefic
6th House	3	–	1	–	2	Benefic
7th House	3	–	2	–	1	Benefic
8th House	2	–	–	–	2	Neutral
9th House	1	–	1	–	–	Benefic
10th House	1	–	–	–	1	Neutral
11th House	3	–	3	–	–	Benefic
12th House	3	–	1	–	2	Benefic

Here we have considered aspects only where the house is not occupied. Also, if there are both benefic and malefic influences on a house, its final nature will depend on the balance between such influences. A given number of benefic influences will cancel an equal number of malefic influences and vice versa. In the chart under consideration, no planet earns the status of a clear-cut malefic in the Saptavargas. There is, therefore, no house in the chart which is supposed to yield purely malefic results. The extent to which a given house would behave as benefic, in comparison to another one, would depend on the actual number of benefic influences operating upon the house. One may be tempted to consider the benefic and malefic nature of the different houses from the actual nature of the occupants or aspectors of a house, without determining the nature of planets from the Saptavargas. The use of Saptavarga, however, makes this exercise more accurate and reliable. It will be seen from the above that houses 1, 5, 11 and to some extent 7 are particularly beneficial and strong in this horoscope.

Timing of Events: The Dasha Scheme

The Sudarshana Chakra must be employed to time the life events of a native. For this purpose, sage Parashara has given a method of working out the *Sudarshana Chakra Dasha*. In this system, each house, starting from the lagna, has a mahadasha (MD) of one year so that all the houses of the chart provide us a cycle of twelve years of MD. The first MD is that of the lagna, the second of the second house, and so on. After twelve years, another cycle of dashas begins from the lagna. A native may run several cycles of this dasha during his lifetime. The MD's in respect of the example chart are tabulated in Table XXXI-3.

Table XXXI-3:
Cycles of Mahadasha: Each house has an MD duration of one year

MD ↓	Year of life	Ending year of MD
Lagna	1, 13, 25, 37, 49, 61	1918, '30, '42, '54, '66, '78'
2nd House	2, 14, 26, 38, 50, 62	1919, '31, '43, '55, '67, '79
3rd House	3, 15, 27, 39, 51, 63	1920, '32, '44, '56, '68, '80
4th House	4, 16, 28, 40, 52, 64	1921, '33, '45, '57, '69, '81
5th House	5, 17, 29, 41, 53, 65	1922, '34, '46, '58, '70, '82
6th House	6, 18, 30, 42, 54, 66	1923, '35, '47, '59, '71, '83
7th House	7, 19, 31, 43, 55, 67	1924, '36, '48, '60, '72, 1984
8th House	8, 20, 32, 44, 56	1925, '37, '49, '61, '73
9th House	9, 21, 33, 45, 57	1926, '38, '50, '62, '74
10th House	10, 22, 34, 46, 58	1927, '39, '51, '63, '75
11th House	11, 23, 35, 47, 59	1928, '40, '52, '64, '76
12th House	12, 24, 36, 48, 60	1929, '41, '53, '65, '77

Within each MD, there are twelve antardashas (AD's), each of a month's duration. The first AD starts from the house represented by the MD. Thus, within each MD, there is an AD represented by each of the twelve houses of the chart, starting from the MD and proceeding in the natural order.

Each AD of a month's duration is further segmented into twelve pratyantardashas (PD's), each of a duration of two-and-a-half days, represented by the twelve houses starting from the house represented by the AD in question.

We thus see here that the twelve houses of the Sudarshana Chakra have their MD's, AD's and PD's in order to enable the astrologer to make specific predictions in respect of each house of the chart and to time these events accurately. It will, however, be seen that twelve years is relatively a short period in the life of a native. Therefore, several cycles of similar dashas would operate within the lifetime of an individual. The life events, however, are not likely to exactly repeat themselves every twelve years. It is, therefore, essential that the Sudarshana dasha indicated here be studied along with the Vimshottari dasha as well as the Gochara (Transits) prevalent at that time.

Interpretation of Dashas: Some Principles

Some important principles appropriate to the interpretation of dashas are being given here. These must be kept in mind while analysing the results from the Sudarshana Chakra.

- The house whose dasha is in operation must be treated as the lagna or the first house. For example, if it is the dasha of the fifth house, the fifth house should be considered as the lagna or the first house and the remaining houses considered from it accordingly, i.e., the sixth house is to be treated as the second house, the seventh as the third house, and so on.

- After a span of twelve years, the MD cycle begins afresh from the lagna.

- For a detailed assessment, not only should the house representing the MD be treated as lagna, but also the houses represented by a given AD or PD. These may be termed as the dasha lagnas.

- Whenever the houses 1, 4, 7, 10, 5, 9 and 8 from a dasha lagna are occupied by benefics, the year or the month or the days represented by that dasha are productive of beneficial results.

- Any house that harbours only Rahu or only Ketu tends to suffer, and yields adverse results only.

- A house occupied by several malefics also yields adverse results.

- Benefics yield good results if they fall in houses other than 2 and 12. They are harmful if they occupy houses 2 and 12.

- Malefics yield desirable results when they occupy houses 3, 6 and 11. Elsewhere, they produce adverse results.

- Since similar MD's, AD's and PD's will operate repeatedly (e.g., same MD every twelve years), the results indicated must be considered along with the results deciphered from an analysis of the Vimshottari dasha as well as Gochara.

- While we have shown how benefic, malefic and neutral nature of houses is to be determined, it is important to also consider the natural beneficence or maleficence of planets while applying the above principles.

- Sage Parashara advocates that one should confirm the Sudarshana Chakra results with those indicated by Ashtakavarga. If both the Sudarshana Chakra and Ashtakavarga indicate similar benefic or malefic results, these will definitely happen. If they vary, only mixed results will come to pass.

Some Observations about our Example Chart

In the chart under consideration, we have seen above that strongly benefic houses are the lagna, the fifth, the seventh and the eleventh houses. Houses two, six, nine and twelve are also benefic, though not strongly so. Houses three, four, eight and ten are neutral. There are no purely malefic houses in this chart. It is thus to be expected that the dashas of houses 1, 5, 7 and 11 would prove particularly significant for the native.

She got married on March 26, 1942 during the dasha of the lagna. This she managed despite a lot of controversy and paternal resistance against it. It was during her lagna dasha ending in November 1966 that she became the first woman Prime Minister of India in a power struggle that subjugated some of the more deserving claimants for the job. Her last phase of lagna dasha, in 1978, was a period of political wilderness and ill health, coinciding with the Vimshottari MD-AD of Saturn-Venus, one the lord of the eighth house and the other the afflicted occupant of the sixth house.

The dasha of her seventh, a maraka, house was adverse for her close relations and for her own self. She lost her mother in 1936. In September 1960, she lost her husband. Her own death too occurred in her seventh house dasha, on October 31, 1984.

In 1964, during the dasha of her eleventh house, she was inducted into the union cabinet as the Minister for Information and Broadcasting, after the death of her father. This was a highly significant landmark in her political career. During her fifth house dasha in 1970, she displayed tremendous strength and managed to sideline some of the powerful political adversaries of hers.

In conclusion, we find that the Sudarshana Chakra of Parashara is an excellent astrological tool that should be used far more extensively than it has been used in the past. It takes into consideration the natal lagna (the physical body), the Chandra lagna (the mind; the mother; also the genetic link) and the Surya lagna (the soul; the father; the ancestors). It thus provides a comprehensive assessment of a man's physical, mental and spiritual make up. It must be employed along with the Vimshottari dasha, Gochara as well as Astakavaraga in order to obtain accurate results.

Index

Made in United States
Cleveland, OH
22 December 2024

12514756R00195